LEADERSHIP AND MANAGEMENT DEVELOPMENT

5th edition

Jeff Gold

Richard Thorpe

Alan Mumford

The Chartered Institute of Personnel and Development is the leading
publisher of books and reports for personnel and training professionals,
students, and all those concerned with the effective management and
development of people at work. For details of all our titles, please contact the
publishing department:
tel: 020 8612 6204
e-mail: publish@cipd.co.uk
The catalogue of all CIPD titles can be viewed on the CIPD website:
www.cipd.co.uk/bookstore

LEADERSHIP AND MANAGEMENT DEVELOPMENT

5th edition

Jeff Gold is Professor of Organisation Learning at Leeds Business School, Leeds Metropolitan University and Fellow of the Northern Leadership Academy.

Richard Thorpe is a Professor of Management Development at Leeds University Business School and currently head of the Management Division. He is a past President of the British Academy of Management and is currently chair of the Society for the Advancement of Management Studies.

Alan Mumford has been involved with management training and development and with other aspects of managerial effectiveness for over 20 years. At present, he is Visiting Professor of Management Development at Interactive Management Centres.

Published by the Chartered Institute of Personnel and Development,
151 The Broadway, London, SW19 1JQ

First edition published 2004
Reprinted 2004, 2006, 2008, 2009
This edition first published 2010
Reprinted 2012

Typeset by Fakenham Photosetting Ltd

Printed in Great Britain by Charlesworth Press, Wakefield

British Library Cataloguing in Publication Data
A catalogue of this manual is available from the British Library

ISBN-13 978 1 84398 244 9

Chartered Institute of Personnel and Development, CIPD House, 151 The Broadway, London, SW19 1JQ

Tel: 020 8612 6200
E-mail: cipd@cipd.co.uk
Website: www.cipd.co.uk
Incorporated by Royal Charter
Registered Charity No. 1079797

Contents

List of Figures and Tables

Preface to the 5th edition

It is more than 20 years since Alan Mumford published the first edition of this book. It was almost the first of its kind and, along with subsequent editions during the 1990s, played a significant role in giving pace, direction and – crucially – a push for action in the development of managers. By the time the last edition appeared, in 2004, management development had become quite strongly established in the UK and elsewhere. There were and still are many ideas, models and theories relating to how managers learn and develop, and the book attempted to capture these so that students studying for academic and professional examinations could be stimulated into learning about the subject of management development but still consider the possibility of action for themselves and others.

One obvious feature of this new edition is a new title: *Leadership and Management Development*. It will also be clear that there are now three authors, and we are most fortunate to have Professor Richard Thorpe from Leeds University on our team. There are some good reasons for the change in title – and this is more than just moving with the times (or increasing the market for the book). There has always been a significant theoretical basis for considering leaders and leadership. As we discuss in Chapter 1, there remain key issues about how and whether leaders need to be seen as different from managers in terms of the evidence about their work and how they can be developed. However, through the 2000s, for good or ill, there has been a trend that it is better and talented leaders who are able to make the right decisions who are needed, first in times of prosperity, and more recently when the issues of recession, global threats to climate and security and sustainability have come to the fore. There is also massive interest in the moral and ethical climate in which decisions are made. However, we argue that nearly all the reasons for the interest in leaders also apply to managers and, indeed, it is rare to find a leader that does not manage nor a manager that does not lead. Hence *Leadership and Management Development* will frequently be informed by the same ideas and models and work from the same evidence from practice.

In this new edition, the 5th, we retain many of the features that will help readers learn about leadership and management development, including specification of learning outcomes, reflect-conclude-plan questions, links to relevant websites, group activities and discussion questions. In addition, in most chapters we provide examples and cases of practice. We have also deepened the coverage in most areas and looked outwards to include consideration of important and emerging topics for leadership and management development. This list draws more on ethics, diversity, e-learning, green and ecological issues, talent management and small and medium enterprises (SMEs). In addition, because they are so important in the ideas that relate to leaders, throughout the book we consider the interest in distributed leadership and globalisation.

We do hope you can consider this book helpful in your studies: it has been written with the new CIPD standards in mind. However – and we have never forgotten the history of this book nor the key influence of Alan Mumford's ideas and insights – we do hope that leaders, managers, professionals and those who have an interest in helping people learn to be more effective will make use of our work in their own practice. Please let us know how you get on.

JEFF GOLD, **j.gold@leedsmet.ac.uk**
RICHARD THORPE, **rt@lubs.leeds.ac.uk**
ALAN MUMFORD

CIPD Students

If you are studying the new CIPD module Leadership and Management Development the following table may be useful in determining how the learning outcomes of that module map to the chapters of this book.

Table mapping the Learning Outcomes of Leadership and Management Development and the CIPD text 'Leadership and Management Development'

Number	Learning Outcome	Mapped to chapters in 'Leadership and Management Development'
1	Explain and critically analyse the concepts of leadership and management and their application in an organisational, social, environmental and multicultural context.	**Chapter 1** Leaders and Managers, Leadership and Management Development **Chapter 11** Diversity and Ecology
2	Evaluate, select and apply a range of approaches to identifying leadership and management development needs in differing organisational contexts.	**Chapter 4** Assessing Development Needs
3	Critically analyse and evaluate approaches to the formulation and implementation of leadership and management development strategies to meet current and future organisational needs.	**Chapter 2** Strategic Leadership and Management Development **Chapter 10** The Future Supply of Leaders and Managers
4	Design, critically evaluate and advise on a range of leadership and management development interventions to implement leadership and management development strategies and plans.	**Chapter 6** Activities for the Development of Leaders and Managers **Chapter 7** Combining Work and Learning
5	Work collaboratively, ethically and effectively to support a partnership approach to leadership and management development.	**Chapter 3** Measuring Leaders and Managers **Chapter 6** Activities for the Development of Leaders and Managers **Chapter 9** Leadership and Management Development and Social Capital
6	Explain and evaluate the role of leadership and management development in enhancing and developing organisational competence.	**Chapter 1** Leaders and Managers, Leadership and Management Development **Chapter 5** Leaders, Managers and Learning **Chapter 8** Evaluating Leadership and Management Development **Chapter 13** Futures Learning for Leaders and Managers

7	Critically assess and evaluate approaches to the development of leadership and management in international and global contexts.	**Chapter 11** Diversity and Ecology
8	Act ethically and professionally with a demonstrated commitment to leadership and management development and to continuous personal and professional development.	**Chapter 3** Measuring Leaders and Managers **Chapter 9** Leadership and Management Development and Social Capital

CHAPTER 1

Leaders and managers, leadership and management development

CHAPTER OUTLINE

LEARNING OUTCOMES

After studying this chapter, you should be able to understand, explain, analyse and evaluate:

- the meaning of leadership and management
- findings in what leaders and managers actually do
- whether leaders and managers are different
- some of the key contextual factors in managing and leading
- alternative definitions of leadership and management development
- various approaches and purposes to developing leaders and managers

INTRODUCTION

Consider the following news item that appeared in *People Management* on 26 March 2009:

HOSPITAL LEADERSHIP FAILINGS

'Appalling' management at an NHS trust contributed to patients' dying needlessly, according to the health service watchdog. The Healthcare Commission said there were deficiencies at virtually every stage in the care of people at Mid Staffordshire NHS Foundation Trust. Insufficient staffing and poor training contributed to higher than expected death rates at Stafford Hospital. Steve Barnett, chief executive of the NHS Confederation, said the findings were 'an extreme example of what happens when leadership fails to focus on the things that really matter'. Health Secretary Alan Johnson apologised for 'a complete failure of management to address serious problems'.

The report is based on an investigation by the Healthcare Commission published in March 2009 (Healthcare Commission 2009) into high mortality rates among patients admitted as emergencies at Mid Staffordshire Hospital, which had held Foundation Trust status since April 2005. Foundation Trusts have been created since 2004 and allow greater freedom and flexibility to hospital trusts to make decisions which are more responsive to local needs. The report found many failings, with much criticism levelled at the leadership and the lack of an open culture that would allow learning.

Can you see why we should be concerned with leadership and management development? The needless death of people in any context could hardly be more serious and here we find responsibility attributed for the failings to leadership. However, throughout the report, the terms 'management' and 'managers' are used as well as 'leadership', so a key issue arises about whether it is management or leadership which is lacking, or both. Certainly in recent years, 'leadership' seems to have become a more popular term – a hot topic of our times, perhaps (Storey 2004), and with it the expectations that those with the title *leader* will 'focus on the things that really matter'. Witness the growth of leadership programmes, leadership centres and frameworks. For example, if you go to the website **http://www.nhsleadershipqualities.nhs.uk/**, you will find the Leadership Qualities Framework of the NHS, setting out the requirements for 'outstanding leadership'. Events in recent years and months have only served to highlight the need for effective leaders, often described as those who are visionary, creative, inspirational, energising and transformational, although we still need people to effectively manage the day-to-day operations, as is very evident in the Mid Staffordshire case above. Thus in the UK as well as elsewhere there have been continuing concerns about the quantity and quality of leaders and managers and the desire to extend good leadership and management practice not only into original areas in manufacturing but also into areas such as professional firms, schools and the public sector generally, small businesses and voluntary and community organisations. Whatever effective leadership and management are, we apparently need more of it (CEML 2002), although as we will suggest, it is difficult to make sweeping generalisations about what leaders and managers need to learn to do to be effective.

LEADERS AND MANAGERS

Given the concern about the quantity and quality of leaders and managers, there are many people in the UK who carry a job title containing the words 'manager' or 'leader', although what these terms indicate can vary from one organisation to another. For example, in a building society we know, Customer Service Teams have a team leader but the Customer Service Department has a department manager who is more senior than the team leaders. Alternatively, some organisations have always distinguished between managers and those at more senior levels by using the title 'executive', as in Chief Executive Officer (CEO), but this term too might also be used at other levels – eg customer service executives. We could add other titles, such as 'co-ordinator' and 'supervisor'. Sometimes a titles game is played. For example, in one university faculty we know, the Faculty Management Team was renamed the Faculty Leadership Team, although no one could discern any noticeable difference in what the team actually did as a consequence.

These issues make it very difficult to be precise about the numbers of leaders and managers and even more difficult to make generalisations about what the people who hold these titles actually do and how they should be developed (Burgoyne *et al* 2004). Nevertheless, some effort has been made at a national level to calculate numbers, and in the UK the *Economic and Labour Market Review* publishes quarterly figures for Employment by Occupation. In December 2007 there were over 29 million people in employment, of which around 4.5 million or 15.2% were recorded as 'managers and senior officials' (not as managers and leaders). Of course, this classification can easily avoid the work of many people who manage and lead in their daily jobs. For example, all professionals and those in skilled occupations are likely to complete activities such as planning, organising and decision-making, which could be seen as managing and leading. This is likely to be the case in many situations where work is knowledge-based and service-driven (Moynagh and Worsley 2005) and most organisations are small or medium-sized (SMEs), where managing and leading are closely tied to everyday working and formal titles have less meaning.

 WEB LINK

Go to **http://www.statistics.gov.uk/elmr/** for the *Economic and Labour Market Review*, where you will find updated figures.

Given the difficulties arising from the titles game, for the purpose of this book the 'leadership' and 'management' parts of Leadership and Management Development (LMD) are taken to mean the description of activities carried out by managers and/or leaders. Leadership or management in the sense of a group of individuals holding power and authority is an important but less useful focus. To say that 'Management here is too autocratic,' or 'The leadership don't know what they are doing' may be a useful precursor to analysis of exactly who has these failings, and therefore what kind of development needs and solutions may emerge. But the use of 'leadership' and 'management' rather in the pejorative way that people talk about 'they' is less useful. A major reason for this is that LMD has consistently overprovided for general statements of need, and generally applicable solutions to those needs. As Burgoyne *et al* (2004) argue, LMD 'works in different ways in different situations' (p.49), so any design for development needs to consider specific circumstances.

1.1[1] REFLECT – CONCLUDE – PLAN

We might argue that the greater the degree of generalisation in LMD and the lower the attention to the particular needs of individuals in particular situations, the less effective LMD will be.

What is your reaction to this generalisation? How applicable is it in your experience of defining management and leadership, and of LMD?

What impact could it have on the provision of effective LMD?

What might you do as a result of your argument?

WHAT LEADERS AND MANAGERS DO

If we turn our attention to considering leadership and management as activities which people enact in work situations, it is common to invoke various studies and theories from the past, completed with varying degrees of rigour, that nevertheless play a major part in what is understood as the body of knowledge we call theory. Management theory usually begins with the work of the American F. W. Taylor, who sought to define the role of managers and is recognised as the pioneer of scientific management. Through analysis of work tasks, managers could find the 'one best way' to control work and eliminate waste – a process referred to as Taylorism. This search for the 'one best way' model of management has continued ever since. Henri Fayol (1949) identified five basic managerial functions – planning, organising, co-ordinating, commanding and controlling, or POC3. Early forms of management education in the UK and the United States used these categorisations, supplemented by additional aspects such as staffing, directing and budgeting. You might recognise the categories as the main areas of coverage and theory presentation in management textbooks. Extensions to Fayol's view, supplemented by the experience of Alfred P. Sloan's *Forty Years in General Motors* (1945) and Max Weber's ideas on bureaucracy (Watson 1980) became in a sense the classical descriptions of managerial work, because they were the first serious attempts. However, Classical Management remains very much the tradition in management education and there remain continuing debates on the value of this tradition in describing management work (Caroll and Gillen 1987).

These classical descriptions of managerial work, however, and derivatives of them, were neither particularly helpful in causing managers better to understand what they needed to do, nor seriously helpful in facilitating the development of managers to meet these requirements. They do not usefully describe in behavioural terms what managers or leaders need to be able to do, and therefore what development actions would be appropriate. Notice also that the focus was on management with implicit implications for leaders but mostly leadership was still seen at the time as something mysterious based on the possession of certain traits or characteristics which were probably inherited – leaders are born, not made. Interestingly, Weber was writing about the 'charismatic authority' of leaders in 1922, although this was not translated into English until 1947. The mystification was and is still very much apparent in the popular mind.

During the 1930s, the famous Hawthorne investigations resulted in what became referred to as the Human Relations School, supported by the application of psychology and behaviour sciences to leadership and management issues during and after World War II. This required leaders and managers to think about key factors such as the influence of groups, the effect of work conditions and the causes of conflict. A subsequent line of thought began to focus rather on the characteristics of managers, such as decisiveness, courage and initiative. This idea of what leaders and managers needed to be able to display through their work was particularly popular as a result of World War II and studies and anecdotes about the kind of leadership displayed. It was during this period that leadership research started to reassess the presupposition that leadership needed to be defined in terms of personality and physical traits – the trait theory approach. Instead, a focus was placed on behaviours that contributed to particular styles of leadership and how a style should vary according to circumstances such as the situation and the behaviour and capabilities of others, usually referred to as followers. The behaviour theory approach to leadership has continued for many years and we do not intend to cover it in depth. Suffice to say that most of the models build on studies at Ohio State or Michigan Universities and work with the dual features of a concern for task and a concern for people allowing a consideration of leadership style. Many leadership courses continue to make use of the diagnostic tools that have emerged from the research and some have now appeared online. The key works to consult are Blake and Mouton (1985), Hersey and Blanchard (1982) and Fiedler (1967). There are similar theories, including path-goal theory (House and Mitchell 1974) and LMX (leader-member exchange) theory (Graen and Uhl-Bien 1995) as well as normative decision theory (Vroom and Yetton 1973).

Combined with Classical Management, Human Relations ideas and theories provide much of the content of what is taught in leadership and management qualifications such as the Master's in Business Administration (MBA) – and note that neither management nor leadership features in the title of this award. The MBA has been a very popular award and the Council for Excellence in Management and Leadership (CEML 2002) highlighted the growth of MBA graduates in the UK to 11,000 in 2000. In addition, in over 100 Business Schools in the UK, over 300,000 students were studying for Business and Administrative qualifications in 2006/07, an increase of 30% since 1996.[2] Despite this growth, there remains significant criticism of formal and theory-led qualifications for leaders and managers, based on the disconnection of such theories from actual practice (Bennis and O'Toole 2005).

The major change in views about, and actions on, what leaders and managers needed to be able to do came through the research of Rosemary Stewart (1975) in the UK, and Henry Mintzberg (1973) and John Kotter (1982) in the United States. Stewart's work is particularly compelling because her research was conducted with hundreds of managers. The main features of her discoveries were:

- Managers do not work according to the neat, well-organised themes of the classical management schools.

- Their activities are characterised by brevity, variety and fragmentation.

- They spend most of their time interacting with other people rather than thinking well-organised thoughts.

- They work at a brisk and continuing pace with little free time.

- So far from being subject to extremely generalised comments about 'what all managers do', there is a substantial variety in the objective demands of managerial jobs.

- In addition to objective differences – for example, between a sales manager and a research manager – personal choices are made by managers which affect what they actually do.

These statements now seem obvious, partly because they so clearly are supported by the experience of those of us who have actually worked as managers.

Mintzberg, in a much smaller but interestingly indicative study, found much the same pattern of pace, variety and fragmentation as Stewart. However, he identified some roles which he believed to be common, particularly for the Chief Executives who were the basis of his studies. Table 1.1 shows the roles.

Table 1.1 Mintzberg's role analysis

Interpersonal roles	Informational roles	Decisional roles
figurehead	monitor	entrepreneur
leader	disseminator	disturbance-handler
liaison	spokesperson	resource allocator
		negotiator

Source: adapted from Mintzberg (1973)

What is interesting is that despite basing his analysis on those in leadership positions, Mintzberg found that the roles also featured a lot of what is considered management. He found that there were three aspects of the work:

- brevity, variety and fragmentation

- more emphasis on verbal communication rather than written

- use of a network of contacts.

Leaders and managers can benefit from discussing, for example, what proportion of time they spend on any of these roles, and other aspects of the significance of what they are doing. Research by Tengblad (2006) on the behaviour of managers in Sweden found similarities to Mintzberg's study but with more time devoted to working with staff in group settings and more time focused on giving information rather than performing administrative duties.

John Kotter (1982) also looked at a relatively small number of senior executives. Like Mintzberg and Stewart he emphasised the degree to which managers were not strategic, reflective or well organised, but he defined five characteristics of effective behaviour, listed below (adapted from Kotter 1982):

- developing an agenda (often different from a formal plan)
- building networks involving other managers, colleagues, direct reports, outsiders
- execution by establishing and working to multiple objectives and maintaining relationships to achieve those objectives, especially by spending time with other people
- working through meetings and dialogues
- spending time with others.

Kotter created a stunningly significant concept – the effectiveness of seemingly inefficient behaviour. The fact that executives rarely plan their days in advance in much detail but rather react to the day's needs through conversations that are short, disjointed and often deal with a variety of issues within the space of a few minutes is seemingly inefficient. These inefficiencies are often the subject of formal management development processes. While not arguing for the wasteful use of time, Kotter observed that apparent waste was not the same as being ineffective. Information and understanding crucial to effectiveness were created often by accidental experiences.

The utility of such accidental opportunities, however, should not dissuade us from attempting to remove the genuine inefficiencies of the ways in which managers use their time. Perhaps those useful accidental experiences can be replaced by useful planned experiences, both in general managerial behaviour and in creating more effective learning experiences from managerial behaviour.

Another major researcher and theorist who has affected the basis of our understanding of what leaders and managers do has been Richard Boyatzis (1982). In his case research with 2,000 managers at different levels and in different kinds of organisations in the United States he identified 18 characteristics or skills which he claimed all successful managers have in common. While at first sight his 18 competencies (see Chapter 3) might be seen as a more sophisticated version of generalised statements about what 'all' managers need to be able to do, in fact he qualified this view to the extent of saying that there will necessarily be variations of requirements in different organisations. Boyatzis indeed specifically recommended that organisations should work on their particular understanding of these characteristics in their own organisations, rather than accepting someone else's general view of the applicability. Specific context is a significant moderating factor.

Boyatzis' ground-breaking study has been followed by a number of equally detailed research studies showing variations on his competencies. The significance of what could be called the 'competency movement' is that it has led to a more refined understanding of what managers ought to do, and in at least some cases to an emphasis on organisations producing their own list more relevant to their particular needs. In Chapter 3 we extend this discussion considerably to show its significance in LMD, but we can posit one conundrum even in this first chapter: the convenience and simplicity of this approach, which requires no additional effort in defining what managers do in one organisation, is likely to be misleading in terms of its effect on developing managers in those competencies which are crucially required by other organisations – or at least identifying and working on the most crucial. Managers live in a changing world, in organisations whose objectives can change, whose priorities can shift. The things which managers have to do effectively must be responsive to these changed circumstances. Thus over the last 25 years and certainly since the work of Boyatzis and Kotter, competition, changes in technology, globalisation and economic crisis require different ways of communication, working with teams within and across organisation boundaries both physically and virtually, and are bound to pose different demands on managers. Thus even organisationally derived competencies as generalised statements about managerial and leadership work in that particular organisation are bound to result in adjustments in both the content of a competence and its level of priority. It is doubtful that any framework of management or leadership can fully account for a process of managing and leading that must remain 'inherently problematic' (Hales 1993, p.15).

Some studies of what managers do provide a more vivid, complex and ambiguous image. Watson (1994) was interested in the reality of management as experienced by managers themselves, and one of the most important conclusions to emerge was the value-laden and moral position of those who perform management roles. As Watson suggests, 'Management is essentially and inherently a social and moral activity' where success is achieved by 'building organisational patterns, cultures and understandings based on relationships of mutual trust and shared obligation among people involved with the organisation' (p.223). Another study by Luthans (1988) pointed to the presence of dubious behaviours such as discussing rumours, hearsay and the grapevine; complaining, griping, and putting others down; politicking; and gamesmanship. Other behaviours included non-work-related chit-chat and informal joshing around.

 WEB LINKS

Watson and Luthans were both using an ethnographic approach to research. As Watson explained, he was able to 'get close to managers as individuals' and involve himself 'in their organisation context' (p.6).

Find out more about ethnographic research at **http://www.questia.com/Index.jsp?CRID= ethnography&OFFID=se1** and **http://www.sas.upenn.edu/anthro/CPIA/methods.html**.

Another image of managers at work is one associated with the importance of conversations and arguing for what is considered to be the right way. Through talk, argument and persuasion, a manager creates meaning with others, providing clarity as the conversations unfolds. It is an ambiguous image because conversations are not always predictable and can take unexpected turns. The manager in practice, according to writers such as Shotter and Cunliffe (2003), needs to be an author. That is, in times of difficulty and flux, as we have been experiencing towards the end of the first decade of the 2000s, leaders and managers are looked to as people who generate order out of chaos, confusion and contradiction. The way this is done is by talking persuasively for the order which they have generated.

ARE LEADERS AND MANAGERS DIFFERENT?

This is a question that has been of interest for many years, especially in recent years when, according to CEML (2002), 'new developments are putting emphasis on leadership abilities' (p.6).

Zaleznik (1977) began a key debate on this issue by asking the question whether leaders and managers were different. Kotter (1990), who as we saw above provided research on effective managers, continued the debate by focusing on what leaders did and encouraging the view that leadership is separate from management – which implies a different level or type of development need. However, he also argued that rather than leadership and management being seen as separate, they need to be understood as complementary to each other with different systems of action, as shown in Table 1.2.

Table 1.2 Leadership and management as systems of action

Management	Leadership
Planning and budgeting Identifying steps to goal achievement and allocating resources to achieve those goals	*Setting a direction* Creating a vision for the future, along with strategies for its realisation
Organising and staffing Identifying jobs and staffing requirements, communicating the plan, and delegating responsibility to job-holders for carrying it out	*Aligning people* Communicating the vision and marshalling support; getting people to believe the management and empowering them with a clear sense of direction, strength and unity
Controlling and problem-solving Installing control systems to correct deviations from the plan, the purpose being to complete routine jobs successfully	*Motivating people* Energising people through need, fulfilment and involvement in the process, including supporting employees' efforts and recognising and rewarding their success. Co-ordination occurs through strong networks of informal relationships

Source: based on Kotter (1990)

A rationale underpinning the separation seems to be that when there is a need for dealing with flux, fast-moving change and complex decision-making, it is leadership that is seen as the requirement. The work of Bennis and Nanus (1985) and Bass (1985) during the 1980s and 1990s makes this point clear by pointing to the need for *transformational* leaders who are visionary, creative, inspirational and energising. By contrast, managers might be seen as more *transactional*, dealing with day-to-day operations. Leadership when defined in relation to management is highlighted as the creative function, with management seen as more routine and mundane. This argument resulted in a range of 'New Paradigm' models of leadership which proved very attractive to many organisations, and still prove so. For example, Bass and Avolio (1990) have developed a well-known Multifactor Leadership Questionnaire (MLQ), allowing the assessment of leaders and managers as transformational and/or transactional.

 WEB LINK

Go to **www.mlq.com.au**. Check the various uses of the MLQ for individuals and groups.

There are now a multitude of institutions, programmes and even academic departments devoted to leadership *rather than* management, working with this separation. It is noticeable that in education, health, public administration and local government, a number of leadership colleges and programmes have been established. In the UK, CEML (2002) identified a particular deficit in leadership skills, and it is leadership that has been highlighted by government reports as the key to effectiveness in the twenty-first century (PIU 2000). In uncertain times, it is leaders who are most needed, to provide direction and maintain engagement and focus (Holbeche 2008).

 WEB LINK

Go to **http://www.ncsl.org.uk/** for the National College of School Leadership.

We do feel, however, that there are a number of problems associated with the separation of leaders and managers which has amounted to something of a glorification of leaders as heroes and the denigration of managers. Firstly, we might suggest that the list of leadership characteristics or behaviours turns out on examination to be very much the kind of list that would be produced in relation to any effective manager. Leadership characteristics such as being a stimulator of thought and action in others, of being creative and 'getting out of the box' and producing direction-changing processes, are surely those we would look for in effective managers. Secondly, to say that these are the requirements for a leader – whereas a manager need only be concerned with the most routine and basic 'transactions' or the least exciting parts of the direction of a unit or organisation

– is demeaning of the managerial context, and of the majority of people who therefore become defined as 'only' managers rather than leaders. Thirdly, there is emerging research which criticises the domination of 'heroic' models that focus on senior staff at higher levels; these might be called the 'distant' leaders. In contrast, there has been interest in how leadership can be found at all levels: 'close' leaders (Alimo-Metcalfe and Alban-Metcalfe 2005). This brings us to a further point. While it is most usual to equate leadership with individual leaders, as an individualising exercise (Wood 2005), this rather misses the possibility of other views of leadership that are concerned with the working of groups, teams and whole units or organisations. These are all possible locations for the working of influence, power, mutual interdependence and collective working. In many organisations and between organisations, work has to occur without a single leader but by people working together and relying on each other. This phenomenon is being recognised as Distributed Leadership (Gronn 2000), and has significant implications for LMD, which we consider later. However, as Bolden (2005) points out, there may have been a misallocation of resources in the attempt to develop leadership capacity if the focus is mainly on individual leaders. Interestingly, there are doubts that we can clearly specify what leadership is and how people can be trained as leaders (Barker 1997).

1.2 REFLECT – CONCLUDE – PLAN

In 1974, Stogdill (1974, p.7) remarked 'There are almost as many definitions of leadership as there are persons who have attempted to define the concept.'

What would be your definition of leadership?

What images do you have of leaders and leadership?

Meet with two others to share your findings and find a joint meaning of leadership.

The uncertainty over specifying leadership has resulted in many different definitions. Here are just a few taken at random:

> Leadership is a process of giving purpose (meaningful direction) to collective effort, and causing willing effort to be expended to achieve purpose.
>
> Jacobs and Jaques (1990, p.281)

> Leadership is a process whereby an individual influences a group of individuals to achieve a common goal.
>
> Northouse (2004, p.3)

> Leadership is the art of mobilizing others to want to struggle for shared aspirations.
>
> Kouzes and Posner (1995, p.30)

You are invited to go onto Google and find as many definitions of leadership as you can – but we advise you to stop at 25. There is little surprise that writers such as Peter Senge (1999) can say, 'There's a snowball's chance in hell of redefining leadership in this day and age' (p.81). This does raise something of a difficulty, especially for those who are tasked with a role as leader and responsibility to act as a leader. As Macbeath (1998) suggests, leaders are often depicted at the apex of things, on top of a hill or at the centre of a complex web of activity. Therefore, if we regard leadership as something different from nominated leaders, it is bound to create problems. We refer to this situation as 'the leader's conundrum', which we state as a position where a nominated leader is expected to be a leader while power and influence are significantly distributed throughout and between organisations. This poses quite a challenge for those involved in LMD, which will be apparent throughout the book.

Because, at an individual level, the terms 'leader' and 'manager' can apply to the same person, depending on the contingent circumstances, we plan to save words by using the word *manager* to cover both leaders and managers. We will make an exception when the research or theory is clearly referencing leaders or managers and, of course, when considering the collective ideas of Distributed Leadership, we will honour that term.

 WEB LINK

The Centre for Leadership Studies at the University of Exeter is obviously trying to collect definitions of leadership. Go to **http://www.leadership-studies.com/lsw/definitions.htm**.

LEADING AND MANAGING IN ORGANISATIONS

It should be evident that much of the discussion about leaders and managers most frequently refers to larger organisations or corporations. For example, Mintzberg's (1973) roles were derived from Chief Executive Officers and a recent CIPD (2008) survey was concerned with 'global leadership' in organisations that 'focused on growth and improving customer relationships' who needed to 'develop high-quality leaders who can manage acquisitions and build new company capabilities' to feed their 'leadership pipeline' (p.2). Such organisations place rationality and efficiency at the heart of their organising principles, and this includes LMD. For example, as we will explore in Chapter 2, having a planned approach to the strategic development of managers might be seen as the goal. This is achieved by careful planning over the long term, the progression of managers through a number of levels within an understanding of roles and requirements, and stable market conditions. Of course, over the last 20 years the assumptions that underpinned this approach have been challenged, and as a consequence even in large organisations there have been some radical changes to structures and work organisation that have implications for managers and LMD. Along with the fact that many people work in the public or quasi-public sector – where public service is the goal, in contrast to the satisfaction of private interests, such as growth and profit – it is important to consider some of the variety that can found in managing and leading in organisations. To do this, we make use of a configuration grid shown as Figure 1.1.

Figure 1.1 A configuration grid

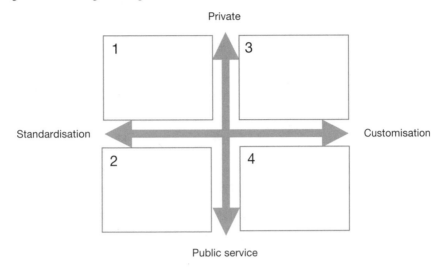

The grid is composed of two dimensions. Firstly, standardisation–customisation, which suggests that organisations can be considered on the extent to which they are configured towards providing products and/or services against a specification by the organisation or the customer. At the extreme of standardisation we can consider the order that is achieved through Fordist and neo-Fordist production approaches based on rational design principles of specialised functions and hierarchic co-ordination. This is the traditional image of work organisation. By contrast, customisation requires a focus on specific and unique requirements of customers. Secondly, on the private–public service dimension, we can consider how work is driven by the satisfaction of private interests, such as profit, shareholder value, growth, and so on or the fulfilment of public service criteria as found in the National Health Service, local government provision, education, and so on. Towards the centre of this dimension we might place various public/private initiatives.

We suggest that there are various ways in which work can be configured. For example, in the 1980s and 1990s patterns of flexible working and pressures to re-engineer organisations to make them more responsive to markets and customers, tended to reduce hierarchic layers and 'flatten' structures, promoting teamworking, often with a requirement for higher skills for employees and a degree of self-management (McClurg 2001). During the 2000s this has been taken further, with interest in high-performance work systems (HPWS). Where this has occurred in the private sector can be summarised as a move from quadrant 1 to quadrant 3 in Figure 1.1. This move also underpins the growth of service-based organisations, responding to customer demand that expects differentiation to meet their particular requirements. Many organisations in the creative and cultural sectors, but also in traditional sectors such as engineering, are using project-based working to achieve this, and this contrasts with hierarchic functional leadership and management (Lindkvist 2004). Project working is seen as a source of learning within and between organisations (DeFillippi 2001), so there is growing interest in how projects are managed and led.

Most organisation units in the UK operate on a small scale employing relatively small numbers of staff. We describe units with nine or fewer employees as *micro-businesses*, and those with 10 to 249 employees as *small and medium-sized enterprises* (SMEs). Such organisations do have a strength in their ability to respond quickly to customer needs, so many would be placed in quadrant 3. Many are family-owned and the direction is strongly connected to the interests and actions of the owner-manager (Gray 2000). Managing and leading in such organisations is also tied up with the desires, aspirations and ambitions of the owners who have overall management responsibility. However, in reality most micros and SMEs are constrained by their size and have short planning horizons compared to their large firm counterparts. Johnson (1999) found that few SMEs had any formal approaches to developing managers, and this is not surprising since most people who manage and lead seem to learn by solving problems and making mistakes (Gibb 1997), rather than through formal LMD.

Most professional organisations can be seen as SMEs although some have grown rather larger than 249 employees – eg the larger firms of accountants and lawyers. Many of the staff are professionally qualified and provide a focused service for their clients (quadrant 3). However, over the years there has been a growth in functional specialisation with some standardised provision of services and management through what Mintzberg (1983) called a 'professional bureaucracy' (quadrant 2). In addition, the professions for many years have been protected from competitive forces. But in recent years there has been a trend towards a more managerial approach which has seen the emergence of the *managed professional business* (Cooper *et al* 1996) with an emphasis on becoming more businesslike in response to changing market demand using the language, techniques and structures of management. Normally organised as partnerships, professional firms since 2006 have been able to form a *limited liability partnership* (LLP), a legal entity in the UK that allows partnerships to enjoy limited liability. Partners become directors of a business, albeit one that attempts to meet the standards expected of a profession. In such organisations, however, staff work with a sufficient degree of discretion and autonomy that make traditional styles of command and control a recipe for conflict and 'it is easy to get into a vicious circle: the manager tries to control things – the professionals sabotage this' (Vermak and Weggeman 1999, p.33).

The issue about professionals as managers – as we have discovered, for example in projects with lawyers – is whether the people who are actually carrying out managerial functions see themselves in such a way. There are specific features about trying to engage in LMD for professionals. Many of them are discussed by Raelin (1986), who examines the differences of view that may occur in the way

LAW FIRM LAUNCHES SCHEME TO TRAIN LEADERS

Law firm Halliwells has launched a management development scheme to help create future leaders. Eighteen of the firm's 160 partners were chosen to take part in the pilot programme, which was developed by Manchester Business School. It comprises four modules: leadership, people resourcing, business development, and finance.

Joanne Edward, learning and development officer, said it was the first time that the law firm, which has more than 1,000 employees, had put in place a succession plan to develop managing partners for the future. 'Lawyers are very good at what they do, but are often put in management roles without

being given the exact skills,' she said. She added that succession and career planning had become important over recent years because the firm had grown considerably in size after a series of mergers.

The modules are delivered through a combination of case studies, group work, individual learning and work-related projects. To complete each module, partners have to take part in a group project – including one on change implementation – present it to the board, and go on to manage it.

Source: adapted from Lucy Phillips, *People Management*, 26 June 2008

professionals see themselves as compared with the way they see people who are more clearly identified as managers. Dawson (1994) also reviews potential clashes in the older professions between what may be perceived as professional standards and ways of behaving and managerial requirements. Nevertheless, a survey of professional associations by Perren (2001), studying those bodies responsible for setting out a profession's specification for membership, suggested that leadership and management were seen as highly relevant for their members, although few went so far as to specify LMD as a requirement. However, some do – for example, the Law Society's Continuing Professional Development (CPD) scheme requires solicitors in England and Wales to complete a compulsory management course with options for further development as managers.

 WEB LINK

Check the CPD requirements of solicitors at **http://www.sra.org.uk/solicitors/cpd/solicitors. page**.

As well as professions, there are emerging many areas of work which must be regarded as concerned with the production and use of knowledge, referred to as knowledge-based organisations (Garvey and Williamson 2002) or knowledge-intensive firms (Newell *et al* 2009). Such organisations focus on the production of knowledge by employing expert 'knowledge workers' to provide solutions for clients (quadrant 3). There is strong emphasis on creating and sharing knowledge within an organisation but also across organisation boundaries. Further, with development of Web 2.0 technologies which allow the creation of architectures for people to share ideas and hold discussion in social networking communities (Martin *et al* 2008), many organisations can operate through the work of virtual teams where interactions mostly occur electronically. Managing and leading a team that relies on electronic interactions between members who can be dispersed geographically throughout the world puts significant emphasis on communication and facilitating interactions (Powell *et al* 2004).

To this point, we have mainly considered the variety of configurations that feature in the top half of Figure 1.1. If we now move towards the public service quadrants, we can note that for a number of years significant efforts have been made to improve the performance of the public sector and various agencies operating with public funding, including the universities. The term 'leadership' is usually preferred, and leadership has been identified as the key requirement in making the step changes necessary for 'modernisation' and effectiveness in the twenty-first century (PIU 2000). This has engendered a degree of standardisation (quadrant 2), set by central government and monitored by achievement against targets and indicators. Thus hospitals have targets and grades, schools are placed in league tables based on examination performance and local authorities are graded. Of course, within the public sector there are many professionally qualified staff who may have difficulty in adopting leadership and management roles or accepting those who do. Generally in the public sector in the UK, as part of the modernisation agenda there has also been a trend of what is called the New Managerialism with an implicit aim of curtailing the power of professionals (Exworthy and Halford 1999).

Recently, however, there has been an attempt to move towards more responsiveness to service-users in the public sector. For example, a recent inquiry into the role, function and funding of local government (Lyons 2007) suggested the need for more discretion and flexibility in local government so that it could engage with local people more effectively. This is a shift towards quadrant 4. An example might be the recent policy on providing support for adults referred to as Personalisation. This allows those who are entitled to support for their care to have more choice and control over what they receive. This is a significant change in the social care system and requires different agencies such as social workers, health workers and care workers to share information and collaborate. Another example would be the policy of Every Child Matters, focusing on the well-being of children. This requires significant collaboration between the agencies that provide services for children – schools, hospitals, police, and so on. Such collaboration would suggest that leadership becomes shared within a group working across their traditional disciplines.

 WEB LINK

Find out more about these policies at **http://www.dh.gov.uk/en/SocialCare/Socialcarereform/ Personalisation/DH_079379** and **http://www.everychildmatters.gov.uk.**

Organising work across disciplines to provide value-added provision for service-users and customers is becoming increasing recognised in both the public services and private sector and sometimes as private/public collaborations. It is clearly a quadrant 4 way of working which Victor and Boynton (1998) refer to as co-configuration. A key idea is to respond to a customer's needs and learn from interactions to add further value. As Victor and Boynton (1998, p.195) suggest,

> Mass customisation … requires the company to sense and respond to the individual customer's needs. But co-configuration work takes this relationship up one level – it brings the value of an intelligent and 'adapting' product.

Learning is crucial to co-configuration. Firstly, as Daniels (2004) suggests, professionals and experts from different disciplines learn to debate and negotiate through dialogue. Secondly, learning occurs through interaction with clients, customers and service-users and is shared with others. Both these requirements suggest a shared responsibility for leadership. In the public sector there is more recognition of the need to work across boundaries, creating partnerships and networks between agencies. Brookes (2008) refers to this as 'new public leadership', with a clear implication for a collective leadership approach. Similarly, Gold and Thorpe (2009) show how lawyers from different specialist departments in a commercial law firm were able to consider client needs strategically, learn from interactions and share knowledge.

In addition to public service bodies and agencies, there are many thousands of community and voluntary sector groups and organisations which we refer to as the *third sector*. They all clearly exist to serve some specific public or community purpose. However, there are large organisations – such as Oxfam and Dr Barnardos – which to some extent are configured for standardisation, enjoying some of the economies of scale that come with size and a degree of specialisation including leadership and management functions. Generally, the third sector lacks organisation, with many groups relying on volunteers, charity funding and managing based on the motivation of participants. The service ethos would suggest consideration of ideas of leadership that reflect such values, like Greenleaf's (1982) idea of 'servant leadership' based on the view that leaders must choose to serve by prioritising the needs of others. Between groups there can be a great deal of informal sharing of ideas supported by networks such as the National Council for Voluntary Organisations. This again suggests that leadership can be considered shared across groups.

A growing part of the third sector consists of businesses with social objectives where profits or 'surpluses' are reinvested in community or environmental projects. These businesses are called *social enterprises*, the best-known example perhaps being the magazine *The Big Issue*, sold by the homeless who can earn money by selling it. The UK Government sees social enterprises as a source of creative but socially and environmentally responsible work, which raises the standards of ethical business and corporate social responsibility (Cabinet Office 2007).

THE ETHICAL LEADER

This does raise an issue of something still rarely addressed in LMD – values and ethics – although there is growing recognition that it should. The ethical dimension in leadership and management has become particularly prominent in the latter part the first decade of the 2000s. Following earlier scandals at Enron, the more recent actions of certain leaders in banking and the financial sector, while not exactly labelled unethical or immoral, have certainly raised questions about the hero status that has been accorded to leaders. Mintzberg in 2004 had already suggested that 'a cult of leadership' could be 'dragging business down', and there is certainly more interest now in ideas around managers who are more authentic, show humility and cultivate spirituality (Bell 2008). Western (2008) identifies a trend towards 'eco-leadership' (p.183) whereby leaders become concerned with ecological and social concerns. Leaders might rely less on functional hierarchical tools of control, and more on relationships, the valuing of differences and diversity, social and environment responsibility, all of which add up to acting ethically.

It is interesting to note that it is mainly leaders who receive the attention for ethics. While managers might be considered neutral and objective in their work, leaders have to make decisions, and such decisions are an expression of their identities and values (Robinson 2010). Therefore, it is argued, such decisions ought to be considered against ethical and moral considerations. According to Brown *et al* (2005, p.120) ethical leadership can be defined as

> the demonstration of normatively appropriate conduct through personal actions and interpersonal relationships, and the promotion of such conduct to followers through two-way communication, reinforcement, and decision-making.

One of the key features of this definition is the emphasis on being seen by others as ethical. Certainly, research suggests that people or 'followers' expect their leaders to have integrity, show honesty and be perceived as trustworthy, and fulfilment of such expectations is predicted to result in willingness to work harder and satisfaction with their leader (Brown and Treviño 2006). As we identify in later chapters, leaders (and managers) are often considered role models for others: any discrepancy between what they say and what they do therefore creates an impression of lacking transparency. Leaders are expected to act in a way that is true to their values and feelings to support an impression of authenticity (Gardner and Schermerhorn 2004).

There seems to be growing pressure for leaders and their organisations to behave more ethically and more responsibly. For example, the Globally Responsible Leadership Initiative at **http://www.grli.org/** seeks to integrate ethics into business and requires leaders to take responsibility for this to ensure long-term sustainability. On paper and on their websites at least, many organisations seem to have made a response through statements and policies for corporate social responsibility (CSR) or corporate responsibility (CR). We explore some of these emerging themes later in the book.

1.3 REFLECT – CONCLUDE – PLAN

Go to **http://group.barclays.com/Sustainability** – *the Barclays Sustainability page.*

What are the key features of Barclays' approach?

What ethical practices is the company seeking to embrace?

What actions can be taken by managers to meet the aspirations presented?

LEADERSHIP AND MANAGEMENT DEVELOPMENT

The variations in configurations of work organisation where leadership and management occurs are bound to raise some important issues for LMD, how it is understood, and what is carried out. As Burgoyne *et al* (2004) suggest, it is difficult to generalise about how managers should be developed because of the variation in situations and context. Nevertheless, in a textbook on LMD you would expect some generalisation and at least some attempt to define what we are considering. Here we can suggest one definition that works, from what is believed to be the correct or best way to manage or lead, found in appropriate ideas and models for managers to put into practice. LMD could be defined as:

> a planned and deliberate process to help leaders and managers become more effective.

This definition does not specify what processes are preferred, only that there is a degree of certainty to allow planning and deliberation. There is also the suggestion of assessing or perhaps measuring the impact of any process. Thus if a manager attends a workshop on managing employee performance, there is enough known about this issue for objectives to be set and a link to be established to see if these are achieved and become part of a manager's actions at work which can then be assessed. However, what we know about what managers really do, does make plans and deliberation problematic. The definition also seems to exclude those unplanned, accidental, undeliberate experiences that so many managers record as a significant part of their development. There are clearly many occasions when managers learn to be effective or otherwise without anyone making plans for this to happen. We suggest that another definition of LMD is:

> a process of learning for leaders and managers through recognised opportunities.

The importance of this definition is that there is no specification for planning and deliberation: whatever is learned needs to be recognised, and often – as we explore in later chapters – this can only be achieved by reflecting on what has been done, either at the moment of action or as part of a review to consider what happened. Both are part of an important process for managers and professionals more generally (Schön 1983). What is done as a consequence, such as a change in behaviour or a new way of understanding, is much less predictable, and this can even occur when prediction is intended. That is, a manager attends a course with pre-set objectives but learns something else that was not pre-set. When this is recognised, we can say it has emerged – but a manager might not have to attend a formal event like a course to achieve this. A great deal of LMD is not 'planned and deliberate', and even more significantly, probably cannot be – although the practice of developers should certainly include attempts to shift at least some experiences from the accidental, informal, undeliberate more towards at least being reviewed and deliberately assessed as learning experiences after the event. The tension between our two definitions suggests a dimension shown as Figure 1.2.

Figure 1.2 Planned and emergent LMD dimension

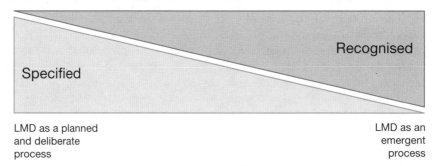

Specified

Recognised

LMD as a planned
and deliberate
process

LMD as an
emergent
process

We see this as a dimension between opposing views of LMD, but there is always a certain degree of overlap too. For example, even when managers attend formal events with clearly set objectives there will be an emergent process operating as stories of experience are shared or people keep up with the latest gossip. Similarly, it is possible to plan for and specify that managers could share what emerges from informal and everyday events, or events can be designed to encourage this. For example, the LMD method of Action Learning (Revans 1982) is to form groups of managers to share their problems, agree to take actions and learn from this process through regular reviews. With such a process, it is difficult to specify objectives or what will be achieved – but it is possible to plan for the process to occur. We deal with this apparent contradiction later in the book.

Without doubt there is a preference for planning and deliberation in LMD. This provides for structure in presentation and delivery, working out timing over a particular period and the allocation of resources. We have often noted the requirement to get LMD plans in place before certain key dates in the financial year, and sometimes a rush to spend money so as not to lose a budget. This is a good example of organisation structures setting the framework for LMD decisions.

Our two definitions incorporate a broad range of processes. For example, LMD covers both events that primarily involve the acquisition of new skills and that are usually the focus of *management training*, and the more formal activity of acquiring knowledge and understanding resulting in accreditation that is usually understood as *management education*. Fox (1997) suggests that the various elements of training, education and development can be linked by the idea of *management learning*. This term is also used by academics in their studies of managers and organisations and how learning occurs at work. In recent years, this has been extended to include leadership learning, professional learning, SME learning, and so on. There is more said about learning and its pivotal role in LMD throughout the book but especially in Chapter 5.

APPROACHES AND PURPOSE TO DEVELOPING LEADERS AND MANAGERS

Definitions help to establish what LMD is about but there also has to be some connection with how LMD can be approached and with an understanding of purpose. In considering choices of approach, there are as we will see many activities that come under the heading of LMD. A search on Google returned 21 million hits for 'management development' and nearly 42 million for 'leadership development' – an indication that LMD is big business. How can we make sense of all this? One source of help is provided by Holman (2000), who has provided a framework for considering approaches to management development which we can also extend to leadership development. The approaches are:

- *academic liberalism* – the pursuit of objective knowledge as principles and theories to be applied rationally and relatively scientifically. Managers have the image of a 'scientist', applying ideas and principles gained from experts. The argument here is that managers need to analyse key issues and use theories and principles to find ways of moving forward. Access to expertise can come through attending seminars, reading, taking programmes such as MBAs, and so on

- *experiential liberalism* – in which, rather than theories, experience is the source of learning that provides ideas and insights which can be used in practice. A crucial skill is to become a 'reflective practitioner' to make learning from experience a deliberate process, perhaps with others in a joint process or by taking responsibility for self-learning and development. As we saw from Figure 1.2, rather than being set a specified formula for learning, managers can use experience from a variety of sources and especially from their own actions set in a particular context. This approach might be seen as more natural and more meaningful to managers (Davies and Easterby-Smith 1983)

- *experiential vocationalism* – in which organisations are where managers practise so what is needed is relevant knowledge and skills, as required. The image is that of a 'competent manager or leader', as defined by an agreed model of competences. Many organisations across many sectors have sought to define the behaviours needed for managers. The result is highly formulated profiles which can be used to set out the requirements for managers as competences, including how behaviours can be measured. In terms of Figure 1.2, we are back at the specified end of the dimension, with the model of competences having some connection with what the organisation is seeking to achieve through LMD

- *experiential critical* – where 'emancipation' is sought by managers by becoming 'critical'. We are moving towards the emergent pole of Figure 1.2, where managers, faced with difficult situations, need to become 'critically reflective' so as to surface and challenge key assumptions that may be preventing progress. There is a combination of using experiences and adopting ideas and techniques drawn from a body of knowledge called critical theory. This does create a tension with the expectation of fast-paced and quick solutions, but perhaps recent events have provided an impetus to this approach (Reynolds and Vince 2007).

Each of these approaches gives rise to a number of models of leadership and management which in turn affect how managers are measured, assessed and developed. They also have implications for who is responsible for LMD, who sets the objectives, and who decides what is to be learned. The tensions that arise from these issues are evident throughout the book.

A key area of debate is around the purposes of LMD. If we start to consider this from a national perspective, there is a sense that LMD must be important. However, as Burgoyne *et al* (2004) found, it is rather difficult to show that LMD is needed for improving UK economic and social outcomes – but they conclude 'with reasonable confidence that leadership and management capability ... enhances performance' (p.2). The Leitch Review of Skills (Leitch 2006) certainly seemed to endorse this by linking an improvement in management skills to the improvement in business performance, although, as Tamkin and Denvir (2006) suggest, we do lack the data necessary at a national level to make the links between leadership and management and performance. Mabey and Ramirez (2005), however, conducted research across European organisations to find an impact on performance from management development, although the link did depend on priority and support from leaders.

Most research is conducted in organisations and one of the most interesting studies by Storey *et al* (1994), comparing processes in the UK and Japan, suggested a number of objectives for management development:

- as a device to engineer organisational change – in particular culture change
- as a tool in pursuit of quality, cost reduction and profitability
- to structure attitudes
- to contribute to the development of a learning organisation
- to assist with self-development.

Although not explicit in their book, their discussion of these purposes enables us to look at the extent to which they may not be mutually supportive or, indeed, might be contradictory of each other. The first four purposes quoted above clearly relate explicitly to organisational needs, whereas the last should contribute to those organisational objectives but in some respects might not do so. It could be in the interests of individuals even acting within a planned LMD system to develop themselves in ways and for needs which are not priorities for the organisation – and indeed might relate to longer-term ambitions outside the organisation. There is scope for confusion here – partly related to definitions of what you mean by 'self-development'.

There are other areas in which confusion about purposes – perhaps enhanced by a failure to agree on the meaning of particular words – may arise. For example, there may be issues about the extent to which LMD policies, systems and actions are designed to create individuals who are wholly in tune with the prevailing beliefs and methods of working in an organisation. Yet at the same time an organisation may claim that it wants to develop managers who are keen on taking initiatives, who will break the mould of current thinking and methods of working, who will introduce styles of behaviour that challenge the existing styles. Such contradictions may appear within LMD programmes. For example, Höpfl and Dawes (1995) reported a programme designed to empower middle managers in a water company so that management style could move directing and controlling toward support and trust. However, as soon as the managers started to make suggestions, senior management perceived themselves under threat, leading to the curtailment of the programme.

Lees (1992) identified some very different reasons why organisations support management development. Apart from the obvious functional purpose of enhancing performance, he also identifies other 'faces' such as *agricultural* – enabling people to develop by 'fertilising' and supporting: 'We need to grow our own managers'; and *organisational inheritance* – which captures the idea that movement between jobs is set by formal criteria for promotion and movement. Lees commented that these formal statements are often at odds with the actuality of what happens. He also suggested that management development was a form of *compensation* – a process through which activities become in some sense a reward for continued employment; and a symbolic *ceremonial* – rituals which confirm the passage of managers through the organisation, and which bind them further into the organisation by celebrating achievement.

Since the early 1990s there has been a significant growth in interest in LMD. Large organisations point to the need to compete, to respond to technological change, and to work globally, requiring managers who are more strategic (Garavan *et al* 1999). As we have suggested, it is no longer something that just occurs in large organisations. Thomson *et al* (1997) found that many organisations were investing in management development in the late 1990s at all levels, and even some SMEs were prepared to do so if they saw a value and purpose. Into the 2000s, as we explore in Chapter 2, the UK government has, through a range of enquiries and reports, seen leadership and management as a key factor in the failure of the UK economy to perform as well as others. The government has sought to stimulate LMD across the public sector, within SMEs and in the third sector too, especially social enterprise.

The recession that started in 2008 has provided revised reasons for attention. The period up to the middle of 2008 had seen considerable interest – especially in large global organisations – in finding, developing and retaining the right talent to feed a 'leadership pipeline' (Conger and Fulmer 2003). A survey of over 13,000 HR professionals and leaders in 76 countries identified growth, improving customer service and improving or leveraging talent as the key business priorities (CIPD 2008), a focus on those with high-potential much in evidence. By late 2008, talent was beginning to be seen as a part of survival. A survey of HR managers in the UK found that there was greater emphasis on leadership and management development (CIPD 2009), with a purpose not just to sustain business during a downturn but to find new ways of doing things when resources are stretched. Rather than continuing with traditional images, there is a need for managers to become 'hands-on' and 'heads-in' (Charan 2009) by accessing intelligence from the whole organisation and adopting an inclusive stance on talent – a return to basics, perhaps, as shown by the *LMD in Practice* below.

LMD IN PRACTICE

'TOUGH LOVE' SCHEME BOOSTS COMPETITIVENESS

Sainsbury's has put 350 of its senior managers through an intensive coaching programme to improve the supermarket's competitiveness and performance. The 'Tough love' programme saw top staff attend three days of workshops to help them develop what the HR department identified as the three most critical behaviours, which were honesty, openness and simplicity.

Of this group, 28 senior managers went on to qualify as accredited 'master coaches', including the director of organisational development and the head of learning and development, Sue Round. She said that the supermarket had made a 'significant investment' in the programme but has saved money in recruitment by helping some deputy managers move into managerial roles without needing an external recruitment process. 'It usually takes six months before people start to add value, so to have someone already in place who knows the company is invaluable,' she added.

Round said some staff who were not performing to a high standard have 'been turned around by the programme – people whom we might otherwise have lost'.

Source: *People Management*, 12 March 2009

It is partly because of recent difficulties and the link made in the public mind to the behaviour of managers in powerful positions in organisations such as Enron, Arthur Andersen and WorldCom in the USA and Northern Rock, Royal Bank of Scotland and HBOS in the UK, that there has been interest in what is referred to as critical leadership and management learning (Rigg 2007). This is a term with a variety of possible meanings and draws on a range of ideas from politics, sociology, psychology and philosophy. They all have the potential to challenge key assumptions relating to the purpose of LMD and the actions of managers.

Critique and critical understanding has informed many researchers of LMD. Over the last 20 years there has been a growing interest in researching LMD. There are now many journals devoted to LMD aimed at both academic and practitioner communities. We are involved in some of these and, as you can see, we are making use of many sources for this book. Some of the key journals are

Management Learning, Journal of Management Development, Leadership and Organisation Development Journal, Action Learning – Research and Practice, Human Resource Development International and *Academy of Management Learning and Education.* In addition, there are conferences across the world that are either devoted to LMD or where LMD is frequently a key feature. There are also professional bodies, such as the British Academy of Management, the Academy of Management and the University Forum for HRD, which seek to advance research and theoretical development in LMD. The Chartered Institute of Personnel and Development (CIPD) also completes research projects for the interest of its professional members.

 WEB LINKS

The website of the British Academy of Management can be found at **www.bam.ac.uk**. For the US Academy of Management, go to **http://www.aomonline.org/**. The University Forum for HRD's website is at **http://www.ufhrd.co.uk/wordpress/**. The CIPD's Management Development resource is located at **http://www.cipd.co.uk/subjects/ lrnanddev/mmtdevelop**, and for its leadership resources, go to **http://www.cipd.co.uk/subjects/maneco/leadership/**.

Of course, the outcomes of researchers form the basis of much of the curriculum for leadership and management programmes in our business schools, although there has also been some concern about what is taught. Sumantra Ghoshal (2005), for example, suggested that the ideas of academics in the business management arena have been partly responsible for some of the 'worst excesses of recent management practices' (p.75), and Bennis and O'Toole (2005) argued that 'business schools are on the wrong track' (p.96), citing the failure of MBA programmes to provide managers with useful skills, for not preparing them adequately for leadership roles, and for not imbuing them with appropriate norms of ethical behaviour. Ferraro *et al* (2005) suggest that the discipline of economics which has provided the basis for business theorising does not value or privilege practice or the plurality of perspectives, or even the creativity and imagination that is often seen as being at the heart of the management process. One consequence of the doubts and confusions relating to research and theories for managers is a growing interest in *evidence-based leadership* and management where managers can make better decisions by learning to find and critically appraise empirical evidence from research (Hamlin 2009).

There are debates among researchers about how LMD can be understood. Burgoyne and Jackson (1997) suggested that a more pluralist understanding is required to appreciate political dynamics and the cultural and symbolic context in which LMD occurs. Mabey and Finch-Lees (2008) more recently argued that research in LMD can be examined under four headings or discourses, each capturing a set of ideas and practices which provide the representations for action and how the field of LMD needs to be considered. The four discourses for researching LMD are:

- *functionalist* – probably the most traditional and mainstream view of LMD which is seen as a means to improve performance, providing skills and knowledge, perhaps as a 'toolkit' to address identified gaps

- *constructivist* – LMD is seen as a way of helping managers make sense of what is happening at work, finding ways of bringing groups together to learn, and jointly constructing meanings to make progress

- *dialogic* – organisations are seen as consisting of many voices and interests, as are managers, who adopt different ways of talking and appropriate identities according to context. Argument and negotiation are required, but ongoing flux and disagreement is likely

- *critical* – organisations are sites of power struggles, domination and subordination. Managers are enabled and constrained, dominating, suppressed and resisting.

How LMD is studied and researched is very much driven by the interests of researchers and the agendas of the institution in which they work. For example, in many universities in the UK, the agenda has been to achieve high research rankings in the Research Assessment Exercise. To do this, researchers have set their sights on publication in peer-reviewed journals, although different journals favour different discourses. However, other researchers of LMD might work in consultancies where their task is to provide solutions for clients. There is less concern with peer review and more concern with practicality. Publication will be focused on practitioner journals, such as *People Management*. In the UK, as we suggested above, there has been a concern to provide research that has an impact on the practice of managers – eg the Advanced Institute of Management and the Economic and Social Research Council.

 WEB LINKS

We suggest that you consult **http://www.aimresearch.org/**; this is the site of the Advanced Institute of Management, which seeks to provide high-quality research to have 'an immediate and significant impact on management practice'. The Economic and Social Research Council's site is **http://www.esrc.ac.uk**. It provides funds and training for research in the social sciences that leads to 'the highest-quality research on the most pressing economic and social issues that we face'.

SUMMARY

- The emphasis in this chapter is on the contingent nature of leadership and management.

- In recent years 'leadership' seems to have become a more popular term – a hot topic of our times.

- There are a range of theories to explain the work of managers but these seem to be disconnected from what managers need to do and what they need to learn.

- There is debate around the differences between leadership and management, with a lot of emphasis on leaders as transformational and managers as transactional.

- There are also debates around the meaning of 'leadership', with too much attention given to individuals as leaders.

- Most ideas in leadership and management development centre on larger organisations in the private sector.

- There is growing interest in leadership and management development in different organisations with different configurations and purposes.

- Definitions of leadership and management development have to embrace informal, accidental learning opportunities as well as formally created ones.

- Organisation ethics and values need to be addressed in the development of managers.

- Leadership and management development can be approached in different ways based on different models of managing and leading.

- Leadership and management development has many purposes, but enhancing performance is usually seen as the prime purpose.

- The Credit Crunch of 2008 has posed new challenges for leaders and managers.

- Leadership and management development is a significant area for research.

QUESTIONS

For discussion

1 How are definitions of leadership and management related to the practice of leaders and managers?

2 *Leaders transform, managers transact.* Discuss.

3 Should leadership development be concentrated on individual leaders?

4 Is leadership and management in a law firm the same as leadership and management in a charity or leadership in a virtual organisation?

5 Should leadership and management development always serve the needs of the organisation?

NOTES

1 The questions posed here take readers through three elements of the learning cycle, which is described in Chapter 5. 'Reflect' is part of the 'Review' element in the cycle.

2 You can check the Higher Education Statistics Agency (HESA) figures online at **http://www.hesa.ac.uk/index.php**.

FURTHER READING

AVOLIO, B. J. and LUTHANS, F. (2006) *The High Impact Leader: Moments matter in accelerating authentic leadership development*. New York: McGraw-Hill

BOLDEN, R. (2007) 'Trends and perspectives in leadership and management development', *Business Leadership Review*, Vol.4, No.2: 1–13

LINSTEAD, S., JEFFCUTT, P. and GRAFTON-SMALL, B. (1996) *Understanding Management*. London: Sage

MINTZBERG, H. (2004) *Managers, Not MBAs: A hard look at the soft practice of managing and management development*. San Francisco: Berrett-Koehler Publishers

WATSON, T. J. (2001) 'The emergent manager and processes of management pre-learning', *Management Learning*, Vol.32, No.2: 221–36

CHAPTER 2

Strategic leadership and management development

CHAPTER OUTLINE

Introduction
The value of leadership and management development in the UK
Strategy and leadership and management development
Evidence and leadership and management development
Learning and strategy
Summary

LEARNING OUTCOMES

After studying this chapter, you should be able to understand, explain, analyse and evaluate:

- the value of LMD to the nation

- the link between LMD and organisation performance

- the link between strategy and LMD

- the significance of evidence-based LMD

- how leadership and management learning may or may not contribute to strategy

- the significance of power in LMD

INTRODUCTION

There is considerable and ongoing debate about the precise meaning of strategy, much of it due to the variety of interpretations of different schools of thought (Caldart and Ricart 2004) and we will refer to some of this discussion below. However, for both the nation and organisations there is a recognised need to do something about the quality of managers so that there is a response to such forces as:

- competitive pressures and globalisation

- economic pressures as a consequence of the 2008 Credit Crunch

- the demands of reform and modernisation in the provision of public services

- the requirements for change, including structures, technology and knowledge production

- the complexities of managing and leading an increasingly diverse and knowledge-based workforce.

Reminding ourselves that the word 'strategy' has its origins in the Greek term *stratēgos*, meaning the commander of an army ranging his troops to face an enemy, we can suggest that these forces represent the 'enemy' and that the 'ranging of the troops' is a call to seek ways to integrate the development of managers with organisation goals. There have been calls to move in this direction for the last 20 years. For example, Constable and McCormick (1987) in a key report made it clear that management development needed to be integral to strategic planning and change. During the 1990s, Thomson *et al* (1997) found in a UK survey of over 900 organisations that management development was not adequately linked to organisation strategies. At a national level, the Council for Excellence in Management and Leadership (CEML 2002), finding dissatisfaction with the quality of leadership and discrepancies between demand and supply of LMD opportunities, saw the need for a strategic body to oversee the field of LMD in order to improve performance. Paradoxically, however, managers are frequently required to learn the skills of thinking strategically, and leaders in particular are expected to display such capabilities of 'big picture sense-making' (Storey 2004, p.24) – not surprisingly, strategy courses are the main form of LMD provided.

Our concern in this chapter is with some of the strategic considerations of LMD. First of all we consider some of the national concerns regarding LMD, and we then relate such concerns to how UK organisations make decisions that provide (or do not) for LMD activity. A key feature of the discussion is the extent to which LMD is linked to considerations of organisation strategy. We will find that one approach is that LMD is valued by some because it helps managers fulfil organisational needs as expressed in its strategic plan. This allows a particular kind of response with a declaration of a policy of how requirements should be met and how the value of any provision should be measured. However, we shall also see that this essentially top-down approach can be contrasted with one that gives emphasis to the way managers learn and develop through the opportunities that occur in the hectic reality of working life. This is a more opportunistic and emergent view, as we identified in Chapter 1, and one that could provide a bottom-up link to strategy. It recognises that the value of LMD is that it could provide an input to strategic considerations as well as being determined by them. However, we also suggest that this optimistic view could be made ineffective by particular value/reward systems which strongly influence what managers learn. We conclude by examining how the values and beliefs that form an organisation's culture have a significant influence on what LMD is provided.

THE VALUE OF LEADERSHIP AND MANAGEMENT DEVELOPMENT IN THE UK

Questions concerning value usually refer to the worth or overall use of some thing or process. In relation to LMD, a key consideration for many organisations and indeed the nation as a whole is the extent to which LMD, whatever its shape or composition, can be shown to improve the capability of managers leading to success of some kind, however judged, in organisation performance and then the nation (Tamkin and Denvir 2006). Underpinning such reasoning is what is often referred to as a 'functional performance rationale' for LMD (Garavan *et al* 1999, p.193), so that there is linear chain of connections between LMD and national economic success, shown as Figure 2.1.

Figure 2.1 The connection between LMD and organisation and national economic success

Leadership and management development

Good managers

Successful performance of managers

Success in organisations

National economic success

At each point in this chain, worth and use might be assessed, feeding what Holmes (1995) rather sceptically refers to as 'the formula for success'. Indeed, one of the key purposes of the evaluation of LMD is to *prove* that claims about the success of LMD at various stages of the chain can be made.[1]

In Chapter 8, on *Evaluating leadership and management development*, we explore various aspects of this link in more detail. However, for the moment it is enough to say that proving the effectiveness of LMD is a difficult process. Very frequently, therefore, more restricted assessments of value are made – eg the number of people attending a training programme or the overall satisfaction of participants at the end of a programme. Sometimes no formal assessment is made at all, so the value of LMD is assessed informally or just becomes an 'act of faith'. The link to an organisation's strategy is for this reason often tenuous or non-existent.

2.1 REFLECT – CONCLUDE – PLAN

Do the various claims in 'the formula for success' seem valid to you? Is it possible to show how LMD leads to better managers, who in turn improve organisation performance, resulting in national economic success?

What evidence is there to support the linear chain of connection?

What could you do to provide better evidence?

NATIONAL CONCERNS

Whatever the complications, adherence to the links within 'the formula for success' in Figure 2.1 have become a taken-for-granted feature of strategic considerations of LMD. Certainly, at national level there have been ongoing concerns about the quantity and quality of managers and the commitment of organisations to LMD stretching right up to the present day. During the 1960s, the publication of the Robbins Report on Higher Education in 1963 identified a lack of management education and recommended the establishment of two postgraduate management schools. Under the guidance of Lord Franks, the two schools were opened in London and Manchester in 1965. In addition, new universities established in the 1960s, such as Lancaster, began to offer management and business qualifications to undergraduates and this extended to polytechnics as they began to open. During the early 1990s the polytechnics became universities and the number of business schools grew significantly, reaching around 120 in the 2000s.

While the number of people with graduate and postgraduate management qualifications began to rise, this did not alleviate concerns about the vast numbers of managers and employees generally who had no qualifications at all and little opportunity for training and development at work. By the 1980s there was continuing concern over the UK's industrial decline, and an under-investment in human capital– usually referred to as 'Britain's training problem' – was identified as one of the causes, along with a failure to modernise capital equipment, poor development practice, outmoded financial structures, an anti-industrial culture and class system, and poor management of strategic change (Sparrow and Pettigrew 1987). Intriguingly, one particular feature of the UK situation was that managers, in contrast with those in other countries, did not value training because it was not perceived as strongly linked to profit (Hayes *et al.*1984). We can discern an important theme here: managers who do not see the value of training and development for themselves are unlikely to see the value of training and development for others. Further, failure to make the link between learning and improving skills and performance could become an accepted feature of an organisation's values and beliefs or culture. It also allows others to blame managers for their lack of support for learning.[2]

The attention given to the education of managers and their continuing development once they started work was one of the key findings of Charles

Handy's Report (1987). Whereas Japan, the USA, Germany and France all took the preparation and development of managers 'seriously' (p.2), Britain did not – apart from some particular exceptions in larger organisations. The findings from the Handy Report were supported by those from the Constable/McCormick Report (1987) and others.[3] Underpinning all such research was the key strategic assumption that there is value in investing in the development of managers because good management provides the foundation for improvements in productivity in organisations and hence, overall national economic prosperity. Some of the key features of both these reports are shown below.

- Over half of UK companies made no provision for the training and development of managers. (Of companies employing more than 1,000 people, one-fifth made no provision for the training of their managers.)

- Over half of companies in West Germany, the USA and Japan gave their managers more than five days' off-the-job training each year. In Britain managers received an average of just one day, most getting none.

- 90,000 entered management each year; very few had any formal management education or training.

- 24% of UK senior management held degrees; the total was close to 85% in the USA and in Japan.

In 1987, Handy set out two problems, one for the short term and one for the long term. In the short term there was a need to improve the competence of existing managers. In the long term Britain needed a pattern of formation for managers so that they were fully prepared for their roles. What happened next?

If the results of surveys in the late 1990s are anything to go by, there seems to have been something of a sea-change in the UK. The survey by Thomson et al (1997) of over 900 organisations using questionnaires and interviews found that management development had been given a higher priority, compared with 1987. This was evidenced by more organisations providing training, only 4% of large companies and 20% of small companies offering no training. The average number of days of formal training per annum per manager had increased to 5.2 days – an apparent five-fold increase since 1987. This particular finding showed little variation according to size of organisation or sector. There was also a claim for more informal development. In addition, there had been an increase in the formal qualifications of managers, 77% of junior managers and 44% of senior managers undertaking qualifications.

However, some words of warning. Various commentators suggested that the general nature of the results hid important variations. For example, some organisations could report large amounts of training and others could report little or none (Thomson et al 2001) with similar patterns for priority, the achievement of objectives and written statements of policy. They suggested that there was little evidence of 'deep thinking' about 'learning processes' of managers or how to make the link to strategy (Thomson et al 1997, p.78). Storey and Tate (2000), in their contrast with Japanese organisations, referred to the 'fickle' characteristic of British provision by which programmes could be cut or changed over time.

For example, there could be a tendency to institute new programmes every few years – leading to 'programmitis' (p.211). There could also be swings in the type of provision. One year the emphasis might be on self-development, followed by its de-emphasis in the next. The result could be confusion and cynicism among managers. Thus, while acknowledging the improvements since 1987, the case for management development was not yet fully proven and the particular need for leadership development only just starting to be recognised.

From 1997, and the election of the Labour Government in the UK with its emphasis on 'education, education, education' and a commitment to the idea of 'lifelong learning', there have been a number of attempts to set out a strategy for skills development at all levels in the country as whole, including LMD. Even though there is a lack of specific evidence between training and economic growth (Machin and Vignoles 2001), the importance of skills was identified as a requirement for national competitiveness and the prevention of social exclusion. A Skills Task Force was set up in 1998 to develop a National Skills Agenda to 'ensure that Britain has the skills needed to sustain high levels of employment, compete in the global marketplace and provide opportunity for all' (NSTF 1998, p.38). To develop such an agenda, 18 research reports were commissioned and two Employer Skills Surveys (ESS) conducted. Management skills were among the areas covered, and the report reinforced much of the previous research that managers in the UK tended to be under-qualified with low levels of qualifications and an inadequate amount of training (Johnson and Winterton 1999). One particular highlight of this report was the attention given to small and medium enterprises (SMEs), to the effect that most managers in SMEs did not hold formal management qualifications, nor did they undertake much management training, although they might recognise the value of this for their business and although much learning about management occurs informally by working on business problems (Gibb 1997). (See also Chapter 12.)

After the STF made its final report in 2000, the work was continued by two national bodies. Firstly, the Performance and Innovation Unit of the Cabinet Office examined Workforce Development, concentrating mainly on lower and intermediate skills. Secondly, management and now leaderships skills were explored by the Council for Excellence in Management and Leadership (CEML).

THE COUNCIL FOR EXCELLENCE IN MANAGEMENT AND LEADERSHIP

CEML was established to 'develop a strategy to ensure that the UK has the managers of the future to match the best in the world' (CEML 2002, p.1) because 'good leadership and management is pivotal to investment, productivity, delivery of service and quality of performance' (p.4). Its work was based on a number of working groups and advisory groups. This provided for a very broad scope and included SMEs, professional bodies, higher education and other bodies such as government agencies, and consultants. More research was commissioned and several reports were produced, providing significant detail and adding to the stock of knowledge provided by previous reports, but also noting some interesting quandaries about managers and their skills. For example, the report on the Management Population in the UK (Williams 2002) found it difficult to identify a reliable measure of the gap in skills at managerial level. Do rising salary levels for managers indicate skills shortages? Possibly, but it could also be the case that managers earn more because they deserve it through adding more value. Further, it would appear that most organisations can fill their managerial posts, although this says little about the quality of those occupying the posts.

Some of the main findings from the work of CEML are listed below (CEML 2002).

- There had been an increase in the award of management qualifications – but there was continuing dissatisfaction with the level and spread of management skills and especially leadership.

- There was no lack of learning opportunities for managers but there were restrictions on the ability to take up those opportunities.

- There was a need to stimulate demand from all organisations and from individuals, and to improve supply by paying attention to what the customer wants and by building links between demand and supply.

- Many organisations were unclear and unfocused about what they needed, which often resulted in dissatisfaction with outcomes.

- Significant amounts of money were being invested in leadership and management development but there were difficulties in showing a positive return.

One result of all the research has been a build-up of a significant amount of knowledge about LMD and the extent to which it is valued in organisations. What becomes readily apparent, as these various research efforts show, is how embedded the notion of the link between LMD and economic improvement has become and how difficult and intractable the problems of evaluating that link remain. There clearly have been some improvements since the 1970s – as the 1997 survey (Thomson *et al* 1997) showed – but there remain widespread concerns about the inadequacies and variations.

The link between leadership and management and national performance, usually measured in terms of productivity growth, is hardly straightforward but it has been the focus of research in recent years. This is important because there are examples of good practice – but in the main, there is still not a great deal of evidence that the value of LMD is proven. Bosworth *et al* (2002) set out to use the results of the 1999 Employer Skills Survey to show the link between the qualifications and proficiency of managers, the strategies adopted by establishments and their performance. Using descriptive statistics and multivariate analysis, the report highlights some very interesting but paradoxical results. Overall, there seemed to be no direct link between management qualifications and performance but evidence for a link between proficiency and performance. It was suggested that this might be due to the acquisition of skills through experience. Taking a macro approach, a report by the strategic expert Michael Porter (2003) on the UK economy suggested that investment, the use of advanced technology and the employment of highly skilled labour were more important and the cause of management capability rather than a consequence. However, this suggestion itself might be too simplistic.

A year-long research survey of 3,000 organisations on performance and productivity by the Work Foundation in the UK (2005) found that leadership and management were among the key factors that contributed to high performance, along with communication, simple processes for fast decision-making and an informal culture to get work done. Interestingly, leadership was not seen as one person forming a vision but rather a process allowing people and teams to decide what needed to be done throughout the organisation – what we referred to as Distributed Leadership in Chapter 1 (Spillane 2006). Other research tends to support these findings, with a clear link between good management practices and performance (AIM 2009), but crucially, organisation context, history and culture – all soft and intangible factors – were key mediating influences on this link, as was competition in product markets. There is clearly a need for more research on the working of all these factors and the role of managers (Siebers *et al* 2008).

This links to the work of Tamkin and Denvir (2006), who have developed a model to show the key elements for impact on organisation performance. The model is shown in Figure 2.2.

Figure 2.2 A model of impact on organisation performance

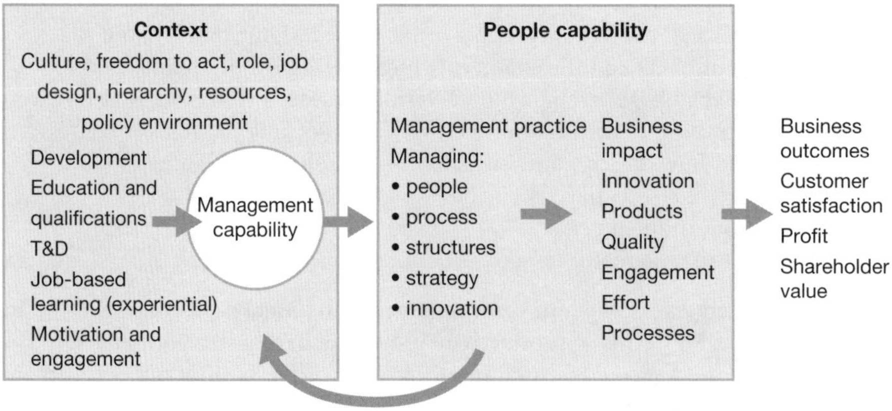

Source: Tamkin and Denvir (2006, p.12)

It is proposed that the model is used to assess the availability of current evidence and identify any gaps so that government policy can be better informed on leadership and management capability. The model specifies the key sections as follows:

- *inputs to management capability* – factors to develop management capability, education, ongoing formal and informal learning, and job experience

- *context* – which includes the HR environment, the presence and operation of rules, the degree of flexibility managers have, and the devolvement of management responsibility
- *management practice* – the processes and practices adopted in terms of managing people, structure, processes, strategy and innovation
- *people capability* – the skills, capabilities and engagement of employees will all mediate the effect of management practice
- *business impact* – product quality, productivity, engagement and effort
- *business outcomes* – the effect of these activities.

The Workplace Employee Relations Survey (WERS) was identified as a key source of data to match against the model, although questions would have to be adapted for this to occur.

 WEB LINK

UK productivity and performance is one of the research themes of the Advanced Institute of Management. Go to **http://www.aimresearch.org/ about-aim** for more details and access to some key papers. The Economic and Social Research Council also finances research into economic performance from a social science perspective. Go to **http://www.esrc.ac. uk/ ESRCInfoCentre/research/EconomicPerformanceDevelopment/** .

In the public sector, for many years LMD was probably even less of a priority. However, with the need to engender reform and modernisation there has been significant attention and resources directed towards the development of leaders. In the UK, the Cabinet Office's Performance and Innovation Unit (PIU 2000) expressed concern at the failure of the public sector to attract and retain the best leaders and stated that there was a need for more 'joined-up' working and support for partnerships. One result of this attention was the establishment of a number of colleges to provide leadership development for various parts of the public sector. There is also a crucial debate about the direction and purpose of LMD in the public sector (see Hartley 2009).

 WEB LINK

Check the provision for leaders at the National College for School Leadership (soon to be the National College for School and Children's Leadership) at **http://www.ncsl.org.uk/**, for further education leadership at The Learning and Skills Improvement Service **http://www.lsis.org.uk/ LSISHome.aspx** and the Fire Service College at **https://firelearn. fireservicecollege.ac.uk** .

The UK Government has also moved towards a more strategic approach for stimulating demand for LMD in SMEs. Based on a recognition that informal learning is more important in an SME, an Action Plan for Small Business (SBS

2004) sought to provide a more 'joined-up' service and a new set of initiatives on a broad front that attempted to stimulate demand using brokers to ensure a match between SME needs and provision. By 2007 it was claimed that the plan had been completed and a new Enterprise Strategy was developed with a range of measures to support SMEs. Similarly, there has been a Social Enterprise Action Plan (Cabinet Office 2007)[4] which aims to foster a culture of social enterprise, improve the business advice, information and support, tackle the barriers to access to finance, and enable social enterprises to work effectively with the government.

The Leitch Review of Skills (Leitch 2006) continued the national push for LMD by highlighting an improvement in management skills and relating it to the improvement in business performance. In the review, the Sector Skills Councils (SSCS) were pinpointed as the bodies to stimulate demand, especially among SMEs. There are 25 SSCs representing employers on skills issues in sectors such as construction, hospitality, engineering and manufacturing. LMD has been identified as an 'all-sector' issue.

 WEB LINK

Find out more about all-sector leadership and management ideas and strategy at
http://www.sfbn-mandl.org.uk/default.htm .

2.2 REFLECT – CONCLUDE – PLAN

There has clearly been an increasing interest in LMD at national levels in England, Wales, Scotland, Northern Ireland and across the UK. However, is there any evidence that it is working?

Find out about the impact of various action plans and strategies for small businesses, social enterprises and SSCs.

What progress has been made and what outcomes achieved? What has been the impact of recession and the Credit Crunch downturn?

STRATEGY AND LEADERSHIP AND MANAGEMENT DEVELOPMENT

In the midst of recession, organisations are urged to maintain their investment in LMD in order to survive (Holbeche 2008) and according to most orthodox views, if LMD is to have any purpose in an organisation, it should be linked and driven by organisation strategy. As organisations attempt to deal with environmental changes such as globalisation, technological change, customer demands and the vagaries of the financial system, LMD can be seen as a 'tool' intended to implement the strategy developed and improve or sustain performance.[5] As Brown (2007) suggests, this would imply that there is some deliberate and conscious process to provide the link between organisation strategy and other levels. A survey by the Chartered Institute of Personnel and Development (CIPD 2002) of nearly 1,000 senior managers found that 86% said, 'integrating management development with the implementation of organisation goals' was the priority in terms of improving the contribution to organisation performance (p.1). The survey found two key purposes:

- *developing managers to sustain the current business model* – Managers need to have the skills to carry out their roles and new managers need to become productive very quickly. Management development provides the means by which an organisation's 'winning proposition' can be sustained

- *developing managers to create future business models* – Because business models have a limited life and stability is becoming more unusual, managers can learn to develop new models. In fast-moving sectors, such as telecommunications, involvement in change initiatives leads to new understandings and new possibilities.

These purposes provide an interesting and contrasting view of the strategic link. The first is perhaps still dominant, apparently more uncomplicated, and reflects the 'functional performance rationale' referred to by Garavan *et al* (1999, p.193), with a causal chain of connection between strategy and performance. Figure 2.3 provides a representation of this view of the link.

The obvious points about the model are that:

- strategy is set in response to an assessment of changes in the environment
- the response is agreed by various stakeholders and interested parties
- the strategy provides guidance on the requirements for managers in terms of numbers, skills and performance requirements
- LMD *policy* translates the requirements to provide LMD *activities*
- the *outcomes* of activities are assessed and valued, providing feedback for organisation strategy.[6]

An example of how an LMD strategy is prompted by environment conditions is the leadership development strategy developed by the NHS Primary Care Trust in Sunderland (see **http://www.sunderland.nhs.uk/TPCT/about_us/board/2005/ nov/docs/enclosure8(p).pdf** [accessed 11 May 2009]). Firstly, it highlights key environmental factors for public sector organisations:

- demands on public services to meet the needs and wishes of customers
- higher expectations on the part of the general public
- increased opportunities and requirements for partnership both across the public sector and with other organisations
- pressure to harness new technology and innovate in delivering public services.

Figure 2.3 A sustaining model of leadership and management development

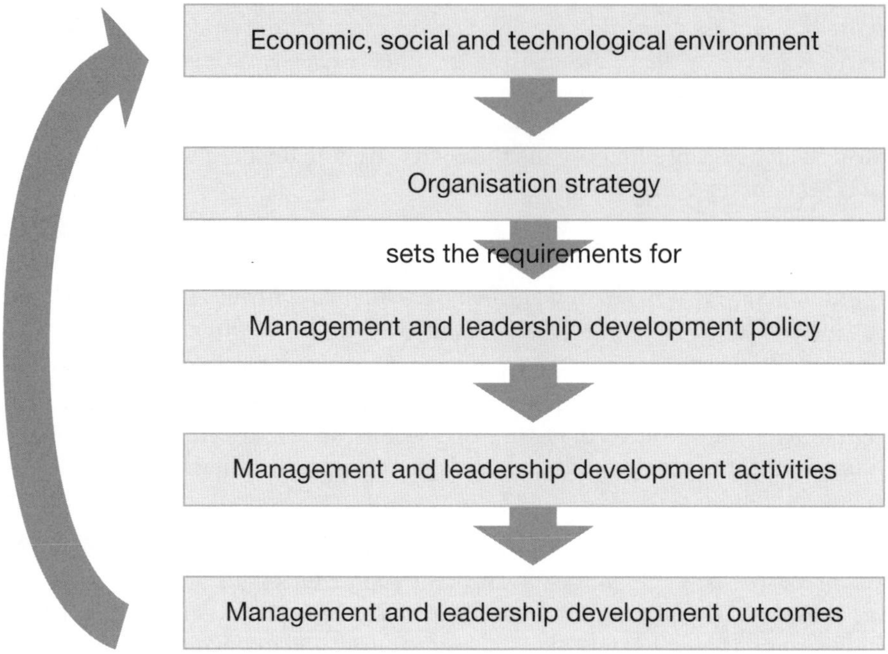

```
┌────────────────────────────────────────────────────┐
│   Economic, social and technological environment    │
└────────────────────────────────────────────────────┘
                         ↓
┌────────────────────────────────────────────────────┐
│              Organisation strategy                  │
└────────────────────────────────────────────────────┘
                  sets the requirements for
┌────────────────────────────────────────────────────┐
│   Management and leadership development policy       │
└────────────────────────────────────────────────────┘
                         ↓
┌────────────────────────────────────────────────────┐
│  Management and leadership development activities    │
└────────────────────────────────────────────────────┘
                         ↓
┌────────────────────────────────────────────────────┐
│  Management and leadership development outcomes      │
└────────────────────────────────────────────────────┘
```

In response, the following elements provide the strategic intent for LMD:

- *aligning leadership development planning with organisational strategy* – involving the identification of the gap between desired future leadership capability and the current position, clarifying how the gap is to be bridged by development activity

- *aligning leadership development with key people management processes* – embedding leadership development strategy and practice within an integrated framework of people management processes

- *evaluating learning and behaviour change* – involving the evaluation of the impact of development activity through assessing individual learning and behaviour change, and its impact on service provision and patient experience

- *evaluating impact on services and objectives* – involving the evaluation of the impact of leadership development activity on services and strategic objectives. It requires systematic approaches to linking the impact of leadership itself on service performance.

Other reasons for forming an LMD strategy would include:

- change of technology, work design and/or organisation structure
- mergers and acquisitions
- entering new markets and providing new services
- responding to identified weaknesses and poor performance.

Of course, any strategy for LMD is subject to disturbances such as the recession from 2008. The *LMD in Practice* below shows how one organisation has responded.

LMD IN PRACTICE

ADJUSTING THE LEADERSHIP DEVELOPMENT STRATEGY AT HML

Tim Spackman, *Organisation Development Manager*

Based in Skipton, North Yorkshire, HML is the UK's leading third-party mortgage administration company, with over 40 clients and £50bn worth of assets under management. It is home to 2,000 employees at four sites.

In an extremely challenging economic environment where the housing and sub-prime mortgage market have collapsed and much trust has been lost in the financial services industry, leadership has never been more important to HML. Our business strategy to respond to these conditions is to focus on quality and continuous improvement to differentiate our service and be the obvious choice for any potential clients looking to outsource. The vision of our senior team has meant we have continued to invest in the long-term health of the organisation to be the best in the market in which we have grown, in preparation for an economic recovery.

There can be opportunities in a recession for agile businesses and we have sought to focus on both income generation through exploring new markets as well as cost control. If we are to lead and innovate,

we need the organisational capability to adapt quickly and effectively, identifying and responding to emerging needs and opportunities. Trust being important to both us and the industry, we have developed new organisation values, including one of trust, as well as seeking to develop the kind of open organisational culture where people feel able to speak freely about concerns and issues affecting our clients' customers.

What this has meant for leadership and management development is an emphasis on developing the behaviours that support our organisational values at all levels of the organisation, coaching as a key leadership style, a focus on tools and techniques to deliver quality and process improvements, and the development of both entrepreneurialism and financial acumen. In an environment where many organisations have cut training budgets, the centrality of leadership to our future success and strategy is recognised through continuing investment in our programmes. We have also developed an edge to our programmes whereby leaders need to demonstrate they are capable of leading their people through a formal accreditation process.

The second purpose, from the CIPD survey (2002) *Developing Managers for Business Performance*, would seem to be more challenging. It provides for the possibility that LMD can have a role in making strategy as well as being determined by it. It is a view which may be becoming more evident, especially where organisations face more unstable and capricious environments. It also embodies a connection to the recent interest in developing a strategy for the management of talent. Michaels *et al* (2001) are usually given credit for the creation of this interest based on the view that organisation success partly depends on attracting and retaining a group of high performers. An organisation can consider its talent more strategically by identifying people of high performance and high potential who join a talent pool to feed the 'talent pipeline' for senior positions. This was a significant theme identified by Tansley *et al* (2007) in detailed studies of nine organisations, as well as the need to attract and retain individuals to meet immediate needs. More recently, attention has switched to the motivation, development and deployment of talent of those already in the organisation (CIPD 2009). While there is certainly a link in any strategy between talent and LMD – including such issues as career development and succession planning (see Chapter 10) – talent management can also involve a more inclusive view of people in organisations: in others words, those who are not destined to be managers and might still occupy pivotal roles in an organisation (Collings and Mellahi 2009).

For many organisations, however, debates about the strategic purpose of LMD are still unlikely and this may be a reflection of the belief about its value to organisation performance. In the 1980s, based on his research in British Rail, Burgoyne suggested that how an organisation responded to management development was an indication of its maturity. Table 2.1 shows Burgoyne's 'ladder of organisation maturity'. (Level 1 is at the bottom.)

The first point to note is that Burgoyne defined management development as 'the management of managerial careers in an organisational context', and managerial careers as 'the biography of a person's managerial worklife'. He said that processes of 'natural' management development happen – they are not deliberately planned or contrived for management development. They are inevitable, usually good, and destined always to be the major provider of management development. However, in most situations they are not enough. In particular, he saw these processes as essentially effective in new entrepreneurial firms, usually small in size. As such organisations need to cope with increasing scale and complexity, natural career structuring and learning alone are not sufficient, so the journey to what he called 'organisational management development maturity' begins.

Beyond Levels 1 and 2, a visible policy for management development provides a form and shape to activities, exemplified by *structural* and *developmental* activities. Structural activities include succession planning, assessment centres and various methods and techniques to allocate managers to specific roles. Developmental activities are those which help a manager learn and develop, such as courses, mentoring, coaching, etc. At Level 4 and beyond, these activities and the policy that provides their integration and co-ordination are strongly connected to corporate policy. In 1988, according to Burgoyne, possibly the majority of organisations were at Levels 1 and 2, and Levels 3 and 4 described the limits of current best practice achieved. Levels 5 and 6 apparently existed as 'occasional achievements often precariously achieved and lost, and often only occurring in some relatively autonomous part of large organisations'.

Table 2.1 Levels of maturity of organisational management development

Level 6 **Strategic development of the management of corporate policy**	Management development processes enhance the nature and quality of corporate policy-forming processes, which they also inform and help implement.
Level 5 **Management development strategy input to corporate policy formation**	Management development processes feed information into corporate policy decision-making processes on the organisation's managerial assets, strengths, weaknesses and potential, and contribute to the forecasting and analysis of the manageability of proposed projects, ventures, changes.
Level 4 **A management development strategy to implement corporate policy**	A management development strategy plays its part in implementing corporate policies through managerial human resource planning, and providing a strategic framework and direction for the tactics of career structure management and of learning, education and training.
Level 3 **Integrated and co-ordinated structural and development tactics**	The specific management development tactics that impinge directly on the individual manager, of career structure management, of assisting learning, are integrated and co-ordinated.
Level 2 **Isolated tactical management development**	There are isolated and *ad hoc* tactical management development activities, of either structural or developmental kinds, or both, in response to local problems, crises, or sporadically identified general problems.
Level 1 **No systematic management development**	No systematic or deliberate management development in structural or developmental sense; total reliance on natural, *laissez-faire* uncontrived processes of management development.

Source: Burgoyne (1988, p.41)

2.3 REFLECT – CONCLUDE – PLAN

Are you able to use Burgoyne's ladder to plot your own organisation's level of maturity?

If you are at Level 4 or below, what steps would be needed to move you further up the ladder?

What action can you take to facilitate this?

Levels 5 and 6 imply that management development can have a reciprocal link to strategy where manager learning is both driven by strategy but also provides an input into strategy-making. It also proposes a link between management development and such ideas as the learning organisation

(Burgoyne and Reynolds 1997), and Burgoyne had a significant involvement with the latter.[7]

During the early 1990s, the move to Levels 5 and 6 seemed to be put on hold: organisations were 'downsizing' and 'de-layering' – processes which put the job security of many managers at risk. At the same time, there were significant changes in many organisations, the managers often being required to take the lead. For example, the implementation of business process re-engineering (BPR) was based on the view of a radical change of business processes by applying information technology to integrate tasks to produce an output of value to the customer. It was often accompanied by the removal of unnecessary processes and layers of bureaucracy so that staff became more empowered to deliver high-quality service and products. Managers were very much involved in identifying the processes but might also suffer the consequences when this resulted in the loss of particular roles and in disruptions to planned career paths (see Chapter 10).

In the public sector there has been a significant shift towards mangerialist language and techniques as part of a response to deregulation and competition. This trend has been referred to as New Managerialism or New Public Management (Pollitt 2000). While this has certainly resulted in a renewed interest in management development in the public sector, involving the establishment of new institutions such as the National College for School Leadership, in general there has been considerable resentment towards managerial processes (Exworthy and Halford 1999).

In the 2000s there was renewed interest in the reciprocal connection between LMD and organisation strategy to enhance a company's sustainability, profitability and competitive advantage as suggested by the 'Developing managers to create future business models' purpose identified by the CIPD (2002) survey cited above. There are indeed examples of how some organisations are seeking or hoping to achieve this. For example, Shell has systematic and integrated processes which focus on business results involving:

- a talent review process – to identify future requirements and assess talent availability by examining the ratio of candidates for every senior level position

- strategy development – an annual process which includes HR considerations and relates business improvement to the 'capabilities required of our managers'. The process allows 'challenging dialogue about leadership and management capability'

- 'potential' assessment – each person is assessed in terms of the job level he or she could ultimately achieve in Shell.

The company runs a range of formal leadership programmes, including Mid-Level and Executive Leadership programmes, to sustain a talent pool of leaders for the future (Ferrarie 2005). It also has partnerships with leading business schools, including Wharton Business School at the University of Pennsylvania where its Group Business Leadership Programme is delivered. Programmes are based on a framework of core competencies such as:

- valuing difference
- delivering results
- building a shared vision
- demonstrating courage
- championing customer focus
- displaying personal effectiveness
- motivating, coaching and developing
- maximising business opportunities
- demonstrating professional mastery.

 WEB LINK

Find out more about Shell's approach to leadership development at **http://www.shell.com/ home/content/careers/professionals/career_progression/professional_leadership_17102006. html** .

For Holbeche (1999), the vital requisite for success is alignment of organisation strategy and employee performance at every level. In this process there needs to be a way of measuring and appraising performance and, as is evident from the example of Shell, allowing strategic changes to be expressed in terms of capabilities required from managers. In many organisations, competency frameworks have been developed to facilitate alignment. As we explore in Chapter 3, competences express the behaviour needed by managers to allow organisation strategy to be achieved. Competences also allow key HR activities such as reward, selection and the identification of LMD needs to be integrated around strategy.

Brown (2005) has shown that strategic management development can stimulate strategic change with new activities and strategies. An organisation can enhance its capability in strategic management as a consequence of strategic LMD. Generally, however, there is little evidence that LMD is connected to strategy in the UK. Part of the reason is related to the low attention ordinarily given to strategic management in the UK, especially to considerations for the medium to long term. Even in organisations where strategic management is seriously considered, often the focus is on profit maximisation and cost minimisation (Coleman and Keep 2001). Skills and HRD are generally a fourth-order consideration, seldom considered either as an input to strategy or as a direct outcome. This is an issue of continuing concern. For example, Clarke *et al* (2004) carried out research to explore the problem of the gap between the recognition of the need for a link between LMD and strategy and its practice. Their focus was specifically on what they called 'business leadership development' (p.275) relating to behaviours and skills such as risk-taking, innovating and anticipating the future. Such skills are usually understood as strategic or 'future-oriented' (p.275). The research revealed agreement on the need for these but little attempt to distinguish such skills from other skills and an unclear strategy for doing so. This was partly attributed to the failure of HR managers or those forming LMD strategy to use business needs as the starting point, perhaps through their lack of understanding of such needs. But it was also attributed to the conservative response of those providing LMD with safe and unchallenging provision that gives priority to short- and medium-term needs. If HR managers and providers of LMD have difficulty in relating their work to organisation strategy, perhaps there is more optimism in considering what is referred to as the *resource-based view* of the firm (Boxall and Purcell 2003), which suggests that successful performance is a function of a firm's core competences which can include skills of the workforce or of part of the workforce (Prahalad and Hamal 1990). Organisational performance can therefore be improved and strategic objectives achieved by focusing development on key groups such as managers.

EVIDENCE AND LEADERSHIP AND MANAGEMENT DEVELOPMENT

One of the most interesting features of the debate concerning LMD and strategy is that there seems to be a difference between the rhetoric of a strategic approach to LMD and the reality. For example, LMD specialists may be keen to point out how they always consider business strategy in whatever they provide, but this may often result in having to be cut back when required by business circumstances (Storey and Tate 2000). Further, Mabey and Thomson (2000), in comparing the views of HRD managers and MBA managers, found a strong difference of views on whether LMD linked to business strategy. A majority of MBA managers saw little link, probably because they had a more precise view of what was meant by strategy. What seems to be evident is that in many cases, even where there is a high priority given to LMD, there is still an adherence to a top-down view of how the connection between strategy and management development should work. What is missing is an appreciation of the everyday dynamics, difficulties and uncertainties that managers learn to cope with and how this can easily diverge from the requirements of expressed strategy. LMD systems can easily become sealed off from the realities that managers face too (Doyle 1995). However, there are other ways the connection can be considered, and what is important is that organisations do have a choice, irrespective of their size, structure and sector. As argued by Mabey and Thomson (2000, p.12):

> enhancing the outcomes of management development is ... within the hands of the organisations themselves and the way they organise and prioritise their management development processes and systems.

To help an organisation decide, there is a growing trend to consider best practice approaches and the evidence of what works in LMD. For example, in their review of literature relating to what might be considered 'best' practices in leadership development, Leskew and Singh (2007) identified six factors regarded as vital for effective leadership development, which could be used to form LMD strategy. The factors are:

- a thorough needs assessment
- the selection of a suitable audience
- the design of an appropriate infrastructure
- the design and implementation of an entire learning system
- an evaluation system
- corresponding actions to reward success and improve on deficiencies.

One of the most vital factors is the support of systems, structures and culture for LMD so that it becomes embedded in the organisation. Here we can consider the importance of a positive HR context, which according to Mabey (2002) is highlighted as the most influential determinant of LMD processes. Drawing further on data from the 1997 survey (Thomson *et al* 1997), Mabey suggested that taking a long-term view about managers was more likely to result in attention given to LMD and the creation of a supportive context that encouraged informal learning which related directly to work experience. Mabey found that HR context – composed of the use of planned career structures, succession planning and fast-tracking – was linked to LMD processes such as policy, diagnosis and review, responsibility and priority given to LMD. It suggested that taking a long-term view about managers is more likely to result in attention to their development over time and viewing their contribution as strategic. Another key finding from the model, and clearly related to the idea of a positive context, was the importance given to informal learning and development. This finding highlights again an important feature of successful LMD which we explore below. Such findings will lend much support to adopting HR practices and giving priority to people (including managers) in strategic considerations. Interestingly, HR managers were often unaware of the amount of development actually occurring because of the difficulty of reporting informal learning, even though it was often seen as effective.

Combining these findings with a further survey in 2004, Mabey (2005) tried to demonstrate how LMD could be linked to organisation measures such as commitment, performance and productivity. Figure 2.4 shows a summary of the links, where the thickness of arrow indicates the strength of the link.

Probably the most important finding was how responsibility for LMD by employers was sustained over time. If managers perceived this, it improved the link between LMD, engagement and performance. In addition, support of the board, the use of competences and the link to business objectives making LMD 'driven strategically' (p.2) were key factors. This is similar to the findings from research across Europe (Mabey and Ramirez 2005), which showed the importance of support and priority for LMD from those in senior positions as crucial for the link of investment in LMD and impact on organisational performance and productivity.

Figure 2.4 How leadership and management development links to organisation performance

Source: adapted from Chartered Management Institute (2005) *Management Development Works: The evidence.* London: CMI.

Using evidence to formulate LMD strategy is connected to the general influence of adoping an evidence-based approach to professional practice (Hamlin 2009). The main sources of such influence have been evidence-based medicine and evidence-based healthcare, which are well-established in these sectors. Hamlin suggests that applying evidence-based approaches to LMD requires:

- systematic feedback of opinions and preferences of managers/leaders and organisations

- good critically reflective evaluation data

- relevant good-quality empirical research of all kinds, including both 'pure' and 'applied' research

- the consensus of recognised professional experts in the field of management/ leadership

- affirmed professional experience that substantiates practice.

Organisations and LMD specialists can enhance the strategy and practice of LMD by using the results of research but also by obtaining ongoing evidence from their own practice by collecting data and reflecting critically on findings. As a result, the facts can be used to make decisions. Rousseau (2006) differentiates between 'big E Evidence' and 'little e evidence' (p.260), where the former is concerned with generalisable cause–effect connections such as that clear and specific goals are better than unclear goals. The latter is organisation-specific evidence that is learned by analysing the facts of particular events, such as customer complaints or salesperson reports. There can also be an interplay between Big E and little e. It is becoming clear that evidence can enhance practice in LMD and the availability of evidence is significantly enhanced by web access.

 WEB LINK

Examine **http://www.business.brookes.ac.uk/research/areas/ coaching&mentoring/**, the home page of the *International Journal of Evidence-Based Coaching and Mentoring*, which is a free-access and international peer-reviewed journal.

LEARNING AND STRATEGY

Gathering evidence from the practice of managers of what works or what can be changed requires an articulation of their learning. Such learning can help form strategy. Consider the following example of how learning from work can become strategic (Mintzberg 1987, p.68):

> A salesman visits a customer. The product isn't quite right, and together they work out some modifications. The salesman returns to the company and puts the changes through. After two or three more rounds, they finally get it right. A new product emerges, which eventually opens up a new market. The company has changed strategic course.

We might add that if the salesman's manager was performing effectively, the manager would be playing a vital role in this process, learning quite naturally through the work with the salesman and the customer, and with a result that has a strategic effect. This example highlights for us the importance of natural and informal learning for managers and how this could work as contrast to the top-down, formal views of strategy and LMD.

If you refer back to Burgoyne's (1988, p.40) 'ladder' model in Table 2.1, the feature of what he described as 'natural' processes and as 'usually good and destined always to be the major provider of management development' seemed to disappear from his model after Level 1. It may be that he meant to imply that such natural processes continued at all levels, but in fact no further attention was paid to them. However, we suggest that natural or informal LMD activities can have a vital role to play in organisations. Indeed, we argue, along with others (Burgoyne and Hodgson 1983; Stuart 1984) that managers cannot help but learn informally and naturally by working on the problems and solutions in a particular work context. While much of this learning will occur in an unplanned manner and often without clear intention or recognition, we argue that it also has a potential to become more deliberate and to feed into an organisation's strategy. We believe that it is important to include both informal and formal learning experiences to capture the totality of LMD in an organisation. However, it should not be too difficult to work out that managers have many opportunities in the performance of their work, which may in turn may result in new organisation strategies.

Organisations can make a stronger link between the learning of managers and their strategy. To do this, we draw on the work of Henry Mintzberg and his colleagues (1998) who, in an intriguingly entitled book called *Strategy Safari*, set out to take us on 'A guided tour through the wilds of strategic management'. At the start of the tour, the authors outline what for many organisations is the orthodox version of strategy as a deliberate and purposeful process passing through distinct phases of formulation, implementation and control. Mintzberg *et al* (1998) suggest that this orthodoxy is represented by a range of techniques and prescriptions developed within three schools of strategic management: the Design School, the Planning School and the Positioning School.[8] Each contributes to a *prescription* of how strategies should be made and carried out, and this could include guidance for the nature and type of LMD provision. However, a key purpose of the book is to contrast prescriptive schools with other approaches which are less prescriptive and pay more attention to *processes* that make strategy (or not). In particular, we draw on two of these schools: the Learning School and the Power School.

The Learning School works on the difficulties of prescriptive approaches and the frequent failure of strategic plans. A crucial feature is attention to the way strategy is formed through ongoing actions and decisions from a variety of sources which lead to small changes at work but eventually a change in direction. In this way, strategy is said to *emerge*, sometimes accidentally and unplanned, through the learning of people in organisations and the work that they do. Much of Mintzberg's work has been concerned with emergent strategy (see Mintzberg and Waters 1985). One particularly striking image, which highlights how strategy can emerge often unconsciously without clear direction, is the idea that strategies are like 'weeds in a garden' which take 'root in all kinds of strange places' (Mintzberg *et al* 1998, p.195). As we noted in Chapter 1, if we apply this to LMD, we can see that managers can learn in any context, probably even unintentionally or by accident. Such learning cannot be planned or pre-determined – indeed, its overall shape and direction may take the organisation away from any attempts to formally specify what managers should learn. Thus an LMD strategy that provides formal activities which are meant to provide an indication of organisation preferences on how managers should perform, can easily become distorted or countered by the emergent processes that occur in everyday activity.

Of course, there is no guarantee that the emergent learning (the weeds) will be fully recognised and translated into strategies from which the organisation may benefit. As Mintzberg *et al* (1998) suggest, 'Real learning takes place at the interface of thought and action, as actors reflect on what they have done' (p.195). This is the prompt for learning where the integration of leadership and management work, and attention to learning from that work, creates the potential for both a critique of existing ideas and actions and the development of new ones. An important part of this is the opportunity to reflect on work completed, and this provides the space for understanding what has happened and for identifying how improvements can be made. Such improvements can relate both to the manager's or leader's performance and to the work carried out. Through successive activity, and reflection, both aspects can work as a bottom-up process to change organisation strategy. An example is shown in the *LMD in Practice* below.

LMD IN PRACTICE

PROJECT MANAGERS LEARNING FROM PROJECTS AT GB BUILDING SOLUTIONS, WAKEFIELD

Louise Ebrey, *Business Improvement Manager*

Most project managers are very focused on their project, but rarely get time to stick their head above the parapet and find out what is happening on other projects around the company. This can mean that mistakes are repeated on many projects and that the benefits of innovation are not realised on all applicable schemes.

Also in some businesses project managers may not feel comfortable admitting that mistakes have occurred, so valuable learning opportunities are lost.

At GB Building Solutions we are very focused on ensuring that we learn lessons from projects in a way which:

- prevents repetition of mistakes
- utilises the advantages of previous innovation
- helps with work-winning by providing examples which give clients confidence in our capability
- gives the participants time to reflect on what they have learnt and how they will apply it in future.

We hold Lessons Learnt sessions on all our projects at key stages throughout the build and on completion. The output from

these is available to all in a very simple easy-to-use database which contains bite-size chunks of relevant information so that project managers can find what they need easily.

As an example, we hold Lessons Learnt sessions on all the projects we have carried out for a national care home provider. Attendees have included their European Construction Director, who was supportive of the process both from our perspective and from his own team's input. Learning from one project led to us rescheduling 30% of the façade and external works on the next project. Instead of providing tunnelled access to the model rooms for prospective purchasers, we provided access through a fully completed central courtyard which enabled visitors to experience what the finished building would be like, gaining much praise from the client and their marketing team. The client believes that this greatly assisted with sales, as prospective residents could get a real feel for where they would be living.

We also use the information from the Lessons Learnt sessions on our bidding, design and preconstruction processes. The earlier the learning can be incorporated into a project, the more benefits the project will gain.

Recognition that managers, and indeed many others at work, can become involved in making strategy through their actions is a feature of the growing interest in what is referred to as strategy-as-practice (Jarzabkowski and Spee 2009). This interest arises from the understanding that strategy is something that people do, and that there is a wide range of practices that contribute to strategy. Some of these are highly formalised and understood as part of the strategy-making process, such as workshops or away-days for the senior team. However, practice can be widened to include many other features of life at work which could produce outcomes for strategy, such as meetings, tele-conferences and interactions such as the salesman in Mintzberg's (1987) example. The strategy-as-practice approach seeks to explore the patterns of action and 'situated phenomena' (Jarzabkowski and Spee 2009, p.84) which produce strategic outcomes.

 WEB LINK

Go to **http://www.s-as-p.org/** for more details of the strategy-as-practice approach. In recent years the idea of emergent strategy has been developed to incorporate ideas on chaos and complexity. You can find out more about these developments at **http://www.santafeassociates. com/** .

If everyday practices of managers can become a feature of making strategy, Mintzberg *et al*'s (1998) presentaton of the Power School is an important reminder that power and politics frequently influence what strategies are formed and, we would suggest, have an important impact on LMD. The process by which new ideas emerge from learning seldom take a smooth path. Such ideas require friends and allies but there may also be contests over resources and the approval of key stakeholders in making ideas work or move on. Increasingly, it is being recognised that talk and the use of language in negotiating and persuading others are vital management skills (Holman and Thorpe 2002). Even in the context of formal strategy-making activities, there are always likely to be certain voices that are more privileged and that dominate others (Gold *et al* 2001).

While the Learning School offered the potential of allowing emergent learning from leadership and management activities to feed into organisation strategy, there is also the possibility that this might be prevented by the working of power and influence in organisations. Thus managers might learn *not* to learn or resist learning. How can LMD be cast as the antithesis of learning? Salaman and Butler (1990) suggested that hierarchic structures and the cultures where managers are located had an effect on managers and their ability to learn through particular value/reward systems. For example, they identified the way power is exercised as a source of what managers must learn, and those behaviours that are rewarded or penalised. This structures much of the everyday experience of managers, causing them to resist change or new forms of behaviour advocated in training courses. Indeed, the gap between new ideas and allowed behaviour can easily breed 'cynicism about courses' (p.187) and, we would argue, about any approach to learning which deviates from what is valued. Managers thus learn what they are supposed to learn and what is in their interests to learn to survive on an everyday basis.

This consideration of the Power School of strategy also prompts awareness that managers always learn and develop in a specific context comprising specific tasks and activities using tangible resources but also composed of values, beliefs, symbols, stories, myths and legends. The latter are usually referred to as organisational culture – an issue which has received considerable attention for the last 30 years and which undoubtedly has played a key role in influencing the nature, style and effectiveness of LMD activity. For example, it is often assumed that a leader will learn from an executive training event, usually at high expense. This assumption is based on a simplification of what is likely to be a complex set of connections associated with the leader and the training, but also the social, political and cultural factors which are usually neglected (Antonacopoulou 2001). Such issues form a fertile field for study by academics who take a critical view of LMD.

 WEB LINK

A Critical Management Studies Conference has been running for several years. You can access all the papers at **http://www.mngt.waikato.ac.nz/ ejrot/** .

SUMMARY

- It is a frequent assumption that there is a linear connection between LMD, good managers and the successful performance of managers, success in organisations and national economic success.

- In the 2000s, a Council for Excellence in Management and Leadership found continuing problems with respect to the ability to undertake learning opportunities, and the amount of LMD in small and medium-sized organisations and the professions.

- LMD can be seen a 'strategic tool' to implement organisation strategy and develop and improve business performance.

- There is a growing trend to consider best practice approaches and the evidence of what works in LMD.

- HRM context has been found to be a key factor in leading to more LMD in an organisation.

- Using evidence to formulate LMD strategy is connected to the general influence of adopting an evidence-based approach to professional practice.

- A learning approach to making strategy highlights how practice and decisions by managers at work can lead to small changes at work but eventually a change in organisational direction.

- Power and influence from different sources through particular value/reward systems may affect the potential of managers to learn.

QUESTIONS

For discussion

1 *Leadership and management development must be aligned to corporate strategy.* Discuss.

2 Can leadership and management development make a difference in times of recession?

3 Research has suggested that 45% of organisations give a high priority to management development in the UK. Why do you think there has been an increase in the priority given to management development, and does this reduce or remove concerns about the quality and quantity of managers in organisations?

4 Is a strategy for talent the same as strategic leadership and management development?

5 Is there a link between leadership and management development and the nation's productivity performance?

6 How can learning from everyday activities become strategic?

GROUP ACTIVITY

Get together in a group of four, in which each person should be familiar with one (preferably different) organisation. Focusing on the organisation, each person should consider some of the key stakeholders in relation to management development in that organisation – for example, the chief executive, the managing director or equivalent, the head of finance, the HR manager, trainers, senior managers, junior managers, staff, etc. Try to identify at least six stakeholders per organisation. Now complete the following:

1 Considering each stakeholder identified in turn, try to identify their expectations and goals for management development and how far they value management development. You may be able to assess these from past meetings, documents or actions. You may have to ask them personally, if possible.

2 Map your findings on a large sheet of paper. Consider how far the stakeholders' interests in management development complement each other and how far they differ. What implications do the findings have for the management development strategy in the organisation?

3 Meet with the other members of your group to share your findings.

4 Prepare a combined presentation on the importance of stakeholder views for management development strategy and implementation.

NOTES

1   In Chapter 8 we examine other purposes of evaluation in LMD.

2   A pamphlet published by the TUC (2002) specifically identified the attitudes of managers as responsible for a failure to adopt a 'high road' approach to competitive success based on high value-added product strategies, high levels

of training and investment, high productivity and high wages and good terms and conditions. Managers might prefer to adopt a 'low road' approach based on control, lack of respect for staff and a belief that their staff cannot cope with greater consultation and participation in decision-making.

3 The Constable/McCormick Report (1987) was the product of four working parties: the Thomson working party – *Perspectives on Management Training and Education: The results of a survey of employers*; the Stoddart working party – *Demand as Perceived by Those Who Have Passed Through a Course of Management Education either Undergraduate or Postgraduate Level*; the Mangham working party – *A Review of Management Education – A Survey of the In-House Activities of Ten Major Companies*; and the Osbaldston working party – *The Supply of Management Education*.

4 In Scotland, the action plan is **Better Business – A strategy and action plan for social enterprise in Scotland**, and the strategy for Wales can be found at **http://new.wales.gov.uk/ topics/housingandcommunity/regeneration/ publications/socialenterprisestrategy?lang=en** .

5 A survey of 900 learning, training and development managers in March 2009 suggested that LMD was important in order to meet business objectives during the recession.

6 The processes of policy formation and auditing LMD might be included in this model. We consider these processes in more detail in Chapters 6 and 3 respectively.

7 The 'learning company' idea was promoted by, among others, the publication of Pedler, M., Burgoyne, J. and Boydell, T. (1991) *The Learning Company: A strategy for sustainable development*, Maidenhead: McGraw-Hill. We consider the learning company/organisation in more detail in Chapter 12.

8 Mintzberg *et al* (1998) refer to ten schools of strategic management, organised into three categories:

Prescriptive	Process	Fit
Design	Entrepreneurial	Configuration
Planning	Cognitive	
Positioning	Learning	
	Power	
	Cultural	
	Environmental	

FURTHER READING

CIPD (2002) *Developing Managers for Business Performance.* London: Chartered Institute of Personnel and Development

CLARKE, M. (1999) 'Management development as a game of meaningless outcomes', *Human Resource Management Journal,* Vol.9, No.2: 38–49

HAMEL, G. (2007) *The Future of Management.* Boston, MA: Harvard Business School

MINTZBERG, H. (2005) *Managers, Not MBAs: A hard look at the soft practice of managing and management development.* San Francisco: Berrett-Koehler Publishers

PFEFFER, J. and SUTTON, R. (2007) *Hard Facts, Dangerous Half-Truths, and Total Nonsense: Profiting from evidence-based management.* Boston, MA: Harvard Business School

CHAPTER 3

Measuring leaders and managers

CHAPTER OUTLINE

Introduction
Models and measures
Leadership and management competences
The leadership and management development audit
Summary

LEARNING OUTCOMES

After studying this chapter, you should be able to understand, explain, analyse and evaluate:

- the difficulties of measuring leadership and management performance

- varying approaches to the meaning, development and use of leadership and management competences in organisations

- the use of competences for measuring leadership and management performance

- the value of a leadership and management development audit

INTRODUCTION

This chapter is concerned with processes and activities that enable an organisation to develop the means to measure leadership and management performance as a precursor to LMD. Three issues are of importance here. One relates to the difficulties inherent in the whole process of measurement, and the need to establish measures that represent an accurate picture of performance – in other words, measures that take account of the system, not simply the function. A second relates to the need for clarity in the manager's job and how it is aligned with the organisation's priorities for success on which any development will be based. This is often not the case, and even senior individuals within an organisation are apt to view priorities very differently unless there are processes in place to ensure there is alignment. Thirdly, if LMD is to be taken forward, organisations need to design and develop processes that embed evaluation at all stages – for example, during the commissioning, design and delivery stage of any development programme so that organisations can be sure that a real difference is being made as a result of the intervention. At the level of the individual this means that there needs to be a job description and some statement of priorities and objectives, while at the organisation level there needs to be a clear understanding of how value is added within the organisation at different stages and different levels and the role of individuals and the competences they require to fulfil these roles. At both levels there also needs to be recognition that the measurement process is a difficult one and often involves the measurement of both quantitative and qualitative aspects that contribute to performance. Also important – as we have witnessed in the most recent banking crisis – is the time period over which the measurement takes place. Normally, the time period is drawn up in three- to twelve-month cycles, with longer-term succession and development programmes extending over several years. Any attempt to develop managers for jobs of which the purpose and nature are unclear, where the constraints and opportunities are unspecified, and where the boundaries are undefined, opens up a risk that focus and commitment is lost in the development process. However, as we have seen in previous chapters, the link between a leader's and manager's job in terms of how it might be performed and the requirements of strategy have often not been well made in many organisations.

MODELS AND MEASURES

One of the big difficulties when measuring leadership and management performance relates to the competing versions that exist of what managers actually do – which is of course is at the heart of any discussion on what might constitute performance. While not all models are explicitly expressed, having some kind of model of what might constitute performance can be extremely helpful in providing a template against which managers might be developed as well as a way by which leaders or managers can be assessed. Any gap identified reveals a need for improvement and the potential for an LMD process. It is best if the models used are stated explicitly, since models of leadership and management are very often understood only implicitly. We argue that the process of making them explicit serves to focus on LMD.

SEARCHING FOR A MODEL

As indicated in Chapter 1, throughout the last century there has been a continual search for universal answers to the question of the nature of leadership and management regardless of sector, size, or stage of development. This search has focused on a range of attributes including the knowledge, skills, abilities, attitudes and behaviours that managers need to possess, and the search continues today. Of note here is the way that at particular stages in this quest different terminology has been used, often merely according to fashion. Certain terms are used before they give way to different terms or expressions that either offer a slightly different emphasis or are simply new forms of expression for the same concept or idea.

So for example we have seen terms such as 'excellence', 'effective', 'competent', 'high-performing' and 'transformational' used. Even though F. W. Taylor lived over 100 years ago, it is his legacy and methods that endure, and of those that followed him, all seeking a scientific explanation for human performance at work. This influence largely through industrial or organisational psychology is the one that has remained strong and has continued to provide scientific explanations for human performance at work, especially the performance of managers and now leaders.

 WEB LINK

The website **http://www.psychnet-uk.com/industrial_psychology/ management_personnel_ training.htm** provides links to many resources relating to organisational and industrial psychology, including various measurement devices that claim scientific status.

Models of leadership and management performance that make claims for being scientific usually provide evidence through any of a variety of measurement devices. The standards that apply to this kind of 'scientific rigour' are usually their reliability and validity. *Reliability* means the extent to which the model remains valid over time, and *validity* means the extent to which it measures aspects of leadership and management. However, one question that might be asked is exactly what model of leadership or management performance is being represented in these frameworks and how might organisations decide which is the appropriate one to use? Firstly, we need to make a distinction between models which apply to all managers in all contexts (or specified subcontexts such as professional organisations, education, health, etc) and those which apply only to managers in particular situations or organisations. The first we see as *generic models* and the second as *organisation-specific models*. For example, there have been various attempts to provide competency models of performance that could be used for all managers, such as the Management and Leadership Standards body in the UK (see below). We might also include as being in the generic category all the efforts made to provide integrated models of leadership and management abilities based on texts and research on leadership and management. For example, Perren and Burgoyne (2002) sought to set out a framework of leadership and management abilities from 'well-known' texts and frameworks as well as from primary data. The result was an integrated management and leadership framework, shown in Figure 3.1.

Organisation-specific approaches, on the other hand, recognise the importance of context, particularly how the expression of abilities or competences needs to reflect the meanings of an individual organisation. Many organisations prefer to develop their own models of leadership and management performance in the belief that the specificity will provide more effective LMD.

A second issue we might consider is what is meant by *performance* in leadership and management. One way of thinking about performance is to consider the

Figure 3.1 Integrated management and leadership framework

Manage and lead people
- Acknowledge and reward others
- Assess and recognise people's potential
- Build teams
- Consult and collaborate
- Deal with politics
- Delegate work and responsibility
- Develop people
- Facilitate and chair meetings
- Handle a diverse workforce
- Know employment rules
- Manage conflict situations
- Manage level above
- Motivate people
- Possess patience and tolerate mistakes
- Provide feedback
- Recruit competent people
- Support people
- Trust people

Think strategically
- Balance agendas
- Challenge the status quo and the opposition
- Develop industry knowledge
- Develop networks
- Focus on customer
- Set goals
- Spot opportunities
- Think conceptually and use reflection
- Think creatively
- Think entrepreneurially
- Think globally
- Think markets
- Think strategically
- Think technologically
- Recruit competent people
- Support people
- Trust people

Lead direction and culture
- Create good organisational communication
- Create shared vision
- Encourage creativity and flexibility
- Handle change
- Handle risk and ambiguity
- Inspire people
- Lead by example
- Manage public relations
- Plan small wins and reinforce

Manage self
- Accept responsibility
- Demonstrate dependability
- Exude enthusiasm
- Handle stress and health issues
- Manage time
- Possess adaptability and flexibility
- Possess drive, passion and capacity to work hard
- Possess personal ethics and values
- Possess self-confidence
- Possess spontaneity
- Possess stamina and perseverance
- Possess tough-mindedness
- Provide good instincts and common sense
- Strive for consistency of approach
- Strive for emotional stability and be emotionally stable
- Strive for self-awareness and development

Manage relationships
- Bargain, sell and negotiate
- Build empathy, relationships and trust
- Create bearing and presence
- Display assertiveness
- Display humour
- Listen to people
- Present self and ideas

Excellence in management and leadership

Manage activities and quality
- Attend to detail
- Audit quality
- Control and monitor activities
- Develop systems and procedures
- Establish priorities
- Evaluate progress
- Monitor, plan and control projects
- Provide practical and technical competence
- Solve problems

Manage information
- Acquire information
- Analyse information
- Make plans
- Manage accounts and finances
- Manage budgets
- Take decisions

Manage resources
- Allocate resources
- Marshall resources
- Safeguard assets

Key   Task abilities   People abilities   Task abilities

Source: Perren and Burgoyne (2002)

relationship between means and ends. From this perspective, a manager starts off with a set of abilities consisting of skills, knowledge and attitudes which are applied to work, and through application achieves particular results or outputs. Between the means and the ends lies the process of leading and managing. Figure 3.2 represents this perspective.

One obvious benefit of this approach is that it is easier to focus on either the means or the ends (or both) when considering how managers might be assessed and their LMD needs determined. A means focus might for example be

Figure 3.2 Performance as a relationship between means and ends

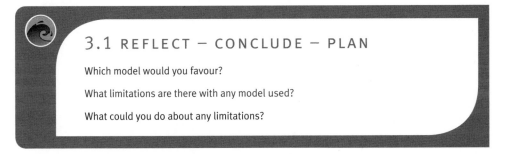

concerned with producing a typology of desired skills, knowledge and attitudes which could be measured. An ends focus might consider either the quantitative or qualitative results achieved and whether these met particular criteria or standards. As a consequence, many models of leadership and management performance tend to favour either a means approach to measurement – for example, inventories of skills and attitudes – or an ends approach – for example, the achievement of objectives and targets, proof against standards.

3.1 REFLECT – CONCLUDE – PLAN

Which model would you favour?

What limitations are there with any model used?

What could you do about any limitations?

The large volume of possible leadership and management abilities and the very many measurement devices for both means and ends does in itself raise considerable doubts about our knowledge and understanding of leadership and management performance. It is perhaps the growing number of measurement devices on offer which constitutes proof that we are beginning to understand that it is only by combining a range of measurements that a more accurate (valid and reliable) picture will emerge. However, a critic might well argue that such measurements are not providing the complete picture at all but instead playing a vital role in constructing it (Astley 1985). For example, a manager might be assessed as being in need of planning skills or as representing a Myers-Briggs type of ISTJ.[1] As we will see, tremendous power is given to those who have the knowledge and expertise to conduct the measurement and assessment of managers relating to such descriptions. This may also lead to responses by managers that the assessments do not always relate to their own experiences or feelings.

One of the reasons for there being a difficulty in measuring performance is because all aspects of the way a leader or manager performs may not always be visible to those undertaking the measurement. The processes of leadership and management almost always occur in a time and place and, as we claimed, almost always with other people. Again, as claimed, such contextual factors have a significant bearing on what managers do – but they also serve to complicate the notion of performance. Further, process is by its nature concerned with dynamic activity often involving groups. As a consequence, it becomes very difficult to isolate the role played by a leader or a manager in this process. However, uncovering aspects of the process should disclose how managers apply their abilities in particular situations and how this is carried out. Attention to process, then, will provide key information about the manager and the needs in specific contexts. One perspective of performance that includes this kind of attention to process has been provided by Leary *et al* (1986). This model argues that effectiveness requires a consideration of inputs, outputs and processes, and that bringing these dimensions together integrates performance offering a 'holistic quality' (p.6). Attention to process will allow an assessment of 'the quality of the connection' between means and ends. A representation of this integrated view is shown in Figure 3.3.

Figure 3.3 An integrated view of performance

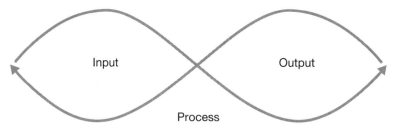

Source: Leary *et al* (1986)

Giving more prominence to process in this way is more likely to relate to a manager's experience of work in a grounded and more authentic manner. Watson (2001) takes up this theme when he speaks of the idea of the 'emergent manager', which highlights this view of management as an ongoing process of interaction. This requires a shift in perspective from a view of a configured world where the needs of individual managers can be objectively assessed towards a more constructed view where movement, processes and relationships between leaders, managers and others are important. Measuring and assessing managers then requires a careful consideration of all the various processes of interaction with others with whom they need to relate. These are some of the reasons for the interest in multi-source feedback and self-assessment, which we consider in Chapter 4. It also highlights the need when assessing LMD for an ongoing process of interaction with those involved, rather than treating them as distant and objective observers.

LEADERSHIP AND MANAGEMENT COMPETENCES[2]

Leadership and management competences (LMCs) are descriptions of behaviours, attributes, skills that managers need to perform their work effectively and/or the outputs to be achieved from such work which can be assessed against performance criteria. It is possible to use such descriptions as a central link in the determination of human resources (HR) activities for leaders, managers and others. Further, the link to strategy is one that can be explicitly made – so, for example, the descriptions that are used in LMC frameworks should be directly connected to an organisation's objectives and, therefore in theory at least, provide the means by which those objectives can be achieved or the outputs which indicate that the objectives have been met. The key point here is that organisational objectives and the various HR activities such as selection, appraisal, training and development and reward can be appropriately aligned (Holbeche 1998). Whiddett and Hollyforde (1999) suggest two important benefits for human resource management:

- Competences can offer a language which describes effectiveness in an organisation. As a consequence, throughout an organisation, common understandings can be gained of those attributes that relate to good leadership or planning.

- Competences allow for a more consistent way of assessing people because all assessors have the same understanding of what competences are required of any given level for any given role.

For nearly 30 years, the idea that competences can be used to set the performance of managers has become an attractive and powerful argument in many organisations across all sectors. The *LMD in Practice* below shows a recent move to bring competences to the work of trainee doctors.

LMD IN PRACTICE

TRAINEE DOCTORS TO GET LESSONS IN LEADERSHIP

All doctors in England and Wales are to learn leadership skills as part of their training for the first time, under new proposals. A competency framework for medical students, identifying the required leadership skills at different stages of their training, has been drawn up by the NHS Institute for Innovation and Improvement.

Students will be expected to demonstrate competency in five areas: personal qualities, working with others, managing services, improving services and setting direction. Trainees will be taught managerial skills through medical scenarios, clinical placements, peer interaction and group learning.

Peter Spurgeon, director of the Institute of Clinical Leadership at the University of Warwick, and leader of the programme, told *PM* that leadership skills were not systematically taught to doctors at the moment. 'We are trying to say that this is part of the normal day-to-day functioning of doctors,' he said. 'We need the medical profession to be positively engaged with improvement and change and we need to give them the skills to manage.' He added: 'There is this culture in the NHS that management and leadership are something we don't want to do. Hopefully, in the future people will actually want to move in this direction.'

The General Medical Council and Postgraduate Medical Training Board intend to integrate the framework into a new curriculum by 2010, making it a mandatory part of medical training. In the meantime, some strategic health authorities have already begun to implement the plans independently. The competency framework will also become part of the appraisal process used by hospitals in the future.

Anna Scott, *People Management*, 16 October 2008, p.10

Bolden and Gosling (2006) have argued that the concept of competency 'has become ubiquitous' (p.147) initially in relation to the assessment and development of managers with an eventual transfer to leaders and others. These authors post a useful warning for anyone considering LMC or competences of any kind – they are a representation and not the real thing. The importance of this will become apparent as we now explore the meaning of LMC.

3.2 REFLECT – CONCLUDE – PLAN

Do you think the idea of competences and related terms such as 'capabilities' or 'attributes' have become 'ubiquitous'?

In whose interest is it to promote and use LMC?

How can you ensure that LMCs are used to support effective LMD?

THE MEANING OF LMC

As we have indicated, LMCs are not a simple concept in that they can be considered in different ways. For example, 'competence' might be related to the behaviours required by a manager, or the skills or attributes they possess, or the outputs of their work. These differences in perspective reflect the various interests and debates that have occurred over the last 25 years relating to how it is best to assess a person's abilities and performance at work. Further, these debates have taken place in a range of disciplines often dependent on the research methods that are believed to offer a better or more accurate 'truth'. So psychologists, educationists, policy-makers, HR and LMD specialists have all taken a view on what we should focus on in order to arrive at and access a competent manager. For simplicity, we can characterise the debate by reference to two approaches: behaviour and standards.

The behaviour approach

The behaviour approach stems principally from the influential study of Boyatzis (1982) in the USA, referred to in Chapter 1. His concern was mainly with the characteristics of effective performance in leadership and management work, which he defined as the results achieved through specific actions by a leader or manager and taking account of the particular policies, procedures and conditions within an organisation. Focusing on specific actions which go on to lead to results, turns the focus of attention to the identification of the characteristics or abilities of the person that enables them to demonstrate the appropriate actions. Thought of in this way, LMCs are therefore those underlying characteristics or abilities[3] a leader or manager brings to a situation which allows him or her to achieve results that are effective. However, because these key underlying characteristics and abilities are difficult to assess directly, most definitions of

LMC concentrate instead on the behaviours of leaders or managers for effective performance. For example, Woodruffe's (1992, p.17) definition is:

> the set of behaviour patterns that the incumbent needs to bring to a position in order to perform its tasks and functions with competence.

The CIPD's (2008, p.1) more recent definition is:

> the behaviours that employees must have, or must acquire, to input into a situation in order to achieve high levels of performance.

One limitation of these definitions is that there is a tendency to focus on individualising performance rather than seeing performance as more of a collective activity that takes place through interaction with others. But it is perhaps worth commenting that Boyatzis was always careful to specify that effective job performance was also affected by the environment and context in which the performance occurred and the particular requirements of the job. The LMCs identified by Boyatzis are shown in Table 3.1.

Table 3.1 Boyatzis' competence clusters

Goal and action cluster	• efficiency orientation • proactivity • diagnostic use of concepts
Leadership cluster	• self-confidence • use of oral presentations • logical thought • conceptualisation
Human resource cluster	• use of socialised power • positive regard • managing group process • accurate self-assessment
Directing subordinates cluster	• developing others • use of unilateral power • spontaneity
Focus on others cluster	• self-control • perceptual objectivity • stamina and responsibility • concern with close relationships

Source: Boyatzis (1982)

The work of Boyatzis and those that followed him led to an increase in interest in management competences and, as is often the way, developers sought generic competences that could be applied in any context – right across the board, in any organisation. This perhaps understandable wish for there to be competences that are generic has led to an ongoing debate about whether this is possible, especially given the growing diversity of managers (Miller *et al* 2001) and the very different contexts of firms. Knowledge and action are often directly related to practice, and the individual practices in different firms in different industries in different stages of development will lead to variation in different competences. Tovey (1993), for example, argued that generic approaches did not take account of specific business needs and critical success factors, with the result that incomplete pictures of performance are formed which miss vital information on values, climate and culture. Further, there are likely to be different clusters of LMC both within organisations and between organisations. Also, there may be very common terms that are used to describe a leader's or manager's tasks – eg decision-making, planning – but these terms often mean different things in different organisations. So as a consequence from the mid-1980s onwards many organisations sought to develop LMC frameworks that reflected the particular characteristics of their organisations as expressed in the language that was used to describe a good manager. These frameworks all required to be constructed by a research process that normally included the following:

- interviews with senior managers to obtain their views on the current and future issues facing the organisation
- observation of managers as well as self-reports (diaries) on what they did and how they spent their time
- interviews with managers to identify particular characteristics relating to both high performance and under-performance. Methods used to achieve this included the critical incident technique, repertory grid and/or behavioural event interview
- focus groups to identify key competences
- the use of benchmarking with other LMC frameworks.

The result of such a process produces a framework of LMC. Table 3.2 provides an example. This was developed for a financial services organisation in the UK – note the way in which the competences are grouped in five clusters.

Each competence is then specified further by the addition of a description and dimensions of the behaviour desired. For example, for the competence 'delivering results', the description might be:

- Sets clear, realistic but challenging objectives for self and others.
- Creates effective plans for self and/or others which contribute towards the achievement of business results.
- Regularly monitors and reviews progress and results.

The dimensions of this competence are:

Dimension 1: Ensures that strategy is converted into operational objectives and ensures delivery of plan.

Dimension 2: Manages the achievement of operational plans.

Dimension 3: Achieves results through peers within own team.

Table 3.2 A leadership and management competences framework for a UK financial services organisation

Personal focus	• self-control • self-development • personal organisation • positive approach
Customer focus	• creating customer service • delivering customer service • continuous improvement
Future focus	• delivering the vision • change and creativity
Business focus	• delivering results • providing solutions • systemic thinking • attention to detail
People focus	• developing people • working with others • influencing • leadership

Cast in this way, managers can be assessed against the dimensions by identifiers of performance ranging from, for example, 'less than effective' to 'fully effective' to 'outstanding'. Outstanding performance might be identified as 'Having an excellent track record of delivering to time and/or matching the resource requirements to the task needs of the task.' For this particular organisation, we are demonstrating that there are clear requirements for leadership and management performance which are aligned with business requirements expressed in language that is meaningful to managers in the business to which they can relate. Also, notice how the focus in this example is on behaviours while still leading to the identification of outputs at different levels of effectiveness. This approach links the behaviour approach to LMC to the standards approach discussed below.

Although many large organisations have developed their own organisation-specific LMC frameworks, building on the work of Boyatzis, there are a wide range of generic frameworks, especially focusing on leadership and particularly the idea of the transformational leader. One of the most well-known frameworks is the Multi-factor Leadership Questionnaire (MLQ) based on the work of Avolio and Bass (2004). The questionnaire seeks to measure the style of a leader against four dimensions:

- transformational leadership
- transactional leadership
- non-transactional leadership styles (passive, avoidant)
- outcomes of leadership (such as effectiveness).

Each dimension is further subdivided. For example, transformational leadership is measured by:

- Builds trust.
- Acts with integrity.
- Inspires others.
- Encourages innovative thinking.
- Coaches people.

Each leader is rated against the dimensions by between eight and 24 others who provide 360-degree anonymous feedback before a report is prepared for the leader. Because of the popularity of the MLQ, the authors have been able to continuously use the data to measure validity and reliability and claim strong predictive qualities of leader performance. However, there are also debates about such claims, with inconsistent research findings (Tejeda *et al* 2001) and the application of the MLQ at different levels in an organisation (Schriesheim *et al* 2009).

In the UK Alimo-Metcalfe and Alban-Metcalfe (2001) developed a Transformational Leadership Questionnaire consisting of 14 dimensions grouped into three clusters. These are:

Leading and developing others

- Showing genuine concern
- Enabling
- Being accessible
- Encouraging change

Personal qualities

- Being honest and consistent
- Acting with integrity
- Being decisive, risk-taking
- Inspiring others
- Resolving complex problems

Leading the organisation

- Networking and achieving
- Focusing team effort
- Builiding shared vision
- Supporting a developmental culture
- Facilitating change sensitively

Once again, a leader is rated by others and a report is provided. One of the interesting features of the TLQ is the claim that it is more inclusive with respect

WEB LINK

Go to **http://www.institute.nhs.uk/assessment_tool/general/medical_ leadership_ competency_framework_-_homepage.html** . This is the homepage of the Medical Leadership Competency framework aimed at doctors so that they can become 'more actively involved in the planning, delivery and transformation of health services'.

to gender and ethnicity and more connected to the need of others (Alimo-Metcalfe and Alban-Metcalfe 2005).

The standards approach

The standards approach to LMC was the outcome of two streams of activity going on in parallel in the UK during the 1980s. One emerged from a government policy initiative in the early 1980s directed towards the development of standards of competence for different occupational areas which would lead to qualifications – later to be called National Vocational Qualifications or NVQs (SVQs in Scotland). The second stream of activity emerged from two influential reports, one written by Charles Handy, the other by John Constable and Roger McCormick. At the time of their writing there was never any intention to produce a 'checklist'-type framework of competences in answer to the reports' highlighting of the relative lack of qualifications held by British managers. But like too many initiatives, the reports were used politically to justify the creation of the idea of a chartered manager. This led to a commitment to an attempt to build long-term improvements in the way British managers were developed through a body known as the Management Charter Initiative (MCI). The MCI sought to achieve two principal objectives:

- the development of a widely acceptable inventory of the main competences required by a manager
- the designation of 'chartered manager' as a professional qualification for those who successfully acquired and demonstrated such competences.

The idea of a chartered manager at that time proved rather contentious, but where there was some agreement was on the need for some effort to be put into policy-making, standard-setting and accrediting management qualifications at a national level in the context of the National Vocational Qualifications (NVQ) framework. These were in turn based on competences that were concerned with a manager's abilitiy to perform effectively within an occupational area to a standard required by employers. The crucial feature and the difference between this approach and others was that a manager would be said to have achieved competence in an aspect of work only if the output of his or her performance met the written standards and performance criteria along with the required evidence. Perhaps it should be said that there was a conscious intention to develop an 'inventory' that would be 'accepted widely'. In other words, the standards approach for managers was concerned with a generic model of competences.

Functional analysis

The standards were developed through a research process called *functional analysis*. This process begins by clarifying the 'key purpose' of management and goes on to explore the 'key roles' that managers have to perform. Each of the identified roles are then broken down into units and elements with competence statements expressed as outcomes, including associated performance criteria, allowing judgement of a manager's ability to carry out a particular element. The result of this process was a generic model of management, first published in 1991, which at the time was claimed 'to reflect the best practices of management'. Since 1991 the model has been revised, and in 2000 responsibility for the management standards in the UK was passed from the MCI to the Management Standards Centre, an independent unit of the Chartered Management Institute, where the work continues. However, the broad structure has remained in line with the NVQ framework in England and Wales and the SVQ framework in Scotland. Coverage to leadership was extended in 2004, and a revised version of the standards was published in 2008. The result is a Key Purpose of management and leadership presented as:

> To ... Provide direction, gain commitment, facilitate change and achieve results through the efficient, creative and responsible deployment of people and other resources.

Based on this definition of Key Purpose, six functional areas are identified, as shown in Figure 3.4.

Each functional area is broken down into

- units of competence
- elements of competence for each unit
- performance criteria for each element.

For example, 'Providing direction' has 12 units, including:

B1: 'Develop and implement operational plans for your area of responsibility', and

B2: 'Map the environment in which your organisation operates'.

For each unit, the outcomes of effective performance are stated along with skills, knowledge and understanding and underpinning behaviour. For example, for B1 there are:

- eight 'Outcomes for effective performance', including 'Balance new ideas with tried and tested solutions'
- nine 'Behaviours which underpin effective performance', including 'You constantly seek to improve performance'
- ten statements of general 'Knowledge and understanding', such as 'How to manage risk'

Figure 3.4 Functional areas of management and leadership standards

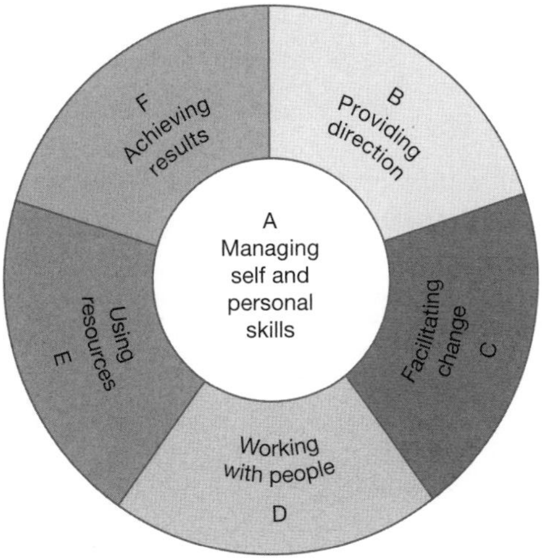

Source: The Management Standards Centre (**http://www.management-standards.org**)

- thirteen statements of 'Industry-/sector-/context-specific knowledge', such as 'Market developments in your sector'.

WEB LINK

Go to **http://www.management-standards.org/**, the homepage of the Management Standards Centre, which is the standards-setting body for the National Occupational Standards for Management and Leadership.

BENEFITS

There have undoubtedly been some benefits derived from the introduction of LMCs. One, for example, noted by Strebler and Bevan (1996), was that LMCs assisted in the identification of training needs and the design of training programmes. This had the result that training programmes were more relevant and allowed for the development of modules of training. Strebler *et al* (1997) also found that the framework facilitated feedback from a range of sources and individuals, and by so doing, added value to the assessment. Winterton and Winterton (1997) found that LMCs led to more coherence in the structure of training and allowed for gaps to be more easily identified in training on the assumption that a well-rounded competent manager needed development in all areas of the framework. LMCs were also found to encourage managers to take more responsibility for the development of others where this is specified as part of the LMC framework (Miller *et al* 2001). Without doubt, LMCs remain a highly popular and well-supported objective view of what managers ought to learn in order to do their work well. It is not surprising therefore that LMCs are probably the foremost models for assessing and developing managers (Bolden and Gosling

2006). Further, recent extensions of LMCs to include emotional intelligence (see below), and social and culture competence (see Chapter 11) have been seen as the way to develop talent and identify 'outstanding performers' (Boyatzis 2008, p.11).

EMOTIONAL INTELLIGENCE

In recent years, the behaviour approach has been augmented by interest in the notion of emotional intelligence (EI). Salovey and Mayer (1990, p.85) defined EI as

> the ability to perceive accurately, appraise, and express emotion; the ability to understand emotion and emotional knowledge; and the ability to regulate emotions to promote emotional and intellectual growth.

However, the key work that brought this idea to leadership and management – but especially leadership – was by Goleman (1998), in which he claimed that successful people with high EI are more able to perceive, understand, and regulate their emotions than unsuccessful people low in EI. Because those high in EI can monitor their feelings as well as the feelings of others, they can use such information to guide action and perform more effectively. The idea quickly gained popularity, and by the early 2000s research suggested that over one-third of employers, mostly in the private sector, had included EI in their competency frameworks (Miller *et al* 2001).

The interest in EI resulted in the appearance of assessment tools, such as Sala's (2002) Emotional Competence Inventory, which allowed for 360-degree feedback and feedback from customers relating to:

- *self-awareness* – self-confidence and accuracy of emotional self-assessments; recognition of emotions, knowing strengths and weaknesses, being open to feedback, and having assurance and presence

- *self-management* – self-control, self-regulation, adaptability, initiative, optimism, achievement; being able to manage one's own emotions, stay composed, focused and poised; having integrity, being trustworthy, ethical and principled; being conscientious, taking responsibility and meeting promises and commitments; being flexible and being open to, and comfortable with, new ideas and information; having achievement drive, commitment, initiative and persistence

- *social awareness* – empathy, organisational awareness, a sense of service; sensing others' feelings and perspectives, anticipating and meeting others' needs; offering feedback, coaching and mentoring; respecting people in an unbiased way; and understanding power relations and networks

- *relationship management* – social skills, inspiration, influence, developing others, fostering team-work, and managing conflict; being persuasive, clear in communication, listening, aiming for mutual understanding, leading by example, initiating and championing change; negotiating disagreements, building bonds and networks, sharing information and resources in a collaborative way, and creating synergies between people.

Very often, EI is included in frameworks for assessing leadership styles, such as the Leadership Dimensions Questionnaire developed by Dulewicz and Higgs (2005), which includes assessment of:

- the 'intellectual' dimensions of critical analysis and judgement, vision and imagination, and strategic perspective

- the 'managerial' dimensions of resource management, engaging communication, empowering, developing, and achieving

- the 'emotional' dimensions of self-awareness, emotional resilience, intuitiveness, interpersonal sensitivity, influence, motivation and conscientiousness.

The *LMD in Practice* below shows how one organisation based its leadership programme on EI.

LMD IN PRACTICE

'EMOTIONAL INTELLIGENCE' ENERGISES NATIONAL GRID

Two-day programme increased self-awareness and improved team motivation

Harriet Wraith

An experimental leadership programme based on 'emotional intelligence' has improved team productivity at one UK firm. The programme, Emotionally Intelligent Leadership, helped to develop four skills among staff at energy provider National Grid: self-awareness, social consciousness, self-management and social skills. Employees attended a two-day workshop to examine the theory and practicalities of the concept.

Speaking at the CIPD's Coaching at Work Conference, Catherine Hamilton, National Grid's diversity and inclusion manager, said the programme had improved leadership skills, team motivation and increased networking opportunities. She admitted that the concept of emotional intelligence had initially attracted pessimism, yet once people went on the course, they became its 'voice', and people were more positive about the idea.

'The cynicism tends to stem from ignorance, or a lack of understanding of the term,' she said.

Source: *People Management* Online, 22 September 2006

WEB LINK

Try the EI quiz at **http://www.haygroup.com/t1/EI/Quiz.aspx** .

There has been much interest in EI – but there are also doubts. It is argued that the measurement of EI in tests is not really measuring anything different from other psychometric tests which incorporate what are referred to as the 'Big Five' personality dimensions of extraversion, agreeableness, openness, conscientiousness and neuroticism (Conte 2005). Further, since they are usually completed as self-reports, there is doubt about their validity. EI tests could be used as part of a development process but they should not be used for selection in the absence of validity evidence.

LMC DIFFICULTIES

Despite the claimed benefits and enduring popularity of LMCs, there have also been some recognised difficulties. Since LMC frameworks' first appearance in the 1980s, there has been an ongoing debate as to whether this approach can really provide accurate (by this we mean valid and reliable) models that reflect the work of managers, and whether competency is an acceptable approach to use in the assessment of LMD needs.

TECHNICAL DIFFICULTIES

Organisations have claimed to introduce LMCs frameworks for a variety of reasons, such as to make the link between organisational objectives and individual objectives clearer or to facilitate organisational change. The organisation's members' response can be varied, often dependent on the organisation's history of initiatives, and sometimes this results in initiative overload. Strebler *et al* (1997) found that individuals can be suspicious about the real purpose of competences, especially when there is a link to pay. There is also a real issue related to the language used – particularly the use of jargon. For example, Rankin (2001) suggested that it is inappropriate language that hampers communication and understanding, and that organisations may need to spend considerably more time training and explaining the use of competency frameworks in order to ensure commitment and their use.

VAGUE TERMS

LMC frameworks may also suffer from the problem of vague terms and of the attributes being sometimes difficult to assess. This partly relates to a continuing lack of clarity over the definition and meaning of 'competence' – is it an aspect of personality such as a trait, characteristic, or skill, etc, or is it an aspect of behaviour or an output to be achieved against a standard? If this is the case, there may be enduring problems concerning the use of LMC as a measure in assessment. For example, the following description is taken from an organisation's LMC framework: 'Acts professionally, keeping personal feelings to one side.'

Using the above example, it might be argued that here we have terms that are difficult to explain and even more difficult to observe and measure. For example, what does it mean to act 'professionally'? How would you know professionalism in respect to feelings, if you saw it? How do we know a manager is able to keep 'personal feelings to one side', and is this something that a manager can learn to do? The issue we are observing here is that LMC does seek to clarify and specify leadership or management work, but there is always the proviso that it is possible to measure performance and developers are able to set objectives for performance improvement and LMD activities. But improving clarification is not without difficulties because leadership and management work is seldom clear-cut and is often carried out under conditions which cannot be controlled. As Bolden and Gosling (2006, p.160) suggest, 'At best a competency framework will only ever be a simple representation of a highly complex and changing landscape.' Seeking to provide descriptions that serve to clarify may also lead to an over-simplification of what is indeed a complex and ambiguous reality – one which managers have to face! This issue is of particular concern where interpersonal performance is involved: something that is difficult to observe and measure directly.

PROLIFERATION OF TERMS AND DOCUMENTS

A further difficulty has emerged from the proliferation of terms and documents which LMC has generated. Over the years LMC frameworks have often produced significant amounts of paper and, even though much of this can now be stored electronically, the result can often be bewildering – all of which managers need to understand and internalise. This is partly due to the manner in which LMCs are produced – how, for example, performance is broken down into parts that add to the whole. This process of 'atomisation' has been a particular issue with the standards approach in the UK, where there have been ongoing concerns that relate to the levels of bureaucracy and paper-chasing to complete management NVQs and a variety of assessment practices (Swailes and Brown 1999). Research by Holman and Hall (1996) into the use of management standards found that assessment had produced a 'tick-box approach' (p.199) and that achievement of standards against performance criteria became an end in itself rather than a means to challenge or change management practice. Grugulis (2000) completed research in private sector orgsanisations that used the standards approach and found that they became 'a distraction from developmental learning, rather than a contribution towards it' (p.89).

SPECIFYING BEHAVIOUR

There is also a problem with the behaviour approach in relation to the specification of categories of behaviour. These can result in a growing number of complex measures that become very difficult to manage and use in assessment – for example, as part of a performance management system (Strebler et al 1997). The behaviour approach ought to have one benefit over the standards approach in the way that LMCs purport to reflect business needs and include a future orientation, whereas the standards approach by definition is concerned with managers' meeting performance criteria which allows assessors to pronounce them competent. This difference was one that was recognised in some of the early commentaries on LMCs in the 1980s (Jacobs 1989). However, this may create tension between the use of LMCs to improve current performance as against specifying the requirements for managers to perform well in the future. Strebler et al (1997) suggested that LMCs can sometimes lead to raised career expectations which the organisation may not necessarily be able to meet.

Paradoxically, the behaviour approach, in its attempt to consider the language and values of an organisation, may also miss some of the technical or professional components that managers may see as essential. Many managers do not regard themselves as general managers but rather as managers within a technical or professional context. These managers are likely to see their work and their development being in both management, and technical and professional areas of capability. A further criticism of the behaviour approach is that it may also serve to reinforce existing notions of effective leadership and management, and this may affect equal opportunities or the trend towards diversity and appreciation of difference within an organisation (see Chapter 11). For example, the language to explain success in leadership and management may reflect particular gender stereotypes. Adams (1996) suggests that there are differences in how men and women may understand successful management styles, and in how behaviour by male managers may be interpreted and categorised differently compared to female managers' behaviour.

THEORETICAL CRITIQUE

Since the early 1980s when the competence movement took hold, there has been an accompanying theoretical critique which seeks to problematise the whole notion of LMCs, questioning their development and underpinning rationale and highlighting certain deleterious effects.

Tools of power and influence

Although there are a variety of strands to the critique, at their heart is a view that LMCs represent another 'one best way' attempt to describe what managers must be and/or do to be competent, effective, or excellent. Furthermore, the language of LMCs evokes a technical orientation which attempts to describe human actions in functional terms (Garavan and McGuire 2001), an expression of an organisation's ideology – to be observed almost like a religion (Finch-Lees et al 2005). LMCs can easily become a tool of power and influence for those who develop competences and those who use them to judge performance.

By adopting a position that particular skills, characteristics, behaviours and outputs can all be tied to the purpose of achieving organisational objectives, claims may be made of neutrality, objectivity and scientific rigour in the process of developing LMCs. This can mean a minimising of the fluid and subjective experience of managers (Lawler 2005). LMCs can therefore easily be seen as a prescription for leadership and management performance which, if applied properly, will lead to improved organisational performance. As one senior manager jokingly responded to the LMCs developed by Watson (1994, p.222): 'This should come in useful when I have to decide which of my first line I am going to sack.'

Reduction to a set of parts

Both the behaviour and standard approaches are seen by many to reduce leadership and management performance into a set of parts – ie skills, knowledge, characteristics, behaviours and/or outputs. The argument means that when combined together the parts will add back to an integrated whole, as if they were a set of building-blocks. However, in this way LMCs break up the job of leadership and management into fragments that potentially can lose the symbolic nature of the role. In addition, it is claimed that LMC has apparently an individualistic focus which foregrounds the development of individuals at the expense of the social and collective. As a consequence, participation in teams, the importance of social capital and so on fail to get the recognition they deserve. This is a particularly true case in the area of leadership where networks and the importance placed on language and rhetoric come to the fore. Boyatzis (1982) and others warned that such a simplistic, individualistic view could not be sustained. Some further limitations stem from the view that because LMCs are the way in which leadership and management performance are defined, all LMD needs stem from competences identified and there can be no other purpose for LMD other than those specified by the LMC framework. From what we know about the nature of leadership in general and managerial work in particular, this seems quite wrong-headed. Managers – as we will see in Chapter 5 – learn in far more complex ways than simply through an emphasis on outputs and assessment against a standard where training and development, underpinned by behavioural psychology (Marshall 1991), leads to effectiveness brought about by behavioural adjustments.

Control of performance

Much of the theoretical main thrust of the critique is concerned with the way LMCs give power to those who seek to control leadership and management performance. Holmes (1995), for example, explains how the way competences are expressed through discourse and language serves not simply to describe and identify them but also to play a key role in constructing them. So that, if LMC describes an attribute for leadership or management performance such as 'Setting clear objectives for self and others', this serves to make legitimate and more sense for those compiling an LMC framework, but the very act of this sense-making produces the manner in which performance will be assessed, and by doing so provides power for those who stand in judgement about what constitutes performance and whether it has been met. Once acceptance has taken place – and usually LMCs are subject to a degree of discussion and argument before acceptance – they become 'accepted as a rational and legitimate way of talking about' performance (Holmes 1995, p.36). Knight and Wilmott (1999) examined the way in which this occurred in the National Health Service in relation to strategy. Those that did not use the 'jargon' or language of strategy were not allowed to play the game, whether or not they were good leaders or managers, and this served to decentralise mainly clinicians.

LMCs as discourse serve then to provide a source for critique by those who take a stance from the work of the French philosopher Michel Foucault. The focus here is how LMCs act as a form of remote governance on leaders or managers who respond by self-regulating their activities according to the values and norms set by the competences. Competent leadership or management performance becomes revealed and known, and it is this seeming transparency which makes it potentially governable and subject to a 'system of domination' (Townley 1993, p.225). The conclusion from this seems to be that the more managers become involved in the use of LMCs, the greater is the possibility that they will accept them as a fact and believe that these are the things that govern their own performance as leaders or managers. However, a Foucaultian analysis points to the historically contingent and fluid nature of any claims about truth in human existence. Thus managers may not recognise themselves within LMC frameworks, but the power of the system to dominate will prevent them from recognising the truth about themselves in any terms other than those specified by the LMCs. In this way, LMCs produce the self-knowledge required for managers to make improvements (Brewis 1996).

 WEB LINK

The work of Michel Foucault has been a very important source of writing for those who wish to take a critical stance towards LMD. If you wish to find out more about Foucault, try **http://www. theory.org.uk/ctr-fou1.htm** .

Salaman and Taylor (2002) concluded that LMCs are widely used in organisations to define or 'redefine' management performance. They found that organisations found it useful to use LMCs to identify and articulate those qualities needed for change – such as customer focus, commercial awareness and market sensitivity – in a variety of contexts. Further, LMCs were seen as a key method of communicating new development requirements for managers, and this often involved appropriate alignment with organisational goals, ensuring coherence. As a consequence, managers are required to take on new responsibilities previously performed by others such as HR. These findings support studies where once qualities have been defined there has been simultaneously an attempt to control and align managers' views in a unified way. This reinforces the view that organisations are 'rational, machine-like, objective and above all consensual' (p.21).

At first glance, then, LMCs would appear to provide the solution to many organisational concerns related to leadership and management performance and improvement through the way they serve to specify either behaviours or standards for leaders and managers. In addition, such specification can be aligned with the overall function of leadership, management and/or organisational strategy. As a means to bring about change, LMCs offer a common language that helps define the qualities needed and/or the outcomes managers need to achieve. Where they fail to meet the requirements specified, LMD needs can be revealed. We have also seen that LMC as a movement has also been subject to an ongoing critique from both a technical standpoint (ie how the competences are identified and specified) and theoretical (ie what they mean and say about the nature of leadership and management). However, one particular point shines through – leadership and management performance is a complex and multifaceted phenomenon frequently characterised by flux, movement, ambiguity and uncertainty which cannot be reduced to or explained by any one typology. Burgoyne (1989, p.60) was one of the first to question how LMCs could account for the 'holistic nature of management', and this question is one that will probably never be answered.

3.3 REFLECT − CONCLUDE − PLAN

How do you respond to the idea that LMCs are a means of control and way of giving power to define performance?

How would you deal with an 'imposition' of an LMC framework?

What can you do to make LMCs work in your favour?

THE LEADERSHIP AND MANAGEMENT DEVELOPMENT AUDIT

There are a number of tensions that might have to be taken into account in the assessment of LMD which it is appropriate to accommodate by an LMD audit. An LMD audit is concerned with the effectiveness and added value of the various aspects of what might be called the LMD system. The idea of *auditing* is borrowed from accountancy and as a term carries with it an image of independence and professionalism. According to Easterby-Smith *et al* (1980, p.12), an audit of management development ought to be 'designed to establish a clear picture of management development within an organisation' through the adoption of an unbiased process which is as neutral as can be designed. Notwithstanding previous comments relating to the difficulties of adopting the objective stance, an LMD audit provides an opportunity for an organisation to find out what managers want, how they feel about what is being provided, and whether the LMD is effective, adding value and in line with organisation requirements.

An LMD audit is a data-gathering exercise concerning the whole LMD framework within an organisation and the operation of the key activities. Because audits are rather intensive activities, involving considerable expense and time as well as the generation of large amounts of data, it is important to establish their purpose and whose expectations must be considered. An LMD audit can serve a variety of purposes, such as assessing needs for LMD, proving added value and/or controlling cost. An audit might also lead to the improvement of LMD activities as a whole. In addition, an LMD audit could be used as an intervention strategy, as a vehicle for initiating activities and interventions (Easterby-Smith *et al* 1980) such as an organisational change programme.

Data that might be considered within an LMD audit comprises information relating to:

- the appraisal of managers
- assessment and development centres
- competency frameworks and models of performance
- assessment tools such as psychometrics
- budget-setting expenditure and control
- training undertaken
- courses attended
- activities such as coaching and mentoring
- evaluation procedures.

Of course we realise that there will be links between each of these activities, and the activities themselves can be thought of as sub-systems within the whole system. For the activity of appraisal, there will be:

- inputs for the activity, such as documents and briefing sheets, the appraisal skills of the interviewer and interviewee
- the process of the activity, such as the interview itself, the documents and resources used
- outcomes of the activity, such as documents with LMD needs identified, feelings about the process.

If an LMD audit is concerned with the gathering and then the analysis of data, it should be possible to identify data sources for each activity and a variety of techniques such as:

- interviews
- surveys
- observations
- documents.

In the light of our previous consideration of multiple interests in LMD, it is evident that an LMD audit can also become rather a political process, different interests vying for influence on the results. For example, if one consequence of an LMD audit is an organisational LMD initiative, the shape of the initiative and its overall aims and objectives will be the concern of different interests affected.

It has become important for LMD to show its connection to organisational strategy, and an LMD audit is likely to provide a means to achieve this. It can serve to prevent LMD activities from becoming isolated from organisational objectives and help those involved in LMD specify clearly how provision contributes. The CIPD (2002) found that the link between business plans and LMD was seldom made, mainly due to the quality of strategic management processes which depended on good-quality information, broad stakeholder involvement, rigorous analysis and debate and clear success criteria. It is suggested that senior managers need to develop their understanding of organisation and management preconditions for business success so that they gain sufficient insight to initiate change or other developments in the organisation. An LMD audit can thus become part of a business, organisation and management review (BOMR) process to provide 'a clear view of the contribution expected from managers to today's and tomorrow's business models and a business-centred brief for managers and developers to work from' (p.19).

WEB LINK

Another approach is to try the Inspirational Leadership tool at **http://www.inspiredleadership. org.uk/** . Its purpose is to enable leaders to be clear about their most natural styles and strengths so that they can shape their roles and those of their teams accordingly.

There are of course other approaches which provide senior managers with a diagnosis of the whole organisation and which can reveal LMD needs. The value of such approaches is that they provide key information which can be used in forming a strategy while at the same time they reveal possible areas for LMD and more generally HRD for the whole organisation. The value of these approaches is that they attempt to assess an organisation against a range of dimensions and often involve a variety of people in debate and discussion.

BALANCED SCORECARD

The *balanced scorecard* is a model developed by Kaplan and Norton (1996) in which managers need a balanced set of performance measures, as is demonstrated in Figure 3.5.

EUROPEAN FOUNDATION FOR QUALITY MANAGEMENT

A further example, the Total Quality Management (TQM) movement which emerged in the 1980s, can be seen as a set of tools or an attempt to bring about lasting change and a culture of continuous improvement. To promote the latter, the European Foundation for Quality Management (EFQM) has developed a model which can be used to assess an organisation against nine criteria of excellence. The crucial feature of the model is that by understanding how the whole organisation works, managers can identify ways to make improvements sometimes by assessing and responding to development needs. It is illustrated in Figure 3.6.

INVESTORS IN PEOPLE

An alternative approach is to use Investors in People (IiP). Since 1991, IiP has provided criteria or a set of 'national' standards which focus more specifically on training and development. Crucially, the standards require the development of a business plan which includes plans to develop all employees and the evaluation

Figure 3.5 Kaplan and Norton's description of the 'balanced scorecard' process

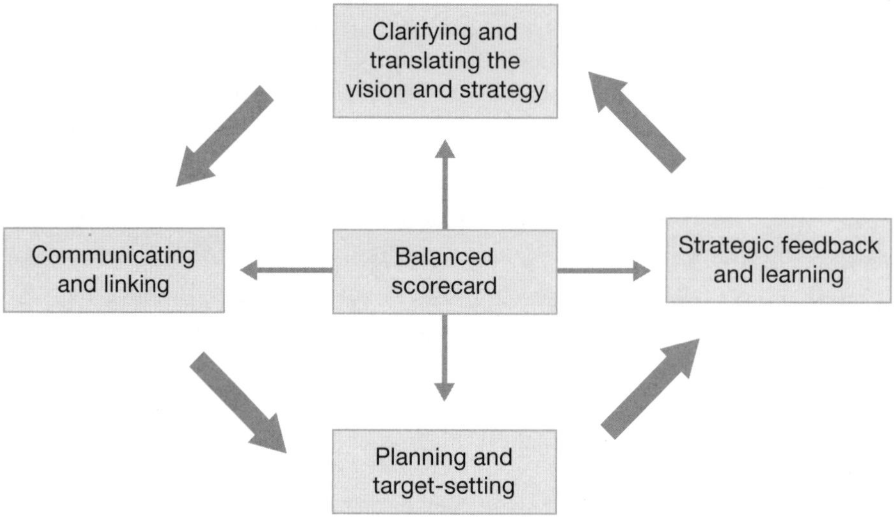

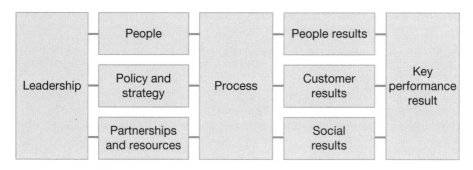

Clarifying and
translating the
vision and strategy

Communicating
and linking

Balanced
scorecard

Strategic feedback
and learning

Planning and
target-setting

Source: adapted and reprinted by permission of *Harvard Business Review*. Exhibit from 'Using the balanced scorecard as a strategic management system', by Robert S. Kaplan and P. Norton, January – February 1996a, p.77. Copyright ©1996 by the President and Fellows of Harvard College; all rights reserved

Figure 3.6 The European Foundation for Quality Management model

Leadership	People	Process	People results	Key performance result
	Policy and strategy		Customer results	
	Partnerships and resources		Social results	

Source: adapted and reprinted with permission from EFQM (2001) *Self-Assessment Guidelines*, European Foundation for Quality Management

of the results. Like the EFQM model, the main benefits from IiP are seen to come when it is used to assess performance requirements and continuous improvement (Alberga *et al* 1997). Recent developments of IiP include a module focused on management and leadership development.

WEB LINK

Further information about EFQM can be found at **http://ww1.efqm.org/ en/** .

The Investors in People website at **http://www.investorsinpeople.co.uk/ Pages/Home.aspx** provides access to copies of the national standard and the latest research on the future of IiP.

You might also visit **http://www.balancedscorecard.org/**, the homepage of the Balanced Scorecard Institute.

SUMMARY

- The link between a leader's or manager's job in terms of how it might be performed and the requirements of strategy has often not been well made in many organisations.

- Models of leadership and management performance can be explicitly stated or implicitly held.

- Leadership or management performance may be considered a relationship between means – skills, knowledge, attitudes – and ends – results and outputs.

- Leadership and management competences seek to link organisational strategy and the performance of managers.

- Organisation-specific approaches to competences recognise the importance of context, particularly how the expression of abilities or competences need to reflect the meanings of an individual organisation.

- There are both technical and theoretical criticisms of leadership and management competences as a 'one best way' attempt to describe performance.

- Leadership and management development audits are used to find out the state of affairs with reference to LMD in an organisation, and to assess the effectiveness of activities.

QUESTIONS

For discussion

1 *If it can't be measured, it can't be managed.* Discuss, with reference to the performance of leaders and managers.

2 Can the performance of managers be measured scientifically?

3 Can leadership and management competences provide an indication of best practice in performance?

4 *Competence is the embodiment of a technically oriented way of thinking.* Discuss, with reference to leadership and management competences.

5 Can leadership and management competences accommodate inclusive and relational perspectives of leadership?

GROUP ACTIVITY

Get together in a group of three.

Then working individually, write down the names of three well-known people you regard as good leaders (for example: Richard Branson or Winston Churchill).

Now against each name write down why you selected this person as a good leader – what did they do that was good?

Meet with the other members of your group to share your findings, and develop an agreed model of good leadership and poor leadership.

NOTES

1 ISTJ stands for 'Introverted Sensing with auxiliary extraverted Thinking' – one of 16 Myers-Briggs 'types' – see **http://www.myersbriggs.org/my-mbti-personality-type/mbti-basics/** .

2 In common with others we will use the term 'competences' to refer to all approaches providing descriptions relating to leadership and management performance.

3 The terms 'characteristics' and 'abilities' include skills, knowledge, understanding, traits, motives, self-image and social role.

 ## FURTHER READING

ALBAN-METCALFE, J. and ALIMO-METCALFE, B. (2007) 'Development of the private sector version of the (Engaging) Transformational Leadership Questionnaire', *Leadership and Organization Development Journal*, Vol.28, No.2: 104–21

CÔTÉ, S. and MINERS, C. T. H. (2006) 'Emotional intelligence, cognitive intelligence, and job performance', *Administrative Science Quarterly*, Vol.51, No.1: 1–28

DREJER, A. (2002) *Strategic Management and Core Competencies: Theory and application*. Westport, CT: Quorum Books

HOFFMAN, T. (1999) 'The meanings of competency', *Journal of European Industrial Training*, Vol.23, No.6: 275–85

CHAPTER 4

Assessing development needs

CHAPTER OUTLINE

Introduction
Performance management systems
Feedback as a key feature in PMS
Development centres
Appraisal
Multi-source feedback
Summary

LEARNING OUTCOMES

After studying this chapter, you should be able to understand, explain, analyse and evaluate:

- approaches to managing the performance of managers through performance management systems

- the importance and value of both giving and receiving feedback when assessing a manager's development needs

- the difference between assessment and development centres

- the various approaches available that enable the appraisal of managers

- the incorporation of LMD needs into personal development plans

INTRODUCTION

The assessment of the development needs of managers is something that requires frequently reconciling with the competing and contested tensions associated with factors such as assessing their needs, how those needs are assessed, and the language that is used when expressing those needs. As we observed in Chapter 3, *Measuring leaders and managers*, the very description of a manager's performance can serve to become a means of controlling performance and defining their identities – often in a very prescriptive way. There are also other tensions. Assessment is inevitably a judgemental process which concerns a manager's performance, and given the multiplicity of purposes or rationales for LMD, there are bound to be competing responses to any judgements made. A key requirement for any assessment is that the main dimensions of work can be defined precisely in performance terms and then measured over time, but that the assessment also allows for a consideration of the constraints faced (Furnham 2004). One obvious point of tension in leadership and management therefore concerns the degree to which judgements about performance are deemed valid by the managers themselves and whether the feedback that is given provokes a defensive response – something that may itself have an adverse impact on performance. Assessing needs in LMD is a prime candidate for Burgoyne and Jackson's (1997) 'arena thesis' by which LMD becomes a mediating device, the aim being for different values to be discussed, perhaps contested, and possibly reconciled and shared.

PERFORMANCE MANAGEMENT SYSTEMS

Performance management for the HR profession has been drawn into centre stage as a means of uncovering and delivering an organisation's strategy (Strebler and Bevan 2001). If strategy and business plans concern an organisation's response to key changes in the environment and signal some response towards future needs and requirements that can then be cascaded throughout the organisation, each section or department is able to set priorities and targets for delivery. Then at every stage in the process managers will be required to determine (with others) those performance requirements that are deemed appropriate, together with how these will be measured. Measurement of performance indicates to others that managers are thinking strategically (Pun and White 2005). In addition, such has been the speed of global and technical change and significant economic disturbance that the goals and targets need to be reviewed and reset on a continual basis. As we saw in Chapter 3, at the level of organisation LMD needs may follow strategic consideration through a process such as balanced scorecard or any other process which provides the organisation with the parameters for measuring progress against and achievement of targets. In this respect, performance management can be said to play a vital role in ensuring that organisational objectives are both communicated and met, and that each person's needs are appropriately aligned with the organisation's objectives. So, for example, when the mobile communications company O_2 prepared its launch in 2002, all its senior managers were assessed against a competence framework developed through a process that had involved structured interviews, data from performance reports and 360-degree feedback and web-based surveys. Each manager was then provided with a personal report including detailed feedback, which identified skills gaps. Coaching sessions aimed at addressing areas of perceived need were provided.

According to Holbeche (1998a), the key elements of performance management are:

- a common understanding of the organisation's goals
- a shared expectation of how individuals can contribute
- employees with the skill and ability to meet expectations
- individuals who are fully committed to the aims of the organisation.

INTEGRATING HRM ACTIVITIES

One important aspect of performance management is the opportunity it represents to create a better integration of a range of HRM activities and to offer an organising mechanism for how such activities can be linked together to better meet an organisation's goals. The CIPD (2005) completed a survey in over 500 UK organisations of performance management activities and the belief that such activities were effective. The responses are shown in Table 4.1.

Table 4.1 The features of performance management

	Organisations (%) using this feature	Organisations (%) using this feature and believing it to be effective
Individual annual appraisal	65	83
Twice-yearly/bi-annual appraisal	27	38
Rolling appraisal	10	21
360-degree appraisal	14	20
Peer appraisal	8	12
Self-appraisal	30	53
Team appraisal	6	10
Subordinate feedback	11	17
Continuous assessment	14	20
Competence assessment	31	39
Objective-setting and review	62	82
Performance-related pay	31	39
Competence-related pay	7	11
Contribution-related pay	4	6
Team pay	3	5
Coaching and/or mentoring	36	46
Career management and/or succession planning	37	47
Personal development plans	62	81

Source: CIPD (2005)

A key task arising from these studies therefore is to show how activities can be linked together in a coherent manner to form a performance management system

(PMS) in which each complements the other to give a more complete picture of performance. It is noticeable in the survey results that annual appraisal, objective-setting and review and personal development plans are considered to be effective. Combined with other features, these can form a performance management cycle, illustrated in Figure 4.1.

Figure 4.1 An integrated performance management cycle

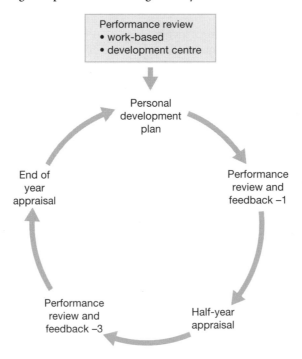

What becomes clear here is that the operation of a PMS relies heavily on the flow of information between the various activities of:

- a work-based review
- development centre attendance
- personal development plans
- performance reviews and feedback
- appraisal.

It is from these processes that managers gain information that enables them to identify how performance might be improved as well as to assess whether the objectives contained within plans are being met. Each PMS therefore requires either a measurement process or metrics to enable decisions to be made, and it is at this stage that the various approaches to measuring managers – especially competences – come to the fore. In Chapter 3, competences were shown to be the vehicle through which a language to describe and assess performance in a consistent manner could be derived. However, a key question remains as to how the information relating to performance will be used. This is the question that reveals an ongoing tension within any PMS – between the need to monitor and control performance, and the need to identify LMD requirements. One particular manifestation of this tension occurs where reward and remuneration is tied to performance. There is a long history of research that serves to highlight the difficulties of relating the performance of managers to monetary reward as well as other rewards, such as promotion. Roy (1952) and Bowery and Thorpe (1986) showed how the linking of performance measures with pay could actually hold down performance or at best lead to undesirable consequences for the priorities the organisation needs for success as a whole. We need to look no further than the payment of bonuses to city traders to see how performing in ways that offer short-term gains can also have disastrous effects on the organisation but also for the national economy as a whole,[1] raising the levels of public sector debt to unprecedented levels. During the 1960s and 1970s there were a variety of schemes, such as Management by Objectives (MBO), which were designed to channel the performance of managers as well as to stimulate their development. However, research into these schemes soon revealed that they were in many ways self-defeating as they were based on a 'reward–punishment psychology' which pressurised managers who had little involvement in the objectives they were to achieve (Levinson 1970). Others considered them a way of offering participation but actually they correspond to a means of control. Fletcher and Williams (1996) have suggested that the equating of performance management with goals or performance-related pay was likely to reduce the effectiveness of performance management, and that job satisfaction and commitment could only be enhanced by approaches which combined a number of activities. This is a finding confirmed by work attempting to explain how the link between HRM and performance occurs (Guest *et al* 2000), although it is becoming clear that HRM works best when attention is paid to how activities are implemented rather than the quantity of activities (Edgar and Geare 2005).

Thorpe and Holloway (2008) in their study of different disciplinary perspectives of performance, identified HRM as having a distinct approach. Houldsworth and Burkenshaw (2008) indicated that there is a trend taking place that moves performance management away from narrowly focusing on the job to a process that begins to incorporate the wider social and economic processes that impinge on the performance of the firm.

One area in which the tension between control and development in a PMS has become evident is government attempts to modernise the provision of public services through Best Value Performance Indicators from April 2000, which have now been replaced by over 150 National Indicators which reflect priority outcomes.

 WEB LINK

Check the latest information on National Indicators at **http://www. communities.gov.uk/ localgovernment/performanceframeworkpartnerships/nationalindicators/** .

FEEDBACK AS A KEY FEATURE IN PMS

In order to assess the development needs of managers a key feature is how they will respond to feedback. Research suggests that this is a very sensitive issue. For example, one of the key findings from a classic piece of research carried out in the 1960s into the impact of feedback on managers during performance appraisal (Meyer *et al* 1965) showed that, on average, there were 13 criticisms during an appraisal interview. This finding explains why appraisals often resulted in defensive behaviour on the part of the managers being appraised. The more criticism a manager received, the more he or she would react defensively by denying shortcomings and blaming others. One way to account for such behaviour was the difference between a person's rating of performance and the degree to which it was confirmed or not by the appraiser. The research showed that most managers rated themselves as above-average before appraisal, and most found the assessment by the appraiser to be less favourable than their own. It was further found that criticism continued to negatively affect performance after the interview.[2]

SELF-AWARENESS

DeNisi and Kluger (2000) reviewed the research between feedback and performance and noted that in 33% of cases there was a negative effect on performance. Feedback can help provide focus to improve performance, but the danger arises when there is an impact on factors such as self-belief or self-esteem which can trigger emotions. Clearly, one of the main aims of feedback to managers is to increase their level of self-awareness and help them to reflect on their strengths and weaknesses as managers so that areas for performance improvement may be recognised and needs for LMD identified. All managers hold views about how well they perform their work, and these views reflect core beliefs that form their self-evaluation. According to Judge *et al* (1997) such beliefs can become relatively enduring and will affect how they operate and respond to events. However, the views and beliefs of managers may not be the views and beliefs held by others, and the aim of feedback is to surface such differences so that greater understanding can be gained and learning takes place (London and Smither 1995). In recent years, managers have been increasingly subjected to feedback from a variety of sources. Here, we perhaps require a distinction to be made between feedback that occurs naturally during the course of everyday working and feedback that is provided more formally. Managers obtain the former from interactions with others and from results achieved in their work but can also obtain considerable amounts of useful feedback for themselves by reviewing and reflecting on their activities as managers. The more formal methods for the provision of feedback include:

- performance reviews and appraisals with managers
- 180-degree or 360-degree feedback from staff, peers, managers, customers and others
- feedback from assessment or development centres.

Through such methods, feedback may be used to identify areas for performance improvement and LMD needs by raising self-awareness, but, as we have noted, there might also be decisions to be made on remuneration and career progression. In all cases it is difficult to escape the judgemental features of feedback which may militate against the manager accepting that he or she has a developmental need.

 WEB LINK

There are many ways to help managers understand the need to increase self-awareness. One of the most popular is the *Johari window*, which explores how feedback and disclosure can be useful to managers (and others). You can find out more about the Johari window at **http://www. mindtools.com/CommSkll/JohariWindow.htm** .

RESPONSE TO FEEDBACK

The response of managers to feedback is affected by their self-evaluation, which Judge *et al* (1997) suggest is indicated by factors such as self-esteem, self-efficacy, locus of control and neuroticism. These psychological traits are built up through life experience and form a sense of value for managers about what they can do and what they have achieved. They provide an important input into how managers negotiate and establish their role and identity as a manager with others (Holman *et al* 2002). It is not surprising therefore that feedback which provides significant challenge to self-evaluation might be resisted or ignored – hence the need to help managers increase their self-awareness. Figure 4.2 shows possible responses to feedback on performance.

Figure 4.2 Response to feedback on performance

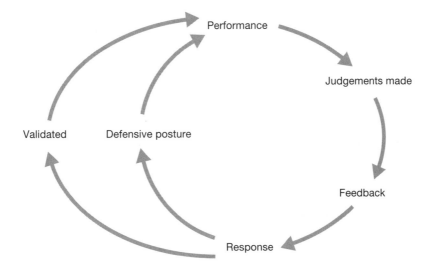

4.1 REFLECT — CONCLUDE — PLAN

Consider one occasion on which you received feedback on your performance.

In what respects was it helpful or unhelpful?

What makes feedback helpful or unhelpful to you?

What could you do to improve the feedback you give to others, and the feedback others offer you?

Of course, not all feedback is negative, and many managers recognise the value of getting feedback and take a proactive stance towards it. Managers can be referred to as 'feedback-seekers', and research by VandeWalle and Cummings (1997) suggested that such behaviour can lead to improved performance. It is argued that a key contributor to feedback-seeking is goal orientation where a distinction is made between:

● learning-goal orientation – the willingness of managers to develop new skills and master new situations

● performance-goal orientation – the seeking by managers to show and prove that their competences are adequate by avoiding negative judgements in favour of positive ones.

Longitudinal research suggests that a learning-goal orientation is positively related to feedback-seeking behaviour and that a performance-goal orientation has a negative effect on feedback-seeking behaviour. The research also suggests that a preoccupation with continually striving to prove that their competency levels were adequate tended to drive out managers' learning and feedback-seeking. Further testing of this idea showed that contextual factors such as leadership could influence goal orientation and, as a consequence, managers' propensity to seek feedback (VandeWalle *et al* 2000).

Cannon and Witherspoon (2005) argue that managers need to understand the dynamics of feedback-giving and -receiving and make their feedback more actionable. This involves 'self-questioning' by observing the impact of giving and receiving feedback and using others to observe how feedback is given or used.

 WEB LINK

If you would like some basic advice on giving feedback, try **http://www. mapnp.org/library/ commskls/feedback/basc_gde.htm** .

A website that provides a link to a page which offers good advice on listening skills is **http:// www.casaa-resources.net/resources/ sourcebook/acquiring-leadership-skills/listening-skills. html** .

DEVELOPMENT CENTRES

According to Ballantyne and Povah (2004, p.142), a *development centre* is:

> the use of assessment centre technology for the identification of strengths and weaknesses to diagnose development needs that will facilitate more effective job performance/career advancement, which in turn contributes to greater organization success.

Both assessment centres (ACs) and development centres (DCs) draw their strength and popularity from a belief in the valid and reliable accuracy of the measurement of performance through the use of psychometric methods and exercises which allow judgements to be made by the trained professionals against particular dimensions relating to performance (Arthur *et al* 2003). In addition, where ACs and DCs are combined with competence frameworks and other models which set out the requirements for performance, they become a link mechanism to support an organisation's strategic approach to HRM and change (Iles 1992). Indeed, as we noted in Chapter 3, leadership and management competences can be seen as a means of sending messages to managers about what counts, and of aligning an organisation's goals with the qualities required of its managers.

Woodruffe (2000) suggests that ACs and DCs have the following common characteristics:

- Their objective is to obtain an indication of an individual's current or potential competence to perform a job.
- The achievement of their objective is through assessment techniques such as exercises and work simulations which capture people's behaviour.

Woodruffe goes on to outline four generalisations about typical centres. These are:

- Participants are observed by assessors – assessors are trained in the use of measurement dimensions such as competences and the skills of rating.
- Assessment is by a combination of methods and includes simulations of the key elements of the work.
- Information is brought together from all the techniques – usually under the language of competence.
- Several participants are assessed at the same time – six is usual to make group exercises feasible.

METHODS AND PURPOSE

Typically, both ACs and DCs use similar methods which yield information about participants. Research by Jackson and Yeates (1993) on DCs in particular found a mix of the following activities:

- ability tests – especially in centres which selected for promotion: this is because ability tests are considered to be good predictors of future performance

- personality questionnaires, including the Occupational Personality Questionnaire and Cattell's 16 PF

- group discussions, involving problem-solving discussions and negotiations

- presentations, based on preparation before the centre

- in-tray exercises, to simulate how managers might tackle or prioritise management work

- role-plays – less common but usually requiring the assessor or someone else to adopt a difficult role or a role in a difficult situation

- other group exercises, including outdoor activities

- individual interviews – mainly to provide feedback and assist in identifying development needs which could lead to the formation of a personal development plan.

As we have indicated, DCs ought to serve different purposes from ACs, although in practice some organisations combine purposes and this can cause confusion among those who participate (Bolton and Gold 1994). Jackson and Yeates (1993) found that a variety of terms are used, such as 'development programme', 'career evaluation programme', 'development workshop' as well as 'AC' or 'DC' which reflected the emphasis of a centre. The research also noted that organisations were using centres for recruitment, for fast-track promotions, for assessing high potential as well as for identifying needs.[3] The crucial questions are whether participants are fully aware of the purpose for which they are carried out, and whether the purpose stated matches the process enacted. As Woodruffe (2000, p.32) argues, 'Assessment centres masquerading as development centres are wolves in sheep's clothing.' He points out that emphasising the purpose of development requires that information generated should be used for development and not to make decisions about a person's potential or future. Individuals who may in the first instance be prepared to participate in a centre where the objective has been stated as their own development may be less prepared to participate if they think that the results of their performance may provide material for judgements made against them at a later date.

The litmus test for the integrity of a DC relates to the use that is made of the information generated. Is the information owned by the assessors on behalf of the organisation to make decisions about participants? Or is the information going primarily to be used for the participant to identify his or her development needs? In most organisations, the answer to this question probably lies somewhere in between pure AC and pure DC, even though this could lead to a blurring of the boundary between assessment and development purposes and uncertainty among managers.

Figure 4.3 shows Woodruffe's (2000) presentation of the differences between centres for development and centres to make decisions about selection.

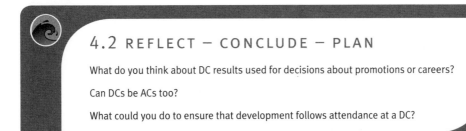

4.2 REFLECT – CONCLUDE – PLAN

What do you think about DC results used for decisions about promotions or careers?

Can DCs be ACs too?

What could you do to ensure that development follows attendance at a DC?

Figure 4.3 A continuum from development centres to selection centres

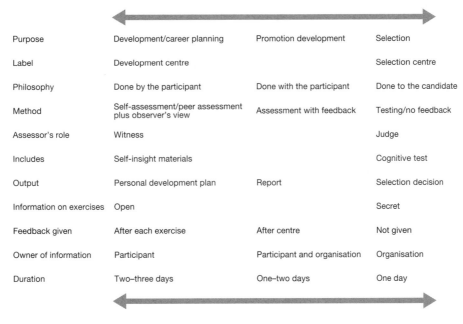

Purpose	Development/career planning	Promotion development	Selection
Label	Development centre		Selection centre
Philosophy	Done by the participant	Done with the participant	Done to the candidate
Method	Self-assessment/peer assessment plus observer's view	Assessment with feedback	Testing/no feedback
Assessor's role	Witness		Judge
Includes	Self-insight materials		Cognitive test
Output	Personal development plan	Report	Selection decision
Information on exercises	Open		Secret
Feedback given	After each exercise	After centre	Not given
Owner of information	Participant	Participant and organisation	Organisation
Duration	Two–three days	One–two days	One day

Source: Woodruffe (2000, p.36)

The *LMD in Practice* below provides an example of an AC which is also used to develop young managers for senior roles.

During the 1990s many organisations moved towards an emphasis on development in centres so that LMD needs could be better identified. Woodruffe (2000) suggested that this was partly a reaction to the judgemental and demotivating features of ACs we have discussed, but also partly as a result of and a reaction to rapid change which required constant revisions to be made to the roles of individuals' performance and the need for managers (and others) to

COCA-COLA'S SIMULATION CENTRE FINDS TOP TALENT

James Brockett

Coca-Cola is using an assessment centre that 'simulates' senior roles to develop talent in its marketing division, group HR director Stevens Sainte-Rose told *PM*. The company invites the best of its global marketing talent to the centre, where they are put through an experience simulating a busy day in the life of a senior marketer. Observing participants' performance under pressure gives the firm a better idea of their suitability for a senior role than simply judging them on their current job, Sainte-Rose said.

'The centre replicates all the stresses that come with being a senior marketer – in fact, we over-stress the day to test out their skills and character,' he said.

The programme, developed over the past 18 months with assessment specialists SHL, was designed with input from senior marketers to make the experience as realistic as possible. Mentors are assigned to participants afterwards.

'Before the programme was introduced, we had a lot of high-performing people in the organisation but we could never really validate whether they were ready to be promoted or not,' Sainte-Rose said. 'It is so important to keep the pipeline of talent flowing.'

There were also more external hires than Sainte-Rose was comfortable with, he said – but the programme has now enabled the firm to fill at least 75% of roles internally. Nine of the 32 employees on the scheme in the past year have already won promotion, taking up posts across the globe. The scheme is set to be replicated in other areas of the company and could also be adapted for use in recruitment, Sainte-Rose said.

Source: *People Management*, 4 October 2007, p.16

engage in continuous learning. DCs can also be a means of retaining staff when promotion opportunities in organisations are limited (Holbeche 1998). The key issues still remain:

- Do DCs lead to an awareness of what managers must learn to improve their performance?

- Does awareness and learning improve performance?

- Does learning and learning-to-learn form a feature of the DC process?

In general, there has been very little research on the value of DCs. One study by Halman and Fletcher (2000) of 111 customer service staff found that attendance at a DC was associated with adjustments made in their self-assessments in line with the ratings of assessors. This was especially the case where participants underrated their performance before the DC. Over-raters on the other hand tended to make fewer and smaller adjustments, possibly relating to their perception that there was less need to improve performance and, therefore, attend to the feedback provided at the DC. An interesting result was obtained from participants who accurately rated their performance – ie where self-assessment matched the ratings of assessors. Following the DC their self-assessment rating increased! This finding suggests a need to identify over-, under- and accurate self-raters as such so that feedback can be adjusted accordingly.

In conclusion, by far the biggest single problem is the difficulty of separating assessment from development. It is clear that the credibility of DCs in part rests on the accepted standing of AC methods and their reliability and validity. However, Carrick and Williams (1999) argued that there are issues relating to validity, and there may also be a problem for some participants relating to attendance which leads to de-motivation as a consequence of the procedures used in the diagnosis of the development needs. Further, for some managers the expected outcome may well be negative, affecting both their willingness to participate and their performance.

APPRAISAL

In many ways appraisal is the Holy Grail of LMD, and in principle it deals with one of the major issues that relates to improvement of leadership and management performance – yet the practice is often perceived to be profoundly unsatisfactory. Appraisal has long been recognised as a political process with potentially negative outcomes (Poon 2004). However, regardless of its reputation, it remains a significant activity in an organisation's attempt to measure, monitor and control the activity of managers. Further, for some, an organisation without appraisal could be considered to be one acting irrationally and ineffectively (Barlow 1989).

PURPOSE

Appraisal schemes are designed to achieve a number of objectives, whether explicitly or not. The possibilities include:

- providing information for succession, talent and resource planning
- providing a basis for improved communication between managers and their staff
- providing clarity of roles and purpose
- identifying and recording performance weaknesses
- providing a basis for the analysis of performance and the identification of required standards and improvements
- identifying potential
- providing mutual feedback between a manager and staff
- providing a basis for training and career counselling
- providing a basis for decision-making or salary.

This list of objectives suggests that appraisal can represent something of a 'panacea' (Taylor 1998, p.185) for organisations. It is important to realise that no single appraisal scheme or appraisal interview will meet all of the above diverse objectives. In addition, some of the objectives actually contradict each other. The best example of this are appraisals related to salary decisions. These are found least effective at engendering useful discussions on performance improvement or, indeed, feedback for managers. Conflicts in purpose of this kind – particularly where a manager is required to make judgements about others – lie at the heart of the difficulties connected with appraisal. In the 1950s, for example, the classic study by McGregor (1957) found that managers disliked 'playing God' (p.89) when they were required to make judgements about the worth of their employees. This finding was replicated in the study by Maier (1985), who found that managers were being asked to adopt inconsistent roles in the appraisal interview – that of both judge and helper. There is also, of course, the study by Meyer *et al* (1965), already mentioned, which suggested that feedback – especially critical feedback – had a tendency to result in defensive behaviour by managers, reduced motivation and *no change in performance.*

APPRAISAL AND LMD NEEDS

Organisations can make a choice to orientate appraisals towards development, but research suggests that in many organisations there is a gap that exists between the desire for a developmental orientation and the achievement of it. For example, a study of appraisal in the NHS found a policy of development and rhetoric in support, but managers appeared to use it to exert their authority and influence through control (Redman *et al* 2000). Training and development always took second place to work objectives, and sometimes did not take place at all. Even when development was discussed, the discussion often occurred in a mechanical and tick-box fashion, although there were also some benefits including setting objectives, personal development plans and mini-reviews of progress towards goals. A similar result was found by Ferlie and McGivern (2007) in their study of appraisal for senior medical professionals where they found that while appraisal could be developmental, it was often reduced to a 'tick-box game' to give the impression that a serious audit of practice was taking place. Some saw appraisal as a waste of time and something to be ignored so that practice could continue as determined by the professionals

At the very least we suggest that discussions related to performance where the objective is to identify LMD needs should be separated from those that focus on pay, and other aspects of reward and promotion. In addition, based on the lessons learned from the problems faced by Management by Objectives, there is a need to focus closely on the process used when setting plans and deciding the criteria for making judgements about performance. In this connection, research by Pettijohn *et al* (2001) found that morale and performance was often diminished if managers do not feel they can control the factors that affect the criteria by which their performance is judged.

Traditional approaches to appraising leadership and management performance usually included a listing of traits or personality attributes. For example, a manager might be assessed on his or her ability to show loyalty, or passion, or determination. Some appraisal schemes might even still include such terms, but attractive as such ideas might be, there is inevitably a difficulty in defining these concepts (one person's loyalty might be another's betrayal), and this has the knock-on effect of making it difficult for appraisers to agree on how they should rate managers – ie there may be a low level of inter-rater reliability. A second problem concerns the value in identifying LMD needs: it might be argued that even if it were possible to recognise whether a manager lacks particular traits, it might not be feasible to create a development solution for all of them.

 WEB LINK

Traits remain a popular way of thinking and talking about managers – especially as leaders. Go to **http://www.mapnp.org/library/ldrship/ traits/htm,** which is a free library of management resources. This particular link is a page devoted to Suggested Traits and Characteristics of Highly Effective Leaders, and contains many further links to articles and resources.

In addition to traits and personality, appraisal discussions also focus on specific types of leadership or management skills – eg planning, time management, building teams, and so on. These of course do have the value of directly relating to LMD activities and processes. In Chapter 3 we saw that the behaviour approach to leadership and management competences (LMCs) was concerned with behaviour patterns which stem from characteristics and abilities that lead to effective performance. There is also the claim that such competences provide an integrating link between PMS and organisation strategy, although there is also evidence that the competences identified are not always included in the appraisal process (Abraham *et al* 2001, p.850). One value of LMCs is that they can be used to develop ratings scales for use in appraisal discussions.

Two distinct forms of ratings scales can be developed:

- behaviour-anchored ratings scales (BARS) – which are descriptions of effective and ineffective performance
- behavioural observation scales (BOS) – which are observable, job-related behaviours that those doing the rating can assess in terms of the frequency in which they occur.

As well as ratings such as these, concerned with performance, there has also been some interest in contextual performance rating which is non-job-specific. These include such features as co-operation and enthusiasm which are seen to contribute to things such as an enhancement of organisational climate. According to Conway (1999), contextual performance is concerned with personality and motivation, although how this kind of performance is demonstrated will require assessment from those who interact with the managers. This opens the door to a growing interest in multi-source feedback (MSF).

MULTI-SOURCE FEEDBACK

Multi-source feedback (MSF) has become increasingly popular (Kettley 1997) as a result of the way it:

- empowers employees and promotes teamwork by allowing them to appraise their managers
- increases the reliability of appraisal feedback and gives more balance to feedback as a consequence of organisations' becoming flatter with fewer spans of control
- reinforces good management behaviour through the way it allows managers to see themselves as others see them, thus raising their self-awareness.

MSF incorporates six types of appraisal of managers:

- appraisal by staff – upward appraisal
- appraisal by fellow managers – peer appraisal
- appraisal by the person in charge – top-down appraisal
- appraisal by the manager and/or staff/peers – 180-degree appraisal
- appraisal by the manager, staff and peers – 360-degree appraisal
- appraisal by the manager, staff, peers, customers, suppliers and others who are in an interdependent relationship with a manager – 540-degree appraisal.

Figure 4.4 shows how MSF can cover all the angles of management performance.

Figure 4.4 Covering the angles of management performance

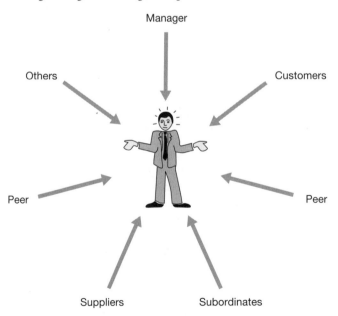

There is an undoubted potential for so many types of feedback all aimed at helping managers to increase their self-awareness and to better identify areas for development, but it can be a very demanding process. As Handy *et al* (1996) found, feedback from people who can observe what a manager does is difficult to deny (p.23):

> 360-degree feedback is scary . . . It asks questions I would have preferred not to have answered. But what is so powerful is that I can no longer pretend that I don't know what is being said about me.

Before we examine these varieties of MSF further, it is important to remember that the process of feedback can provoke a variety of responses from managers. Context plays an important part in the receptiveness of managers to MSF. One key issue is the way MSF works in connection with other HR processes such as development (Brutus and Derayeh 2002), and where there is support from peers and senior managers which leads to LMD, MSF is likely to be viewed more positively. Particularly important from any MSF process is using the results to set goals for action based on those results, and coaching has been found to be effective for this activity (Luthans and Peterson 2004).

As we suggested above, all managers value who they are, what they can do and what they have achieved. This would suggest that MSF must include another angle of appraisal – self-appraisal.

SELF-APPRAISAL

Self-appraisal is based on the simple notion that the best person to make an assessment and judgement about a manager's performance and therefore able to determine his or her development needs is the manager himself/herself. Following Campbell and Lee (1988), it might be suggested that self-appraisal has four steps:

1 The manager has beliefs and ideas about what the work requires and what needs to be done to meet goals.

2 The manager attempts to meet work requirements and goals informed by these beliefs and ideas.

3 The manager judges whether particular behaviours best achieve the desired results.

4 The manager uses judgement to reinforce or change these beliefs and ideas about the work requirements and what needs to be done.

It might also be suggested here that others – such as the individual's superior, his/her staff, and so on – also need to move through the same steps in order to make their judgements about the performance of a manager, albeit from different angles. One of the crucial factors in the success of self-appraisal concerns whether, as we have already indicated, the orientation is towards evaluation for performance control or for development. Where the emphasis is on the former, and especially where self-appraisal judgements about performance are contrasted with the ratings of others, there are likely to be discrepancies. Campbell and Lee identified three types of discrepancy:

- *informational* – disagreements about work to be done, how it is done, and the standards to be used in judging results
- *cognitive* – the simplification of complex behaviour and performance, resulting in differing perceptions about what actually happened
- *affective* – the triggering of defence mechanisms as a consequence of the evaluative nature of appraisal, resulting in bias and distortion in the interpreting of appraisal data.

None of this needs to be surprising, especially if we remember some of the earlier research findings on appraisal in which most individuals tend to overrate their performance and inflate their self-appraisal (Meyer 1980). These distortions and others are likely to be present in all forms of MSF, especially where evaluation for the control of performance is the main purpose. However, where development is at the fore, self-appraisal may be more effective. Managers may, for example, be modest about their ratings and more critical if the purpose is for development. Further, with the use of LMCs, self-appraisal can focus on specific behaviours in particular contexts rather than on general impressions. For instance, the following self-appraisal items relating to 'education, training and development staff'[4] are taken from the LMC framework of a software company in the UK. Managers were asked to rate themselves on a scale of 1 to 5 against these statements:

a) I take responsibility for the effective induction of new staff.

b) I am able to identify the training needs of new staff and agree a training plan.

c) I understand how to evaluate the effectiveness of training.

UPWARD APPRAISAL

Of course, it is quite natural that leaders or managers would wish to include the views of others within the organisation as part of an MSF process. If we now consider upward appraisal, we can show how the staff might consider the same issues as the manager. In respect of the three competencies listed above, for example, they might consider them in the following context:

a) My manager takes responsibility for the effective induction of new staff.

b) My manager is able to identify the training needs of new staff and incorporate them into an agreed training plan.

c) My manager understands how to evaluate the effectiveness of the training and development undertaken.

It would seem important that staff have a clear view of the manager's role if upward appraisal is to be used. It is not difficult to imagine how the feedback from performance evaluations might well differ from feedback from development activities. Managers might be fearful of such appraisals for a number of reasons:

- It undermines their managerial authority.

- It potentially disturbs current working relationships.

- It might foster unhealthy rivalry between managers as they compete to gain the best ratings.

Antonioni (1994) suggested that staff view upward appraisal in a more positive way when it is anonymous, and fear reprisal if constructive feedback is its main function. He discovered there was also a tendency to give more positive feedback when staff were not anonymous, which might result in fewer development needs being identified. In addition, upward appraisal can often be used as a stepping-stone to the more adventurous models of 360-degree/540-degree appraisal. This would open the opportunity for a more voluntary approach to be taken in which managers could identify the staff they wish to ask for feedback. This appears to have been the approach reported by Jones (1996), where an initial voluntary process eventually evolved into a mandatory 360-degree feedback system. For Jones, feedback from staff led to 'very open and honest feedback about his behaviour and approach to managing', but he also conceded that they had been 'rather too kind' (p.48). How managers respond to upward appraisal may also depend on the current ratings of managers. Reilly *et al* (1996) found that where managers had low or moderate ratings, and feedback from staff was sustained over time, an improvement in management performance did occur. Managers who already had high ratings showed less improvement than those that had lower ratings. The important feature promoted by upward appraisal was an increased awareness of the behaviours measured and the communication of the fact that an improvement in these areas was an expectation being used. However, we recognise that the overall climate may militate against such a process. For example, Atwater *et al* (2000) found that feedback from staff had low impact on managers in the context of an organisational change intervention that they thought had been cynically introduced. Managers tended to respond more positively to high ratings manifested by a reinforcement of their commitment to staff, but low ratings led to a reduced commitment.

More recently, Dierendonck *et al* (2007) considered the impact of upward feedback on leadership behaviour over four months in respect of 17 managers who participated in an LMD programme in the NHS. In addition, 29 managers who also participated in the programme but did not receive upward feedback were placed in a control group. The leadership behaviours rated included coaching/support, commitment to quality, communication, fairness, and integrity/respect. It was found, however, that upward feedback had only a small positive effect, and the main finding for both groups was the general discrepancy between the managers' higher self-ratings and the ratings by staff. Some managers did reduce their ratings as a result but did not change behaviour.

PEER APPRAISAL

From a developmental perspective, feedback from peers can be very important to a manager – even critical feedback often being seen as helpful. In contrast, where feedback is used for decisions not relating to their development, it can lead to rivalries and jealousies. Bettenhausen and Fedor (1997) found that peer appraisal was viewed positively when used for development but negatively when it was used for evaluation. Peiperl (2001) argued that peer appraisal is difficult simply because of its paradoxical nature. For example, because managers often have to engage closely with other managers – their peers – they tend to give positive feedback so as to not disturb the relationship or damage their career. They might, however, be prepared to give feedback on an informal basis, as part of everyday working conversation, but are less inclined to do so in a formal way. Similarly, peers often work as part of a team and contribute as part of a larger collective, yet appraisal is almost exclusively undertaken on an individual basis. Peers may be required to make comparisons between individuals, and this also serves to harm the workings of the team. When the team is low-performing, fears arising from feedback can lead to resistance and the avoidance of blame.

One particularly thriving area of peer appraisal and review is among professional workers such as doctors, medical staff and teachers. For example, Colthart *et al* (2008) completed a survey of over 600 GPs in Scotland. While some reported limited or no benefit, 33% reported undertaking further learning as a result of the appraisal

360-DEGREE APPRAISAL

Clearly, the move from upward and peer appraisal to a more rounded view of 360-degree appraisal requires a shift in confidence and overall trust. Because the outcome can potentially be deeply negative and demoralising for the target managers, most organisations have introduced 360-degree feedback extremely carefully. Fletcher (1998) found that 360-degree appraisal could become unworkable very quickly if used for evaluation purposes. This has led some organisations to dispense with it in as little as two years. Usually, the approach provides for feedback from three sources: line manager, peers, and direct staff. Some organisations also attempt to go outside the firm and to obtain information from clients or customers (540-degree appraisal). Going outside adds value, but gaining support from outside the organisation is even more difficult. So although 360-degree appraisal provides better feedback, it is not without its difficulties. A sample that is representative would probably be a minimum of eight people. However, the most important issue is that the feedback presents not only a broader view of the manager but potentially a more accurate one. The validity of the comments of course depends in part on the rating items that are constructed, and also on guarantees to respondents of anonymity. This comparison of the views of others together with a self-appraisal has the potential to produce surprising results, sometimes positively and sometimes negatively. However, it is also possible that validity can give way to ambiguity, contradiction and confusion when each respondent offers a different perspective on a manager's performance.

Once again, it is important here to establish the purpose of the 360-degree appraisal. Is it to evaluate performance, to provide information in order to remunerate or reward, or to allow managers to identify their LMD needs? Chivers and Darling (1999), in a study of six organisations, found that development was the main purpose and that it was usually incorporated into new or existing LMD programmes. In one of the organisations, 360-degree appraisal was seen as one of the catalysts in the development of a new culture. They also found that there was little attempt to link the process to remuneration and reward, although it is always possible to incorporate the information generated into ongoing discussions that feature as part of an organisation's performance management system. What seems to be vital is to make the objectives clear and explicit so that managers do not regard the process as unfocused and confusing (Handy *et al* 1996). Where the objectives are stated as for the purpose of learning and development but managers suspect that there may be other hidden objectives, they are likely to regard the process more cynically and respond at best ambivalently and at worst negatively to the results (Atwater *et al* 2000). Readers should not forget that 360-degree appraisals do require time: most feedback is paper-based, although there are many examples emerging of online or electronic versions. They all use some form of rating scale. On this latter point managers may well find that feedback mediated by a computer is experienced as less daunting and less emotionally fraught, allowing for a more objective analysis. Where the process is incorporated into a programme or as part of a development centre, it will also be necessary to use trained facilitators or to hire external experts to be able to soothe undue sensitivity.

Smither *et al* (2005) have sought to assess the impact of MSF on performance over time. The research was based on 24 studies but found only small improvements which could be explained by MSF. They highlighted the following factors as important in affecting performance improvement:

- feedback characteristics
- initial reactions to feedback
- personality
- feedback orientation
- perceived need for change
- beliefs about change
- goal-setting
- taking action.

More recently, Smither *et al* (2008) considered the impact on 145 managers nine months after MSF. It was found that managers tend to recall strengths rather than weaknesses, suggesting a need for a more regular review. While certain areas were more likely to be recalled – such as earning others' respect, being sensitive to others' feelings, being patient, and production orientation – generally, there was little evidence that recall of MSF led to performance improvement. This highlights again the need to consider wider features of context. Finally, we found no evidence that recall of MSF was related to subsequent improvement in MSF. These features are confirmed by other studies of 360-degree feedback such as Garavan and McCarthy (2007), who suggest that MSF has to be considered part of the organisational context including culture and the broader LMD system. It was found that managers often reported lack of interest by others such as their immediate line managers. We can see a lack of interest as a form of feedback – but one that could be considered ambiguous at best and demoralising at worst.

4.3 REFLECT – CONCLUDE – PLAN

What would your reaction be to a lack of interest by your boss if you had identified learning needs following MSF?

What could you do to prepare for eliciting interest?

There is no doubt that 360-degree appraisal can be a powerful LMD process, but as with other approaches it is likely to fail unless a meaningful follow-through is agreed in advance. In development terms, managers will need to be in a position where they can identify areas of improvement which can be met by LMD activities. The *LMD in Practice* opposite provides an example of one leader's view of 360-degree feedback.

PERSONAL DEVELOPMENT PLANS

Usually, one outcome of assessment and appraisal is the establishment of an action plan, or perhaps more formally, a personal development plan (PDP). This might be composed of objectives and activities for learning and development, but it could also include aspects related to a manager's performance. What is crucial, though, is that a PDP should involve managers in a genuine discussion with their superior about LMD, including those opportunities for career development and progression within the organisation (see Chapter 10). Mumford (2001) suggests that there are benefits from PDPs for both the individual being developed and the manager. This is shown in Table 4.2.

Table 4.2 The benefits of PDPs

Benefits for the individual manager	Benefits for the manager's manager
• Increased ability to develop performance • Reduced stress about untackled gaps in personal performance • Increased chance of holding on to a desired current job • Increased potential of job enlargement • Clearer process for establishing personal aspirations • Clear process for establishing a commitment on the part of the higher manager and the organisation to the development of the manager cadre within the organisation	• Reduced problems of performance • Increased use of additional opportunities for effective work within the unit • Reduced belief that a manager's manager does not support development • More individuals capable of dealing with new or difficult tasks or more complete jobs

Source: adapted from Mumford (2001)

LMD IN PRACTICE

LAW FIRM LAUNCHES SCHEME TO TRAIN LEADERS

ERIC'S EXPERIENCE OF LEADERSHIP 360 PLUS

Eric is a departmental head within the European Commission, with 24 direct reports, and is an economist by profession. As part of his development he attended the Leadership Programme at Henley Business School during which he participated in Leadership 360 Plus. Within the Commission, claims Eric, 'We don't take each other to task,' and consequently 'the 360 process is a good means of getting feedback.' He sees the 360 'as a snapshot at a moment in time'. Although he was not used to 'the quantification of other people's perceptions', Eric was 'impressed by how charts could accurately indicate personal performance'.

Eric's first reaction to receiving his profile was one of concern. 'There is always an element of worry when first glancing at feedback – but it is important not just to look at absolute figures but to look through the figures. Because there is a great variation in responses between superiors, colleagues and staff, the first question I ask myself is: "What do I agree with?"' This questioning style is very typical of Eric's approach, and when 'looking through the figures', other questions occur to him: 'Are the diamonds too far to the right relative to the bar chart? Why does my manager see me in a different light than my staff? What themes are emerging?'

Such questioning led Eric to conclude that 'I found that I was perceived as being rather dominant in meetings – probably reinforced by a loud, deep voice which is difficult to change. Having self-knowledge and being aware is fundamental to personal change.' Consequently, 'I was determined to speak more slowly and to listen more attentively in meetings.'

Eric set learning priorities by highlighting gaps and analysing phrases. 'Basically, I ask myself a lot of questions. For example: "What does accountability mean?" The answer emerges from my role within the organisation. Managers have different levels of accountability. So what does accountability mean for me? What do I actually do? For whom am I responsible? Am I pushing people too far? These sorts of questions increase my awareness and lead to personal change. Thus, for instance, rather than wear a formal suit and white shirt, which may reinforce perceptions of me being overconfident, I wear less formal clothes and a coloured shirt to give a more relaxed appearance. These changes I can make – but I can't change my personality. Perhaps I focus too much on the negative!'

This case study is provided by Peter Holt (peter.holt@leadingpeople.co.uk) who is a member of the Visiting Faculty at Henley Business School. He contributes to their Leadership Programme and designs and organises Leadership 360 Plus. The case is real but Eric is a pseudonym.

WEB LINK

Go to **http://www.psychtesting.org.uk/downloadfile.cfm?file_uuid= E39E0206-1143-DFD0-7EAD-34EE9316F322&ext=pdf** for access to an online version of the Best Practice Guidelines for 360-degree feedback.

We suggest that a PDP, whatever the process used, must be constructed on a meaningful understanding of the gap between performance requirements

4.4 REFLECT – CONCLUDE – PLAN

What methods of assessing development needs are most attractive to you?

How effective are such methods?

What features from this chapter might be used to improve how development needs are assessed?

and achievements. The performance focus and the realities of the work being undertaken by managers is fundamental, as is the joint discussion and involvement with their line manager. A PDP, formally stated, also represents a commitment by the organisation towards its LMD policy, and the key mechanism seems to be line managers' involvement and support (Thomson *et al* 2001). The outcomes agreed in a PDP also need to link back to an organisation's performance management system, and it is this return to ongoing activity which will determine whether assessment and appraisal processes for managers become accepted within the organisation.

CONTRADICTIONS AND TENSIONS

Throughout this chapter we have highlighted at various stages of our explanation how the contradictions and tensions that exist between the purposes of assessment frequently lead to different interpretations with unpredictable consequences. It is very difficult to escape from the view that assessment and appraisal as it so often is practised is a means of controlling a manager's performance, even when senior managers employ the narrative of learning and development. One possible consequence is that assessment and appraisal processes become rituals rather than the serious means of assessing LMD needs that they perhaps ought to be. Ritual was one of themes identified by Barlow (1989) in his study of appraisal in a petrochemical organisation. The following quotation by a manager from the study (Barlow 1989, pp.505–7) illustrates the point:

> I think success is having the ear of higher management. To be noticed by higher management, and having opinions asked for, often. Appraisal forms are no use. It's what's left out rather than what's put in that's important.

One of Barlow's key points is that appraisal presents a view that an organisation makes decisions in an efficient and rational fashion while at the same time constructing a 'façade' (p.512) behind which 'real' decisions can be made about managers and their development. Other writers have used the work of the French philosopher Michel Foucault in order to frame their critique of appraisal. Here, managers become 'knowable, calculable and administrable' objects (Miller and Rose 1990, p.5). One of the images utilised by Foucault is the idea of the 'Panopticon' – a model prison in which all prisoners can be seen by a guard but prisoners cannot the see the guard or other prisoners.[5] Crucially, the prisoners know they can be seen, even though they cannot tell how it is done, and the knowledge of this allows them to be 'dominated'. The Panopticon is designed to ensure 'surveillance' (Foucault 1980, p.148). If this image is translated into appraisal, it is argued that the various devices used to appraise and assess managers – such as BARS, BOS, standards, MSF questionnaires – serve to exert a power over them in setting an ideal or a 'norm' to be achieved. Managers for their part learn to accept such measurements as a means of finding out what they have to do to improve their performance, including the identification of LMD needs. Thus, even where the attention is seemingly on learning and development, managers are still subject to a 'disciplinary power' set by others who are able to use the 'appraisal technology . . . to gauge where the appraisee "stands"' (Newton and Findlay 1996, p.48).

SUMMARY

- Assessing LMD needs requires judgements to be made concerning a manager's performance, and there are fundamental difficulties concerning who makes the judgements, how they do it, and whether the judgements are regarded as valid by managers.

- Performance management systems (PMS) offer the opportunity to align aspects related to an organisation's objectives within a manager's performance requirements and measurements.

- An aim of feedback to managers is to increase their self-awareness of their strengths and weaknesses and to identify issues for performance improvement and requirements for LMD.

- Development centres (DCs) can play a role in helping managers assess LMD needs – however, their similarity to assessment centres (ACs) often provokes doubts that their purpose is not always developmental.

- Appraisal lies at the heart of a formal approach to assessing LMD needs, although there remain difficulties in separating the purpose of appraisal between control, development and other unintended outcomes.

- Multi-source feedback (MSF) allows managers to receive feedback about their performance from different perspectives.

- The assessment process should result in an action plan or personal development plan, but implementation requires support in the workplace and a positive learning environment.

- Critical views of assessment and appraisal point to its ritualistic nature and its hidden features whereby power can be exerted over others.

QUESTIONS

For discussion

1 Is 'performance management' likely to follow the same road as Management by Objectives? What is the contribution of talent management?

2 *All feedback to managers should allow them to make their own assessment of the need to improve their performance.* Discuss.

3 Can clear distinctions be made between assessment centres and development centres?

4 Can managers ever really identify their own LMD needs accurately?

5 What are the key requirements for a successful scheme of multi-source feedback?

6 *The appraisal of managers is a ritual and a 'façade'.* Discuss.

GROUP ACTIVITY

Get together in a group of four.

As a group, consider the following types of leader, manager, and professional staff:

- managers in a fast-moving fresh-food-processing factory that must meet clear targets on a daily basis
- the leader of a global drugs company
- accountants who are required to manage a variety of clients but must meet monthly targets for their chargeable time spent with clients
- teachers in a large school in an inner city area where difficulties occur in relation to both the attendance and the achievements of pupils.

For each type of leader, manager and professional, what do you consider to be the best approach to managing their performance?

Consider how their learning and development needs might best be identified and appraised, including the overall approach used, the means of assessment, methods of feedback, and the involvement of others.

In each case evaluate the requirements for the successful implementation of an appraisal for their development

Prepare a joint presentation of your findings.

NOTES

1 A number of banks and financial institutions have sacrificed their independence and are now effectively state-owned.

2 Despite the undoubted influence of this study, we should also mention that it has been criticised on the grounds of 'criteria contamination' – managers who made 'above-average criticisms' also rated subsequent 'low goal achievement': see Newton and Findlay (1996).

3 Other purposes identified were to bring people of the same level together and to foster team spirit.

4 There were 13 competences in the framework but managers were able to focus on up to three at any one time.

5 The Panopticon is drawn from the work of Jeremy Bentham, the founder of British Utilitarianism in Victorian England. You can find out more about Bentham at **http://cepa.newschool.edu/het/profiles/bentham.htm** .

FURTHER READING

ATWATER, L., BRETT, J. and CHARLES, A. (2007) 'Multisource feedback: lessons learned and implications for practice', *Human Resource Management*, Vol.46, No.2: 285–307

BALLANTYNE, I. and POVAH, N. (2004) *Assessment and Development Centres.* Aldershot: Gower

BONO, J. and COLBERT, A. (2005) 'Understanding responses to multi-source feedback: the role of core self-evaluations', *Personnel Psychology*, Vol.58: 171–203

BRUTUS, S., FLEENOR, J. W. and LONDON, M. (1998) 'Does 360-degree feedback work in different industries?', *Journal of Management Development*, Vol.17, No.3: 177–90

FLETCHER, C. (2001) 'Performance appraisal and management: the developing research agenda', *Journal of Occupational and Organizational Psychology*, Vol.74: 473–87

MABEY, C. (2001) 'Closing the circle: Participant views of a 360-degree feedback programme', *Human Resource Management Journal*, Vol.11, No.1: 41–53

RYAN, A. M, BRUTUS, S., GREGURAS, G. J. and HAKEL, M. D. (2000) 'Receptivity to assessment-based feedback for management development', *Journal of Management Development*, Vol.19, No.4: 252–76

CHAPTER 5

Leaders, managers and learning

CHAPTER OUTLINE

Introduction
Effectiveness in LMD
What do we mean by 'learning'?
Theories and models of leadership and management learning
The value of reflection
Learning to learn
Summary

LEARNING OUTCOMES

After studying this chapter, you should be able to understand, explain, analyse and evaluate:

- the meaning of effectiveness in LMD
- the main features of how and why managers might learn
- the major theories that explain how managers might learn
- the importance of reflection in learning
- the meaning of learning to learn

INTRODUCTION

As Sadler-Smith (2006, p.2) points out, 'learning is at the heart of *organisation*' and an understanding of how managers learn is a key consideration when creating effective LMD programmes. This is a topic about which there have been a number of fundamental misconceptions in relation to what managers do. The approach so often adopted has been a behavioural approach, where recipes are sought about what managers should do, or how they should behave, and the information transferred to them in formal ways such as in lectures. Such one-way communication has led to two things: the frustration of managers, and a concern that what is being transferred might not always be relevant to all managers in all situations. As a partial response, teaching approaches have embraced active simulations, with course designers attempting to provide a variety of learning processes. Variety in developmental pedagogies was seen as a good thing, since managers faced with a variety of approaches to learning would be far more likely to remain interested – but perhaps more fundamentally there were the beginnings of an understanding that not every manager learned and acquired knowledge in exactly the same way.

It should come as no surprise that managers differ in their response to programmes. What is also the case is that managers differ in their ability to learn from particular kinds of opportunities and learning environments at work. What we can conclude from the above observations is that in the same way individuals differ in their preferences for opera and pop music, or for different kinds of sporting activity, managers will be likely to differ in their learning preferences. The question for LMD is how these differences in preference as well as differences between the ways managers conduct their work can be taken into account. The aim of this chapter is to provide some indications as to how it might be achieved.

EFFECTIVENESS IN LMD

In Chapter 1 two definitions of LMD were presented. The first was 'a planned and deliberate process to help managers become more effective', and the second was 'a process of learning for managers through recognised opportunities'. In the first, the idea of effectiveness is stated as an outcome of LMD, while in the second it is rather hidden, although we do know from the research of writers such as Kotter (1982), Mintzberg (1973) and Stewart (1975) that managers do learn to be effective, but not necessarily as planned and designed for by others. What we now want to build on is how we might extend the idea of effectiveness to the LMD itself, and we suggest that this might be achieved by bringing together three aspects:

- a definition of effective leadership and managerial behaviour that is based on contingency theory (what is likely to be effective will relate to certain factors concerning the organisation, the individual and the environment)

- the development of those processes which will improve leadership and managerial effectiveness under certain conditions

- identifying those learning processes which are effective for managers.

These factors are presented visually in Figure 5.1. What we want to suggest is that this 'effectiveness triangle' for LMD does not rely on any particular kind of development, nor does it suggest what an effective learning process should be – rather, it focuses these two aspects on effective leadership or managerial behaviour.

Based on the contingent nature of leadership and management, we have to recognise that there is no one single approach that can be applied to all managers in every organisation. What is effective behaviour for one may be less effective for

Figure 5.1 A triangle of effectiveness

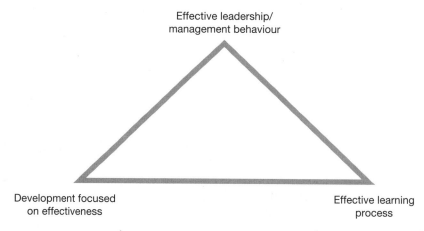

another. As a consequence, it is crucial to assist managers in assessing their LMD needs based on concepts of effectiveness that are meaningful to them. This leads to the second aspect of the triangle, where LMD is depicted as being required to meet the needs of managers and the actions they have to develop to achieve results, rather than simply detached generalisations that relate to skills or abstract presentations of knowledge and theories. We argue here that the emphasis on generalised skills and knowledge, especially in off-the-job LMD, often leads to problems in the transfer of learning (Gilpin-Jackson and Bushe 2007). For LMD to be effective, managers must respond to real situations and real problems so that results can be identified as being the results of actions.

A VICIOUS LEARNING SEQUENCE

Many managers have had training or educational experiences that they feel are useful, and they subsequently repeat these experiences. However, an equivalent number have had poor or even bad experiences which have put them off formal LMD. This is the 'vicious learning sequence', shown in Figure 5.2.

5.1 REFLECT — CONCLUDE — PLAN

How far does this vicious learning sequence relate to your own experience of formal learning?

If you experienced these difficulties, how did you attempt to overcome them?

How successful have you been, or what might you do on future occasions when attending any formal learning activities?

Figure 5.2 The vicious learning sequence

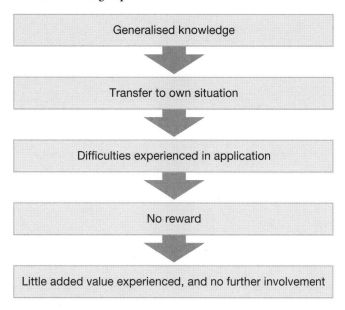

A VIRTUOUS LEARNING CYCLE

To try to avoid the very worst effects of this vicious learning sequence, we argue that attention needs to be paid to developing the conditions for a cycle of virtuous learning, where there is an effective focus for development that leads to an increased perception of relevance for the activity and, as a consequence, greater transferability of the learning, which leads to increased satisfaction and reward. This in turn will hopefully lead to increased enthusiasm for learning and support for others to learn. The cycle is shown in Figure 5.3.

As an example of how a virtuous learning cycle might work, consider the *LMD in Practice* below.

LMD IN PRACTICE

ACTION TO ACHIEVE OBJECTIVES

A company which had revised its sales objectives and organisational structure had some concern that the managers involved might not have the skills necessary to achieve the changed objectives. As a result of analysis conducted with them it became clear that although in all probability a number of them were lacking in some skills, the more crucial problem related to the fact that although they were apparently committed to the revised objectives, they had not fully set up a process of action that would achieve them. The prime concern therefore in relation to effectiveness was not the skills sales management had, but rather the identification of specific actions required to achieve the broad objectives agreed, and the skills involved in their implementation.

Figure 5.3 A virtuous learning cycle

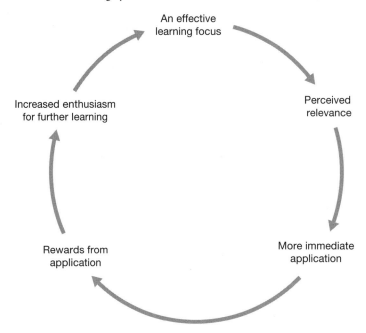

By attending to what managers understand as the requirement for effectiveness, and by focusing LMD on such requirements, there is a stronger likelihood that leaders and managers will identify those actions that might be implemented in their work. However, although these are necessary conditions for effectiveness, they are not sufficient. Individuals are far more likely to learn if they perceive the potential benefits of that learning for them. Attwood (2002) provides a list of what these benefits might be, which includes such things as recognition and advancement.

WHAT DO WE MEAN BY 'LEARNING'?

There are many different definitions of learning. The following, offered by Kolb (1984), has been of particular importance in the story of how of LMD has developed:

> Learning is the process whereby knowledge is created through the transformation of experience.

One difficulty with this definition is that it seems to emphasise only knowledge without necessarily leading to a change in behaviour.

If we assume that any learning is a function of the interaction (or behaviour) of the individual in their environment or

$$L = f(b, e),$$

we can see that expressed in this way a change in behaviour can have an effect on the environment in the same way a change in the environment can have an effect on the individual. Another view is offered by the work of Reg Revans (1982) and the formula

$$L = P + Q,$$

where P is programmed knowledge, and Q is questioning insight. This suggests, as we have already indicated, that knowledge only takes a person so far – what is required is challenge, this time in the form of questioning by others or critical reflection by the individuals themselves. Moreover – and Revans was a champion of this move – action must be taken for learning to be possible. We will be exploring these notions further, but for the moment the definition we are using is from Honey and Mumford (1996):

> Learning has happened when people can demonstrate that they know something they did not know before (insights and realisations, as well as facts) and/or when they can do something they could not do before (skills).

This definition combines knowledge, skills, and insights into a definition and provides practical utility in the understanding of learning as well as of its effective implementation and change in behaviour. These categories can then be used to define what an individual or group of individuals need to learn, as well as help them analyse what it is they have learned. Both aspects we believe are crucial to effective LMD. The use of the term 'insights' also has great resonance for managers (Hackman and Wageman 2007). Individuals, who have reviewed their learning experiences quite often highlight what we might characterise as 'Aha!' insights. These insights appear to us much more useful than the element more usually referred to as 'attitudes' which used to be regarded as one of the objectives of much formal training. Attempts to develop different attitudes in people has always been problematic in the sense that if attitudes were changed, they were also changed through a mixture of knowledge, skill and insight experiences.

The definition of learning has two further implications. Firstly, if managers have achieved knowledge, skills and/or insight, learning will be the end result. So that whatever is achieved, the noun *learning* becomes applicable. Secondly, to achieve a successful end result requires a process through which managers acquire knowledge, skills or insight. In varying degrees they become engaged in activities in which the verb *to learn* is deemed to be appropriate. This distinction between the verb to 'learn' and the noun 'learning' often leads to difficulties and misunderstandings. One particular problem relates to learning as a process where an activity is complex and difficult to observe or capture. There is often a preference for a focus on outcomes – *learning* as a noun – which often stands as a proxy for the process of learning. This issue becomes even more important when the variety of different approaches to learning are considered. For example, training and education is a formally structured process where the aim is to enable managers to learn. Others approaches, however, involve managers learning from experiences at work (and of course also in their lives outside work). Here, learning occurs naturally in a non-structured manner, informally as part of an everyday process (Stuart 1984). The formal experiences – education and training – can be seen as inputs designed and controlled by educators and trainers which are intended to add new learning or replace inappropriate learning, whereas informal – or what Eraut (2000) refers to as 'non-formal' – learning involves 'learning from experience' both within and outside work. This is seen as of special importance in leadership, managerial and professional development. However, such learning can occur without recognition, remaining implicit with little or no conscious awareness that learning has happened or is being used (Reber 2003). What we perhaps need to do is to see managerial learning as being much more concerned with helping managers to learn more effectively from their work experiences rather than necessarily attempting to replicate or replace these naturally occurring opportunities by off-the-job experiences (see Chapter 7). This requires identifying and recognising learning events and somehow structuring the learning process around them.

IS 'LEARNING' DIFFERENT FROM 'DEVELOPMENT'?

Usually these different words mean different things founded around a person's short-term needs contrasted with his or her needs for the future. The former was learning, the latter development. One useful distinction, however, was suggested by Chris Argyris (1991), who distinguished between 'single-loop learning' and 'double-loop learning' (see below). Single-loop learning refers to the use of existing knowledge or patterns of behaviour to find answers to problems, whereas double-loop learning indicates the need for a return to find principles and the abandonment of preconceived ways of solving the problem until all factors and solutions have been considered. This concept of the single and double loop is similar to what Engeström (2001) refers to as 'expansive learning', what Bateson (1983) called 'level three learning', and what Senge (1992) called 'generative learning'. Such ideas are used to engage managers in deep learning. It requires an exposure of underlying values so they can be challenged to allow new meanings to be considered. This can allow creativity to flourish and is seen as a requirement of the development of transformational leadership (Nailon *et al* 2007).

5.2 REFLECT – CONCLUDE – PLAN

Consider how learning takes place in your life.

Do you think there is a need for more deep learning?

How might you extend the learning that takes place beyond short-term task learning?

THEORIES AND MODELS OF LEADERSHIP AND MANAGEMENT LEARNING

The famous American psychologist Kurt Lewin[1] once proclaimed that there was nothing so practical as a good theory. In tune with this view we now consider a number of theoretical ideas and key writers in the field that serve to illustrate how theories can have impact and shape behaviour. The theories that provide the basis for explanations for how managers learn can be characterised as being either 'behaviourist', 'cognitive', 'experiential' or 'sociocultural'. This categorisation is based on the extent to which they can be said to have had an influence on practice.

 WEB LINK

If you want to explore a wide variety of learning theories, try **http://www. emtech.net/learning_ theories.htm** or **http://tip.psychology.org/ theories.html** .

For much of the twentieth century learning theories were developed in relation to the behaviour of children. From the 1960s, however, there was recognition that adults needed to be considered rather differently. For example, the work of Malcolm Knowles (1984, 1998) identified the differences in how adults learn ('andragogy') and how young people are taught ('pedagogy'). Gradually this was drawn to the attention of leadership and management developers and educators. In his view:

- The learner is largely self-directed but has a conditioned expectation to want to be dependent and to be taught.

- The learner arrives with experience, which in effect means that with many kinds of learning, adults are themselves a very rich resource for each other, and that in any group there is a wide range of experience.

- Adults are ready to learn when they have a need to perform better in some aspect of their lives.

- For the most part, adults do not learn for the sake of learning – they learn in order to be able to perform a task, solve a problem or live in a more satisfying way.

- Although adults will respond to some external motivators (eg a better job, a salary increase), the more potent motivators are internal – self-esteem, recognition, greater self-confidence, self-actualisation.

Keep these points in mind as you consider the theories.

BEHAVIOURIST AND COGNITIVIST THEORIES

Although managers are clearly adults and should be considered to be self-directed learners who are less dependent on instruction, it remains the case that the influence of behaviourist and cognitive theories remains and can be found in many LMD approaches. Based on the work of psychologists such as Pavlov (1927) and Skinner (1974) and a whole host of others, the key ideas are that learners are passive and that a change in behaviour requires stimulation from elsewhere which, if correct, is reinforced by feedback. Thoughts and feelings are secondary to behaviour change. Instructors can therefore design their stimulation in advance and specify the change desired in the form of objectives towards which progress can then be measured in the responses of the learners. Where the response does not meet the requirements, corrective feedback can be provided until the right response is produced. Practice can play a role in this process. We can see the influence of some of this reasoning in some approaches to LMD, especially where skills with definitions of required behaviour are part of the measurement process. For example, in Chapter 3 we examined the development of National Occupational Standards for Management and Leadership as a standards-based competence framework in which competences are specified in terms of outcomes and the behaviours required. Of course, many training activities in LMD are also specified with objectives or outcomes.

Another influence from behaviourism is the role of reinforcement or feedback in learning. Being able to practise new skills is understood as a requirement for transferring learning from training to work. If we consider the vicious learning sequence in Figure 5.2, we know how demoralising the lack of opportunity to practise new skills can be. Of course, feedback that is corrective can also be interpreted as criticism. Some managers are proactive 'feedback-seekers' (VandeWalle and Cummings 1997). However, others may be less keen to receive criticism. In other words, managers do have the ability to think about responses to what happens to them, and how they do this is the concern of cognitivist learning theories. Such theories consider the way learners process information through thinking and memory. Inputs are registered through senses and processed before being stored for future use and behaviour or rejected. Managers are inevitably exposed to continuous supplies of information – we do, after all, live in a knowledge society – so there is a great risk of overload and a need to organise the storage of processed information. The term *schema* is used to denote this process by which information is organised into patterns which can be used to attend to what is happening (Derry 1996). So managers might be helped to build their cognitive schema, organising what is known into meaningful patterns, allowing new insights and useful actions in difficult situations (Sadler-Smith 2006).

One interesting development of cognitive theory is the devising of tests that provide an assessment of the way managers might habitually process information. This is the idea of cognitive style, and one of the best-known tests is the Cognitive Styles Index, developed by Allinson and Hayes (1996) and used specifically in organisational settings. The test is scored against two ways of processing information, labelled 'analytical' and 'intuitive', shown in Figure 5.4.

A preference for analytical thinking would result in more structured decision-making based on systematic investigation using step-by-step models and

Figure 5.4 Cognitive processing styles

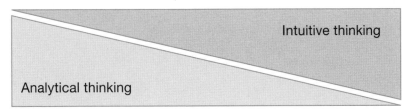

Intuitive thinking

Analytical thinking

formulas. An intuitive preference would result in more open approaches to decision-making, taking more factors into account in working on problems and being prepared for more creative possibilities. While such preferences might be seen as contrasting opposites, recent suggestions present each pole as a dimension, so a manager might have a combination of high intuition *and* high analytical ability, which would indicate versatility in processing information and openness to a range of factors but also a mindset that is structured and systematic (Hodgkinson and Clarke 2007).

Other measures of how the brain processes information include Herrmann's (1996) 'whole brain' model and the Herrmann Brain Dominance Instrument (HBDI), and the Kirton Adaption-Innovation Inventory (Kirton 1999).

 WEB LINK

Read more about the Herrmann Brain Dominance Instrument at **http://www.hbdi.com/ WholeBrainProductsAndServices/thehbdi.cfm,** and about the Kirton Adaptation-Innovation Inventory at **http://www. kaicentre.com/** .

EXPERIENTIAL LEARNING

Research in both behaviourist and cognitive learning has continued, but over the last 30 years – and especially in LMD – there has been interest in the interaction of managers and their context or environment, and the way they can make use of experience. Prominent among such interactionist theories is Kolb's Experiential Learning Theory or KELT (Kolb 1984). Arguably, his most powerful impact has been through his notion of a learning cycle.[2] Figure 5.5 shows the stages of the cycle.

The learning cycle is often quoted to show what ought to be happening within any designed learning experience. It is interesting to note here that rather less frequently quoted are examples of what should be happening in relation to workplace learning. Kolb's unique contribution was not only the identification of the fact that some individuals have strong preferences for learning in one way but not in another, but also his creation of an instrument to measure these preferences – the Learning Styles Inventory (LSI). According to Kolb, learning occurs by grasping an experience and transforming it. Thus at CE (in Figure 5.5) an experience is sensed, and then transformed through reflection (RO), leading

Figure 5.5 Kolb's learning cycle

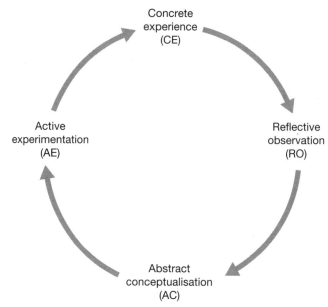

Source: Kolb (1984)

to the emergence of ideas (AC) and extended into the world of work by taking action (AE). As a consequence, learning in the cycle embraces both process and outcomes. While the LSI was originally criticised on technical grounds, its reliability significantly improved in later versions. Further, this approach to thinking about learning has great significance in LMD and in HRD more generally. It has also provided the basis for the work of Honey and Mumford (1996).

Honey and Mumford built on the work of Lewin and Kolb in respect of contemplating learning as a virtuous learning cycle. They also embraced Kolb's fundamentally analytical proposition about the relationship between different learning styles at different stages of the cycle. The models they developed, however, are different from Kolb's in that their learning cycle (Figure 5.6) incorporates a 'Planning the next steps' stage replacing Kolb's 'Active experimentation'.

Kolb seemed to imply that action takes place without planning, emerging as a result of a thoughtful learning process. A second major difference in both the theory and practice is that whereas Kolb's original theory and construct was based on the proposition that differences could be identified as polar opposites – eg between abstract conceptualisation and concrete experience – his own research seemed to show that such polar opposites were not observable in practice. A third difference relates to how Honey and Mumford identify their learning cycle as applying to all kinds of learning activity, whereas Kolb explicitly specified an 'experiential learning cycle'. This has been interpreted, perhaps wrongly, as meaning that his cycle applies only to learning from particular kinds

Figure 5.6 Honey and Mumford's learning cycle and learning styles

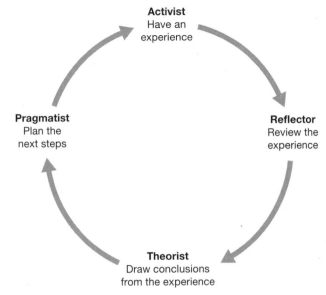

Source: Honey and Mumford ((2006)

of activity. The Honey and Mumford learning cycle on the other hand proposes that, for example, learning can occur when a lecturer provides conclusions – where there is neither an experience nor a review that occurs before the lecturer offers conclusions.

The learning cycle is clearly a simplified version of what happens in a learning process. The notion of identifying individual learning preferences, developed by Honey and Mumford's Learning Styles Questionnaire, is still widely used in LMD. Table 5.1 provides abbreviated versions of preferred ways of learning for the four styles identified.

The models discussed above have been shown to be extremely important in the design of learning experiences, and for enabling individuals to develop the important 'meta quality' (Pedler *et al* 1994) – the ability to learn to learn. One important finding was that 35% of individuals have a single, strong preference on how to learn. This does not suggest that managers are unable to learn outside these preferences, but it does help to explain why some individuals have unsatisfactory learning experiences.

It needs to be recognised that the results of the LSQ are indicative, not prescriptive, and learning styles are capable of being changed. Changes can occur in style as a result of changes in the learner's work environment or through explicit development processes (see *Learning to learn* below).

Since KELT and Honey and Mumford's variation appeared, research on learning styles has grown quite rapidly, with a wide expansion of the idea of styles. There is a well-organised network in Europe – the European Learning Styles Information Network (ELSIN) – which supports an annual conference providing an outlet for

Table 5.1 Honey and Mumford's learning styles

Activists	Reflectors
learn best from relatively short 'here-and-now' tasks. These may be managerial activities on the job or courses – activities such as business games and competitive teamwork exercises. They learn less well from situations involving a passive role, such as listening to lectures or reading.	learn best from activities in which they are able to stand back, listen, and observe. They like collecting information and being given the opportunity to think about it. They learn less well when they are rushed into things without the opportunity to plan.
Theorists	**Pragmatists**
learn best when they can review things in terms of a system, a concept, a model or a theory. They are interested in and absorb ideas even where they may be distant from current reality. They learn less well from activities presented without this kind of explicit or implicit design.	learn best when there is an obvious link between the subject matter and the problem or opportunity on the job. They like being exposed to techniques or processes which can be applied in their immediate circumstances. They learn less well from learning events which seem distant from their own reality. 'Does it apply in my situation?'

5.3 REFLECT – CONCLUDE – PLAN

Read the descriptions of learning preferences in Honey and Mumford's learning styles in Table 5.1.

Which do you feel is/are your preferred style or styles of learning, and which do you prefer more, which do you prefer less?

How do you think you can use your learning preference?

What can you do to help others understand their own learning preferences?

this research. One of the more interesting models was developed by Lynn Curry (1987) who reviewed a number of cognitive and learning styles instruments to produce a three-layered onion model, shown as Figure 5. 7.

The outer layers show preferences for instruction, and the inner layers measure information-processing style and cognitive personality style. The centre of the onion controls learning behaviour through the middle layer of information-processing, but social and environmental preferences could be more adaptable based on a learner's choice but influenced by interaction.

Learning styles, preferences and the concept of the learning cycle, whether based on Kolb's LSI, Honey and Mumford's LSQ, or any other typology, have proved to be a very popular approach to helping managers engage in LMD activities, but although they appear to have significant face validity with many managers and LMD providers, there have been criticisms. The LSI, for example, has been

Figure 5.7 Curry's 'onion' model of learning styles

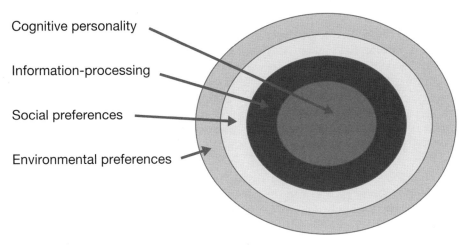

Cognitive personality

Information-processing

Social preferences

Environmental preferences

Source: Curry (1987)

criticised for its lack of reliability and construct validity (Allinson and Hayes 1988). The measurement of learning styles has also been criticised as lacking in rigorous research and made difficult by 'conceptual and semantic confusion' (Moran 1991, p.241). Coffield *et al* (2004) completed a study which started with 71 learning styles instruments which they reduced to the 13 seen as most influential. Based on their examination of each instrument's theoretical origins, definitions of terms, questionnaire, the claims made by the author(s), external studies of these claims and independent empirical evidence of the impact on teaching and learning, they suggested that only two could be recommended in higher education – and none for post-16 education. Nearly all the instruments lack independent validation.

Reynolds (1997) also provided a broad-ranging critique, but his key argument is that the learning styles approach tends to decontextualise learning and give prominence to individuals. Styles or preferences (and by implication, non-preferences) can become seen as 'psychological concepts', which excludes consideration of the complexity of the organisational environment, and the social. But it can also serve to stereotype and label managers in particular ways. Reynolds (p.128) feels that 'the individualistic discourse' has become 'common sense' in LMD, expressed in the competences movement – as we discussed earlier – and other 'forms of credentialism'. He suggests that learning styles can be avoided by considering the following questions:

- What is learning?
- What learning experiences have been beneficial to you?
- Do you tend to avoid certain ways or opportunities for learning?

● How can others be of help to you in enabling you to enhance both your learning and your self-development?

Holman *et al* (1997) also suggest that there is a need to counter the idea of a manager as an individual or 'isolated monad' (p.140) separated from social context.[3] Their analysis gives particular emphasis to the importance of social conditions, the use of language and other tools of mediation and, especially, conversations with others essential for managers to develop and understand in carrying out their roles as managers and also for learning. These points are developed further below when we consider sociocultural learning. Before we do that, it is worth considering Bandura's (1977) Social Learning Theory (SLT), which provides a link between cognitive and behavioural theories of learning and interaction with the environment. Bandura suggested that there is an ongoing process between the behaviour of a person, their psychological processes and the environment. Learning often involves modelling what others do by observing their behaviour and attitudes. For example, if a manager observes a senior manager at a meeting, modelling might occur if there is value in doing so and the model is seen as someone with similar attributes. Through image and words, the behaviour is used in mental rehearsal until it is reproduced in an appropriate situation. Managers are also likely to be seen as models by others. Another feature of SLT is the idea of self-efficacy, concerned with the conviction a person has about their ability to complete a behaviour in a particular setting. For example, if a leader does not believe he can make a speech to staff in a crisis, this indicates low self-efficacy and the leader might avoid situations where this behaviour is needed. Self-efficacy is a useful idea in helping managers apply learning at work after an LMD event.

SOCIO-CULTURAL THEORIES

Such theories take the impact of context and environment further. Many are based on the work of Lev Vygotsky (1978), a Russian psychologist who was writing and working in the Soviet era. There are two key features of this kind of theory to consider. Firstly, there is the idea that all action occurs in a context which is cultural and social. Figure 5.8 shows what is referred to as Vygotsky's action triangle.

A person in action, the Subject, always has a goal, whether explicit or not. A manager preparing a report is taking action, so the goal is perhaps to complete the report before midnight. The achievement of any goal requires 'mediating tools', and this is a crucial contribution of the theory because tools enable the completion of an action. For example, the tools for a report are physical – such as a laptop – but also psychological or intellectual tools, which Vygotsky (1982, p.137) described as:

> systems for counting, mnemonic techniques, algebraic symbol systems, works of art, writing, schemes, diagrams, maps, and technical drawings, all sorts of conventional signs, and so on.

Figure 5.8 Vygotsky's action triangle

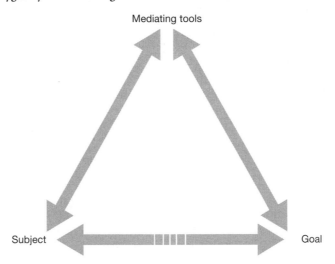

Both physical and intellectual tools enable a manager to complete the action. In particular, the manager writes the report using words and numbers, so language is crucial to action, as well as the laptop. Indeed, the quality of the report depends on how the tools are used. Crucially, to use tools, the manager has to learn them and then use them in action, so learning is very much about acquiring new tools for action. One of the key aspects of this way of considering learning is how tools, which are socially and culturally provided, can help a manager, but also provide constraint. A manager is only as good as the tools available. In another move, Vygotsky also shows how tools can impact on the subject – that is, they may reverse the action by playing a part in how a person may see himself or herself. For example, clothes are a social and cultural tool and may affect how a leader wants to be seen. Tools affect the self-understanding of managers, for good or ill. Learning is very much a disturbance to this, and new tools – both physical and intellectual – may need to be accepted by managers before they are used in action.

A second idea from Vygotsky is the 'zone of proximal development', or ZPD. For new action to be tried, support may be needed in the form of help and guidance. Such support must consider where a person is now in terms of what is known, what can be done based on the desires and interests of the learner, and what is an acceptable level of potential movement. There is a limit to such movement, and this is the boundary of the ZPD. The value of this understanding is to consider how far a manager learning a new skill can be stretched. If the move is too far, beyond the boundary, failure is likely. However, successful achievement expands the repertoire of the manager and allows a new ZPD to be established.

Related to Vygotsky's ideas is the work of Lave and Wenger (1991), who argue for a situated approach to learning, especially through participation in everyday activities. Learning, they argue, occurs through practice obtained from work which is usually informal and incidental. This they equate to 'natural' learning

WEB LINK

Vygotsky's ideas are beginning to impact on LMD, but have had more influence in schools. Go to
http://www.gtce.org.uk/teachers/rft/ vygotsky1203/ .

(p.47). They consider that there is an explicit difference between 'learning and intentional instruction' (p.40), where the former is focused on work practices. Fox (1997) summarised the following key elements of situated learning:

- People who perform work belong to a 'community of practice', and it is within that community that learning occurs 'naturally'.

- A community of practice has embedded within it an apprenticeship system which may be formal or informal, in which novices learn to participate by assisting more experienced members. Novices are 'legitimate' but on the 'periphery' of a community. They can observe skilled practitioners and then copy and learn.

- Communities are dependent on other communities and are part of a network of communities.

Although Lave and Wenger were not explicitly concerned with LMD, the concept of situated learning and the role played by communities of practice in the knowledge production within organisations and management was a feature of their work. Of note must be the importance played by everyday activities, which served to create 'natural learning' for managers by means of what Fox refers to as 'the learning iceberg'. This metaphor indicates that so much of a developer's attention is placed on the observable and manageable, yet a great deal of significant learning and development for managers takes place 'below the surface' hidden from view. The process is complex, difficult to measure and is less visible. So the theory essentially suggests that managers and those who wish to become managers need to consider how they might learn through their work and participation in practice, by watching, doing, talking and, especially, sharing stories. Through these processes they practise making sense of their ideas to their communities, and it is through practice they learn, often tacitly, what is acceptable or not. In addition, this kind of learning is situational, contingent and improvisational, and when faced with a problem or difficulty, managers construct new possibilities for practice (Brown and Duiguid 1991). Of course, one of the challenges they face in order that learning-in-practice occurs is that it occurs not just in their own communities but also across communities. By definition, such learning needs to be contextual and relational, and this requires an explanation of the cultural and the historical influences in relation to activity – dimensions suggested by the Finnish academic Yrjö Engeström (1987).

WEB LINK

For an overview of situated learning, try **http://tip.psychology.org/ lave.html** . For further details on communities of practice, go to **http://www.infed.org/biblio/communities_of_practice.htm** .

5.4 REFLECT – CONCLUDE – PLAN

Consider how your personal experience of learning relates to the theories discussed.

If you have designed learning experiences before, in what ways did any of these theories impact on your design?

How important do you think it to be to have an explicit theory of learning in your work?

Is there further information you want to acquire about any of the theories?

THE VALUE OF REFLECTION

A shared concern for both the Kolb and the Honey and Mumford learning cycle models and perhaps other theories is conscious and frequent reflection about experience. In recent years the importance of the reflective components explicit in models has been recognised as a crucial if not determining feature of LMD. However, as we have indicated, it is still a sadly absent component in the working and learning practices of many managers, particularly as theories emphasising the importance and significance of reflection were developed by individuals such as Donald Schön (1983) and later by Jack Mezirow (1990).

THE REFLECTIVE PRACTITIONER

Schön identified the possibilities that reflection might offer the studies of management practice. He highlighted tacit knowledge, which he referred to as 'reflection-in-action' – the ability to respond spontaneously to surprises through improvised routines that required little thought. Conceptually, he contrasted such 'knowing' with 'technical rationality' the object of which was problem-solving, so as to regain control. He referred to the routine as 'programmatic descriptions' of knowledge that consisted of formulable propositions which increase in generality and abstraction. For Schön (1987, p.4) what is required is 'not a blind adherence to *one* method [emphasis in the original]' but rather that through reflection-in-action a manager could solve new problems and equip himself or herself to 'change the situation for the better'. Indeed, by becoming 'reflective practitioners' as he referred to them, managers could generate new insights and invent new ways of working in practice. Today the notion of reflective practice has become extremely significant for leaders, managers and professionals, and for many developers forms the basis of frameworks of *continuing professional development* (see Chapter 11). It is argued that reflective practitioners can cope with difficulty and change. The argument made is that those managers who have learned how to become reflective practitioners are those who are able to cope with contradiction, ambiguity and change.

Schön was a close collaborator of Chris Argyris (1991), who made three major contributions. The first was the distinction between 'single-loop' and 'double-loop' learning that we mentioned earlier. Single-loop learning he defined as learning that is able to correct errors through the changing of routine behaviour. It is characterised as being incremental and adaptive, rather like a thermostat that is set to turn on the heat if the room temperature drops below a comfortable level. Double-loop learning, on the other hand, corrects errors by examining the underlying principles of a problem in the values and policies of the organisation. Continuing the metaphor, double-loop learning can be seen to require an intelligent thermostat that can evaluate whether or not the 'comfortable level' is the right temperature for optimum efficiency. Whereas single-loop learning involves enabling people to develop knowledge and skills appropriate to and defined by present circumstances, double-loop learning involves redefining the nature of the problems faced (by an individual or organisation) and learning how to cope with the new – transformed – understanding.

A second contribution Argyris makes concerns the notion of theories, as we have hinted above. Here, he distinguishes between espoused theories and theories-in-use. The former represent what is said and believed about what we do and what we will do; the latter are theories used by managers which account for what is actually done and reflect the theories which determine what we do. There is frequently a gap between the two, and this is very noticeable to others.

Argyris's third contribution relates to the concept of defensive routines. Double-loop learning, as we have described, involves challenging the status quo. Understanding the difference between our espoused theory and our actual theory in use requires individuals to examine both the fact and the reasons for the difference. Argyris argues that what prevents either of these processes happening is that both individuals and organisations develop defensive routines. These are both the conscious and unconscious, stated and unstated, ways in which the examination of underlying themes, issues, problems, and beliefs are avoided. Argyris develops a view that suggests that it is the very existence of defensive routines that causes individuals and organisations to be unwilling ever to question whether these defensive routines are being employed.

 WEB LINK

Read more about Donald Schön at **http://www.infed.org/thinkers/et-schon.htm** . Go to **http://tip.psychology.org/argyris.html** for more detail on Argyris's notion of double-loop learning.

CRITICAL REFLECTION

Mezirow (1990) further developed the idea of reflection by emphasising the requirement that reflection should not only serve to create improved understanding of experiences but should also seriously critique them as well. Through a critically reflective process, an individual can become more aware of and open to the perspectives of others, less defensive, and by so doing make acceptance of new ideas possible. These are the features of what Mezirow refers to as 'transformative learning'. Mezirow explained that the opportunities for such learning arise when individuals face situations that are different from their previous experiences and understandings. Through a process of critical reflection a manager can go further and examine his or her feelings, beliefs and actions and even the assumptions that underpin them. Transformation is said to occur through the challenge brought to bear on these assumptions and the attendant identification of new possibilities for thinking, feeling and associated action.

Drawing on the ideas of Mezirow and other writers in the field of adult education, the notion of a manager as a critically reflective practitioner has taken hold, especially among academics who consider leadership and management needs to have a critical dimension and should not as a practice simply be taken for granted – particularly in changing times and times of difficulty. The now established field of *management learning* (Burgoyne and Reynolds 1997) has explored different versions of the meaning of the term 'critical', and there is even a domain of management referred to as *critical management studies* (Fournier and Grey 2000).[4] One approach to critical thinking is presented by Mingers (2000):

- to critique rhetoric – whether arguments and propositions are sound in a logical sense

- to critique tradition – a scepticism of conventional wisdom and long-standing practices

- to critique authority – be sceptical of one dominant view and be open to a plurality of views, and

- to critique knowledge – recognise that knowledge is never value-free and objective.

These four aspects of critical thinking are used by Gold *et al* (2002) in a programme for managers who engaged in critical reflection of work experiences by examining their claims and beliefs through the lens of argument analysis, a framework suggested by Toulmin (1958). What they found was that managers were able to think more critically and take a more considered approach to their work – and even their lives. As a consequence, they became more aware of their own views of the situations they faced as well as the perspectives of others. Some managers were even able to uncover beliefs about their behaviour and to begin to question their feelings, and this was especially the case when reflecting on difficult experiences. In turn this led to new actions and increased confidence – they also became increasingly aware of how different views of the same situation could arise. The study has been picked up by Argyris (2006) as an example of how tools (in this case Toulmin's model) help managers to think and become more reflective.

WEB LINK

Further details about Jack Mezirow can be found at **http://www.nl.edu/ academics/cas/ace/ resources/jackmezirow.cfm** .

Antonacopoulou (2004) offers a wide-ranging review of reflective and reflexive critique on an MBA programme. She extends Mingers's presentation to include:

- the critique of simplification, and
- the critique of identity.

The first, the critique of simplification, is an attempt to move managers beyond simple cause-and-effect thinking which underpins many ideas such as 'more pay means harder work'. This kind of thinking would bypass the complexity of an issue which includes politics and social factors. The second, the critique of identity, highlights how subjectivity and identity are bound to influence thought and actions as well as emotions. Helping managers embrace critique, especially of their own assumptions, is a challenge to normally accepted certainties. Chia and Morgan (1996) saw this as a process that would allow managers to embrace 'the management of life in all its complexions' (p.41) and consider their 'ignorance'. They suggested that managers needed to consider philosophy as a route to 'challenge the mental abstractions which are confused for truth', and this is what is meant by reflexive critique. The *LMD in Practice* opposite shows the findings from one manager who completed a reflexive critique of his work.

LEARNING TO LEARN

In recent years a great deal of emphasis has been placed on individual responsibility in relation to learning and development as opposed to simply seeing the responsibility being on others to provide it. Learning is now promoted as part of government policy through agendas for Lifelong Learning which, according to Green (2002) have become a 'dominant and organising discourse in education and training policy' (p.611). Much is made of the developments in knowledge-intensive work as part of the knowledge economy and knowledge society (Rohrbach 2007). An underlying principle in much of this activity is that individuals are more likely to work more effectively at their learning needs if they have contributed substantially to identifying what their needs are, and also if they are encouraged to work on identifying what those needs are through processes which they have themselves identified, or at least over which they have a substantial degree of choice. Authors such as Brookfield (1986) in relation to self-directed learning, Cunningham (1999) in relation to self-managed learning, and Pedler *et al* (2006) in relation to self-development (see Chapter 7) have written extensively in these areas.

The idea that individuals should take more responsibility for their own development is a welcome one. Part of that responsibility will be more effectively

REFLEXIVE CRITIQUE AT WORK

David Nicholson, *HML Plc, Skipton*

I have been keeping learning logs for some time now, recording both what I have done and what I will do with it in the future. The project, however, gave me an opportunity to gain a different perspective. I was able to reflect on the actions of others (and my reactions to these) and to express my thoughts and opinions.

The idea of looking at the underlying beliefs, values and prejudices that my words indicated was difficult to do at first, but has led to some interesting discoveries. Looking back at the whole process, there are some clear patterns and recurring themes to my reasoning. What has surprised me is the existence of strong values that I tend to conceal from those I work with. I had strong prejudices about asking for and being given help – prejudices that could be summed up by the old civil service mantra of 'never asking for a job and never refusing one'. The process

brought out for me the strength of this feeling and how it affects my dealings with members of my team.

Another area that came out as a theme was how I deal with uncertainty. This also proved to be a problem that I had with the process generally. I initially found it difficult to direct any of my thoughts to a more external outcome, and generally found the process to be quite internal. What then came out was that my tendency towards uncertainty is exacerbated by internalising my thoughts, and on the occasions when I have converted the thoughts into external actions the levels of uncertainty have been reduced. This took some time to come to light, though.

Having now identified some of my deeper-set prejudices, I have been able to use them to rationalise my viewpoint and have also been able to challenge and push them to expand my leadership style and techniques of dealing with others.

5.5 REFLECT – CONCLUDE – PLAN

Are you able to be reflexively critical?

Under what conditions would reflexive critique be important for you?

How can you learn reflexive critique?

exercised if individuals themselves understand how they learn and make better use of learning experiences, particularly if they can become more conscious of themselves, their needs and the needs of others. Attwood (2002) highlighted this issue by saying that 'learning to learn is the most fundamental learning of all.' The logic of this, particularly in the context of increased personal responsibility for learning, is that effective learning depends on individuals' recognising and consciously using the learning skills involved. Unfortunately, this is an area in which lip service is too often paid. Brochures, for example, may include a heading in their prospectuses yet fail to provide the means whereby reflection can realistically take place. Mumford's definition of 'learning to learn' (2001) is a process through which individuals or groups understand the principle of effective learning, and acquire and continuously improve the disciplines and skills necessary to achieve learning.

Although throughout this section we have concerned ourselves with recommending that individuals be encouraged to pay attention to learning how to learn, those individuals in leadership and managerial positions will often be responsible for the learning of others. Managers therefore need to understand how a learning-to-learn philosophy might be engaged so that the learning of others can be made as effective for the others as for themselves.

5.6 REFLECT – CONCLUDE – PLAN

Do you agree with the statement 'Learning to learn is one of the most fundamental aspects of learning for everyone'? What is the basis for your agreement or disagreement?

In your view, how important is it to make learning to learn an explicit element in any learning experience?

What are the features of learning to learn that you give priority?

How important do you consider learning reviews and learning logs to be?

How might you implement any conclusions you have reached when reading this section, and any conclusions arising from these questions?

Throughout this chapter, implicit assumptions have been made to the effect that learning is beneficial for managers, organisations and society as a whole. However, it does seem to be the case that some managers do not consciously seek to learn or are actively prevented from learning. There may be a number of reasons why this might be, and we have indicated these in both this and previous editions. They include:

- a lack of recognition that a learning need exists
- a lack of assessment of the relevant needs
- a lack of understanding on the part of the organisation that learning must be given a high priority in order to be effective
- the presence of defensive routines which actively prevent learning
- the failure of managers to give stimulus, encouragement and help.

Further attention to barriers to learning is offered in the following chapters.

WEB LINK

You can read the Declaration on Learning at **http://www.mwls.co.uk/ learndec.htm** .

SUMMARY

- Managers differ in their likely response to any particular learning process.

- Effectiveness in LMD requires a contingent definition of effective leadership or managerial behaviour, where development is focused on results, and the identifying of the learning processes which are more effective for managers is recognised.

- Learning is both a process and an outcome concerned with knowledge, skills and insights.

- There is a growing range of learning theories for use in LMD.

- Managers most usually learn in a context of practice.

- Reflection is recognised as being crucial in order to both critique and improve practice.

- Increasingly, managers and others are being asked to take responsibility for their own learning.

QUESTIONS

For discussion

1 Below are three statements relating to the significance of theory in the development of managers. What is your response to each one?

'There is nothing so practical as a good theory' (Kurt Lewin)

'Theory without practice is empty, and practice without theory is blind' (Patricia Cross)

'Practice, at the end of the day, needs theories to shape it. Theory, on the other hand, is tested and developed through practice' (John Burgoyne and Mike Reynolds).

2 Which of the above statements do you consider the most significant in relation to the theories outlined in this chapter?

3 Can you develop an argument for suggesting that theory is unimportant in LMD, important only to a small number of 'experts in learning'?

4 Is a manager's learning transferable?

5 Why should leaders and managers reflect on their practice? How critical should their reflection be?

6 How can managers be encouraged to learn to learn – and why should they be?

Get together in a group of three.

Working individually, consider the illustration below, which shows a range of factors that influence learning and development.

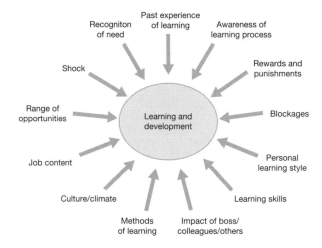

Select the three most important influences on your own learning and development. These can be influences both positive and negative.

Prepare notes for discussion in your group on the influences you have selected.

Be prepared to explain why their impact on you was positive or negative.

NOTES

1 Kurt Lewin is regarded as one of the most important social psychologists of the last century. You can read more about him at **http://psychology.about. com/od/ profilesofmajorthinkers/p/bio_lewin.htm** .

2 Kolb acknowledges precursors in Kurt Lewin and John Dewey – check the Center for Dewey Studies at **http://www.siu.edu/~deweyctr/** .

3 Holman *et al* (1997) were using ideas from Social Constructionism and activity theory.

4 You can examine the proceedings of the Critical Management Studies Conferences at the site of the electronic *Journal of Radical Organisation Theory* at **http://www.mngt.waikato. ac.nz/ejrot/** .

FURTHER READING

ARMSTRONG, S. and MAHMUD, A. (2008) 'Experiential learning and the acquisition of managerial tacit knowledge', *Academy of Management Learning and Education*, Vol.7, No.2: 189–208

BOYATZIS, R.(2006) 'An overview of intentional change from a complexity perspective', *Journal of Management Development*, Vol.25, No.7: 607–23

GOLD, J., THORPE, R. and HOLT, R. (2007) 'Reading, writing and reasoning: the three Rs of manager learning', in J. STEWART and R. HILL (eds) *Management Development: Perspectives from practice and research*. London: Routledge

VINCE, R. and REYNOLDS, M. (2004) *Organizing Reflection*. Aldershot: Ashgate Publishing

CHAPTER 6

Activities for the development of leaders and managers

CHAPTER OUTLINE

Introduction
Proposing an LMD policy
A typology of LMD activities
Specified activities for individuals
Emergent activities for individuals
Specified activities for collective leadership
Emergent activities for collective leadership
E-learning
Summary

LEARNING OUTCOMES

After studying this chapter, you should be able to understand, explain, analyse and evaluate:

- the importance of a written LMD policy

- different activities of LMD

- the possibilities for e-learning in LMD

- the difference between specified and emergent LMD activities

- the difference between individual and collective LMD

INTRODUCTION

There has been an explosion in the amount of provision and the number of activities that purport to develop managers and leaders. The report by CEML (2002) found a large supply of LMD opportunities, but it suggested that such supply was 'mixed on quality' and presented a 'confusing plethora of options' which was not 'sufficiently customised to meet the specific requirements of the organisation or of the individual' (p.4). This finding does not surprise us because the work of managers is contingent on contextual factors such as structure, culture, technology and the situation faced; it is therefore difficult to provide generalised statements about what managers should do. As Burgoyne *et al* (2004) argue, LMD 'works in different ways in different situations' (p.49), so any design for development needs to consider specific circumstances. A further issue relating to leadership is the recognition that there may have been an over-emphasis on individuals as leaders at the expense of the development of leadership capacity, taking a more distributed view of leadership (Bolden 2005). There is an important contrast and choice for any organisations considering LMD (Day 2001): there could be:

- emphasis on individual leaders enhancing an organisation's human capital in terms of developing particular skills, knowledge and attributes of those in formal roles,

or

- there could be an emphasis on activities that build relationships and networks between leaders and others to enable a sharing of ideas and influence, enhancing an organisation's social capital.

A further choice relates to types of LMD activities, and most people normally understand this to mean those that are planned and deliberate, such as attending a course on interviewing or strategic thinking, doing an MBA or having a formal mentor. Such activities may be of value in themselves, but they also exclude many of the experiences that are particularly real for managers. The exclusion of those preponderant and powerful experiences leads to a diminished persuasiveness in talking to managers about LMD. As we argued in Chapter 1, much of LMD occurs informally or even accidentally, so there has to be a recognition of how such events can be recognised and used to best effect. Firstly, we will consider the importance of an LMD policy in organisations.

PROPOSING AN LMD POLICY

In Chapter 2 it was suggested that LMD gains purpose by showing a link to organisational strategy and that LMD policy explicitly translates the requirements into activities: it is a central symbol and indicator of intentions. Managers may not agree with its contents, and like many policy statements in HRM, it may represent an espoused view rather than enacted practice (Purcell and Hutchinson 2007). Nevertheless, as noted by Thomson *et al* (2001), organisations which had formal policies were likely to provide more activities than those without. Mabey (2002), building on these findings, showed that policy contributed to a positive HR context that took both formal and informal LMD seriously. Some organisations will have an objective that all management appointments should be filled by people developed by the organisation itself. Others will have set some target figure for recruitment from outside, or will set different targets for different jobs. With the onset of recession during 2008, many organisations were giving attention to their talent management systems, identifying individuals' high potential or roles which are of value to an organisation (CIPD 2009).

Formal LMD will normally include the following items:

- a statement of the purpose of LMD
- a statement about the processes to be used in identifying and developing managers and leaders.

Emphasis is usually given to performance management including appraisal processes, or a development needs analysis for individuals (see Chapters 3 and 4), the type of performance review/appraisal to be conducted, the philosophy behind it, and the way in which it should contribute to the identification and development needs may be set out. Variants such as 360-degree appraisal may be introduced. Where organisations separate appraisal and the identification of development needs (see Chapter 4), timetables will be set out for the achievement of these tasks. Training or guidebooks and DVDs about how to conduct these processes may well be provided, frequently via an organisation's intranet or *virtual learning environment* (VLE).

Guidance on the kind of learning activities which may be provided has progressed beyond the identification of training courses in an internal catalogue, to guidance on some of the processes centred on and around the job, such as mentoring and coaching and online guidance as part of a company intranet service.

Spackman (2010) provides an example of how a policy for LMD is derived from strategy in his organisation HML, a third-party mortgage administration company in the UK with 2,000 employees. He makes it clear that LMD and talent management are considered very much together, and policy development is aligned with organisation development, fearing that any policy will become meaningless unless implementation is evident. The policy outlines the company's leadership ideals of:

- leading self
- leading people
- leading the business.

The core principles that are used to design activities are

- individuals learn at their own pace and in differing ways
- individuals focus their development best by owning their learning
- individuals learn more quickly through real actions
- individuals learn in context to their environment
- individuals cannot develop leadership without developing followership
- individuals' learning takes them somewhere unique
- individuals' learning creates 'thinking performers'.

The design makes use of an integrated framework of activities for LMD based on a background consisting of competencies, performance management and 360-degree feedback. The activities include such formal programmes as:

- aspiring leaders – a structured 12-month programme for front-line employees who have leadership potential

- growing leaders – core elements for all new managers, consisting of coaching, performance improvement, recruitment and selection, and discipline and capability

- leadership development programme – for middle and senior managers, over 12 months consisting of action learning, modules in finance, lean processes of service provision, commercial awareness and coaching – led by senior managers and business experts

- talent development – for high potentials and rising stars, consisting of career goal-setting, business projects and mentoring.

6.1 REFLECT – CONCLUDE – PLAN

Should an organisation have a written LMD policy?

What is needed for it to operate effectively?

How could you ensure that the policy becomes enacted practice rather than merely espoused?

WEB LINK

Find out about the leadership policy of the Association of Chief Executives of Voluntary Organisations at **http://www.acevo.org/ index.cfm/display_page/Policy_leadership** and about their activities at their Third Sector leadership centre at **http://www.thirdsectorleadership. org** .

A TYPOLOGY OF LMD ACTIVITIES

In Chapter 1 we suggested in our definitions of LMD that there ought to be a consideration of approaches which could be specified in advance in terms of models and skills to be learned and approaches which are concerned with recognising learning as they emerge in events. We presented this in Figure 1.2 as a dimension between contrasting views of LMD. We also indicated the overlap so that even in specified events where there is clarity about objectives, there would also be an emergent process occurring, usually informally between the participants. Similarly, informal learning that cannot be specified can be recognised and to a certain degree formalised. For example, we note in the example from HML above that coaching and mentoring are included in their programme. Even in the most planned and organised system, there is a great deal of 'natural' LMD. Managers often talk about informal and unplanned experiences as 'explicit, powerful, relevant and realistic', and as the main source of their development. Davies (2008), for example, considers how managers were able to draw on experiences of 'exceptional events' as the source of significant learning. Yet the same experiences can also be fragmentary, inefficient, and subject to the winds of circumstance – that is, they are not recognised.

The dimension between specified and recognised LMD is one way of considering activities. Another angle to consider is who becomes the unit for consideration of provision of activities. There has been growing recognition of the importance of distributed leadership (Gronn 2000) and even some evidence that it works, particularly in educational settings (Leithwood *et al* 2008). Distributed leadership is concerned with the dispersal or sharing of influence in order to complete different tasks at work – for example, through teams or projects across and between organisations. This suggests that different people can be leaders at some time, although this may not always be recognised by those formally in leader positions. It could be argued that in professional or knowledge-based organisations, and in geographically dispersed organisations, it is a necessity for all leaders to understand distributed leadership (Ross *et al* 2005) as a dimension between a concentration on individual leaders and distribution and dispersal towards a more collective view. This is shown as Figure 6.1.

As can be seen, once the unit for attention changes from single individuals, other configurations from LMD come into view. For example, it is not difficult to recognise the need for leadership couples (Gronn and Hamilton 2004), extended perhaps to small teams of three or four that share responsibility. Further along the dimension, teams within and across organisations distribute leadership, becoming, according to Barry (1991, p.31), 'bossless' or self-managed. As a final step, but probably difficult to understand, requiring a different 'way of thinking about leadership' (Bennett *et al* 2003, p.2), is the idea that the whole organisation can be considered to be a collective endeavour with leadership shared among many as work is performed. For example, Lumby's (2003) studies in colleges revealed leadership as a 'community exercise' (p.292). The key task for those formally appointed leaders is to ensure alignment with purpose, because influence and power may be working against this (Harris 2008).

6.2 REFLECT – CONCLUDE – PLAN

Consider the last time you worked in a team.

How did shared leadership occur?

Was shared leadership vital for success, or did it constrain individuals?

How could the team learn to share leadership better?

Figure 6.1 Concentration and distribution in LMD

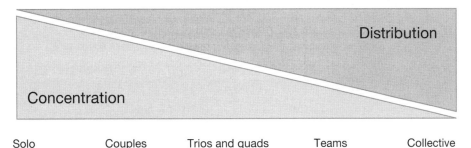

| Solo | Couples | Trios and quads | Teams | Collective |

Source: Ross *et al* (2005, p.131)

 WEB LINK

You might like to explore the Distributed Leadership Study at **http://www.sesp.northwestern.edu/dls/** which provides access to a collection of research projects that examine leadership practice in schools in Chicago.

If we now combine the two dimensions together, we are able to form a typology that attempts to portray conceptually the totality of LMD in an organisation and various activities that could be provided. This is shown as Figure 6.2.

Working with Figure 6.2, we propose to explore the different quadrants to identify some of the activities available for LMD. We would emphasise that our coverage will inevitably be partial and broad in scope. The reason for this, as a short search on Google will demonstrate, is that there is a vast range of possible activities and methods that come under the heading of LMD. For example, Huczynski (2001) presents an 'encyclopaedia' of more than 700 methods. We might suggest that such is the mystery and vagueness surrounding management and, especially, leadership that it becomes possible to match many activities to LMD from different fields and disciplines.

SPECIFIED ACTIVITIES FOR INDIVIDUALS

TRAINING EVENTS AND COURSES

Activities in Quadrant 1 are concerned with the development of managers as individuals, even where they participate in teams, groups and projects. These will be concerned with the enhancement of an organisation's human capital basis. Activities in this quadrant – and such activities traditionally form the basis of most LMD programmes – are mainly based on an understood model

Figure 6.2 A typology of LMD activities

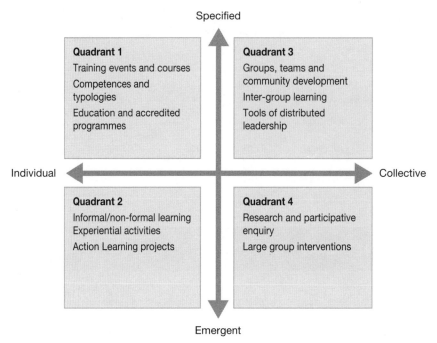

Source: adapted from Rodgers *et al* (2003)

of management, informed by 'best practice', so there is clarity about what will be learned in terms of skills, knowledge, attributes or competences. Delivery can occur either off-site or in-house as part of an organisation's own set of programmes for managers. Most LMD programmes focus on individuals, often using explicit or even implicit models of manager attributes, behaviours and skills composed of a mixture of competences, psychometric assessment of personality, emotional intelligence, team management profiles and training events around particular skills or issues. For effective provision, activities need to contain the key elements of manager-centred learning, which we regard as:

- managerial reality
- building on experience
- using familiar learning processes
- continued learning
- preferred approaches to learning.

The focus for activities ought to be reality, not only because it is real but because it engages the attention of managers. It is more sensible to build the design and content of specified LMD on the experience that managers have when they arrive on a course. It takes longer and may be less exciting for the tutor – but it is more effective. Although one of the great virtues of formal training and education is precisely that it focuses on learning rather than just managing and leading, the achieved learning will be small if the process is too different and distant from what they usually do or need to do in the future. Since managers do not customarily spend their time listening to lectures, even brilliantly delivered lectures may not attract them. If they spend their time reviewing historical case studies of practices in other organisations, a learning process based on this starts with some major disadvantages. Perhaps most powerfully of all, if the learning process, of whatever nature, is seen as something that is likely to be useful only on a course, not in real life, learning will be limited. Further difficulties can arise when 'there is a difference between what an individual recognises as development needs and what the organisation defines as what managers need' (Antonacopoulou 1999).

 WEB LINK

The Association of Management Education and Development (AMED) is a network for people interested in management and organisation development practice. The website is **http://www. amed.org.uk/** .

Research by Storey (2004) identified three interventions which fit into this quadrant and are frequently provided for leaders. These are:

- learning about leadership and organisations – mainly traditional ideas and theories, delivered in business schools and training workshops

- self-analysis, team analysis and leadership styles – completed by individuals to create understanding of current styles but these can also include psychometric tests that can link to feedback and coaching in Quadrant 2

- top-level strategy courses – often aimed at the higher-level leaders, delivered as executive courses or masterclasses. They can be very expensive, depending on where they are delivered and who delivers.

Similarly, recent research in Finland by Suutari and Viitala (2008) of 878 responses by managers to an Internet-based survey found that training programmes were the most common method of participation, both internally and outside the company. Most of this was short term, lasting between one and three days. Many training programmes for managers focus on what are referred to as 'soft skills' (Crosbie 2005), such as communication, collaboration, coaching, personal effectiveness, teamwork and, as considered below, emotional intelligence. In all cases, learning is not just a case of acquiring knowledge but also practising new behaviours and receiving feedback.

COMPETENCES AND TYPOLOGIES

Many organisations work with competency frameworks to provide the focus for activities. IDS (2003) reviewed programmes in five UK public and private organisations and found a recognition of the need for different competences for distinguishing between management and leadership. The frameworks formed the basis for individuals to identify their LMD needs. The research suggested that change orientation, drive for excellence, impact and influence, strategic thinking and customer focus all featured strongly. In addition, there has been considerable interest in activities to help leaders and managers enhance their emotional intelligence (EI). For example, Rubin *et al* (2005) found that the ability to recognise emotion, maintain 'positive affect', and demonstrate agreeableness, positively predicted transformational leadership in a large biotechnology/ agricultural company. Stein *et al* (2009) suggest that leaders need different EI skills for different areas of work. For managing others, the EI skills of optimism, self-regard and impulse control would be of most importance; for the task of managing organisation growth or performance, EI skills of problem-solving and flexibility become more prominent.

As well as competences, there are a variety of typologies of skills and attributes, often accompanied by a questionnaire, which allow managers to assess their own styles and preferences. Some of these are very well known, such as:

- Blake and Mouton's managerial grid (Blake and Mouton 1964)
- Hersey-Blanchard's situational leadership styles questionnaire (Hersey and Blanchard 1981)
- Bass and Avolio's Multi-factor Leadership Questionnaire (Bass and Avolio 1997)
- the Transformational Leadership Questionnaire (Alimo-Metcalfe and Alban-Metcalfe 2001)
- Belbin's Team Role Inventory (Belbin 1981).

Each of these is based on a theory, developed into a model, which is then tested to produce empirical support for the value of using the assessment in LMD. As we have suggested in Chapter 3, there are disputes about the claims for reliability and validity of such assessments (Aritzeta *et al* 2007). However, managers often like to complete questionnaires that reveal their style, preferred roles, and so on. There seems to be intuitive appeal and face validity for managers and leaders, despite doubts of researchers (Fisher *et al* 1996).

EDUCATION AND ACCREDITED PROGRAMMES

An important source of activities in Quadrant 1 are the large number of higher and further education institutions and others that offer programmes for LMD, usually but not always leading to accreditation. In the past, education has been defined as a broadly based and broadly directed process aimed at the whole person and total career, while training has been seen as the specific process of helping managers to learn things appropriate to particular circumstances, within specific organisations or industries. The distinction also broadly followed location: education was what happened in the further/higher education system, and training was what happened in management centres. The distinction, if ever true, seems now to have largely lost its meaning (Holman 2000). Although training centres probably tend to focus more on issues that are practical and specifically related to organisational needs, they also often see themselves as educating a manager or leader for his or her total life. Similarly, education centres have increasingly taken on responsibility for developing managers who meet the specific needs of their particular organisations. The major business schools, when first set up, took a distinctly lofty and distant view about the desirability of doing in-company work (except as private ventures by senior faculty). Now many make a virtue of – and a great deal of money from – doing such work.

One distinctive characteristic of programmes leading to awards in higher education especially is the attention given to trying to inculcate knowledge rather than to develop skills, since the former is much easier to assess, and academic judgements about performance on knowledge are easier to justify than comments about levels of skill. A study carried out by CEML (2002a) suggested that there is little evidence that management qualifications improve organisational performance although there is likely to be a benefit to individual managers and their careers. At undergraduate level there is a good demand for business and management degrees and graduates become eminently employable, although such a degree is not a requirement for management work. MBA programmes receive disproportionate attention in discussion about management education because they are the longest and most ambitious attempt to develop managers by structured processes. In the UK most business schools now offer MBA qualifications, and demand for the MBA has grown, many UK-based students (80%) opting for a part-time or distance-learning approach (CEML 2002a). The MBA is presented as a high-quality qualification, with an approval process developed by the Association of MBAs (AMBA). However, there are continuing concerns about the application of theoretical teaching and the practice of managers (CEML 2002a). In the United States there have been major concerns about the actual results achieved by 100,000 MBA graduates a year, and this concern has been expressed not so much by concerned industrialists as by academic researchers like Behrman and Levin (1984). Henry Mintzberg (2004) and Pfeffer and Fong (2002) criticise MBA programmes as being too oriented towards skills of analysis rather than skills of implementation. Bennis and O'Toole (2005) claim that business schools, particularly represented in the MBA, have been too focused on 'scientific' research and analysis and less concerned with qualities such as judgement and abilities that can accommodate the complexities of organisational life. They point to the way that textbook models and cases used in MBA teaching are too abstract and removed from the real experience of managing and leading.

Further concerns come from those who take a more critical stance towards management education more generally (Grey 1996) – indeed, it is claimed that management education faces a 'crisis of confidence' (p.11). The key argument is that such education purports to provide managers with 'useful knowledge'; it should instead 'expand and challenge the intellectual world' of managers (p.14), including the complex moral and political dimensions of that world.

WEB LINK

AMBA's website is located at **http://www.mbaworld.com/** . From there you can check their criteria for accrediting MBA programmes at **http://www.mbaworld.com/templates/mba/ images/accreditation/pdf/MBA_criteria_0807.pdf** .

If you would like to consider a free online management development programme with ten modules, try **http:///www.managementhelp.org/ fp_progs/org_dev.htm#anchor704607** .

THE JOB

Probably the most common form of LMD in organisations relates to a plan to use the job as the starting point. This may well start with the kind of appraisal and performance review discussed in Chapter 3, followed by a formal personal development plan (Chapter 4). Table 6.1 gives a large-scale view of opportunities in and around the job. Within each major opportunity there are a number of different learning activities involved. In this chapter we deal with the first two major opportunities – in Chapter 9 we look at issues around coaching and mentoring.

Table 6.1 Formally planned learning opportunities at work

Changes in the job	Changes in job content	Within the job
• promotion • doing the same job but with a different function or product: job rotation • secondment	• stretching the boundaries of the job by extra responsibility and tasks • special projects • committees or task groups • junior boards	• being coached • being counselled • monitoring and direct feedback by manager • being mentored

Firstly, changes in the job. There are significant differences in the nature of the opportunities provided by different types of change, and in the nature of the difficulties involved in taking up the opportunities: Figure 6.3 shows some of the possibilities. Moving into a new job with an existing or new employer poses the same development issues. What is the new manager or leader to learn, at what pace, and through what processes? As Figure 6.3 indicates, the most difficult move of all – yet the one with the most potential for learning – is promotion into a new organisation. Some kind of induction programme will usually be arranged. The new manager will meet new colleagues and will probably be given a tour of working facilities. There may be arrangements to meet a range of customers, suppliers and other useful contacts. In essence the manager has to learn about the nature and purpose of the organisation – 'getting to know the business'.

Then there is the need to find out about internal relationships: the politics of the business, the way in which people work together or avoid working together. Finally, there is the outside world, the people and organisations serviced.

There can be particular difficulties in areas of professional or knowledge-based work where experts in one form of work are promoted into management

Figure 6.3 Learning problems in job moves

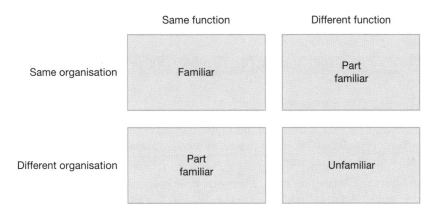

positions. For example, Sambrook (2006) in a study of the movement from nursing roles into management positions in the NHS found some conflict between being a nurse and then a manager. This was partly the consequence of nurses' valuing their professional identities as nurses.

Secondment can be a useful LMD job move and can be recognised as part of an organisation's succession plan (Kur and Bunning 2002) or talent management strategy. A secondment may in certain instances have a dual learning objective. For example, secondment of a manager or leader from industry to work in the civil service normally has a double objective – the individual learns from exposure to a different culture, a different environment, a different way of doing things. At a secondary level the organisation sponsoring the secondee learns about how the civil service operates, and may therefore learn how to deal with it more effectively.

Changes in the job content ought to be formally recognised as LMD but too often opportunities are provided without any effective development taking place. Thus a manager may be given additional responsibilities or a greater weight of responsibility. This is stretching boundaries and acquiring new tasks. An example of this would be that of a sales director handing over to a sales manager the responsibility for a major national account previously handled by the director. Another would be delegating to a subordinate manager the task of producing a report, visiting an important customer or negotiating with a trade union. Crucial here, as highlighted by Davies and Easterby-Smith (1983), is that managers who have to face new situations and difficulties, where their existing behaviours are not adequate, will need to learn to cope. However, such learning must be recognised by senior managers in order to become 'legitimate' (p.181). Senior managers most frequently assign managers to special committees/working parties or task forces for purely managerial reasons. The senior manager wants a particular expert on the subject or a representative from a particular area in the business or somebody who is known to have the ear of somebody important. Managers can stay in their existing jobs but be given experience simulating the work of their board of directors through a 'junior board'. They may be given the same information as the board on a particular issue, and/or be required to make recommendations to the board.

EMERGENT ACTIVITIES FOR INDIVIDUALS

INFORMAL LEARNING

When asked how they learn to do their jobs, managers frequently reply that they 'learn from experience'. There are clear reasons why managers often find informal processes more effective than formal ones. These include:

- the content of development programmes, especially courses, which is experienced as unreal, irrelevant to the manager's priorities or difficult to transfer from a course to work
- processes of learning that too often reflect the interest of course designers and tutors rather than those of participants
- processes that do not take into account different individual learning preferences.

Informal learning usually occurs by accident or incidentally, through everyday experience and practice (Marsick and Watkins 1990), although such experiences are not always recognised in LMD. With such activities, managers have not been encouraged and helped to go through the process of assessing and planning what to do about the learning experience, as suggested by Kolb's learning cycle (1984). They need to be encouraged to look at their experiences in those terms. Similarly, the 'situated learning' approach of Lave and Wenger (1991) supports the importance of natural learning within the context of practice and legitimacy received for learning through the social relations of a community of practitioners.

Informal learning is difficult to uncover – rather like the submerged part of an iceberg (Coffield 2002). Eraut (2000, p.12) prefers the term 'non-formal' learning to contrast with formal learning. He sets out three types of non-formal learning:

- *implicit learning* – learning that occurs without intention and awareness at the time it has taken place but becomes part of experience, used unconsciously in future events
- *reactive learning* – learning that occurs spontaneously in response to events: there might be awareness that learning has occurred but there is little time to consider it except through reflection
- *deliberative learning* – learning from events that is recognised through reviewing and reflecting on actions, and time is provided to allow this to happen.

Managers can be helped to make their learning deliberative, recognising some of the experienced processes at work and beyond as learning experiences that could be improved with a significant benefit to themselves and their organisation. Help can come from a variety of sources including coaches, mentors and others through 360-degree feedback. Some of these sources are considered in more detail in Chapter 9.

Some typical informal learning opportunities for managers are listed below (adapted from Honey and Mumford 1995):

- analysing mistakes
- attending conferences or seminars
- being coached or counselled
- being mentored
- budgeting
- championing and/or managing changes
- covering for holidays
- dealings with colleagues and peers
- dealings with staff
- dealings with a boss
- domestic life
- familiar tasks
- giving a presentation
- interacting with social networking technologies
- interviewing
- job change in a new function
- job change within the same function
- job rotation
- making decisions
- meetings
- negotiating
- networking
- performance appraisals
- planning project work
- reading
- same job but with additional responsibilities
- secondments
- solving problems
- unfamiliar tasks/work
- working in groups/teams
- working with consultants

In Chapter 7 we propose ways by which such learning from informal opportunities can be transformed into more effective LMD.

6.3 REFLECT – CONCLUDE – PLAN

Identify a recent informal learning experience.

How did you learn from this opportunity?

Could your learning have been improved?

How can you ensure that you learn more effectively from such opportunities more regularly?

Any attention to informal learning must, however, be accompanied by a recognition of major deficiencies.

They include:

- *idealisation* – Attitudes and behaviours may predominate which say that past experience is so valued and appropriate that it is all that is necessary. Effective learning involves building successfully on properly understood past experience, not treating it as the only process of merit.

- *narrowness* – It is possible for work experience to be extremely narrow in terms of jobs, functions, kinds of organisation and sizes of organisation. While effective LMD is more likely to focus on the specific than the general, this does not mean that a manager in retail needs to know nothing about, for instance, production processes.

- *obsolescence* – Painful and perhaps carefully acquired experience of how to do work may well become out of date.

Of course, people develop skills from the 'natural' process of doing the job, and finding out whether the way they do it works. If it does, they understandably assume that they have a skill. However, the skill they have acquired may be either inappropriate or at an insufficiently high performance level. At worst it may even be the wrong kind of skill. One example is the process of interviewing. The skills that managers deploy in selection interviewing have often been acquired from the experience of being interviewed themselves, and then of interviewing others. Their level of skill is often, however, well below what they need to interview effectively. You might also recall the Power School of strategy that we mentioned in Chapter 2 and the structures of everyday experience where the most important message might be 'Learn not to learn!' (Salaman and Butler 1990). In a similar vein, informal learning always occurs in a context where politics, contests and tensions may exert inhibiting influences on managers (Garrick 1998).

EXPERIENTIAL ACTIVITIES

Learning informally from everyday opportunities and incidents probably represents the most prevalent form of LMD. It is emergent in the sense that it is unplanned and lacks the intention for learning, although it still has to be recognised for it to be valued as learning. Making learning from any experience more deliberate has been of considerable interest in LMD. For example, Antonacopoulou and Bento (2004) propose that those appointed as leaders need to accept a 'learning leadership' (p.82) approach to their development; this, we suggest, involves using experiences and seeking feedback, forming and trying new ideas and behaviour. What is understood as experience can vary along a range from the everyday lives of managers, which is ever-present, to the provision of activities by others which is meant to provide stimulation of some kind. To a certain extent, the latter can be planned and may even be specified in terms of learning objectives or outcomes, although the value of experiential learning is the emergent sense-making that depends on the response and interpretation of managers to whatever is selected as experience. However, such interpretations are never neutral and are subject to the cultural, social and political factors that provide part of the context for activity (Swan 2007).

According to Reynolds and Vince (2007), experiential learning can be used to stimulate the involvement of managers so that they can reflect on aspects of managing. It is argued that through active participation, managers can reveal a complex range of forces involved in their work, all part of the 'underground organisation' (p.6). Exposure to challenging activities allows emotions to be revealed and new possibilities for action to be considered as a critique of previous ways of working. Experiential learning may be less certain, especially where there are assumptions that specified outcomes can be achieved, but this is not seen as a drawback – it is a parallel to the lives or 'lived experience' of managers and leaders. This does pose difficulties for those that seek to use experiential learning within accredited programmes like MBAs. However, many academics have incorporated experiential activities within their LMD courses, even if this provides the potential for critique of the traditional curriculum for managers.

One well-known form of experiential activity for LMD is the use of the outdoors. Owing much to military approaches to training (Adair 2005), outdoor management development (OMD) has been used by many organisations although there are doubts about the transfer of learning from what is inevitably an off-site activity back to work (Ibbetson and Newell 1999) – but this is an issue that applies to all off-site LMD and one we consider more carefully in Chapter 8.

OMD can focus on personal development providing physical and psychological challenges for participants which, if completed successfully, result in a boost to self-confidence, and a willingness to undertake even greater challenges. In addition to this personal focus, OMD often is used to consider key management issues such as working in teams, leading and managing complex tasks such as cultural change using a mix of different activities such as problem-solving, abseiling, rafting, caving, and so on. Crucially – and this is always a tension – it is important to balance the doing of a task with the chance to discuss, analyse and reflect on its completion and derive learning from it (Honey and Lobley 1986). A further tension is the extent to which OMD programmes are concerned with and designed around generalised understanding and awareness for individuals or specific issues related to the organisation (Burke and Collins 2004).

For many, OMD represents a powerful space for LMD which enables an explicit use of Kolb's (1984) learning cycle. Experience is used for reflection and discussion followed by working out what can be taken forward into the next task (Bank 1994). Badger *et al* (1997) point to the use of learning styles to help participants work on problems in OMD, and this allows managers to relate how they work on tasks to a model of problem management presented by Kolb (1982), shown as Figure 6.4.

Figure 6.4 A problem management cycle

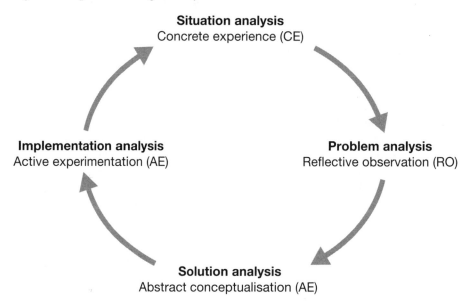

Source: adapted from Kolb (1982)

Managers can consider their relative learning preferences against effectiveness in managing problems presented as challenges during OMD. For example, difficult and ambiguous problems require more attention to problem-setting in the situation analysis stage but participants may avoid this because of preferences for action. The *LMD in Practice* opposite provides an example of one manager's experience of OMD.

An additional model that is well known in OMD focuses on the requirements for action by leaders with relevance to particular tasks in particular situations. This is Adair's (2005) action-centred leadership (ACL) model, shown as Figure 6.5.

The model puts a leader in a situation, working with a group that needs to achieve a recognised task. A group or team exists to work together towards

MY EXPERIENCE OF OMD

Stratis Koutsoukos, *Leeds Business School*

I work as Deputy Director and Senior Research Fellow of a European economic policy and business research and consultancy unit based at a university Business School. I lead the European branch of the unit, which requires me to win new research and consultancy contracts, respond to the client and their needs and manage what are often multi-disciplinary cross-faculty and university teams to deliver the contracts.

The Bavarian training was a team-based experience that was unique in many ways. Marketed as an outdoor leadership training programme, under different configurations it is in many ways a 'running experiment' for the university associated with the annual staff development festival.

Working in a team-based environment was by no means new to me. A necessity in the occupation, I have both led teams and been part of them, and I feel that I have learnt to identify my role within such teams with ease. In the expedition in Bavaria, however, the basic rules upon which I have based the biggest part of my team and leadership experiences were altogether different. To start with, the knowledge area and the abilities relevant to the exercise were not as clearly defined and were much broader. For instance, is it about the technical knowledge of climbing and hiking, is it about basic fitness and human physiology, or is a knowledge of oneself and how one copes and reacts in adversity that is more important? Is it about an emergent model of leadership, or about map-reading skills? And if anything, what is the final desired outcome? Clearly,

the degree of complexity between choices and decisions made on behalf of others and the relative consequences are less contained than in the highly pressured yet better-defined environment of research and consultancy. Finally, the week was filled with many team-based 'new experiences' from snowshoe-walking to orienteering in the Alps – hiking, sledging, abseiling, winter survival skill education, and basic avalanche training. The evening team bonding, which again added a dimension of complexity, also created a basis on which most members of the group were at the same level with each other – all of us 'learners'.

I found overall the event a very humbling experience and an enjoyable one. Certainly, it allowed me to reflect on how I approach new knowledge and experiences, how I personally react to the initial fear of the unknown, and how I can harness the dynamic and support of a group situation to better overcome my personal fears and weaknesses. I question wholeheartedly the wisdom of calling such programmes overtly 'leadership' ones. Like so many other skills, I believe this is one that can only be cultivated at a very early stage in life and that too often concentrating on the iconic 'leader element' distracts us from the real substance of the argument which is about delivery within teams. Ultimately, I feel that the most significant skill and attribute for the expedition is not being a leader or extremely fit athletically, or a good fundraiser or ideas-generator, but instead it is about knowing oneself well and truly, and being prepared to acknowledge that this is an ongoing lifelong process.

some common objective relating to the task. As Adair recognises, however, there can be a disconnection between the need of the task and the life of the group, which like an 'iceberg' (p.14) is mostly hidden from view. This can cover the norms and values present derived from past experience and history.

Figure 6.5 Action-centred leadership

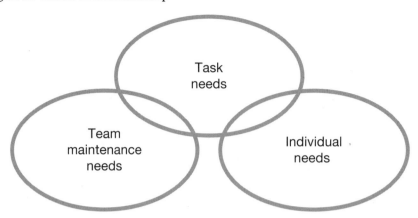

Source: Adair (2005, p.15)

Together these form the basis of a team maintenance need. Then there are the needs of individuals, which may or may not be in tune with the team or the needs of the task for all sorts of reasons. These three considerations must be taken together, each connecting to the other areas. The job or 'function' of the leader is to ensure that this occurs. For example, at the RAF College where ACL is used in leadership training, each area of need is broken into actions such as:

Task – defining the task, making a plan, adjusting the plan

Team – setting standards, building team spirit, appointing sub-leaders

Individual – attending to personal problems, encouraging individuals.

6.4 REFLECT – CONCLUDE – PLAN

Could the ACL model be applied to any task you face?

What actions are required for each area of need?

What will you do to apply the ACL model to your next group task?

WEB LINK

Go to **http://www.johnadair.co.uk/** for more information on action-centred learning and links to papers by John Adair.

For some really interesting stories of managers' experiences of using the outdoors in LMD, go to **http://reviewing.co.uk/research/ple_sum.htm** .

While action and the outdoors would seem to complement each other, there is also recognition that escaping to somewhere peaceful and quiet – and a long way from the work context – can provide a space for personal reflection and personal awareness. Watson and Vasilieva (2007) describe an outdoor leadership programme where, instead of problem-solving activities, the space was used as a retreat to engage in 'wilderness thinking' (p.243). Rather than compete against the challenge of the outdoors, participants complete reflective exercises as individuals and in teams which promote personal awareness. Evaluation of 100 participants shows that, with the support of coaching after the retreat, the programme provided a 'catalyst for sustainable change' (p.243).

Viewing the outdoors as a retreat where managers can find time to reflect and reconsider their lives does seem to connect to religious ideas for spiritual growth. In recent years there has been a growth in providing workshops, seminars and training that seek to allow managers to get in touch with their inner selves so they can be more effective in the outer world of their work. This is referred to as 'spiritual management development' (SMD) (Bell and Taylor 2004). SMD programmes are based on the view that managers can achieve their goals through personal growth through a focus on the inner self through such techniques as meditation, hypnosis, visioning, therapeutic touch, yoga and walking on fire. Spiritual development enables a transcendence over the physical world, it is claimed, and allows a fulfilment of human potential which, as Bell and Taylor suggest, is 'implicitly religious' (p.461). Like OMD, SMD also faces the difficulty of disconnection from the organisation context and everyday life: it becomes the individual's responsibility to make something happen.

While OMD is an important source of LMD, over the last 20 years there have been attempts to use other kinds of provision from other arenas to provide a stimulus for learning. The crucial move is whether lessons from one facet of life can be applied in the world of organisations. One example is drama, and for many years the idea that an organisation is like a theatre with a stage, actors and audience – referred to as the 'dramaturgical metaphor' (Clark 2008) – has attracted interest. As an extension, this way of thinking has been applied to LMD. For example Olivier and Verity (2008) use 'mythodrama' in LMD as a way of providing insight into people and organisations. As they explain, *mytho-* is concerned with stories and insights into human nature from writers such as Shakespeare, and *-drama* is the method for delivery and making an impact. They use:

Henry V – as an inspirational leader

Julius Caesar – to understand power, politics and influence

Macbeth – to explore the danger of derailing behaviours

The Tempest – to understand the dynamics of leading change, and

As You Like It – for positive culture change.

Progammes are developed by theatre-trained facilitators who are able to work with the purpose and meaning of a play such as *Henry V*, making these relevant to participants, who also act out key features.

In addition to drama, LMD has been delivered by using ideas from music, comedy and the arts generally. There is also an attraction in using sport not only in terms of ideas but also as the source of experience. A search on Google will show a large variety of connections, for example, between golf and leadership development.

PROJECTS

Projects can be a powerful development tool for managers (Smith and Dodds 1993). The manager in a new job can take up a major project as a development process – for example: 'Find out why repeat orders have declined by 28% in the last six months.' A secondment can include a project or, indeed, be totally dedicated to one. For example, 'We are seconding you to charity X for six months. Your project is to review their management control systems, and produce a report for the chairman of their council.' Projects can also be identified within the existing job: 'We want you to do an investigation into the forecasts actually used by sales, marketing and production. Why do they have different forecasts, and what problems result?'

Projects can provide major potential developmental benefits. They often involve managers in looking at a wider range of issues, in greater depth, across a wider range of functions, than might otherwise be encountered. At their best, even within a formal development context, projects of the kind described here should be real rather than invented purely for development. In some cases they carry responsibility for implementation as well as recommendation, in which case they provide for the strongest form of development (see Chapter 7 on Action Learning). There is growing recognition of project-based learning for managers and others in organisations. Ayas and Zeniuk (2001) suggest that such learning provides a way of thinking beyond the short term, allowing for knowledge creation and sharing. However, and critically, such a process is not without difficulty and accounts for the emergent features of project-based learning. For example, Scarbrough et al (2004) argue that there are limits in how much learning from a project can be transferred to other parts of an organisation. They suggest that there is a 'learning boundary' (p.1583) between a project and the rest of the organisation which becomes particularly marked when changes in practice are the outcome of a project that need to be implemented elsewhere. So it is quite possible for learning to occur within a project which then becomes constrained if applied elsewhere. Managers who undertake projects as part of their development will need help to consider how the barriers to application can be overcome; they will also need to reflect critically on their approach to bringing change to organisations. (See Chapter 7 for a consideration of reflection and critical thinking.)

SPECIFIED ACTIVITIES FOR COLLECTIVE LEADERSHIP

Quadrant 3 embraces activities that view LMD as more than the development of human capital with a focus on individual skills. As Iles and Preece (2006) argue, it involves the development of:

- social capital – defined by Nahapiet and Ghoshal (1998) as 'the sum of actual and potential resources within, available through and derived from the network of relationships possessed by an individual or social unit' (p.243)

- leadership capability – defined by Day (2001) as 'expanding the collective capacity of organisational members to engage effectively in leadership roles and processes' (p.582).

Spillane (2006) sees distributed leadership as a reciprocal process of interdependence and the work of multiple leaders although, as Gronn (2008) suggests, there are a variety of different practices that fall under the heading of leadership, so the term 'distributed' might be considered an ultimate position along the individual/collective dimension. Between the extremes of solo and distributed leadership are a 'mix' of leadership configurations such as couples, trios, groups and teams which Gronn sees as more accurately represented by the term 'hybrid' (p.152). From this perspective, we start to embrace activities that develop an understanding of combined patterns of leadership.

GROUPS, TEAMS AND COMMUNITIES

Much of the research on distributed leadership has been gathered in schools where systematic reviews of the evidence on the impact of individual school leaders on pupil learning outcomes was found to be indirect, relying on the influence of staff and others for success (Bell *et al* 2002). Further work in schools highlights both the importance of traditional leadership from the top – the vertical processes – and the sharing of leadership based on interdependent work – the lateral processes (Harris 2008). Recent research by Leithwood *et al* (2007) points to the specification of working with groups and teams to allocate tasks in order to create alignment between them. While a group can be considered as any combination of two or more people who see themselves under the same heading or category, a team is characterised by recognised interdependence between those people who combine efforts in pursuit of a common goal (Stewart 1999).

Group and team development programmes, which may well make use of various typologies of roles (Quadrant 1) and experiential learning events such as OMD (Quadrant 2), seek to engender a climate for shared meanings and activity. Anderson and West's (1994) Team Climate Inventory assesses team dynamics and shared perceptions for team practice, including:

- communication – how members interact, and the structure and style of team meetings

- participation – in decision-making and other activities

- safety – how safe people feel, and how much interpersonal trust there is

- cohesiveness – how cohesive the team perceives itself to be, and is perceived by others

- task style – how the team approaches tasks and pursues objectives

- vision – the team's vision or mission, and objectives and targets
- innovativeness – how creative the team is.

Group and team-building requires two key processes – a design process, and then an ongoing learning process. Tuckman (1965) has provided a well-known set of stages for group development consisting of:

- *forming* (characterised by dependence on the 'leader')
- *storming* (independence/counter-dependence)
- *norming* (interdependence)

and

- *performing* stages (interdependence).

Tuckman later added that teams also have an *adjourning/mourning* stage (exit, break-up, moving on).

Thus the first step is to bring a group of individuals together. Exactly who is involved is based on the purpose of the team and the tasks to be performed, so a key decision is a matching of individuals to the specialisms required (Edmondson *et al* 2001). This process raises one of the first points of tension in team-building which relates to the paradoxical and contradictory possibilities when individuals are brought together in a team. As pointed out by Donnellon (1996), a team needs differences between individuals in terms of their knowledge, skills and experiences but also the integration of such differences to fulfil the purpose of the team. This is not easy to do, and team-building requires recognition of the tensions that can arise. Donnellon identifies four manifestations of tensions in teams:

- individuality – individuals make contributions based on their skills and knowledge, but such contributions need to be accepted in the team
- identity – people develop as individuals, albeit in social contexts, but acquire a status based on qualifications, skills and membership of groups such as professional associations, but they are required to adopt a new identity when joining a team
- interdependence – a team must learn to depend on each other but also needs individuals to use their skills and understanding in team activity, thus maintaining a degree of independence
- trust – a key aspect of team-work is trust between members – but can others be trusted?

Recently, the idea of coaching has been applied to team development. While it is usually seen as a one-to-one LMD activity, as Clutterbuck (2007) argues it can also be applied to teams. Team coaching is defined (p.77) as:

> Helping the team improve performance, and the processes by which performance is achieved, through reflection and dialogue.

6.5 REFLECT – CONCLUDE – PLAN

How far do Donnellon's tensions occur in any group or team that you are (or have been) a member of?

Share your findings with other members of this team.

How could an understanding of these tensions help you develop teams in the future?

Team coaching is inevitably more complex than individual coaching, with key dimensions relating to:

- confidentiality
- the scope of the relationship
- the speed of decision-making.

A team coach is likely to be 'inside' the team, where dialogue is more frequent and more intensive (Clutterbuck 2007).

In addition to groups and teams, some organisations seek to develop *communities of practice* to enhance the creation and sharing of knowledge. While such communities were originally recognised as the source of informal and improvised learning based on the practice of a group in a local context (Lave and Wenger 1991), with leadership very much in the hands of the group, recently there have been attempts made to create such communities and orient their efforts towards 'their companies' success' (Wenger and Snyder 2000, p.145).

INTER-GROUP LEARNING

Although most team-building activities are aimed at single teams and the internal relationships within the team, increasingly it is important to recognise that there is value in considering relationships between teams within and between organisations. Iles and Auluck (1988), for example, show how a process of 'organisational mirroring' allows one team or department to receive feedback from other teams.

Particular challenges arise when collaborative working is required from at least two teams or members from those teams where each team has differing values, cultures and disciplines. In recent years, for example, different agencies involved in complex issues such as child safety are required by policies to work together to share knowledge, make decisions and co-ordinate actions for service delivery. Since each team can be seen as a figuration of shared leadership, inter-group work might be perceived as an example of what Victor and Boynton (1998, p.195) referred to as co-configuration. For Daniels (2004), the skills of debate and dialogue are regarded as important for co-configuration, as are the skills of learning from interactions with customers and service users. Joint training is considered to be an important means enabling inter-group activity (Tomlinson 2003).

TOOLS OF DISTRIBUTED LEADERSHIP

As the research on distributed leadership has progressed, there have appeared a number of suggested processes or techniques which can be prescribed to help people understand the way leadership is shared across an organisation or between groups. For example, the Distributed Leadership Study in the USA developed a number of instruments for school improvement. The study aimed to understand leadership as a practice to improve instruction and classroom work. One instrument, focusing on mathematics teaching in middle-school grades, was the School Staff Network Survey which allowed an examination of leadership that influenced teaching practice.

Distributed leadership and the various configurations of influence represent a challenge to orthodox notions of individualised management and leadership. Understanding how patterns of practice are contributing and aligned towards a common purpose requires an understanding of collective units such as teams, departments, or the whole organisation. Depending on the size of the unit, such an understanding will need to include the voice of many others who are active participants in the unit. Gronn (2000) advocated the use of Engeström's (1987) model of activity systems and cultural history activity theory. This considers the work of individuals and their interdependence with others within a context. As work is completed, individuals become entangled in a web of influences, all affected by the history and culture. It is within situations of work that leadership becomes distributed and influence is exerted to achieve outcomes that are successful or otherwise. How this occurs can be learned by the use of the model but also allows interaction with the understanding and voices of others involved in work. Learning distributed leadership can be both specified and emergent LMD (Gold *et al* 2007) but is essential for alignment of practices for positive organisation change and performance (Harris 2008).

 WEB LINK

For more information on the instruments from the Distributed Leadership Study, go to **http://www.sesp.northwestern.edu/dls/instruments/** . For details of cultural history activity theory, go to **http://www.edu.helsinki. fi/activity/pages/chatanddwr/chat/,** the site of the Center for Activity Theory and Developmental Work Research.

EMERGENT ACTIVITIES FOR COLLECTIVE LEADERSHIP

RESEARCH AND PARTICIPATIVE ENQUIRY

Bennett *et al* (2003) suggest that distributed leadership is an 'emergent property of a group or network of individuals in which group members pool their expertise' (p.3). As a consequence, much of the influence that is exercised can be hidden from view or operate without the awareness of formally appointed managers and leaders. For example, one of the first studies of communities of practice within organisations highlighted the way groups worked and learned according to local norms, values and stories about what works, and much of this was at variance with what managers believed (Brown and Duguid 1991). In schools, it was research seeking to identify successful leadership that revealed distribution through collaborative and joint working (Day *et al* 2000). If distributed leadership is a way of thinking about any organisation, particularly those aspects concerned with leading in practice at all levels, researching practice is a way of revealing emergent aspects (Spillane *et al* 2008). One activity is to use the tools of distributed leadership suggested in Quadrant 3. While these can be seen as specified activities, the findings are likely to be a surprise but they will allow managers to learn about local networks and communities which form the social capital of an organisation. Understanding how these operate allows the possibility of intervention to enhance organisation purpose and alignment.

Research and enquiry can be highly action-oriented and involve many others in a process, especially during times of change. For example, Action Research is concerned with researching to take action in relation to make improvements to a difficult problem. Managers play two roles: that of researcher and that of interventionist (Eden and Huxham 1996). Action Research becomes a participative enquiry when those under study become actively involved in the study throughout the process and are involved in the discussion of findings and the next actions. According to Whyte (1991), Participatory Action Research (PAR) has three important features:

- organisation or community members are active in the process of research and construction of meaning with researchers

- actions are jointly determined in a process of continuous learning

- the outcomes of the process, the learning, serve the interests of action-taking and research-making.

PAR gives particular attention to the ongoing and jointly determined process of collective meaning-making, so we can see its connections to distributed leadership.

A similar approach to participative research is found in Appreciative Enquiry (AE) (Reed 2007), which considers how people in an organisation view what works and what they value in what they do. This allows interesting and different ideas to emerge and show how different voices can exert an influence on an organisation's future. The focus is very much against failure and problems and for considering success. According to the work of Cooperrider *et al* (2000), AE considers the 'best in people, their organisations and the relevant world around them' (p.5). As a process, the whole organisation is considered for involvement in change, which moves with the process of inquiry. Four parts of a cycle – the 4-D Cycle – provide guidance:

- Discovery – conversations about possibilities

- Dreaming – ideas and stories for the future and what might be

- Designing – asserting the ambitions into plans for the future

- Delivery – action planning around specific activities, tasks and processes.

An example of the use of AE can be found at Keers (2007), where an inquiry into workplace culture was completed at O$_2$, the mobile phone company. Staff were asked what they like about working at the company. A viral approach was used by working with 10 staff who approached 2,000 other staff informally over four months. Key positive themes emerged, such as Great Relationships and It's the Little Things That Count, which were then used as the basis for 100 interviews which resulted in changes. A noticeable improvement in staff satisfaction was recorded soon after change in practice and management behaviour became incorporated into the AE process.

LARGE GROUP INTERVENTIONS

AE can employ a number of techniques, including methods for 'whole systems change' which bring everyone who has an interest in an issue together into an event to find possible changes. Such events can make use of large group interventions, of which the best-known are Open Space Technology and Future Search Conferences.

The aim of large group interventions is to provide a momentum for change based on the commitment of participants who have a key role in generating ideas and implementing actions to make change work. It also recognises that those closest to a problem are likely to have critical information that can enrich the change strategy. This avoids the top-down 'cascade' approaches that are often employed by managers but usually fail to gain commitment and are open to distortion.

The purpose of Open Space Technology (Owen 2008) is to allow discussion of a complex issue or question by those who have an interest so as to explore the possibility of collaborative action based on what emerges. The event can last from half a day to three days. For example, in 2009 an Open Space event in Barnsley which posed the question 'What kind of leadership do we need in Yorkshire?' attracted over 75 participants for a one-day event. Because the issue is complex, there are no single answers to the question. Instead, there is a chance for participants to set their own agenda based on what they want to offer as possible contributions. Open Space begins with a plenary of all participants who are able to make offers of contributions at particular times during the event. Space is provided to allow delivery of offers and choices are made, but then it is entirely up to the participants to decide what happens. As one of the key principles states, 'Whatever happens is the only thing that could have happened.' Participants are also allowed to follow the 'law of two feet' which states:

> If at any time you find yourself in any situation where you are neither learning nor contributing, use your two feet. Go to some other place where you may learn and contribute.

During the conference, a record of events is usually kept and this becomes the conference proceedings at the end, distributed among all participants. A key benefit of using Open Space is the opportunity for different voices to be heard and allowing the formation of new networks of collaboration. These all enhance an organisation's or community's leadership capability. The *LMD in Practice* below considers one person's view of the Barnsley event.

BARNSLEY OPEN SPACE

LMD IN PRACTICE

David Taylor, *The Edge Coaching* and *Wakefield College*

I was at the Open Space event held in Barnsley and run by the West Yorkshire Lifelong Learning Network. At the event I set up a group to explore what kind of learning opportunities we need to create for leaders as we deal with the volatile climate in which we operate. The group was inspiring in its ability to create a meaningful conversation where people were able to contribute and be listened to rather than be argued against by people wanting to be 'right' about their particular views.

The themes that came through regarding learning that leaders need to do was interesting. It was all about being able to connect with people in an open way, communicate openly, be able to listen to 360-degree feedback, be able to coach and be able to access the intelligence of

emotion and feeling. There was also a theme around going outside our comfort zones and not just sticking to what and who we know.

I found this very heartening – people know what they need leaders to be like. They know that so often we don't create opportunities for enabling leaders to develop these skills. We are in an area that has nothing to do with Business degrees, MBAs, etc, etc. In many ways the best leadership development is in effective people and self-development skills. We need to develop the systems and structures in our businesses to facilitate this kind of development in our leaders. We need to do it at this time especially as our old ways are being so strongly challenged by what we have created financially and socially and spiritually.

In a similar way Future Search Conferences (Weisbord and Janoff 2000) attempt to bring about system-wide change based on the preferred futures of participants. Through conversations, common ground emerges for action and new approaches rather than resolving differences or reaching conflict resolution on every issue. Usually lasting two to three days with between 10 and 100 participants, Future Search Conferences are based on the following principles:

1 The 'whole system' is in the room, either directly present or represented. This might involve a single department or unit, the whole organisation, or the system of which the focal organisation is a part (eg customers, suppliers, distributors, etc).

2 Diversity enhances understanding and action.

3 There are no 'experts' but

   – people with information

   – people with resources/authority

   – people affected.

Participants who are close to issues and therefore have valuable knowledge and influence are able to explore their past and present to create conditions for future action. All information and ideas are visible to everyone all the time, and self-managed discussions including action plans take place from individual, organisational and global perspectives. The conference tries to map the present in all its messy complexity – what participants are proud of, sorry for, and so on.

Warzynski (2004) reports on the use of Future Search at Cornell University within the Department of Population Medicine and Diagnostic Sciences. The purpose was to develop joint understanding to provide information for the strategic plan. Thirty-nine participants attended a one-day conference, preceded by an email survey of key questions relating to the future of the Department. The conference produced goals, strategies and action plans for the future which, as one participant reported (p.110), provided:

> more meaningful results than I anticipated in a short time. It was a good and refreshing experience, meeting and working with others in the Department, identifying common issues to move the Department and the diagnostic lab into the future. There is more in common among colleagues than there are differences.

 WEB LINK

Find out more about Open Space at **http://www.openspaceworld.org/ cgi/wiki. cgi?AboutOpenSpace** and about Future Space Conferences at **http://www.futuresearch.net/ method/whatis/index.cfm** . Other large group interventions include World Café at **http://www. theworldcafe. com/** and Syntegration at **http://www.syntegrity.com/** .

Large group interventions pose quite a challenge to individual managers and leaders. Firstly, they are quite difficult to organise in terms of timings and logistics. Open Space, for example, needs just that – space for activities to occur. Secondly, there can be no certainty of the outcome since the processes imply a strong degree of self-management and direction by the participants, but this is distributed leadership in action, so those with formal authority have to trust the process and appreciate what emerges. Thirdly, large group interventions create equality and democracy in terms of who is allowed to speak, participate and exert influence, and there also needs to be an acceptance that whatever emerges will become a contribution of value to an organisation or community. It is the minimum that can be expected if those in nominated leader positions are to deal with what we called the leader's conundrum in Chapter 1. We would also argue that in making such a response, both individual and organisation leadership capacity are enhanced.

E-LEARNING

The term 'e-learning' has a number of possible meanings. For example, Sambrook (2003) sees e-learning as any activity of learning that is supported by information and communication technologies (ICT). The CIPD (2004) would agree with this view but allocates more attention to 'connectivity' and the importance of the purpose of training in organisations. However, in the light of the different definitions of LMD in Chapter 1 which differentiated between planned and emergent approaches, we would suggest that given the current exposure of most managers to connected technologies and their use of it on a regular basis, we have to recognise the informal and unplanned possibilities of e-learning too.

We also have to recognise that it has long been possible for managers to learn at a distance, and, as argued by Stewart (2010), e-learning has to be linked to historical attempts to enable learning at a distance through correspondence courses, such as the CIPD's open learning route to qualifications and the Open University's MBA programme. According to Stewart, key features of such programmes are:

- The learner is not immediately or continuously in the presence of or supervised by a trainer or tutor.

- The learner does, though, benefit from the services of a training or tutoring organisation.

- Such services may include support from a distance provided by a trainer or tutor.

- Such services always include learning materials provided by the training or tutoring organisation.

- Such materials can be a variety of forms and media, and courses usually utilise a mix of these forms and media.

Distance-learning has offered flexibility and autonomy to learners, and it has continued with advances in ICT and, of course, connectivity via the Web. This has created new possibilities that extend distance-learning towards e-learning, including mixing approaches such as the idea of blended learning by which connected ICT can be matched with paper-based material or DVDs and audio. Early evaluation of the benefits of e-learning included the ability to learn 'just in time' at the learner's pace and convenience, and the provision of updatable materials with reductions in delivery costs (Pollard and Hillage 2001). Managers have thus been able to bypass a number of hurdles in accessing LMD materials and articles via the Internet, many of them freely available. Of course, a key skill for managers is learning how to search and choose from the vast amount of material now available. Such has been the generative power of ICT that there has been an explosion in the availability of new information and knowledge, with rapid dissemination. Some organisations such as Motorola, BAE and Heineken have responded to this growth by creating corporate universities (CUs), and so there has been some attempt to formalise the access of managers to such materials. Gibb (2008) suggests that the purpose of a CU is to provide 'strategically relevant [learning] solutions for each job family within a corporation' (p.143). It has been argued that a CU reflects an organisation's strategic priority for learning, which aligns activities such as LMD across a widely dispersed global workforce (Paton *et al* 2005). The deliberate use of the word 'university' does seem to suggest an attempt to promote learning excellence and raise its status, although critics have been concerned that most CUs are simply re-badged training departments (Walton 2005). Leaders and managers are seen as critical to the success of formal e-learning programmes in organisations (McPherson and Nunes 2008).

The implied formality of LMD through CUs and the more recent extension in the provision of Virtual Learning Environments (VLEs) is both enhanced but also threatened by the emergence of Web 2.0 technology and social networking (CIPD 2008), which allows managers to join online groups and build their own networks, communities or even alternative identities in Second Life! In addition, and in combination, perhaps, we are increasingly able to access online information and link with communities or preferred individuals (eg Twitter) through mobile phones and wifi-enabled laptops. This form of mobile learning or m-learning (Sambrook 2003; Stewart 2010) cannot be formally controlled by an organisation but does enable managers to engage with others, any time and anywhere.

There is probably no limit to the amount of material that will be available to managers via various electronic or wifi connections. This is the stuff of e-learning (Rossett 2002) but it still has to be engaged with or 'stirred' in a process of LMD. Stewart (2010) recommends using a blended approach partly because e-learning alone has not yet been shown to be effective. He suggests that other methods such as coaching and mentoring can be used in combination with e-learning so that LMD is more focused on individual requirements and action can be considered for workplace application.

 WEB LINK

Blended learning and e-learning both require some degree of moderation. A well-known model is Salmon's five-stage model at **http://www.atimod. com/e-moderating/5stage.shtml** .

SUMMARY

- An LMD policy is a symbol of an organisation's intentions and contributes to a positive HR context to support LMD.

- Many organisations are giving attention to their talent management systems, identifying individuals' high potential or roles which are of value to the organisation.

- LMD activities have to include both formal and informal learning processes, specified, emergent, individual and collective activities.

- Training programmes and courses, both internally and outside an organisation, are a common method of participation in LMD.

- Many organisations work with competency frameworks to provide the focus for activities.

- There are a large number of higher and further education institutions and others that offer programmes for LMD, usually leading to accreditation.

- The use of the job for LMD involves planned opportunities such as promotion and secondment.

- Leaders and managers often find informal processes more effective than formal ones.

- Experiential learning can be used to stimulate the involvement of managers so that they can reflect on aspects of managing and leading.

- Projects can be a powerful development tool for managers and leaders.

- Group and team development programmes seek to engender a climate for shared meanings and activity.

- There are a number of ideas and tools for learning distributed leadership.

- E-learning in LMD is more effective when blended with other methods.

QUESTIONS

For discussion

1 Why should an organisation develop a formally stated LMD policy?

2 How convinced are you that the balance between informal and formal development ought to be changed?

3 What is the value of e-learning in LMD?

4 Should a leader learn to understand distributed leadership?

5 What is the value of using the outdoors in LMD?

6 What LMD activities are needed for the creation of ethical leaders?

GROUP ACTIVITY

Get together in a group of four to work on the following case study.

You have been asked by the training director of a large chemical organisation to investigate the effectiveness of outdoor management development and then suggest how most value can be obtained from sending all managers on such a programme.

Use the web to gather data.

● Go to http://www.aee.org/ . This is home page of the Association for Experiential Education. It provides research findings on outdoor development and links to other pages.
● Also, http://www.geocities.com/dr_adventure/activitypage.html is a page of activities for the outdoors.
● A resource for reviewing outdoor management development can be found at http://reviewing.co.uk/index.htm .

Finally, prepare a presentation based on your findings.

FURTHER READING

BOYATZIS, R., COWEN, S. and KOLB, D. (1995) *Innovation in Professional Education*. San Francisco: Jossey Bass

KOZLOWSKI, S. W. J., WATOLA, D. J., JENSEN, J. M., KIM, B. H. and BOTERO, I. C. (2009) 'Developing adaptive teams: a theory of dynamic team leadership', in E. SALAS, G. F. GOODWIN and C. S. BURKE (eds) *Team Effectiveness in Complex Organizations: Cross-disciplinary perspectives*. London/New York/Philadelphia: CRC Press

MANN, T. (2007) *Facilitation: An art, science, skill – or all three? Build your expertise in facilitation*. Bradford: Resource Productions

WEISBORD, M. (2008) *Future Search: An action guide to finding common ground in organizations and communities*. Sydney: ReadHowYouWant.com

CHAPTER 7

Combining work and learning

CHAPTER OUTLINE

Introduction
Work- and practice-based learning
Practice and knowledge
Opportunities for practice-based learning
Support for and barriers to practice-based learning
Effective learning from reflection
Self-development
Learning in groups and Action Learning
Summary

LEARNING OUTCOMES

After studying this chapter, you should be able to understand, explain, analyse and evaluate:

- the importance of work and practice-based learning

- how managers can combine work and learning

- the contribution of practice-based learning to knowledge creation

- the range of learning opportunities available to managers

- the support for and barriers to learning, and how to surmount them

- the use of learning reviews and techniques of reflection

- the use of self-development and Action Learning

INTRODUCTION

The contingent process of leadership and management practice suggests that LMD could be most beneficial if it were grounded in the lived experience of managers and meaningful to what they actually do. Further, because managers often face work of complexity and ambiguity in the context of rapid change and turbulence, knowledge and skills acquired on a more formal course, for example, may soon become redundant and out of date. Managers need to learn frequently and in the context of their practice. This is an approach to LMD that has received growing interest under the heading of Workplace Learning, which considers how the workplace provides space, an environment and a climate for learning on an everyday basis (Billett 2006).

As we described in Chapter 6, informal learning occurs within managerial activities. We referred to Eraut's (2000) preference for the term 'non-formal' learning consisting of:

- implicit learning – learning that occurs without intention and awareness at the time it has taken place but becomes part of experience, used unconsciously in future events

- reactive learning – learning that occurs spontaneously in response to events: there might be awareness that learning has occurred but there is little time to consider it except through reflection

- deliberative learning – learning from events that is recognised through reviewing and reflecting on actions, and time is provided to allow this to happen.

In the first type, implicit learning, we can see that managers would hardly recognise that learning has occurred – and this might also be the case for the second type, reactive learning. In both cases, work practice and task performance would be the intention. However, LMD still occurs, because learning in such circumstances is real, direct and occurs *naturally* (Burgoyne and Hodgson 1983). Kempster (2009) suggests that it is within the lived experiences of practice that leaders learn, and that their practice can be developed in line with the requirements and context of their organisations. In addition, natural learning is frequently the path managers follow in order to move into leadership positions. Yet such learning is usually unconscious and possibly insufficient – although this might not be recognised as a problem. Indeed, coming to build up and rely on what is termed one's tacit knowledge (see below) and understanding, acquired through the experience of doing work including being with and observing others, is considered to be the source of successful management and leadership (Argyris 1999).

In this chapter we look at the ways to make non-formal learning more deliberative so that natural learning processes can become integrated LMD (Mumford 1987). This means that LMD can shift its focus from the classroom or training location to the site of practice, and that managers consciously become work- or practice-based learners (Raelin 2007).

WORK- AND PRACTICE-BASED LEARNING

Managerial work is replete with opportunities for learning. Learning through the job as a method is particularly attractive because it derives from imperatives around the job. This contrasts with many other forms of learning which are seen as being driven by a development agenda that may or may not have been set by the individual involved. As Raelin (2004) argues, in many cases the provider of LMD is usually working from a 'list . . . of what attributes it takes to be a good leader' (p. 131). In contrast, he suggests the use of *work-based learning* (WBL) which focuses on the actions and tasks that form a manager's practice while simultaneously allowing for the questioning of the assumptions relating to practice and making the recognition of new thoughts and ideas deliberate. Where the focus of attention is a specific action or practice, we might refer to this as *practice-based learning* (PBL). Both terms are used when there is a deliberate attempt by managers to combine their work with learning.

WBL and PBL occur most commonly when managers are faced with problems, difficulties and situations that are perceived as new or different. As argued by Davies and Easterby-Smith (1983, p.180):

> Managers develop primarily through confrontations with novel situations and problems where their existing repertoire of behaviours is inadequate and where they have to develop new ways of dealing with these situations.

Problems and difficulties relating to work can be particularly motivational for learning and even allow consideration of theories which become relevant. WBL then allows the combination or blending of theory with actions (Raelin 1997). In recent years there has been a growing trend to provide accreditation for WBL programmes for managers. Boud and Solomon (2001) suggest that WBL qualifications are characterised by such factors as:

- a learner-centred and managed curriculum
- recognition of learning already possessed by individuals
- design in partnership with the learner and sponsoring organisations
- a focus on work-based projects which are significant for the learner, the academic institution and the organisation.

Of course, WBL programmes that are accredited by universities have to conform to quality-assurance requirements, and this can create tensions with the need for clarity and certainty that characterise traditional programmes based on particular inputs that are deemed a requirement for managers to know or do. Nevertheless, there are some good examples of WBL programmes now operating for managers.

 WEB LINK

Go to **http://www.mdx.ac.uk/wbl/index.asp** for the homepage of the Institute of Work-Based Learning at Middlesex University. WBL projects can be continued up to doctorate level. For an example go to **http://www.mdx.ac.uk/wbl/business/value.asp** .

Rounce *et al* (2007) provide an example of an approach to developing leadership for senior health and social care professionals through WBL, and the tensions and difficulties involved. The programme involved a partnership between different universities and other stakeholders, each with their own view of the possible content of the programme – their own 'list'. However, eventually, the key ideas of WBL were asserted that more attention needed to be given to the work of participants and the context in which they worked. Participants completed work-based projects which were also submitted for accreditation. Thus there were benefits to the workplace, including patients in hospitals, although interestingly – and an issue we consider below – some participants were not always able to specify the benefits. The blending of practice with theories provided 'rigour' and 'focus' which 'added value to the finished work' (p.221).

Projects or written assignments are common features of blending in WBL. To initiate such a process, there needs to be a process to allow managers to explore the particular features of their practice that they wish to attend to. The explicit intention in WBL is to allow managers to identify an aspect of their work they see as important and in need of attention. This becomes the focus for analysis, which initially results in an articulation and declaration of the crucial questions that require attention and a prioritisation of these questions that need an answer. Posing questions forms the basis of a 'learning contract' which also specifies the actions that must be taken to answer questions, the resources and timings, and crucially, how findings will be reviewed and assessed (see Knowles 1986).

As you might recognise, this process has some resonance with Kolb's learning cycle but with more attention given to identifying a problem of interest and importance to managers. Indeed, an important contribution by Kolb (1982) was to combine his experiential theory of learning with problem management. As he suggested (p.110), the primary skill

> is the ability to manage the problem-solving process in such a way that important problems are identified and solutions of high quality are found and carried out with the full commitment of organisation members.

What is particularly interesting about this view is that it gives attention to different aspects of a task. Managers face problems of varying degrees of difficulty, but depending on how the task is understood, they need to consider:

- finding and defining problems
- analysing and understanding the possible causes
- deciding on appropriate solutions
- working with others to plan and implement actions
- using the results to decide the next steps.

One important aspect of this view is that managers may focus on solving problems at the expense of finding the right problems. Schön (1983) also focused on the importance of 'problem-setting', which he saw (p.40) as a process in which, interactively (along with everyone who must solve it), we name the things to which we will attend and frame the context in which we will attend to them.

Kolb claimed that the skills for problem management can be shown in relation to the phases of his learning cycle, as we showed in Chapter 6 (Figure 6.4). As Kolb explained, these cycles provide managers with a normative process, and where there was ineffectiveness in managing problems, it could be due to constraints in the organisation context or skill limitations and particular habits. For example, a low preference towards the Concrete Experience stage of the cycle could also mean a failure to give full attention to problem-setting. Alternatively, a stronger orientation towards Abstract Conceptualisation could lead to a focus on solutions rather than problem-setting and problem analysis.

Mumford (1997) also saw a connection between dealing with the reality of tasks and the learning cycle. So we could say that leading and managing is learning, linked conceptually and practically through the learning cycle cast as a task cycle, as shown in Figure 7.1.

Figure 7.1 Task and learning cycles

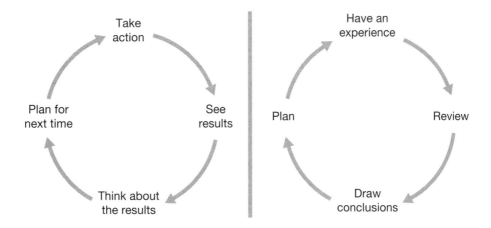

Source: adapted from Mumford (1997)

The combination of the two cycles can encourage managers to see that when asked to work through a task, they can also relate it to how they learn and their preferences for learning. Managers can give consciousness to both learning and working on a task. This becomes especially meaningful when facing problems. The *LMD in Practice* overleaf is based on a manager who set a learning contract and then used the learning and task cycles to work with problems over a three-week period.

The combination of approaches to learning and tasks faced, especially current problems, can be a very powerful way to help managers begin and continue

TASK AND LEARNING CYCLES IN OPERATION

I went through the learning cycle many times, each time arriving back at another problem having solved one. I was very aware that as I progressed over the three weeks, one does not go around the cycle before another problem appears. More problems can arise when reflecting and conceptualising. I learnt that provided I completed the cycle with each problem, it was possible to deal with more than one problem at once. One problem or learning opportunity cannot be kept separate from others, as Mintzberg suggested when he talked about the variety of tasks completed by a manager in a day. I was constantly dealing with a variety of problems and using different skills and learning styles to deal with them.

7.1 REFLECT – CONCLUDE – PLAN

What is your reaction to the example above?

How can you learn better from your everyday tasks?

What help will you need to do that?

a process of LMD. Many managers may not see the value of academic and theoretical views of their work, but they do appreciate help with their difficulties. Gold and Holman (2001) provide an example where learning was still prominent for a group of managers, although they preferred not to use a model of learning styles. Instead, they posed simple questions relating to a manager's preferences in relation to a work problem. This helped managers explore the meanings that they held about the situation and the particular value-orientations they held. Through talk and challenge, managers could consider new possibilities for action in work, through which they could continue this process. As we explain below, a vital aspect of this or any other LMD process that combines work and learning is the importance given to reflection as a way of both reviewing actions taken and generating new ideas, but also critiquing assumptions that underpin practice.

PRACTICE AND KNOWLEDGE

While WBL considers the broad range of possible approaches to combining work and learning, there is also considerable interest in the way managers can learn from their work practice, or PBL. As managers engage in practice, they are able to draw on ways of knowing that enable them to complete tasks, successfully or otherwise. Here it is customary to distinguish between two forms of knowing, first highlighted by Ryle (1949/84):

- 'knowing what' – concerned with conceptual and abstraction that can be made explicit and communicable, based on facts and explanations
- 'knowing how' – personal, based on knowing what to do according to the requirements of a situation.

The former is easily understood as knowledge because it is usually explicit and codified, found in theories and explanations appearing in books, journals, papers and through search engines on the Internet. Such knowledge forms the content of the key ideas for practice of any area of professional expertise, such as being a doctor, engineer, and so on – although, as we suggested in Chapter 1, there are disputes about whether managers are professionals. Nevertheless, there is a strong body of knowledge which is available for those who wish to become managers. 'Knowing what' is a form of knowledge that is highly valued in our society, and acquiring qualifications is a mark of having 'got' the necessary knowledge. However, it is recognised that 'knowing what' is insufficient and has to be combined with 'knowing how', which is knowing that is developed over years of practice, usually naturally, but very necessary for practice. By contrast, such knowledge is tacit and according to Polanyi (1967) 'cannot be put into words' (p.6) or can only be done so with difficulty. For example, consider how you know a face in the distance within a large crowd. However, tacit knowledge is widely recognised as vital for expert practice (Dreyfus and Dreyfus 1986), and as the source of new ideas, new insights and new ways of working which can be integrated into practice. The term 'tacit knowledge' remains ambiguous and, as suggested by Beckett and Hager (2002), can have several meanings ranging from knowledge that cannot be put into words to knowledge that can be explained with difficulty or the secrets of those with craft skills or intuitions. Collins (2001), who studied the work of scientists, identified some additional types of tacit knowledge such as 'ostensive knowledge', concerned with conveying information by direct pointing or demonstrating or feeling, and 'unrecognised knowledge', concerned with habits passed on without recognising how important these are.

7.2 REFLECT – CONCLUDE – PLAN

What kind of tacit knowing are you using when reading this question?

How can you consider tacit knowing in any other work practice?

What knowledge that emerges from your practice might be shared with others?

A key point to consider is that some tacit knowledge can be expressed and shared through talk, stories and conversations with others, even though it still might be recognised officially as knowledge. This sharing of knowledge lies at the heart of situated learning theory and the development of *communities of practice* (Lave and Wenger 1991). The sharing process is situated in the practice of work in a particular context but is often concerned with what works and what is effective.

WEB LINK

Find out more about Michael Polanyi and tacit knowledge at **http://www. infed.org/thinkers/ polanyi.htm** . Also go to **http://www.cardiff.ac.uk/ socsi/contactsandpeople/harrycollins/ expertise-project/expertise.html** for Harry Collins' site on expertise. From here you can read more about what he calls 'beer-mat knowledge' and his Periodic Table of Expertise.

The importance of tacit knowing as managers (and others) engage in practice is also recognised in various models that seek to link individual learning with collective learning by groups or whole organisations. For example, Crossan *et al* (1999) suggest a model of organisation learning (OL) involving four processes of creating and applying knowledge. Their '4-Is model' involves:

- intuiting – individuals see patterns in their experience which provide new insights

- interpreting – individuals explain their insights to themselves and then others

- integrating – the group shares in the understanding and takes action

- institutionalising – the learning at individual and group levels becomes organisational through 'systems, structures, procedures and strategy' (p.525).

Although these may appear to be stages or even a complete cycle of learning, it is accepted that power and politics can influence the moves from one process to another (Lawrence *et al* 2005). For example, new ideas from intuiting may not be accepted for interpretation. Indeed, there may be traditions and preferences for what is acceptable for consideration. Managers need to develop skills to influence others and understand the values within the different contexts and cultures of any organisation.

Nonaka *et al* (2000) provide another model of OL for knowledge creation which is presented as a spiral of knowing that passes through conversion modes. These make up the SECI model, which again begins with sharing tacit knowledge:

- Socialisation – tacit knowledge of individuals shared with others

- Externalisation – conversion of tacit knowledge into explicit metaphors, analogies, concepts and models

- Combination – new knowledge is combined with existing knowledge

- Internalisation – whatever emerges from combination is enacted and becomes part of behaviour and accepted.

Context can enable or inhibit the conversions, and this is conceptualised by Nonaka *et al* as a context of shared space for knowledge creation which they refer to as 'Ba'. Such space can be physical such as an office, or virtual such as email or wiki, or even mental through the sharing of experiences.

Models of OL which take a collective view of learning and knowledge do tend to assume a unified single version of life at work – an assumption that creates

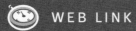

WEB LINK

Find out more about the concept of 'Ba' at **http://www.polia-consulting.com/A-Japanese-approach-of-KM-the-Ba.html** .

comfort for many managers. However, as the idea of communities of practice reminds us, it is work practice that is the source of knowing and of the creation of knowledge, and this occurs locally in a specific context. There is a need for a practice-based understanding of how this occurs (Nicolini *et al* 2003), which brings us back to PBL for managers.

OPPORTUNITIES FOR PRACTICE-BASED LEARNING

Spender (2008) sees an important connection between knowledge creation and learning through the idea of *knowledge-as-practice* which, he argues, is a good way to consider difficulties, failures or simply 'not-knowing or knowledge-absence' (p.166). Recognition of this can trigger a search for new opportunities, and since managers often have to work with difficult issues or where they are likely to make mistakes, such opportunities are likely to occur frequently. Weick (1995) distinguishes between problems and difficulties which are fairly structured and easily solved and problems of equivocality where there are different views about what is happening in a situation such that no single solution is likely to be successful. Similarly Rittell and Webber (1973) provide a typology of problems. Firstly, there are tame problems, which may be complicated but are resolvable probably because they have happened before, so it is a question of finding a solution from existing knowledge. Managers must have a process to do this. Then there are wicked problems, which are complex and do not have a clear solution and existing knowledge is insufficient. There may not be a solution as such and the problem could become intractable with no right answer. The process needed is to understand the problem better by asking good questions – something that is very much at the heart of LMD activity called Action Learning (see below). Managers face many problems of equivocality or wicked problems, such as how to manage employees with different goals and expectations, building teams with different cultural backgrounds, and planning for changes that might include making acquisitions, the relocation of production facilities, re-engineering work design, and so on. One consequence of attempting to treat wicked problems as if they were tame and structured problems is that managers will make mistakes. Because mistakes are such an inevitable feature of the complex changing world, it is certainly the case that there are plenty of mistakes which provide opportunities to learn. It is a weakness of research in LMD that so little has been written about what and how individuals learn from difficulty. However, we would suggest that difficulties represent superb opportunities to engage in PBL, with a special emphasis on reflection and learning to learn.

WEB LINK

Karl Weick's answer for managers facing difficulties was 'Complicate yourself'. Read more at **http://www.wired.com/wired/archive/4.04/ Weick_pr.html** .

Because managers are usually considered by others as knowledgeable and expert, they are often called upon to make on-the-spot decisions and take action. There is little time for careful deliberation, and Beckett (2000) nicely refers to such moments as 'hot' actions (p.42). At such moments of practice, there will always be some degree of uncertainty and a feeling of 'going into the unknown', so a risk is being taken. It is at the moment of enactment that managers may recognise what is being achieved and whether the action has been successful. They are able to catch a glimpse of some aspect of tacit knowing that they are able now to speak about, and it is through the speaking that new understanding becomes articulated. Of course, things may not proceed as expected. So they begin to come under pressure (Beckett and Hager 2002), but because managers are still expected to perform, they will find ways of adapting and adjusting in order to keep going. This provides an extended opportunity for seeing new ways of acting which, through talk and other means, can be shared with others.

Managers can become proactive about finding opportunities for LMD as part of their everyday experience. Honey and Mumford (1996) use the term 'opportunist learner' to describe the individual who recognises and uses opportunities to learn from the wide variety of activities in which that individual is engaged. Table 7.1 shows some of the opportunities.

Research by McCall *et al* (1988) in the United States, obtained by interviewing 191 managers, attests to the importance of 'lessons of experience' based on opportunities, although mostly such lessons were not set up as development experiences in any serious way, nor were they reviewed afterwards as learning experiences. The research noted that line assignments accounted for 60% of experiences, hardships accounted for 20%, and what they called 'notable people' accounted for 20%.

McCall *et al* established five key events as precipitating learning at work. They were:

- participation in projects or task forces
- switching job from line to staff
- starting from scratch – eg a new plant or function
- turning jobs around
- taking a leap in a job to something broader or very different.

Mumford (1988) found that managers described the same kind of experiences, but it was only during the interviews completed for research that the questions they were asked were in many ways those that should have been asked of them

Table 7.1 Learning opportunities for managers

Situations within the organisation	Situations outside the organisation	Walking the floor
meetings	voluntary work	virtual visits
tasks, familiar	domestic life	visioning
tasks, unfamiliar	industry committees	strategic planning
task force	professional meetings	problem diagnosis
customer visit	sports club	decision-making
visit to plant/office	processes	selling
managing change	coaching	**People**
social occasions	counselling	senior managers
foreign travel	listening	mentor
acquisitions and mergers	modelling	staff
closing something down	problem-solving	network contacts
	observing	peers
	questioning	consultants
	reading	family and friends
	negotiating	
	mentoring	
	public speaking	
	reviewing/auditing	
	clarifying responsibilities	

at or immediately after the time at which they had the experience. Some, indeed, made an action note about what they should now do in relation to their own future experiences. Kempster (2009a) found a similar pattern among 30 managers from small businesses, third-sector organisations and large private organisations. In fact it appears that little has changed since the research in the 1980s – that is, there is little awareness by managers of what they have learned until the interview by the researcher prompts a retrospective consideration which provides some clarity of what they have done and where they are going.

Kempster during his interviews also found useful data on the way managers learned under the influence of 'notable people', as described by McCall *et al* (1988). Learning by observing the practice of others is a recognised factor of Social Learning Theory as presented by Albert Bandura (1986). By observing others, especially experts (Raelin 2007), we gain ideas of what can be done which provide guidance for action when required. Such others therefore provide a form of modelling or vicarious learning for managers which enables them to work out how to avoid mistakes in their own practice because they have spent some time considering how to perform. Managers learn from models and in turn act as models for others, but usually without awareness (Manz and Sims 1981). In his research, Kempster (2009a) found that managers could identify the influence of others on their practice where they gave more importance to the ideas of leadership and management. For example, small business managers gave less importance to such ideas in contrast to those employed by others, and this diminished the influence of others on their practice as managers, although they did recognise the influence of others such as their families on what they did.

7.3 REFLECT – CONCLUDE – PLAN

Think back over the last five years. Who has had the most influence on your learning? How did you learn from them?

Which 'notable others' would you currently consider for helping you to learn?

What can you do to enable this?

The case for converting these experiences from incidental learning into something more deliberate is that an additional benefit is drawn from something which is occurring anyway – a bonus with no substantial cost.

Consider the following example of informal, accidental learning:

> I was a shift manager on a new production line in our plant. The line involved quite a bit of new technology and we had a number of problems with it. My immediate manager was a very ingenious guy with an engineering background. Every problem that came up he seemed to have an answer for, but the problems kept coming up. His boss, the production director, called all three shift managers and our manager to his office. He had two flipcharts. One he marked 'Problems'; the other he divided into two columns, 'Causes apparent' and 'Causes deeper?' After 40 minutes with him we did not come out with a single answer, whereas five minutes with our manager always produced an answer. The difference was that we came out with the questions we needed to pursue in order to produce really effective answers. I learned two things – one was about looking deeper into problems, and the other was about how to make the best use of the intelligence of five people working together.

Examples like this are just the tip of a very large iceberg with so much under the surface not seen but present and yet to be discovered. The informal and accidental learning involved in the case mentioned above could have been enhanced by either seeing in advance what kind of learning possibilities were contained within the experience (prospective learning) or looking at the experiences afterwards (retrospective learning). Effective LMD arises from using either or both of the retrospective and prospective ways of learning more frequently and more effectively. A crucial part of effective learning from projects, for example, is to construct a method in setting up and reviewing the projects which emphasises questions about what has been learned during and at the end of them. In addition, of course, there has to be a supportive learning environment around those attempting to learn from informal opportunities.

SUPPORT FOR AND BARRIERS TO PRACTICE-BASED LEARNING

Managers always practise within a context which provides a rich source of everyday possibilities for learning. Marsick and Watkins (2001) have provided a model for using such possibilities, shown as Figure 7.2.

Figure 7.2 A model for informal and incidental learning

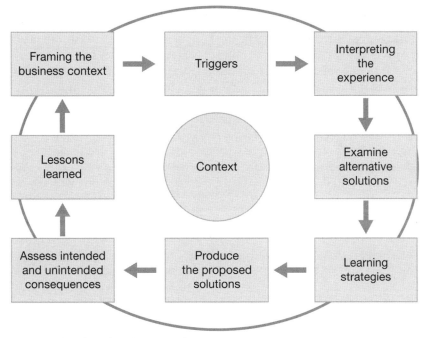

Source: Marsick and Watkins (2001, p.29)

The model shows how learning begins with some kind of trigger, perhaps in the form of a challenge, a problem or a surprise. Such triggers might also be provided by more formal LMD events such as a seminar or outdoor programme. However, the crucial feature is the way such experiences are interpreted to create sufficient dissatisfaction to require some kind of further examination and assessment. Such interpretations will depend on the learning orientation of managers (Nevis *et al* 1995), a social-psychological mechanism which accounts for how experience is evaluated, what is accepted or rejected and what action is taken. It is important to stress how learning orientation is supported (or not) by organisation structure, strategy, resources, processes and the attitudes of others, including managers. These are all aspects of an organisation's learning climate (see below and Chapter 8). Thus, as Marsick and Watkins (2001) suggest, progress is unlikely to proceed smoothly as a sequence but rather as 'ebb and flow' (p.29).

A key feature of support will be the working of relationships (Marsick 2009) and there are usually a significant number of people who can help individuals with their development (see Chapter 9). A fundamental feature of such support necessary for PBL is, as we have emphasised throughout, that individuals should have been encouraged through some structured learning-to-learn process to understand *how* they learn. The concepts we advanced above relating, for example, to the close association between the problem management/task cycle and the learning cycle is particularly relevant, as are situated learning theory and Vygotsky's socio-cultural theory.

However, even without support individuals can often create their own learning, taking responsibility to continue learning at work. The ideas involved in self-development (see below) certainly help with this, and whatever the formal support given to them as learners by their organisations, individuals can take their own initiatives in creating learning opportunities. If they can do so, we can also introduce here the more sophisticated version of the learning cycle – the learning spiral (see Figure 7.3). PBL is more likely to involve the learning spiral, which emphasises that as you go through continuous pieces of work – for example, a project – the learning you have secured at one stage is developed and employed and further reviewed at a later stage. One of the important aspects of this, which we will pick up again in Chapter 9 on helpers, is that those involved in helping other individuals to learn not only help to structure the experience but to assist learners in dealing perhaps with those aspects of learning with which those individuals are least comfortable – quite often, for example, by encouraging more reflection.

Figure 7.3 The learning spiral

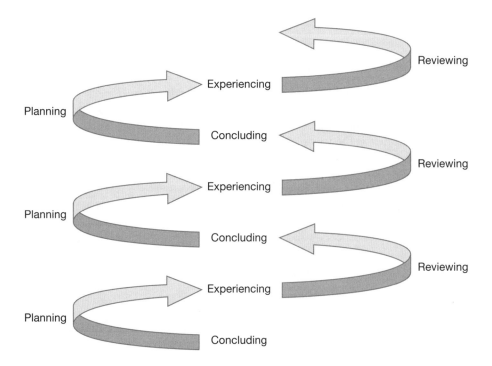

7.4 REFLECT — CONCLUDE — PLAN

Identify a learning experience you would categorise as informal.

What do you think you learned from that experience at the time? Do you think you could have learned more?

How might you convert the experience into something more deliberative?

What steps might you take to turn single-event learning into a learning spiral?

The defining feature that makes PBL more deliberate is obviously that it may be envisaged beforehand as a learning opportunity, and is certainly reviewed during and after the experience as learning. As the research suggested earlier, managers did not realise fully at the time what they learned – it is only in subsequent discussion that more learning has been identified and perhaps therefore used. In addition, learning which is used impacts on context and usually requires sharing knowledge with others – just as the proposition that feedback is important as a crucial aspect of individual improvement is similarly difficult in implementation. Dixon (1998) helpfully reviews many of the crucial issues around sharing, presenting both her own ideas and their association with those of others such as Argyris (1982, 1991; defensive routines) and Mezirow (1990; critical reflection). In her view, dialogue is a means for the co-creation of meaning: 'Each individual has internalised the perspectives of others and thus is enriched by a sense of whole' (p.10). While sceptical about the extent to which such exchanges are transferred from courses to real work, she identifies for example Action Learning (see below) as one of the ways in which sharing is designed and encouraged.

There may be personal or organisational barriers to effectively combining work and learning:

- The apparent naturalness of learning through practice can lead to some impatience with efforts to make it a more disciplined process through deliberation.

- While the work itself creates a huge variety of opportunities, the recognition of them or the motivational need to learn from them may be strong or weak in relation to any particular opportunity.

- It is fundamental to the leadership and management of any organisation that managers learn from mistakes. Unfortunately, this learning may be inhibited by personal or organisational constraints on identifying what has gone wrong. Nor are the lessons always accurately drawn, perhaps because of a failure to analyse a problem, its context and the actions taken to overcome it with sufficient rigour.

Clearly, it is important for managers to recognise such difficulties and to confront them as part of a process of learning.

Several of the possible barriers come from what is often referred to as 'the learning environment or climate'. Fuller and Unwin (2003), for example, refer to the idea of a learning environment which can be considered as a continuum from expansive to restrictive, where expansive environments are characterised by access to learning and qualifications, career progression, the valuing of skills and knowledge, and crucially, managers as facilitators. Temporal (1978, p.95) referred to the learning climate as a 'collection of variables – physical and psycho-social – subjectively perceived by managers'. The important feature of such variables is that they can prevent managers from learning. Physical barriers to learning occur in the work that a manager is required to do. Paradoxically, a major barrier to combining work and learning is precisely the strength of learning from real work activities. If the task is the priority, it often overwhelms the necessary disciplines such as allocating time to the consideration of the learning that could be or has been achieved. An associated element is the fact that managers idenitfy themselves through their work roles, and often do not like being described orally in associated literature as 'learners'. Other barriers come from the overall structure of the organisation and the way that tasks are allocated. Managers will also feel limited where the pace of activity and time-scales for planning and delivery are intensified. Of course, the actual physical setting of work may prevent deliberate learning.

A second set of variables form psycho-social barriers to learning. These arise from a prevailing culture in which the particular relationships that managers are a part of prevent learning or only support a particular kind of learning. They may experience negative attitudes and the exertion of influence which prevents new ideas from being tested – 'You can't do that here!' (Honey and Mumford 1996).

 WEB LINK

Try the Campaign for Learning's quiz at **http://www.campaign-for-learning.org.uk/law_survey/law_survey.asp** .

Variables that form the learning climate will influence and interact with a manager's own barriers to or prejudices for learning. Such internal barriers have been classified by Temporal (1978) as:

- *perceptual* – managers cannot see problems or recognise what is happening in a situation, and have a limited view of learning possibilities
- *cultural* – managers cut themselves off from possible LMD activities by a set of norms and values which have been internalised, regarding what is right/wrong, possible/not possible, and so on
- *emotional-motivational* – managers feel insecure and become reluctant to try new behaviours. They may avoid MD situations where they feel threatened
- *expressive* – managers have poor listening, speaking or presentation skills. They may avoid participating in group activities.

Unhelpful emotions may particularly inhibit learning. While emotion can be a positive factor that leads to people pursuing something worthwhile and feeling good about the pursuit, undoubtedly for some managers in some situations emotion massively inhibits learning. Although learning can be stimulated by challenges and difficulties, those same situational aspects may inhibit learning where they promote anxiety. Emotion is specific to the moment, and can therefore be a significant inhibition on learning from precisely those specific and of-the-moment work activities which in principle provide learning. Emotion can be created by an individual's general anxiety level, fear about what he or she does not know and the implications of not knowing, and past negative experiences of learning. Snell (1988) described both some emotional aspects and, still more helpfully, how to try to reduce the pain and/or discomfort involved. Vince (2002) found that even in events designed to promote learning it is possible for emotion to provide a block and become embedded within political processes that affect the learning climate. Fineman (1997) argued that working life is inevitably emotional, and that learning to be a manager requires the acquisition of an emotional literacy. Managers as learners also have emotions, and clearly the recent interest in emotional intelligence for managers is concerned with enabling abilities to identify, understand, use and manage emotions in self and others (Mayer and Salovey 1997) (see Chapter 3).

What becomes apparent when we consider both the variables of the learning environment or climate and these internal barriers, is that any desired form of LMD must contain within it the possibility of overcoming barriers to learning. Failure to do so threatens the effectiveness of LMD.

EFFECTIVE LEARNING FROM REFLECTION

The availability of opportunities for LMD both at work and beyond, including the everyday difficulties faced and mistakes made, can only become deliberate sources of learning if some process of review and reflection is undertaken. As argued by Sadler-Smith (2006), both action and reflection are ways by which managers 'can engage more directly and effectively with their worlds' (p.185). In many organisations, the issue is whether and how people are encouraged to learn from difficulties and mistakes. Significantly, we know from experience that managers face problems on a daily basis and often these problems are solved by quick responses. Solving problems is expected by others, so it is a requirement that a solution is provided, but this will depend on how managers analyse the situation (Grint 2005). Managers, even those considered expert, can be caught out by a short-sighted view of problems based on past experience, failing to see the complexity or ambiguity of the situation. In such cases they need to 'consider their ignorance' (Chia and Morgan 1996, p.41), challenging their understanding of the world and of how such understanding was formed, and be helped to consider new possibilities. This requires a degree of critical reflection, as we suggested in Chapter 5.

If difficulties and mistakes are to provide opportunities for effective learning, a crucial contribution must be made through structured reflection on experience –

7.5 REFLECT – CONCLUDE – PLAN

Do you agree that effective learning from mistakes and difficulty is an important issue in LMD?

Look at your own experiences and those of other people. What do you think have been the constraints on learning from these events?

How do you think this learning can be improved through action taken by yourself or by others?

and an important issue is the extent to which reviews are conducted to encourage critical reflection as described by Mezirow (1990) or by Argyris in encouraging double-loop learning and the avoidance of defensive routines (1982, 1991). As we saw above, managers have internal barriers, and such barriers – which affect learning preferences and approaches to the dealing with problems – are underpinned by a manager's meaning perspective combined with a range of organisational and work factors. Reflection therefore provides an opportunity for consideration of what happened in events but also for surfacing attitudes and meaning perspectives to reveal assumptions. The latter process is the start of a self-questioning process by managers referred to as reflexivity (Cunliffe and Jun 2005). The potential here is for managers to test the validity of assumptions, and gain insight and understanding about their actions and the nature of the problems and difficulties faced. They can become aware of limitations and open to new and alternative perspectives.

A learning review provides for the construction or reconstruction of meaning from an experience. It achieves this through a process of recording, recall and reasoning. It is a process of reflection: 'the process of stepping back from an experience to ponder carefully and persistently its meaning to the self through the development of inferences' (Daudelin 1996, p.38). It is a method of facilitating LMD that is:

- conscious

- structured

- planned.

There are a variety of ways of reflecting on experience such as sitting and thinking about events, going for a jog or just talking with others. However, we feel that a more deliberate approach is required and that a review should be written because writing is a way of bringing past events into present consideration but with a detachment from speaking. This allows for the possibility of interpretation and reconsidered understanding (Gold *et al* 2007). One well-known method of reflection is the completion of a learning log. It is a written record designed to facilitate the learning review. Its purpose is:

- to record or capture experience of events

- to encourage managers to think about what has been recorded

- to encourage managers to decide what the experience has meant to them
- to enable managers to consider how to move from understanding to action.

Thus, as with many diaries, the prime intention may be simply to record, but from a learning point of view this is an unhelpfully restricted purpose. Many managers will be more persuaded to keep a learning log if it is directed at least partly at identifying reasons for what has been recorded, and possibilities for further action. The learning log may exist in handwritten, PC or laptop form.

Learning logs are also a form of story-telling, and Gold *et al* (2002) suggest that managers can become critical reflectors by recording their experiences in the form of stories which make use of a managers' abilities to think in narrative terms. Polkinghorne (1997) argues that narrative is an important way experience is made meaningful. By writing out stories of important events, including difficult situations or mistakes, managers can re-present the complexity of their work, including the views and actions of different characters, connected by a plot into a whole. Stories are a primary means by which managers can make sense of reality; they can also be a resource for talking over and making sense of what is happening with others (Weick 2005). An important aspect of any story, told from a personal point of view, is the beliefs and values presented. For managers to understand these for further critique, Gold *et al* used argument analysis based on the work of Toulmin (1958). After writing a story of an experience, particular claims can be identified and evidence sought to support the claims.

WEB LINK

You can find out more about the growing interest in story-telling on the Internet. Try the Society for Story-telling at **http://www.sfs.org.uk** . David Boje's fascinating study of story-telling in organisations can be found at his own website, **http://web.nmsu.edu/~dboje/** . The following site gives details of the Toulmin method of analysing arguments: **http://www-rohan.sdsu. edu/~digger/305/toulmin_model.htm** .

Learning logs and story-telling can both be used to develop the skill of *meta-reflection* whereby managers are able to understand key patterns and themes of behaviour that occur over time so that areas for improvement can be identified along with new opportunities for LMD. One such process is to chart a number of logs or stories on a single side of A3 paper, as shown in Figure 7.4.

This particular chart is based on stages of the learning cycle, showing how events are linked together through a number of learning logs with patterns, themes and insights emerging as further reflection occurs by completing the chart. These appear in the top left corner of the chart. This can also include any assumptions made which can be checked for validity. The bottom right corner shows possible development needs. The richness of the process is based on the number of logs made, which allows more themes to emerge. What is also important is that individual managers maintain control over the whole process – it can thereby

Figure 7.4 A learning chart

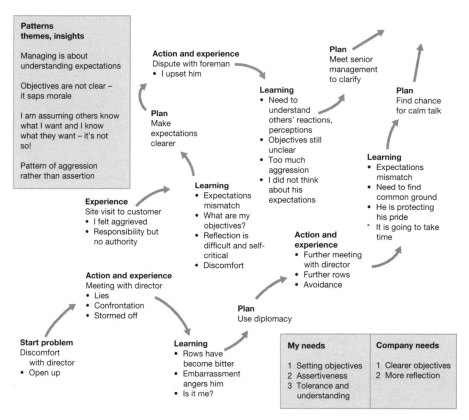

add to their self-development (see below), but learning can also be shared with others.

An interesting development in recent years is the movement of reflection from its usual place as an individual activity towards a shared or collective process. According to Vince and Reynolds (2010), a more organisational view of reflection allows more consideration of the social and political processes. It also allows the generation of knowledge which can be captured and the identification of barriers to learning. They outline a process of 'public reflection' which allows managers to become aware of the consequences of their behaviour, the gap between what they say and do, the biases or prejudices they hold, and in addition allows for the exploration of new activities. In particular, the contextual aspects of power and authority can be made more visible and subject to challenge and negotiation.

WEB LINK

For more ideas about reviewing and reflection, try **http://reviewing.co.uk/** . This is an online active reviewing guide with links, articles, reviews and a lot more.

SELF-DEVELOPMENT

Self-development for managers emerged during the 1970s and 1980s, partly as a response to problems related to management training courses in which providers would determine what managers learned. During such times, the vicious learning sequence that we established in Chapter 5 was especially in evidence. Megginson and Pedler (1992, p.3) see self-development as a process in which 'learners take the primary responsibility for choosing what, when and how to learn'. They also suggest that this implies a certain freedom in choosing what *not* to learn, although this may raise certain tensions with others in the organisation. Self-development has also been seen as part of a wider view of how adults should determine their own needs for learning and taking command of the direction of that learning (Brookfield 1995). In recent years, such ideas have become more prominent as more leaders, managers and professionals are pushed to engage in continuous professional development and take more responsibility for career development (see Chapter 11).

There are many techniques and resources for self-development (Pedler *et al* 2001), but once again there is the issue of whether managers are willing and able to take responsibility. Some of the processes that we have covered in this chapter – such as relating learning to current problems and tasks, reflecting on experiences, surfacing assumptions and revealing patterns of behaviour – can be used to help managers become aware of what they want to learn and how. They can also come to a similar understanding by attending a development centre and using the feedback from other assessment processes where information is used to help them determine LMD needs.

Review and reflection play a crucial role in self-development not simply to analyse experiences and record learning but also to explore the learning process itself. This provides a link to many ideas relating to development, although we prefer to differentiate between qualities of learning and the ability to learn to learn. For example, there is interest in helping managers to learn to think in more complex ways (cognitive complexity – see Streufert and Swezey 1986). This would enable managers to view problems from different perspectives so that different ideas can be considered. They are also able to tolerate ambiguity and less likely to make mistakes in their behaviour. To learn such skills managers need to engage in activities that stretch them beyond their current capabilities (Bartunek and Louis 1989). Stretching tasks can be set by others, or they can find new opportunities, taking a risk and allowing experimentation with new actions. The more difficult the situation faced, the more a manager may need to explore the underlying patterns of belief which Schön and Rein (1994) refer to as a 'frame', or the way a manager perceives reality. Challenging and changing such perceptions (reframing) cannot be imposed although managers can be shocked into new views of their situations and their abilities. However, the prime method for reframing comes where a manager, through critical reflection, finds new meanings and understanding for action.

In recent years, there has been interest in how leaders in particular can embrace honesty by being 'true to oneself' (Harter 2002), show integrity and restore trust from others where it has been lost. This is related to the idea of authenticity in leadership which, according to George (2003), requires leaders to demonstrate passion for their purpose, consistently practise values and lead with hearts by building relationships over and for the long term. Research of over 125 leaders who had a reputation for authenticity and effectiveness found that the crucial factors in their development were learning from their life story and a commitment to self-development by becoming self-aware from experiences (George *et al* 2007). Authentic leaders act on their awareness, sometimes taking risk, but balance their values with the desire for rewards and ensure that they have a strong team based on trust. Recently, Walumbwa *et al* (2008) have sought to use the emerging research to develop an Authentic Leadership Questionnaire which includes a strong recognition of the need for self-development and self-awareness as well as fostering a positive ethical climate.

 WEB LINK

Other approaches for helping managers learn to learn include:

personal construct psychology and the repertory grid at **http://www.brint.com/PCT.htm** and **http://www.repgrid.com/pcp** .

neuro-linguistic programming (NLP) at **http://www.nlpinfo.com** and **http://www.anlp.org** .

Myers-Briggs Type Indicators at **http://www.teamtechnology.co.uk/ myers-briggs-type-indicator-home.html** .

You might also check the Centre for Self-Managed Learning at **http://www.selfmanagedlearning. org** .

LEARNING IN GROUPS AND ACTION LEARNING

Self-development was never meant to be a solo process of learning. Managers always undertake LMD in relation to some context, and this can be made more deliberate by making groups the unit of development. This represents a clear movement from individuals as the focus of LMD towards more collective and distributed configurations (Gronn 2009). We deliberately use the word 'groups' rather than 'teams' because there are groups that are not teams. The situation may be that of direct colleagues working together closely for a specific purpose, who may actually be described as a leadership or management team. Or they may be a collection of individuals brought together to exchange information with no accountability or specific job purpose. Mumford (1997) says that group learning is achieved through 'the three-legged stool' – task, process and learning:

- knowledge, skills and insight gained by and through the task – As an example, a product launch might provide knowledge about customers, skills in carrying out analysis, and insights into how a particular sales message was delivered.

- knowledge, skills and insight gained about the process through which the task was tackled – The group carrying out a task might learn about how different members interacted with each other, how the meetings were managed, how successfully different contributions were taken in and used.

- knowledge, skill and insight about learning gained by participants understanding how they have learned from the task and the process – The group might set up regular and structured processes through which it assesses not only what has been learned from task and process, but how it is going about learning – eg through explicitly following the learning cycle.

There are different ways of looking at the kind of learning achieved. One differentiation is that learning is:

- about self

- about others

- from others

- about the processes of this particular group

- about group processes in general.

Knowledge, skills and insights may be generated in any of these categories.

Another form of analysis would be concerned with different levels of learning. In one form a group might be concerned to generate knowledge of a relatively objective type such as 'What are the different approaches to marketing used by the participants in this group?' In contrast, the group might be concerned with much more risky sharing of knowledge such as 'You never seem to be really interested in anyone else's point of view.' The question of the level at which knowledge is sought, skills are intended to be developed, or insights pursued is crucial. It may be that interpersonal issues are considered not open for discussion. As Argyris (1982) has argued, on individual, group and organisational levels the fact that some issues are not discussed can itself be unmentionable.

7.6 REFLECT – CONCLUDE – PLAN

In what ways have experiences in groups helped or hindered your learning?

What lesson do you draw from those experiences?

What action could you take to improve learning in groups in which you are involved?

Any attempt to combine work and learning is bound to have an impact on others, both positive and negative, but also to require their collaboration. One approach to LMD which makes such collaboration more formal but does not squeeze out the importance of informal and emergent learning is Action Learning (AL). The characteristics of AL were never set out in a single statement by its progenitor, Reg Revans. Indeed, he once wrote that 'The day Action Learning becomes explicable in words alone will be the day to abandon the practice of it' (Revans 1982, p.626). However, a useful definition is provided by Pedler (1996, p.9):

> Action Learning is a method of problem-solving and learning in groups to bring about change for individuals, teams and organisations. It works to build the relationships which help any organisation improve existing operations and learn and innovate for the future.

McLaughlin and Thorpe (1993) argue that AL can be viewed as a philosophy and set of beliefs representing a different 'world view' (p.20) by which managers must take responsibility for their own development (as in self-development). They contrast AL with traditional management education, as shown in Table 7.2.

AL does take a variety of stances and forms, and there is a debate about what is and what is not AL (Simpson and Bourner 2007). AL has been used by groups to tackle a particular project or task, which may be set by others but is defined and directed by the group. There are also examples of Virtual Action Learning making use of Web 2.0 technologies to hold meetings online with messaging used to maintain contact. Mostly, however, AL is concerned with managers who face difficult problems, as we noted earlier – that is, problems that can be called intractable or wicked or equivocal, where the solution is unknown so the manager does not know what to do. It is in such situations that the key elements of AL come into play. As identified by Pedler (2008) these are:

> A *Person* who has a *Problem* which is presented to a *Set* of others to provide challenge and support through questions, leading to *Action* on the problem in a work setting.

A key assumption is that leaders and managers can overcome problems that are important to them by working in a group or 'set' as 'comrades in adversity' (Revans 1982, p.636) who agree to meet over a period of time for three hours or more each time. They agree to help each other by asking questions, discussion, exposure to critical comment and allowing time for reflection and planning action. Managers then work on real tasks and projects, which ensures that action and learning occur in a work context, and through participation in a set and reflection they gain an understanding of power and politics in organisation.

The process is not without risk, and for Revans it was vital that managers understood change in themselves, expressed as the 'principle of insufficient mandate' (p.545):

Table 7.2 Action Learning contrasted with traditional management education

	Traditional management education	Action Learning
World view	There is some notion of correct management practice established through research that defines the curriculum.	The curriculum is defined by the manager or organisation.
	Managers should learn theories and models derived from research.	Managers should join a 'set' tutored by a facilitator, in which each member is in a similar position, where they learn to solve problems, learn management competencies and develop self.
	Self-development is unimportant.	Self-development is very important.
	The world is something to learn about.	The world is somewhere to act and to change.
Practical objective	Management development is *to* the manager.	Management development is *by* the manager.
	Experts are seen as the highest form of knowledge.	Experts are viewed with caution.
	Experts decide what should be learned, when, and how much.	The manager takes responsibility for his/her own development in deciding what to learn, including how and when to stop, and to value what has been learned.
	Management education requires the distillation of approved research and ideas, which people then relate to how they might use them to either do things differently or do different things.	Management education is delivered via self-development in tackling problems with set support to manage change and build management competencies.
	Models, concepts, ideas are provided to offer tools for thinking and action.	Models, concepts, ideas are developed in response to problems.
	Learning is individualist.	Learning is social – 'comrades in adversity'.
Manifestation	Theoretically oriented research.	Practically oriented research.
	It is held that a properly tested theory is able to offer reliable knowledge, which allows situations to be predicted, and ideally brought about. This requires prior knowledge of past models both to test and to use as foundations for new theories.	It is based on the somewhat paradoxical assumption that one of the best ways of understanding issues relating to organisations, people and self as manager is an attempt to change them.

Source: McLaughlin and Thorpe (1993)

> Managers unable to command change in themselves cannot constructively change the conditions in which they command others.

This is interesting and possibly archaic language with respect to the work of managers, but the sense that managers must see a connection between their own learning and change as well as learning and change in others certainly resonates with recent images of managers and the ethical dimension to their work. Invoking Napoleon's well-known aphorism, 'There are no bad soldiers, only bad officers!', Revans (1998) suggested that 'This is a truth ... now crossing the minds of the responsible all around the globe' (p.25).

While Revans (1982) did not employ recognised learning theories, he has made some useful contributions which we see as pragmatic and heuristic explanations for managers who participate in AL. Firstly, there is the key idea of

$$L \geq C,$$

where **L** is learning, and **C** is the rate of change in the environment. Revans' key point is that managers must learn at least as fast as changes in their environment, and failure to do so would lead to trouble.

Secondly, he suggested that learning could best be understood through the following equation:

$$L = P + Q,$$

where **P** is programmed knowledge or answers already available to known problems, and **Q** is questioning insight or the consideration of new possibilities through questions to difficult problems.

Although Revans' prime attention has been to the questioning insight element of the equation through Action Learning, and has occasionally seemed to dismiss the importance of **P**, the equation neatly captures the view that the acquisition of knowledge by itself is likely to be unsatisfactory and certainly unlikely to lead to subsequent action. This equation provides a fascinating question for any method of learning. Is it pure **P** or pure **Q**, or does it combine the two in some form? Certainly, in an age of knowledge, there tends to be an emphasis on what is known and available in codified form. If you need information about air flights or research on air cabin crew behaviour, it would not take too long to access what is available. However, intractable and difficult problems cannot rely on such knowledge, and this is where questioning insight becomes valuable. Questions from others in a set in response to presentation of a problem allow the formulation of ideas to be tried at work, and such action can in turn be reviewed and declared as learning, even perhaps presented in a codified form as a new **P**. Others such as Vince (2004) suggest an extension of the formula to:

$$L = P + Q + O,$$

where **O** is organising insight. This suggests that AL needs to consider the effect and implications of action on organisation factors and dynamics. For example, politics and power aspects can hinder action but AL can also play a role in revealing the assumptions that underpin constraints. Recently, there has been interest in developing a more critical approach to AL (Trehan and Pedler 2009) which makes more explicit the tensions, power dynamics, emotions and dominance factors that exist with the set, but also within organisations. Trehan and Rigg (2007), for example, argue that AL can provide a means for collaboration and partnership working such as networks that cross organisation boundaries, all of which require a surfacing of assumptions and a questioning approach to engender dialogue and shared decision-making. The *LMD in Practice* below shows how one organisation created a network of AL sets, with significant results.

ENERGISING FOR ACTION – A HEALTHY OPTION?

Dr Mandy Chivers, *Assistant Chief Executive (Learning & Development), Mersey Care NHS Trust*

Mersey Care NHS Trust, one of three specialist mental health trusts, has taken a radically different approach to organisational and cultural transformation using emergence and Action Learning. Key to this has been the development of a novel new role as Assistant Chief Executive to work outside organisational conventions and managerial arrangements, while having the delegated authority from the Chief Executive.

What started as a conversation between the Chief Executive and a clinical leader who was completing a PhD at the time into 'What makes a good organisation' became a movement and campaign for improvement in mental health care. A belief that Action Learning creates an opportunity to gain a profound understanding of purpose, and acting on that purpose within the context of challenging environments. The World Health Organisation suggests 'Good health is not the absence of disease but a positive concept emphasising personal and social resources, as well as physical, mental and spiritual capacities.' So too organisational health. There is a subtle but vitally important difference between stopping things being bad and helping them to be good. Therefore this wasn't seen as a comfortable option in a difficult world, but rather an intention to shift thinking and encourage behaviours, energy and actions which aspired to more than day-to-day problem-solving. A different kind of conversation and pattern of engagement.

Opportunistically we formed a small group, sharing the author's conversations and experience. The group discovered a common purpose, articulated as our commitment to improve services, to take action and to share our learning. No attempt was made to control this, to determine the agendas or desired outcomes. We simply gave people the opportunity and protected the space to allow them some freedom to think together and then take action.

What happened next was unexpected and unplanned. Over a twelve-month period there was an explosion of interest and activity, radiating outwards from the core group at the centre, resulting in a whole system learning event, a strategy for learning and the development of a handbook to support future sets (see the diagram below).

Corporately, Action Learning has been a significant contributor to the achievement of the organisation. We have moved from 64% to 81% patient satisfaction in five years; we have been described by the Healthcare Commission as the most improved Trust in the country; we have stabilised a service that had had ten chief executives in 11 years, three critical national reports and political proposals to close. We have a national reputation for involving service users and carers, and perhaps as significant as all those material achievements, the sense seven years ago of the 'poverty of expectation' has disappeared.

At the outset we established that Action Learning was *a* strategy and not *the* strategy. There has been a large investment in good-quality conventional management which has created a strong foundation for the Trust. Can we say that we wouldn't have made as much progress without the Action Learning strategy? Certainly – and we can add that in value-for-money terms it is probably the most cost-effective strategy too.

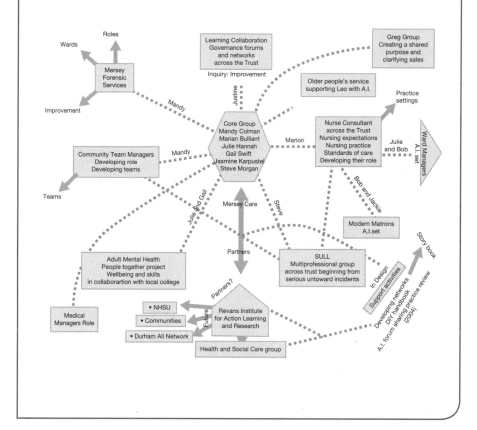

WEB LINK

Go to **http://www.ifal.org.uk/** for the homepage of the International Foundation for Action Learning. Information about the Revans Academy at Manchester University can be found at **http://www.mbs.ac.uk/ research/revans_academy/revans-academy.aspx** . For papers on Action Learning and Action Research, try **http://www.scu.edu.au/schools/ gcm/ar/arp/actlearn.html** .

SUMMARY

- It is the work, the job, the task and its problems that are the prime features for LMD, in contrast to most other approaches where the central feature of the method is the learning content.

- While the work itself creates such a variety of opportunities, managers may or may not learn deliberately from events. Learning may be implicit or reactive instead.

- *Work-based learning* (WBL) is an approach to LMD which broadly focuses on the actions and tasks that form a manager's practice. Where the focus is the specific action or practice, this is referred to as *practice-based-learning* (PBL).

- Managers can use problems in combination with learning preferences to combine work and learning.

- The practice of managers draws on tacit knowledge which is vital for expert practice. Sharing knowledge with others can lead to organisation learning.

- Managers can become proactive about finding opportunities for LMD as part of their everyday experience.

- Learning from difficulties or mistakes provides strong opportunities for development through reflection and learning to learn.

- Although an opportunity to learn is available, there may be personal or organisational barriers to learning effectively through the job.

- A key feature of support will be the working of relationships, and there are usually a significant number of people who can help individuals with their development.

- Structured planning makes it possible to identify learning opportunities – prospective learning must be supported by retrospective learning via learning reviews and reflective techniques such as learning logs and stories.

- Self-development allows managers freedom to choose what and how they learn.

- Action Learning enables managers to work in sets (select groups) on issues of importance to them and to collaborate with others.

QUESTIONS

For discussion

1 What are the key organisational and personal factors that can ensure the effective combination of work and learning for managers?

2 What kind of support in learning and developing at work do leaders and managers need?

3 How can organisational barriers to learning be overcome?

4 *Both self-development and Action Learning are too focused on individual managers*. Discuss.

5 Do managers need to engage in critical reflection? What are the requirements?

6 Do managers need to be 'shocked' into learning to learn? What are the dangers and the prospects?

GROUP ACTIVITY

A leader/manager's place of work and real issues are increasingly being seen as a source of learning. Apart from Action Learning, other approaches include:

- *problem-based learning*
- *Action Research*
- *Action Science*
- *participatory Action Research.*

Get together in a group of four.

Use the Internet and other sources to find more information on each of these approaches to LMD. Pay particular attention to:

- the main features of each approach and how they are incorporated into programmes of learning
- examples of practice and evidence of the effectiveness
- ethical and moral aspects.

Meet to integrate your findings and prepare to report back.

FURTHER READING

BOUD, D. and GARRICK, J. (eds) (1999) *Understanding Learning at Work*. London: Routledge

DAVIES, L. (2008) *Informal Learning*. Aldershot: Gower

GABRIEL, Y. (2000) *Storytelling in Organizations*. Oxford: Oxford University Press

LEE, M. (2003) *HRD in a Complex World*. London: Routledge

MEGGINSON, D. (1996) 'Planned and emergent learning', *Management Learning*, Vol.27, No.4: 411–28

RAELIN, J. (2008) *Work-Based Learning: Bridging knowledge and action in the workplace*. San Francisco, CA: John Wiley & Sons

CHAPTER 8

Evaluating leadership and management development

CHAPTER OUTLINE

Introduction
Meanings, purpose and approach
Systematic and systems models
Holistic models
Transfer of learning
Summary

LEARNING OUTCOMES

After studying this chapter, you should be able to understand, explain, analyse and evaluate:

- the purpose of and various approaches to the evaluation of leadership and management development

- different models of evaluation and ways of collecting evaluation data

- the key factors that influence the transfer of learning

- the role of an organisation's learning climate

INTRODUCTION

At a time when resources for investment in LMD and human resource development (HRD) more generally are bound to be questioned, there needs to be more attention on demonstrating the value that such an investment adds to an organisation's performance. Indeed, there seems to have been a trend to show the value of activities, which one commentator has suggested represents a 'new social epidemic of evaluation' (Preskill 2008, p.179). Nevertheless, it is important that attention is paid to evaluation because if there is competition for resources for investment, those involved in LMD must compete for these resources –

and showing the value of LMD activities is one way of doing this. This makes evaluation very much a political activity (Kim and Cervero 2007). Recently, Anderson (2007) has highlighted the importance of aligning learning processes closely with the strategic priorities of the organisation. Figure 8.1 shows the key links in demonstrating the value of learning processes.

Figure 8.1 The value of learning and evaluation

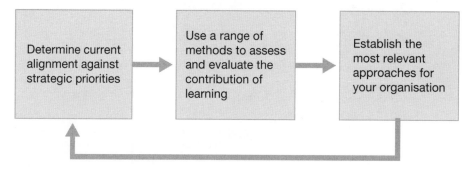

Source: Anderson (2007, p.5)

In some respects the challenge for evaluation of LMD is straightforward – as argued by Thorpe *et al* (2009), we have to learn the lessons of what has worked, and what does not, and apply these lessons now and in the future. However, for LMD specialists and HRD professionals to provide evaluation to meet this challenge remains difficult (Russ-Eft and Preskill 2005). As we saw in Chapter 2, there has been on ongoing concern on whether LMD, in whatever shape or form it is delivered, could be shown to result in an improvement of leadership and management performance. We also suggested that the reasoning behind this view was based on what Garavan *et al* (1999, p.193) referred to as a 'functional performance rationale'. The argument here is that a linear connection between LMD, good managers, their successful performance, success in organisations and, even, national economic success can be proposed and sought. It therefore follows that evaluation must be concerned with proving the validity of claims relating to such a connection. However, it has long been recognised that proving impact as a kind of cause-and-effect relationship is far from easy in LMD (Smith 1993), not least because of the difficulty of isolating the variables that are required to make any claim of a successful link, once managers return to the complexity of their everyday lives. As we also saw in Chapter 7, so much LMD occurs informally and tacitly, which adds further to the challenge of evaluation.

This has not prevented a continuing effort to find the evidence, but more often than not, it can lead organisations to try to evaluate LMD with limited methods based on a general lack of knowledge and understanding about evaluation ideas. The result is that most evaluation is cursory, largely retrospective, and it is left to chance whether LMD activities can be shown to contribute to leadership and management effectiveness and organisation results. In this chapter we attempt to explain why this is so, and to show how – by taking the time to consider key questions relating to the purpose of evaluation and overall approach – it is possible to develop a strategy for evaluating LMD that also considers how it can become a 'prospective' process (Anderson 2010) by contributing to learning for leaders, managers and the organisation as a whole.

MEANINGS, PURPOSE AND APPROACH

A single meaning for the term 'evaluation' is not easy to find. As Weiss (1972, p.1) suggested, evaluation is 'an elastic word that stretches to cover judgements of many kinds'. For example, Hannum *et al* (2006) define 'evaluation' as 'A process of enquiry for collecting and synthesising information and evidence' (p.6), while Goldstein (1993) saw the collection of information as 'necessary to make effective decisions related to the selection, value and modification of various instructional activities' (p.181). One starting point perhaps is the old French word *évaluer* meaning 'to value'. We might therefore suggest that one meaning of 'evaluating' in LMD is concerned with judgements relating to the *value* of particular LMD products and processes. Taken in this way, we can see that evaluating is closely connected with people's view of LMD and the criteria used to make judgements. Since LMD is inevitably the concern of a variety of people with different interests, we can also see that the judgements they make about LMD and the criteria used to form such judgements will strongly influence the value they will seek. This will inevitably affect the purpose of evaluation and the overall approach, including the methods used. Harrison (2005), for example, argues that 'collaboration with key partners' (p.144) is a crucial feature of participation in evaluation.

Placing a value on LMD can occur at different points in time. Valuing may begin before, during and/or after delivery. We can also distinguish between the evaluation of programmes of LMD activities and the evaluation of the activities themselves. This distinction gives rise to a number of other terms relating to evaluation. For example, if we consider the managers who participate in activities, we would expect them to arrive at an event with a set of expectations, sometimes formulated as explicit objectives in terms of what each manager wants to know or do better on completion of the activity. For such managers, what may be important is that those expectations are met, and these set the criteria for judgements of value. Evaluation might therefore be concerned specifically with the extent to which an activity meets the expectations and objectives specified – this is referred to as 'internal validation'. We would also expect providers of LMD activities to be interested in this kind of evaluation, although an immediate issue arises on the extent to which managers do set objectives for their participation and whether these match the objectives set by providers. One particular interest for providers, especially when they are testing a new product or process, is in being able to show that managers achieve particular objectives set. Of course, they would wish to show that such achievement occurs with different managers in a variety of settings, thus demonstrating the reliability and validity of the activity in a systematic or scientific manner.

A chief executive might be interested in internal validation but probably more interested in whether internally valid activities contribute to organisation performance and the various criteria of effectiveness. This requires an answer to the question whether the objectives of LMD activities relate sufficiently to organisation objectives – an aspect of evaluation that is referred to as 'external validation'.

A finance director might take this further. The crucial questions would concern whether LMD activities provided financial benefits for an organisation that were greater than the cost of providing the activities. Evaluation therefore means undertaking a cost benefit analysis so that value-added can be proved, usually in financial terms. This 'return on investment' (ROI) view of evaluation has always been difficult to carry out in most areas of LMD and, more widely, in HRD and is seen as something of a Holy Grail (Russ-Eft and Preskill 2005). It would require some measurement of performance, preferably quantitative and financial, before attending an event or participating in a programme and at various times afterwards too. Where a number of managers participated in the same activities, measurements could be used to show statistically that benefits achieved were due to participating in LMD activities rather than by chance.

Anderson (2007) suggests that organisations need to develop a pattern of measurements or metrics so that evaluation can meet different interests. Her research found there was a need for:

- learning function measures – assessing efficiency and effectiveness of the learning function

- return on expectation measures – assessing the extent to which the anticipated benefits of the learning investment have been realised

- return on investment measures – assessment of the benefits of learning and training interventions compared with the costs incurred

- benchmark and capacity measures – evaluation of HR processes and performance through a comparison with internal or external standards of 'good practice' or 'excellence'.

There may be a desire to consider all such meanings in a single framework, to allow the different interests of leaders, managers and others to be met. The importance of any metrics established is how relevant they are in providing data for showing the value of LMD and other learning activities.

 WEB LINK

Evaluation is a vibrant field of activity and you may be interested to learn more about its theory and broader practice. Try the UK Evaluation Society's page at **http://www.evaluation.org.uk/**, and the American Evaluation Association's, which can be found at **http://www.eval.org/** .

A particularly useful starting point with access to resources and many other sites is the Virtual Library on Evaluation at **http://www.policy-evaluation.org/** .

FORMATIVE AND SUMMATIVE EVALUATION

The various meanings of 'evaluation' have tended to focus on the outcomes of LMD activities. However, we should also consider that such activities involve managers in a learning process, and this will affect their expectations and the value they derive from it. It suggests also that such value can change throughout their participation and that objectives at the start of the process are not the same during the process and on completion of it. Here we could make use of a distinction that is frequently made in education (Tessmer 1993) between 'summative evaluation', which occurs on completion of an activity, and 'formative evaluation', which occurs while the activity is happening either to improve it and/or to enhance the experience of the participants and the value they gain. Similarly, Rackham (1973) made a useful distinction between 'long-cycle' and 'short-cycle' evaluation, in which long-cycle evaluation is concerned with a whole programme whereas short-cycle evaluation is concerned with quick feedback for participants within a programme.

These variations in the meaning of the term 'evaluation' and the presence of different interests make evaluation a complex process since it has to take account of and respond to the different interests and their judgements, which are always value-laden and frequently permeated by organisational politics (Easterby-Smith 1994).

8.1 REFLECT – CONCLUDE – PLAN

What are the meanings of 'evaluation' in your college or organisation?

How do such meanings affect the way evaluation is carried out?

What can you do to make the meaning of evaluation relevant to you?

PURPOSE

A broad distinction can be made between evaluation as a form of research and evaluation as a provider of practical knowledge which can help decision-making. The former is the concern of those who seek to explore and explain social activities to provide generalisable hypotheses, models and theories of the working of particular features of the world. The latter is more concerned with providing information about programmes and activities in response to various interests so that decisions can be made and actions taken. While these two perspectives towards research and the practical lead to differences in methods and approach, there is considerable overlap between them (Clarke 1999). In general, evaluation in LMD is oriented towards the practical perspective, but there are also examples of research-oriented evaluation, many of which are found in the references for this book. For example, Finch-Lees *et al* (2005) completed a study that evaluates competency or capability-based management development (CBMD) based on the issue about concerns about its purpose while at the same time they considered why practitioners of LMD seem to remain committed to using the approach. As we have seen in Chapter 3, there have been ongoing debates about competencies or capabilities for over 20 years. Finch-Lees *et al* sought to explore this apparent tension by taking a more critical stance in order to fill what they saw as gaps in our knowledge by 'analysing CBMD as both an ideology and a quasi-religious discourse' (p.1188). The focus was a UK-based multinational company which employed CBMD in its programmes. A research question was posed for their evaluation – 'Which interests are being served by the company's capability-based approach to management development?' – and data was collected through interviews and documents. A key finding after analysis was that CBMD seemed to be based on assumptions which could not be proved but were nevertheless believed. Such assumptions therefore could be seen as ideological and 'quasi-religiously faith-based' (p.1215) serving interests that could be both productive and repressive. Of course, such a study may or may not be seen as relevant to those using CBMD who might prefer evaluation research to provide useful lessons. For example, practitioner journals such as *People Management* frequently publish case study articles of successful LMD, although you might also question the possible distortions that could be present in the way data is used.

Easterby-Smith (1994) suggests that there are four consistent purposes that can be identified for evaluating LMD. These are:

- proving
- improving
- learning
- controlling.

The first purpose – proving – is probably the most obvious and logical. Evaluation is concerned with showing that a particular outcome has been achieved as a result of LMD activities. The proving purpose also matches conventional wisdom on how evaluation should proceed, informed by models of evaluation that suggest that data can be collected systematically and rigorously as though the impact of LMD activities occurred in a linear fashion. Thus the purpose of proving could be applied at all levels of evaluation and, in theory, provide satisfaction for all stakeholders. However, there may be difficulties in making the necessary links in LMD, especially once the influence of contextual factors of the workplace are taken into account. As argued by Thorpe *et al* (2009), LMD can create conditions where things can change in unknown ways and therefore works through 'generative' causation rather than 'successionist' causation where things are predictable and outcomes are known in advance.

The second purpose – improving – arises partly from some of the difficulties of proving the impact of LMD. In the absence of a definitive link between LMD and, for example, organisational outcomes, it might be argued that the least that should be done is to make sure that evaluation contributes to the improvement of activities.

The purposes of proving and improving provide data that allow decisions to be made about LMD. For example, if a programme proves to meet objectives, it could be repeated, and if it proves not to, information from evaluation might help providers decide how to improve it. The third purpose – learning – however, focuses on how data can be used by managers and others as part of the learning process within LMD events. For example, it is often difficult to specify how climbing a mountain or crossing a river can relate to the work of a manager. But through a process of review, such as completing a learning log or conducting a discussion, managers are able to evaluate the experience and identify key learning points. It is important to stress the focus of learning – that is, that whatever data is generated in reviews, it is part of the process. Possible confusions may arise if such data is also used for other purposes such as proving.

The control purpose of evaluation is a reminder that LMD events seldom take place without some aspect of surveillance, whether in the form of financial control via a budget or the need to show that LMD provision operates within particular boundaries with respect to content and delivery.

There is also another related purpose – influence. Evaluation provides data which can be manipulated to ensure a persuasive portrayal of LMD for particular reasons. For example, a programme might be evaluated in such a way as to ensure the continuation of the programme or used to extend the influence of providers. Thus Kim and Cervero (2007a) show how the evaluation of an LMD programme in a Korean organisation was completed by HRD practitioners by producing a report which eliminated negative comments about the programme in order to enhance their influence in the organisation. This is a reminder that information collected as part of evaluation can be presented as a revelation of real facts or the 'truth' (Clarke 1999).

While the choice of evaluation purpose in LMD is significant, there is frequently a requirement to respond to a variety of different needs, and this may result in a mix of purposes. Easterby-Smith (1994) suggests that purpose can be decided on the grounds of expediency, where an activity is under threat, or by prioritising the interests of stakeholders.

APPROACH

Allied to the purpose of evaluation are issues relating to:

- the approach taken concerning what data is collected
- who it is collected from, when and how
- the analysis and presentation of results
- the evaluation methodology and the strategy adopted to meet the purposes.

Methodology will partly depend on the beliefs held about what happens in LMD and how what is happening can come to be known. There are significant debates relating to evaluation methodology, and at the heart of the debate are questions about what is meant by 'knowledge' and what is a reliable claim to 'know' something.

Two broad approaches to the issue of methodology can be identified:

- positivist methodologies
- phenomenological methodologies.[1]

The two categorisations are underpinned by very different sets of assumptions made about the world and the explanations that can be developed.

To explain the relevance and possibilities for the evaluation of LMD, we will consider methodology in relation to an organisational example. The company in question, a software project management company, was seeking to enhance a 'coaching culture' among managers and team leaders. A programme for 30 managers and team leaders was set up with the overall aim of enhancing managers' coaching skills and the ability of team leaders to improve team performance. The programme ran over 10 weeks with an initial training event, followed by work application and reviews. The evaluation design needed to be rigorous in seeking to prove the effectiveness of the programme but had also to be useful to trainers and participants.

Considering the overall methodology, the key ideas of *positivism* are:

- the world exists externally and objectively
- knowledge of this world can only be based on observation and measurement of its properties.

The first idea is a statement about the reality of LMD, and especially the view of it. As a positivist, you would believe that the activities you wish to understand do exist, and that you can separate them sufficiently from other factors. Thus, the coaching programme would actually take place with real managers and team leaders.

The second idea is based on the view that if LMD activities exist, the only valid way to claim knowledge about their value is to observe and measure. If you cannot do that, how could you claim to know it? For example, to explain the behaviour of coaches and team leaders at work following training, there must be a way of measuring and observing what happens in terms of skills, the application of knowledge and the values of participants. You can believe that managers and team leaders really have values which affect their performance, but how do you know this? Can you observe and measure values?

Positivist evaluation is also closely aligned with what is referred to as 'the scientific method' in research, from which a number of implications for evaluation can be derived:

- The evaluator is independent of what is observed and measured, and his or her values and subjective opinion are held in check.
- Observations and measurements provide knowledge which can be used to produce generalisations about what is happening.
- Generalisations can be used to make claims about cause and effect, anticipate what will happen, and, if necessary, control events.

The important values of rationality and objectivity make a positivist view so attractive in evaluating LMD, particularly the emphasis on seeking data that systematically provides a logical flow of cause and effect – ie to suggest that LMD events lead to particular outcomes. Thus in the coaching programme, an external evaluator sought to find out what was happening both during and after the initial training, with an attempt to measure impact on the performance of participants.

8.2 REFLECT – CONCLUDE – PLAN

Think of a recent learning event you attended. Write out a description of the event, striving to maintain independence as an evaluator.

What do you conclude about maintaining independence in your observations of what happened?

What can you do to enhance accuracy?

Phenomenological methodologies in evaluating LMD are concerned with understanding how a leader or manager's behaviour is formed from meanings held by a manager (and others) in the various situations that he or she faces as part of an LMD event and beyond. In the coaching programme, the starting point of phenomenological evaluation is that managers and team leaders define and interpret what goes on around them and make their own sense of coaching. They use their own interpretations to evaluate the usefulness of coaching in terms of what they consider to be important. Throughout their participation, new interpretations are made, new meanings may be constructed,[2] and the value given to coaching may change. Further, there are likely to be a variety of interpretations, meanings and values for different managers from the same coaching activities. For example, both managers and team leaders will share informal evaluation through anecdotes which show the benefits or otherwise of the experience. The passing on of anecdotes or stories is probably the most common form of evaluation and could significantly affect the success and value given to LMD.

For the evaluator, a consequence of accepting the phenomenological approach is that it is difficult to make generalisations of cause and effect in relation to the coaching programme. Rather, a multiplicity of values exists – there are many voices, including the evaluator's, and what is seen as social reality is a social construction. The way this construction is built up and sustained by managers and team leaders is a legitimate issue for evaluation. Indeed, it is within the ongoing events before, during and after the programme that meanings are made, and actions are carried out and valued. The evaluator can seek to access such meanings to gain a richer understanding of the programme and provide feedback for use by the participants.

The contrasting approaches give rise to a wide variety of evaluation methodologies, models and methods. The sponsors of the coaching programme were happy for an evaluation design which encompassed aspects of both approaches, as shown in Figure 8.2.

In the programme positivist methods are used at various stages for measurement, observation and assessment of impact during and beyond the duration of the programme. Phenomenological methods are used to gain access to the meanings of participants at all stages of the programme, including the formative reviews[3] and the final review which allow learning to be used to enhance action and implementation and to collect qualitative data relating to participants' valuation of the experience.

Figure 8.2 Evaluation design for a coaching programme

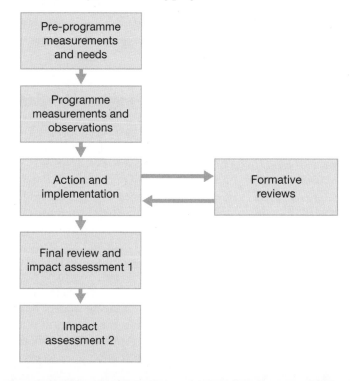

  WEB LINK

The website **http://www.intute.ac.uk/socialsciences/** provides access to Intute: Social Sciences, with information and links to many resources on evaluation methodology and methods.

SYSTEMATIC AND SYSTEMS MODELS

The differing perspectives offered by positivism and phenomenology provide evaluators of LMD with different schools of thought to inform the choice of evaluation models and methods. In the UK, for many years, a systematic model of training and evaluation has been regarded as the orthodoxy. A typical presentation of this model is shown as Figure 8.3.

The four-stage model emphasises the need to evaluate at the conclusion of activities. Data collected can then be analysed and decisions made on the value of the activities and the extent to which the objectives set were valid. This model has become deeply ingrained into the thinking of organisations as a way of proving the effectiveness of activities. Further, the model can incorporate a feedback loop from evaluation back to identifying needs and specifying objectives. Thus, as well as being systematic and logical, the model is also systemic in that feedback provides information about activities so that necessary improvements can be made.

Figure 8.3 A systematic model of training

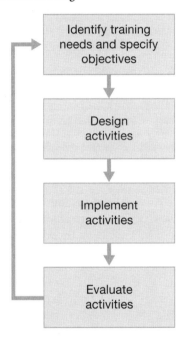

There are some obvious consequences of this model for the evaluation of LMD. Firstly, evaluation appears as the final stage of a process, probably training or some other formal programme. This tends to mean that the evaluation of LMD activities becomes something of a ritual and perhaps an afterthought. Usually it is completed after the close of the 'official' activities with a certain amount of pressure to do it quickly before departing.[4] The favoured technique in such situations is to issue a questionnaire to obtain overall reactions to the activities (a 'reactionnaire') and collect data on enjoyment ('happiness' or just 'happy' sheets). The consequence is that data gathered may be subject to bias and distortion, dependent on the feelings of the group at the time of completion (Smith 1990). Secondly, LMD providers may be able to influence matters so that adverse reactions are screened out or regarded as anomalous. Thus, starting from the premise that 'good activities' are provided, good activities must lead to good experiences for participants and positive evaluation, as shown in the 'happiness' sheets. Negative evaluation can be disregarded.

The restriction of this view of evaluation has long been recognised and has prompted various attempts to adjust the model so that evaluation occurs not just at the end of a course. Kirkpatrick's (1983) model is a well-known approach where evaluation can take place at different stages or levels as shown in Figure 8.4.

Figure 8.4 Evaluation of LMD at different stages

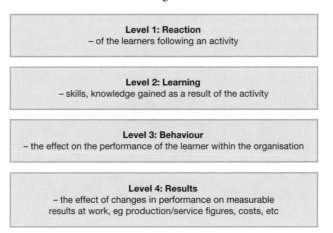

Level 1: Reaction
– of the learners following an activity

Level 2: Learning
– skills, knowledge gained as a result of the activity

Level 3: Behaviour
– the effect on the performance of the learner within the organisation

Level 4: Results
– the effect of changes in performance on measurable results at work, eg production/service figures, costs, etc

Source: adapted from Kirkpatrick (1983)

This model has become the conventional wisdom of evaluation showing how data gathered at different levels can be linked in a chain of consequences (Hamblin 1974). Thus, if evaluation of LMD occurs at the *reactions* level, this can be used to evaluate at the next level of learning. If it can be evaluated that a manager has learned new skills, it might then be possible to evaluate at the next level of behaviour and eventually at Level 4: Results. Beyond this level, Phillips (1996) added a Level 5 to enable a cost–benefit analysis to measure net programme benefits (NPB) by calculating programme benefits divided by programme cost. The beauty of this view is that it could provide a direct link between LMD and an organisation's results, so long as each level of evaluation is completed in sequence. The *LMD in Practice* opposite shows how this model informed the design of evaluation for a programme of training by Skills for Justice Sector Skills Council.

Further elaboration of the Kirkpatrick model was provided by Warr *et al* (1970), who presented an integrated model of evaluation covering all stages of LMD activity. The CIRO model covers:

● Context – the organisational situation that requires change through training

● Inputs – the methods used to meet training objectives

● Reactions – of managers to their training

● Outputs – immediate, intermediate (behaviour in the work context) and ultimate (the impact on organisation results).

LMD IN PRACTICE

EVALUATION OF FACILITATION TRAINING

The aim of the evaluation was to:

- explore the administration and management of the programme

- explore the programme design and facilitation process, what worked well and what was less successful

- explore the learning and knowledge which participants had gained.

The evaluation also explored the extent to which the programme had met underlying aims, which were:

- facilitating cross-boundary working

- improving mutual insight into carrying out responsibilities at a senior level in the public sector

- providing personal development in a challenging and supportive environment.

The evaluation design included both quantitative and qualitative methodology.

Delegates completed evaluation questionnaires designed to assess how the set-up workshop and overall programme had been received (Level 1, Kirkpatrick) and the benefits and learning obtained (Level 2, Kirkpatrick). Throughout the programme the candidates were assessed on their application of the knowledge (Level 2, Kirkpatrick) and identified learning through a process of reflective review (Level 2, Kirkpatrick).

Source: The Leadership Association, 2008

This version provides a basis to evaluate stages other than those that follow the end of LMD activity. Because there are so many factors that could affect the performance of participants once they return to work, it was suggested by Warr *et al* (1970) that trainers might have difficulty in linking training to outputs beyond the activities themselves. Trainers might do better, therefore, to evaluate the context that produces the need for training and the effect of their activities, the inputs, as the training happens. In this way, trainers can ensure that training meets the requirements of managers and make improvements as required. Of particular importance is the idea that evaluation can provide feedback for learning so that opportunities for work application can be identified (Burgoyne and Singh 1977) and stimulate practice-based-learning. Figure 8.5 shows an example of an evaluation log that was used to help managers who attended a training event identify opportunities for action as the event took place. The log was completed in duplicate to allow the collection of data for the evaluators. A further stage of data collection was added to evaluate outputs.

Evaluation at different stages throughout LMD allows the use of a wide variety of data collection techniques ranging from the quick (and dirty?) to the more complex and sophisticated. Table 8.1 shows some suggestions for evaluation techniques at each stage.

 WEB LINK

If you are seeking further tools and techniques for evaluation, a good starting point is the National Evaluation Project, Resources for Evaluators at **http://www.lancs.ac.uk/fss/projects/edres/itsn-eval** . For a more training-oriented website try **http://reviewing.co.uk/** .

Figure 8.5 An evaluation log

My expectations for today:	Why I have these expectations:
Ideas I am getting:	
Action points:	Event evaluation On a scale of 1 to 6 where 1 is not satisfied and 6 is highly satisfied, how satisfied are you that the event meets your expectations? The administration prior to the event? The administration at the event? The event facilitation? The venue? Comments

Table 8.1 Techniques of evaluation

Context (before LMD)	Interviews and questionnaires, briefings, written tests, 360-degree assessment
Inputs (during LMD)	Session reviews, questionnaires, written and practical tests, observation of behaviour, interviews, repertory grids[5]
Reactions (to LMD)	Questionnaires, interviews
Outputs (following LMD)	Interviews, questionnaires, debriefing meetings, 360-degree feedback, appraisal, performance measures, results measurements

The systematic model of evaluation and the various elaborations would appear to have a strong appeal – however, in LMD a number of difficulties can be highlighted:

- The systematic model is mainly applied to training, but this is just one feature of LMD. As we have indicated throughout this book, LMD incorporates many activities including formal education programmes and learning at work, deliberate or otherwise.

- Managers can undertake a blend of LMD activities (Voci and Young 2001) such as class-based training and web-based programmes, and these often overlap or occur in relation to each other. Identifying the effect of one activity may be contaminated by the effect of other activities.

- Managers learn in different ways. We have indicated that learning preferences can affect how managers respond to activities. There are also time-lags for some managers in responding to LMD activities.

- Leadership and management work always occurs in a context (Osborn *et al* 2002). Even when managers have been able to improve their knowledge and skills, unless they are able to implement what they have learned, it may be impossible to link the effects of LMD to changes in behaviour. Ideally, an evaluator would seek to minimise the impact of random or unknown factors – however, this is impossible in leadership and management work where a wide range of variables are likely to affect behaviour and performance.[6]

The incorporation of feedback allows evaluation to occur more frequently and for more data to be collected and used. It also allows evaluators to respond to activities and participants during activities (Bramley 1999) – a feature of holistic evaluation which we consider below. However, even a systems model of evaluation has its limitations.

Even if adjustments are made in response to feedback, the adjustments may be limited by the language of the feedback and prevent more critical or radical responses. This is a feature of what Easterby-Smith (1994, p.35) calls the 'systems fallacy'. Negative feedback may explain that participants dislike a technique and may provide a way of improving the technique – but a provider may continue to use the technique. What is not provided is an alternative technique or a true decision on whether such techniques should be used at all. Easterby-Smith also suggests that the systems model tends to focus on outcomes, which assumes a mechanistic view of how managers learn. Further, the model assumes that LMD starts with objectives with little reference to the status of such objectives, to who set them, or to how they might change or be disregarded during the unfolding of activities.

More generally, there are doubts about the applicability of the systemic idea or metaphor to the complexity, uncertainty and difficulties of reality – especially the reality of organisations. Specifically, can the systems model of evaluation capture the multiple values that are present in LMD in all its forms? Could it, for instance, cope with conflicting values, dilemmas and paradoxes and power relations? Evaluation models must therefore accord with the complexity these factors bring.[7]

HOLISTIC MODELS

The difficulties inherent in systematic and systemic models have resulted in a move to understand different perceptions, respond to requirements, and make improvements rather than directly prove the success of LMD (Simpson and Lyddon 1995). There is an acceptance that within any situation there is likely to be a variety of different meanings both within LMD events and beyond as part of a wider system. Evaluation models therefore need to be more holistic in order to take account of how the wider system impacts on LMD and vice versa. Thorpe *et al* (2009) argue for models of evaluation in LMD that acknowledge the importance of cause-and-effect connections in evaluation but also consider how learning is occurring within the LMD events and, crucially, the impact of the wider system or context. Figure 8.6 shows a representation of holistic evaluation.

Figure 8.6 Holistic evaluation

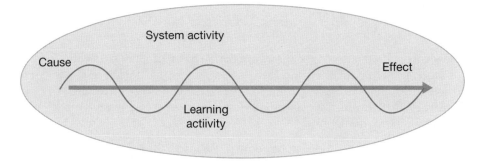

Source: Thorpe *et al* (2009)

A key concern is to help managers find ways to make action possible in LMD, especially in the face of the difficulties and complexities facing managers within a work context. One approach is to associate the taking of action with the evaluation of action taken through Action Evaluation (Rothman 1997). Action Evaluation (AE) has its roots in organisation development (OD) and Action Research, and was developed during the 1990s with a particular orientation towards the resolution of conflict. However, it also emerged as an evaluation methodology for complex situations in organisations composed of multiple stakeholders each with their own interests, which allow stakeholders to share understandings and which therefore make the achievement of success more likely. The stages of AE can be represented by a simple cycle, as shown in Figure 8.7.

At first glance, AE would seem to have some similarity to the systems model of evaluation that we explored earlier in this chapter. However, the approach has some important differentiators. A key feature is the stage of setting goals where AE is concerned, asking the various stakeholders to identify their goals and express values and motivations attached to the goals. By participating in such a process, the various parties are able to move to shared agreement about goals. In this way, goals of the different stakeholders become explicit. Actions emerge from goals set and can then be evaluated. That is, the goals set become the source of feedback to participants and the source of reflection. Reiteration and a continuous focus on defining/redefining goals and what is required for success make AE responsive to context and an integral part of the learning process. Similarly, in Action Learning evaluation is integrated into the learning process.

Figure 8.7 An Action Evaluation cycle

An example is provided by Pedler (1996) from a programme with head teachers. Evaluation consisted of:

- using a stakeholder map to identify critical success factors for projects
- visits to each other's schools to check on how far stakeholder criteria had been met and what benefits had been achieved – eg attendance at open evenings, communication between staff members, use and practice of techniques, interviews with stakeholders
- regular reviews and developmental evaluation within learning sets
- a final summarising evaluation on the worth of the programme.

More recently, Pedler and Trehan (2008) have argued how Action Learning – with its concern with difficult and complex problems that are linked to context – can also provide a good source of data for research. AL engenders engagement with others within a context, seeking to find a way forward and has an in-built evaluation method of review.

 WEB LINK

You can find out more about Action Evaluation at **http://www.ariagroup. com/libraryC3.html** .

You can follow an online programme of Action Research and evaluation at **http://www.scu.edu. au/schools/gcm/ar/areol/areolind.html** .

It becomes crucial to consider the impact of system activities through the interests of different groups or stakeholders and how these will affect their requirements for evaluation. It would not be surprising to find conflicts of interest between stakeholders, and this can create difficulties in meeting requirements. Evaluation that attempts to take account of various perspectives and respond to their requirements has been called 'responsive evaluation' (Stake 1975). Of particular importance is the attention that is given to cultural and contextual factors within evaluation and a revision of the purpose of evaluation away from proving towards feedback, learning and use. Thus Patton (1997) presents a model of utilisation-focused evaluation, the key characteristic of which (p.21) is:

> Involving specific people who can and will use information that enables them to establish direction for, commitment to, and ownership of evaluation every step along the way.

By involving stakeholders, the evaluator is active, reactive and adaptive to decision-makers and those who will make use of evaluation information. As stated by Patton (p.21), 'The evaluator facilitates judgement and decision-making by intended users rather than acting as a distant, independent judge.' Users are able to act on the evaluation findings because the findings meet their requirements and they have a personal interest in those findings. Evaluation is mainly formative and begins by analysing the context. This is particularly important in LMD, and it allows evaluation to occur throughout an LMD process. Tasks of utilisation-focused evaluation include:

- the development of relationships with intended users so that it is understood what kind of evaluation is required

- the facilitation of meetings between stakeholders to examine findings, assess progress against expectations and reconsider the next steps

- the organisation of dialogues about the evaluation data where there are different interpretations.

One key task is to identify the key stakeholders, their desires and interests, the roles they will play and the various situational factors that will affect how evaluation will occur and be used. The *LMD in Practice* opposite provides an example of evaluation that sought to involve different stakeholders.

Such approaches to evaluation inevitably require more attention to participation and collaboration. LMD events usually carry the prospect of action and making a difference to any workplace, but there are always difficulties in enabling a transfer of learning (see below). Much of this difficulty is related to limiting factors within the context. However, if a learning stance is adopted in evaluation, it becomes possible to make stronger connections between LMD and continuous learning in organisations. This is the approach suggested by presenting evaluation as a form of evaluative enquiry (Torres 2006; Torres *et al* 2005). It does require managers themselves to see the importance of evaluation and data generated as part of a process to generate actions but also to reflectively consider why action may not be occurring – they must 'practise what they preach' (Torres 2006, p.546). Linking LMD to organisation learning requires, as Torres *et al* note:

- using evaluation findings as feedback to make changes

- integrating changes with work activities and the organisation's systems, culture, leadership and communication infrastructure

- an attempt to bring about alignment of meanings, values and feelings through asking questions, surfacing assumptions and allowing dialogue.

A DEVELOPMENT PROGRAMME FOR SMALL BUSINESS MANAGERS

The development programme took place across England from September 2004 until April 2006 and allowed managers to obtain a grant of up to £1,000 towards any development identified following an in-depth assessment.

The aims of the evaluation were to:

- measure the impact of the programme on the participants' own performance

- measure the impact of the programme on their respective organisations

- assess how effective the brokerage models have been from the customer perspective

- inform policy on the way in which leadership and management provision can be embedded in Train to Gain.

The methodology consisted of:

- a postal/email survey of all local LSCs and Business Links

- six partnership case studies and telephone follow-up with ten Business Links

- stakeholder interviews with programme managers at the Centre for Enterprise

- a telephone survey of 500 participants on the programme and in-depth case studies with 20 participants

- a telephone survey of 216 intermediary organisations and a control group survey with 100 organisations.

Source: LSC (2006)

The learning orientation of evaluation becomes continuous when actions taken provide feedback which can be analysed for making sense and meaning of what is happening so that new actions can be considered. Evaluative enquiry can also be linked to Appreciative Enquiry (see Chapter 6), which seeks to consider the whole organisation in a process of change. Coghlan *et al* (2003) and Preskill and Catsambas (2006) highlight the similarities between learning-oriented evaluation and Appreciative Enquiry such as asking questions, dialogue, integration of action into work and the use of data as feedback to generate new decisions on action. With Appreciative Enquiry there is a clear intention to ask questions about success, positive experiences and best practice which allow images of what to do next. In this process, there is an invitation to enter the murky waters of how leaders, managers and others value LMD and how such values change throughout the experience of LMD and beyond. It is not always easy to gain access to values but story-telling and what is referred to as narrative evaluation[8] (Abma 2000) provide an opportunity.

Stories can be significant in evaluation because stories of personal experience provide an opportunity to give an interpretation and meaning to events. In addition, stories told capture uniqueness and richness of experience. So leaders, managers and others will be able to present feelings and emotions relating to their experiences of events and working life by story-telling. Narrative evaluation provides a more formal attempt to make use of the anecdotes that surround LMD but are rarely captured. Narrative evaluation is a complex approach – but it is its complexity that makes it attractive for the capture of the value of the dynamic and often ambiguous learning activities that form LMD and organisation activities. Further, evaluation through story-telling can be highly participative since stories told orally or written are a means of reflecting to make sense of participation, revealing key arguments and values which can provide leaders, managers and others with new ways of understanding and ideas for actions (Gold *et al* 2002).

WEB LINK

Go to **http://appreciativeinquiry.case.edu/**, the homepage of the 'AI Commons' – a worldwide portal devoted to the sharing of academic resources and practical tools on Appreciative Inquiry.

Narrative evaluation is strongly connected to 'narrative analysis' and the work of William Labov. Go to his homepage at **http://www.ling. upenn.edu/~wlabov/home.html** .

TRANSFER OF LEARNING

Formal LMD most usually occurs away from the workplace but with the potential to help managers bring new skills back to the organisation. However, managers face problems in how to ensure that learning is transferred back into their performance at work, so that it becomes part of their practice. These problems are concerned with what is referred to as the transfer of learning.[9] If we take a simple approach to the evaluation of LMD, we might ask the following crucial questions:

- Can managers show they have learned something?
- Can managers apply what they have learned?
- Can someone show that the organisation has benefited?

Answering such questions raises the following key points to consider in the transfer of learning:

- Managers do learn new skills, ideas and attitudes.
- Managers are able to apply learning to work in various ways.
- The application is sustained over time leading to some impact.

Baldwin and Ford (1988) provided a framework for this process, and an adapted version is shown as Figure 8.8.

The value of the framework is the prominence it gives to some of the key factors that affect transfer of learning. Transfer occurs when skills, knowledge and attitudes are not only learned and retained but also generalised sufficiently for application in various work activities and maintained by further application over time. The framework suggests that learning, retention, generalisation and maintenance are all influenced by leader and manager characteristics and the work environment. Thus, even where LMD activities are well designed for positive learning and retention – with good reaction-level evaluation – it is still

Figure 8.8 A framework for the transfer of learning

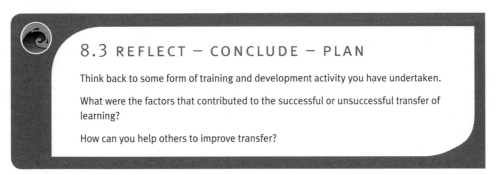

Source: adapted from Baldwin and Ford (1988)

possible that transfer will be inhibited by a lack of motivation on the part of managers. There may also be a lack of opportunity to use the learning and/or no support from others such as peers and senior managers; these are crucial features of what is referred to as an organisation's learning climate (see Chapter 7 and below).

8.3 REFLECT – CONCLUDE – PLAN

Think back to some form of training and development activity you have undertaken.

What were the factors that contributed to the successful or unsuccessful transfer of learning?

How can you help others to improve transfer?

The issue of transfer has remained important in LMD and HRD (Ford and Weissbein 1997). Holton *et al* (1997) refer to the influences as the 'transfer system' and have developed a Learning Transfer System Inventory (LTSI). This helps an organisation diagnose the factors that affect transfer, including what might prevent transfer. The items in the inventory (Holton *et al* 2007) relate to:

- motivational factors relating to expectations that people have about applying new skills

- secondary influences concerning the degree of preparedness of learners and belief or conviction by learners of their ability to use skills, referred to as self-efficacy (see below)

- environmental elements such as supervisor support or sanctions and peer support
- ability elements relating to the opportunity to apply new skills, the energy and workload of learners and the way training is designed to link to work performance.

All of these are assessed by the LTSI and plans can be made to ensure that help can be provided to support managers and their learning. Kirwan and Birchall (2006) provide a useful test of the LTSI in relation to a programme for nurse managers in Ireland.

LEADER AND MANAGER CHARACTERISTICS

Motivational factors, personality, readiness to learn and existing abilities will influence learning and retention and overall transfer. Huczynski (1977) suggested that it was the individual working with self-interest that made the key decisions about transfer, although this was on the basis of an 'inner debate' (p.98) that took into account the organisational context. There are a number of ways to consider leader and manager characteristics. One approach is to examine learner readiness based on how prepared a person is to participate in events, and how they prefer to learn. Better still is to help managers understand their learning orientation, including how they may prefer not to learn. If a manager, for example, prefers to avoid trying new actions, or planning new actions which involve others, and so on, this preference will influence how that manager might participate in LMD, learn from participation, and attempt to transfer ideas and skills back into practice.

In addition to learning preferences, there are other ways to consider characteristics. For example, a study by Cheng (2000) considered the following key elements from an MBA programme to examine transfer of learning:

- a measure of personality type to indicate a degree of ambition to succeed and achievement striving
- the 'locus of control', which measures the inner belief that rewards and outcomes in life are controlled by a person's own actions or by outside forces
- self-efficacy, which corresponds to a person's confidence that he or she can carry out certain behaviours and deal with threatening situations.

Self-efficacy has been particularly interesting, especially in the context of how managers cope with difficulties in trying to apply ideas or use skills. This refers to the conviction that a manager has about his/her ability to execute the behaviour needed to produce particular outcomes (Bandura 1977). Robertson and Sadri (1993) suggested that high self-efficacy is associated with high performance and low self-efficacy is associated with poor performance. For example, if a leader does not believe he or she is able to chair a meeting, it indicates low self-efficacy for chairing meetings. So even if this skill is 'learned' on a training course, the leader may try to avoid using it because of fear and inhibition, and if the leader is forced to chair a meeting, the low self-efficacy may result in poor performance and reinforce the negative expectations about chairing meetings held by the leader. Indeed, the leader may even be more pessimistic about carrying out such a task in the future. Accordingly, it may be important to prepare managers for the possibility of dealing with difficult applications of new skills and ideas so that they can cope and prevent the negative impact on self-efficacy. Marx (1982) referred to this process of preparation as 'relapse prevention'. By becoming aware of high-risk situations in advance and developing coping skills, self-efficacy can be enhanced so that when a difficult situation arises, a manager will believe that success can be achieved, and through accomplishment, will use the skill again, leading to generalisation and maintenance.

Recently, Tams (2008) completed research into what she referred to as a 'person-centered' (p.167) perspective of self-efficacy which considers how people think about their ability to perform a task. She completed 145 interviews with 74 people in various settings. After analysing the data, two dimensions were revealed concerning how self-efficacy was constructed. Firstly, there was a dimension of attending and reflecting, in which the former considers the use of cues in the environment as sources of self-efficacy, and the latter as making sense and re-interpreting the cues. Secondly, there is a dimension concerning focus of thinking covering information for doing a task and information about the social environment by observing and interacting with others. Figure 8.9 shows a variety of possibilities for constructing self-efficacy.

The value of this analysis is the help it can provide leaders, managers and providers of LMD to consider carefully how confidence to perform can be advanced. For example, 'attending to one's doing' requires 'focusing on the task' and/or 'generalising previous experience'. Thus a leader might consider how judgements are made about task completion and the steps taken to do this. Such judgements tend be based on self-evaluations rather than set as standards by others. A leader might also form an analogy between what has been completed in the past and the present task. There is also consideration of how the responses of others, especially negative feedback, can be managed better so as to enhance self-efficacy rather than diminish it.

WEB LINK

For more information about self-efficacy, try **http://www.des.emory.edu/ mfp/BanEncy.html** .

A general measurement of self-efficacy can be found at **http://userpage. fu-berlin.de/~health/ selfscal.htm** .

THE LEARNING CLIMATE

Leader and manager characteristics influence and are influenced by external factors that form part of an organisation's context. In particular, we are interested in that part of context which impacts on how a manager learns: the learning climate. In Chapter 7 it was suggested that the learning climate is composed

Figure 8.9 Possibilities for constructing self-efficacy

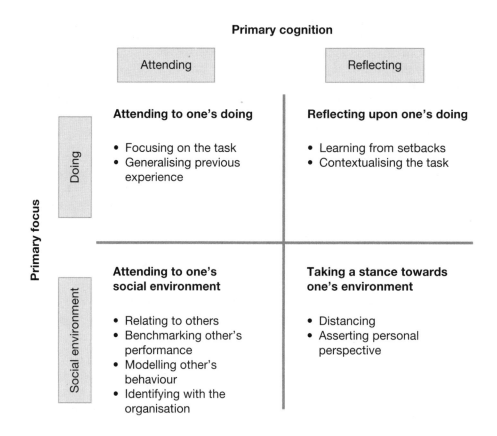

Source: Tams (2008, p.173)

of perceived variables that affect a manager and others in whether they realise learning potential (Temporal 1978). With reference to the transfer of learning, it is a reminder that LMD does not begin with attendance at a formal event. Managers work, assess needs for LMD and identify how needs will be met all in a context, and they return to that context after attending events that should have been designed to meet their needs.

Features of a positive learning climate for managers include:

- the structuring of work to match and stretch capabilities
- ongoing discussions to set objectives and review performance focused sufficiently on development
- LMD events and activities identified to match requirements
- opportunities to use new skills and learning on return to work, together with support from others to investigate how work can be extended or deepened to allow application
- ongoing coaching and informal support.

One of the key factors identified in research (Ford *et al* 1992) is that opportunities to use new skills can be created, and this is connected with the degree of autonomy within work. Essentially, this would require support from superior managers. An implication here is that managers who receive support should also support others, thereby reinforcing a positive learning climate (Axtell *et al* 1997). We would also expect to find the positive HRM context involving the use of planned career structures, succession planning and fast-tracking which were found by Mabey (2002) to contribute significantly to LMD in organisations, along with an importance given to informal learning and development or practice-based learning.

In identifying the key features of a positive learning climate, we should not forget that many managers face less favourable circumstances. Instead of support, they find themselves blocked by factors such as lack of autonomy in their work, insufficient stretch to allow the application of learning, and psycho-social factors such as the negative reactions of others and a lack of help from superiors. At best, managers returning from formal LMD events might be greeted by ambivalence or mild disinterest; at worst, power and politics may prevent any attempts to try something different, leading to disillusion about LMD in general and overall cynicism.

EVALUATION AND TRANSFER

This consideration of transfer of learning suggests that there are a number of ways evaluation can be utilised:

- The organisational context will influence who undertakes LMD, and how and what LMD is undertaken. Through audits and other organisational review processes (see Chapter 3), contextual factors can be influenced to support effectiveness.

- LMD needs can be identified through discussions with superiors and feedback from others in the organisational context. LMD should be driven by a manager's problems and by business issues. Preparation for attending LMD may include a plan on how to apply learning on return to work.

- The goals set by managers for LMD provide information for providers.

- Consideration for transfer begins during a programme by identifying possible new ideas, setting goals and/or identifying what is needed to manage transfer and how to cope with difficulties in transfer.

- Reviews with managers soon after their return to work should identify the need for support for transfer.

- Further reviews will allow new ideas for transfer to emerge after a programme.

If evaluation for learning becomes the main purpose by providing feedback for managers and others, it facilitates the transfer of learning and continues it as an ongoing process. In this way, an organisation engages in 'evaluation capacity building' (Preskill 2008, p.129), and one important consequence of this is that evaluation becomes purposeful in enhancing an organisation's learning climate.

It has been a feature of many organisational approaches to change, organisational learning, the 'learning company' and knowledge production and management. By taking a whole-organisation approach, evaluating LMD can become an integrated and continuous activity rather than an add-on at the end of courses.

Clearly, evaluation is a complex activity. The temptation not to make a serious effort is understandable. If there is no serious attempt, LMD will live – or die – by anecdotes and stories: a most uncertain basis. At the least, we advocate a form of evaluation which assesses whether people have learned something from an activity.

SUMMARY

- Proving the value of an investment in LMD is a key purpose of evaluation, but is difficult to achieve.

- In LMD, evaluation is concerned with criteria-based judgements relating to its value. Placing a value on LMD can be done by a variety of stakeholders and can occur at different points in time.

- The main purposes of evaluation in LMD are *proving*, *improving*, *learning*, *controlling* and *influencing*.

- There are significant debates concerning evaluation methodology affecting what data is collected, who it is collected from, when and how it is collected, and the analysis and presentation of results.

- Evaluation can occur at different stages to form a chain of consequences, seeking to provide a direct link between LMD and organisational results.

- Holistic models of evaluation are concerned with understanding and meeting the needs of different stakeholders and how LMD can enhance continuous learning and improvement in an organisation.

- Many managers face difficulties in transferring learning from LMD into their work – this is the transfer of learning problem.

- There are a number of ways evaluation can be used to support the transfer of learning and allow 'evaluation capacity building'.

QUESTIONS

For discussion

1 Should evaluating LMD be more than an 'act of faith'? If so, why?

2 Can evaluation be designed to prove the *added value* of LMD?

3 How can competing interests in LMD be reconciled through evaluation?

4 *Evaluation of LMD serves no purpose unless results lead to action.* Discuss.

5 Is transfer of learning an issue only for off-the-job LMD?

6 How do organisational power and politics affect LMD?

Get together in a group of five.

Working individually, look back at Figure 8.5, the evaluation log, and make a usable copy for yourself.

Identify an event in the next week where you can use the log.

Attend the event and use the log.

Report back with your findings to your group. What actions have you identified, and what will you now do?

NOTES

1 The different approaches are sometimes referred to as quantitative and qualitative evaluation. However, we avoid such a distinction here. Quantitative methods may be used in phenomenological approaches, and qualitative methods may be used in positivist approaches.

2 The phenomenological approach may also be referred to as a 'constructivist' approach (see Easterby-Smith 1994, p.23).

3 Formative reviews were learning reviews held every two weeks, using learning logs and stories which were posted on a secure web location so that the evaluator could access such data.

4 Anecdotal evidence suggests that participants while recognising the need to evaluate would rather go home, especially where activities have been completed off-site and participants become 'demob-happy'.

5 The repertory grid is a multi-purpose technique based on 'personal construct' psychology. The technique can be used to gather data about a leader or manager's personal meanings in relation to a particular issue and aspects of that issue. In LMD, a grid could be used to evaluate attitudes towards activities, situations and people and how these might change during LMD.

6 The Kirkpatrick model has been subjected to considerable criticism – see Tamkin *et al* (2002).

7 Some systems approaches do claim to be able to cope with the complexity of human activity. See Gold (2001) for an examination of 'soft systems methodology' in management learning, and the Systems Dynamics Society at **http://www.systemdynamics.org/** .

8 'Narrative' is a broader term covering a wide variety of forms such as myths, fables, tragedy, painting, pantomimes . . . as well as stories. See Gabriel (2000).

9 Sometimes called the transfer of training, since it is off-the-job programmes which suffer most from lack of transfer.

FURTHER READING

ANDERSON, L. (2010) 'Evaluation', in J. GOLD, R. THORPE and A. MUMFORD (eds) *The Handbook of Leadership and Management Development*. Aldershot: Gower

HALE, R. (2003) 'How training can add real value to the business: Part 1', *Industrial and Commercial Training*, Vol.35, No.1: 29–32

HANNUM, K., MARTINEAU, J. and REINELT, C. (eds) (2006) *The Handbook of Leadership Development Evaluation*. Hoboken, NJ: John Wiley

KESNER, I. F. (2003) 'Leadership development: perk or priority', *Harvard Business Review*, May: 29–36

OLSEN, J. H. (1998) 'The evaluation and enhancement of training transfer', *International Journal of Training and Development*, Vol.2, No.1: 61–75

TAMKIN, P., YARNELL, J. and KERRIN, M. (2002) *Kirpatrick and Beyond: A review of models of training evaluation*. Brighton: Institute for Employment Studies

CHAPTER 9

Leadership and management development and social capital

CHAPTER OUTLINE

Introduction
The development of social capital
The direct manager
Coaching
Mentoring
Beyond coaching and mentoring
Summary

LEARNING OUTCOMES

After studying this chapter, you should be able to understand, explain, analyse and evaluate:

- the importance of social capital development in LMD
- the role of direct managers in supporting LMD for others
- the importance of coaching and mentoring in LMD
- the use of a wider network in LMD

INTRODUCTION

Until the early 1990s it was often assumed that the prime responsibility for ensuring that managers developed lay with the managers themselves. It was also recognised that although managers frequently worked with teams and relied on networks of contacts to achieve particular outcomes, it was as individuals that managers should receive attention for LMD. However, partly as a result of interest in the importance of informal learning and the ideas relating to situated learning, there has been growing attention paid to the social context of learning and the role of others in encouraging, delivering and monitoring LMD both formally and informally. Indeed, with the growing interest in leadership configurations (Gronn 2009), it is recognised that LMD needs to have as much to do with what Day (2001) referred to as 'expanding the collective capacity of organisational members to engage effectively in leadership roles and processes' (p.582), as with the focus on individual skills and competence. As Day suggests, while developing individuals is an investment in human capital, recognition of interdependence and the role of others and networks in LMD is an investment in social capital. We will argue that others can be particularly significant in LMD, and that this is becoming increasingly recognised. For example, there has been a strong interest in providing help for managers through coaching and mentoring. A survey by the CIPD (2009) identified coaching as an effective practice by nearly 50% of respondents as part of developing a learning culture across organisations. However, like all opportunities in LMD, the offer of help, requests for help and the ways in which these are received are substantially affected by personal feelings, present and past relationships, leadership and managerial styles and learning orientations. Further, organisational culture – especially in its attitude to mistakes – affects how social capital develops in particular the degree of trust, mutual respect and commitment. As we have noted earlier, the effect of power may indicate to managers exactly how much or how little help they can expect in LMD and the limits on learning. National culture, ethnicity or gender can also affect both the 'what' and the 'how' of relationships. In general, the success of most relationships is improved when the participants in the relationship recognise that learning is reciprocal and the effectiveness of help is improved by the adoption of learning structures and disciplines, especially in an understanding of the learning process and specific objectives within relationships.

THE DEVELOPMENT OF SOCIAL CAPITAL

As we have indicated throughout this book, leadership and management work is characterised by frequent and ongoing interactions with others. It was Kotter (1982) who noted that managers get their work done by building networks involving others and spending time within relationships. Day and O'Connor (2003) argue for more attention to be given to the process of leadership development, especially its relational aspects, noting that the practice of leadership frequently runs ahead of research. We would argue that given the varied contexts where management is practised that we identified in Chapter 1, this is bound to occur.

The value of relationships with others has been increasingly recognised as a form of social capital, defined by Nahapiet and Ghoshal (1998, p.243) as the

> sum of actual and potential resources embedded within, available through and derived from the network of relationships possessed by an individual or social unit.

For Adler and Kwon (2002), social capital is concerned with 'goodwill available to individuals and groups' (p.23) which arise from interactions and relations.

As a consequence, 'information, influence, and solidarity' become available as resources (p.23). Others such as Burt (2000) focus on the network structure and network ties, arguing that 'Better-connected people enjoy higher returns' (p.347), so if we consider how many managers can also access networks of networks via Web 2.0 facilities such as Facebook, Plaxo, LinkedIn and Myspace, there probably has never been a better time for building networks. However, it may also be important for organisations to provide opportunities for developing social capital through resources, space for meetings and time for connections to be made (Cohen and Prusak 2001). Such recognition may at least have some influence on how social capital develops, although complete control of this is never possible or even desired.

These views of relationship development highlight the importance of investing time in building trust and respect with others whose help can then be called upon when needed, which simultaneously enhances both social and human capital (Whetten and Cameron 2005). McCullum and O'Donnell (2009) highlight the mutually enhancing interdependence between human and social capital and the key characteristics of each, as shown in Figure 9.1.

Figure 9.1 Human and social capital characteristics

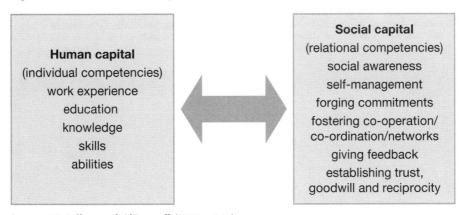

Source: McCullum and O'Donnell (2009, p.155)

An obvious consequence of considering this process is to give more attention to connections, relationships and interactions as learning opportunities for social capital development (Tymon and Stumpf 2003). Yet, as found by McCullum and O'Donnell (2009) in their review of five leadership studies, there was still mainly a focus on human capital and less attention given to social capital. However, a moment's reflection by any manager will reveal the extensive range of connections that can provide a contribution to LMD. Often such help is provided within formal processes, such as assessing needs, creating and reviewing personal development plans and attending LMD events. But help may be less formal in processes such as coaching and mentoring, which can often support practice-based learning. In particular, others can be very influential in providing support for the transfer of learning and overcoming both internal and external barriers to learning (see Chapter 6). The range of potential connections for LMD is set out in Table 9.1.

Table 9.1 The range of potential connections for LMD

On the job	Off the job
direct manager	tutors/trainers/facilitators
manager's manager	consultants
colleagues/peers	friends
direct reports	partner
mentors	participants in events
clients	participants in professional activities
internal advisers	participants in voluntary activities
external advisers	Web 2.0 networks
teams and project groups	

Source: adapted from Mumford (1997)

WEB LINK

Find out more about social capital at **http://www.infed.org/biblio/ social_capital.htm** .

A key writer is Robert Putnam at Harvard University, and you can read about his views on social capital at **http://www.infed.org/thinkers/ putnam.htm** .

9.1 REFLECT – CONCLUDE – PLAN

Can you identify the value of your social capital? Who can help you in terms of providing access to important information or influence, and who will come to help you if you need it?

What do you need to do to develop your social capital?

How can you help others to develop theirs?

THE DIRECT MANAGER

For a long time formal LMD schemes or policies described line managers as being 'responsible for developing their subordinates'. This was primarily to be achieved by appraising the performance of their subordinates, thereby identifying what were often referred to as 'training needs', although as we suggested in Chapter 4, there was a danger that this process would become little more than a ritual, and that the real decisions about LMD would take place elsewhere. London (1986) identified the 'boss' as the controller of important situational factors that affect career development for managers and opportunities to advance. He found that there were variations in whether they were treated as a person to meet current needs or as a resource for the future. Recent survey evidence

(CIPD 2009) suggests that only 34% of respondents felt that senior or line managers had the main responsibility for determining learning and development needs, although 47% saw coaching by line managers as an effective learning and development practice, the use of which has increased over the last two years.

Organisations are at different levels of recognition and action in terms of what they expect of line managers in developing others. Some still give exclusive attention through formal processes of development, through structured LMD systems and procedures, organised through human resource or development specialists. Others try to influence the use of learning opportunities on the job, integrating formal and informal development. The line manager has the potential to convert the cliché about learning from experience into a more effective development process. But the central characteristic of the role of line managers as a method of LMD will increasingly be based on the recognition that development is drawn from tasks, highlighting the importance of coaching (see below). The line manager is also influential in the learning of new managers once they are in post. Watson and Harris (1999) found that 'being thrown in at the deep end' was the main learning experience, combined with watching others as role models. The process was 'slow, often painful' (p.107), typical of unplanned approaches to LMD.

An effective LMD process not only encourages direct managers to take up formal responsibility, but would also encourage them to improve the contribution they make in their day-to-day informal relationships. Processes necessary for converting the direct manager's contribution from formal activities to those within the context of practice are shown in Table 9.2.

Table 9.2 The direct manager's contribution to LMD

Within a formal system of development	Within the context of practice
• appraising performance	• using activities as learning
• appraising potential	• establishing learning goals
• analysing development needs and goals	• accepting risks in subordinate performance
• recognising opportunities	• monitoring learning achievement
• facilitating those opportunities	• providing feedback on performance
• giving learning a priority	• acting as a model of leader and managerial behaviour
• formal roles as a coach	• acting as a model of learning behaviour
	• using learning preferences
	• offering help
	• coaching directly

Each of these processes provides direct managers with an opportunity for what D'Abate et al (2003) refer to as 'developmental interactions' (p.360). It suggests that such opportunities can occur on planned occasions with time allocated for completion and even some degree of sanctioned monitoring, but also on occasions which are brief, more difficult to recognise and yet potentially very powerful for those involved.

We argue that there are good reasons a direct manager may have for choosing to engage in developmental interactions with their reportees, such as:

- Improving performance is necessary to overcome problems, to meet the needs of the organisation.

- Improving the performance of an individual would reflect favourably on the manager's own managerial ability.

- Satisfaction is derived directly from helping someone to grow and fulfil potential.

- The manager's own skills, knowledge and insights would be developed as a result of discussions with others.

- The manager would be meeting the requirements of the organisation, which are to the effect that direct involvement in development activities with their reportees is a 'good thing' and is a measure of perceived managerial effectiveness within the organisation.

- Choosing to provide support for developing others is a crucial act in the creation of a learning and development culture.

- Developing the skills of another can help to take problems off the leader or manager's desk, which in turn affords more space to do other things.

Perhaps the least satisfactory reason for direct managers to offer help on learning is that a policy, system, form or workbook requires them to undertake the task. If the only reason direct managers have for undertaking development is to satisfy the system, it is likely to be the system that will be satisfied, not the potential learners. As the CIPD's (2007) research on coaching in organisations makes clear, trust is a crucial feature of interactions with support for line managers from development staff, even though the process is usually personalised and focused specifically on interactions with a reportee.

An example of the direct manager's large-scale provision of learning opportunities can be seen in the history of one of the biggest and most successful companies in the United States, GE. Jack Welch describes (2001) both the way in which he was developed in order to become chief executive officer, and the process he used for developing others through a specific programme to succeed him. Although there were differences in what happened for him and what he provided for others, essentially the point worth emphasising here is the personal involvement of the two chief executive officers, and their focus on providing different kinds of learning opportunity to stretch and test out their potential successors.

The collective of managers, and particularly the board of directors/governor/ trustees, has the responsibility for actually determining the nature of LMD in their organisation. Their responsibility for the total system – again usually seen purely in terms of the formal processes set up for the organisation as a whole – is also important, although different in kind from that discussed so far. The general rather than personal involvement of the direct manager in the total system includes:

- helping to determine the formal LMD system, and perhaps contributing to a written policy

- giving evidence of the priority attached to LMD by allocating resources, participating in decision-making meetings and courses

- giving personal evidence of interest by calling for reports on what has been done and evaluating results, by discussing development issues with managers at various levels on both a formal and an informal basis, by making achieved development of direct reports one of the criteria for selection for promotion.

Honey and Mumford (1995) have identified four roles for direct managers. They focus on the specific actions which direct managers must undertake:

- *role model* – explicitly demonstrating through behaviour and actions an enthusiasm for learning and development

- *provider* – consciously and generously providing learning and/or development opportunities for others, and active support/encouragement whenever the opportunities are taken up

- *systems provider* – building learning into the system so that it is integrated with normal work processes and is firmly on the conscious agenda

- *champion* – promoting the importance of learning for other parts of the organisation and the organisation as a whole.

COACHING

Recent survey reports show that coaching is used in 69% of organisations, but for public sector and larger organisations with more than 5,000 staff, the figures are 71% and 83% respectively (CIPD 2009). For 55% of respondents, coaching was seen as a part of LMD initiatives perhaps as a way of leading and managing talented staff during a downturn where developing and motivating staff is regarded as a way of providing differentiation between organisations (CIPD 2009a). Coaching is a popular process of LMD and, we suggest, carries a nice double benefit for any organisation:

- Managers who are coached by others are likely to improve their performance.

- Managers who coach others are likely to learn as they do this, and this can also improve their performance.

Boyatzis *et al* (2006) add a further benefit by suggesting that leaders can increase their sustainability by the experience of compassion when they coach others, and this will also relieve stress.

According to Garvey *et al*'s (2009) historical investigation, the term 'coaching' was used as a pun in Thackeray's novel *Pendennis* as in 'I'm coaching there', meaning travelling in a coach with a tutor. Thus the term 'coaching' came to mean providing tutor support for students so they could complete their exams. The term soon transferred to the sporting arena of boating and rowing, and from there to other sports. Its transfer to management in organisations is associated with the aim of improving performance (Evered and Selmen 1989). This occurred during the 1950s and 1960s where it was a feature of Human Relations thinking to use psychological understanding to motivate staff and help them self-actualise. Western (2008) also sees coaching as strongly linked to counselling and therapy, often as part of 'remedial' work such that if coaching was recommended, it was because 'you needed "fixing"' (p.99). Thus there was and probably remains some stigma attached to coaching in organisations because of its negative associations.

The processes of coaching and counselling can easily become confused – probably because they are, in fact, difficult to separate. Counselling may clearly be taking place when a manager discusses issues of domestic significance and difficulty. It may still be counselling when the discussion centres on problems with personal relationships at work. But is it counselling or coaching if the discussion focuses on how a person's aggressive instincts towards the head of another department can be reduced to a level acceptable to both sides? A discussion about an individual's career may also be counselling. The extremes of coaching and counselling are distinguishable, yet both of them require rather similar skills in areas of common interest. Some leaders or managers will be able to make direct statements under either coaching or counselling umbrellas, while being unable to carry out a gentler non-evaluative process under either heading.

9.2 REFLECT – CONCLUDE – PLAN

Is it possible to separate the personal from the public in discussions about work, performance and learning?

What skills are needed to ensure a 'non-evaluative process'?

How can you help others to develop theirs?

In recent years, as we have noted in this book, there has been more attention given to the importance of emotions, values, feelings, etc. Managers have been pressed to develop emotional intelligence (Goleman 1996) requiring awareness and sensitivity to their own emotions and emotions in others. Clearly, coaching carries a strong possibility for emotional displays. The role of emotions in coaching is still relatively under-researched, partly because of the private nature of discussions. However, as Bachkirova and Cox (2007) suggest, managers need to be aware of their emotions in coaching and a failure to do this could have an 'undermining' impact on the 'value of coaching' (p.609).

During the 1970s and 1980s, coaching also focused on employee development as part of a general movement to increase management responsibility for learning and development at work.[1] Megginson and Boydell (1979, p.5) defined coaching as:

A process in which a manager, through direct discussion and guided activity, helps a colleague to solve a problem, or to do a task better than would otherwise have been the case.

This definition remains useful because:

- it refers to guided activity
- it is aimed at solving a problem
- it talks about colleagues, with the useful indication that the manager can be working with peers as well as with direct reports
- it helps to distinguish coaching from counselling and therapy.

In the modern context, coaching is recognised as a crucial means to achieve results in the context of rapid change (Parsloe 1999) and can be carried out by a wide variety of people, including managers but also peers and teams within organisations as well as a growing number of executive and life coaches who earn their living by selling coaching to organisations and individuals. A coaching profession seems to be emerging (Hamlin 2009) although, like many professions, it is not yet fully formed. There are also confusions about the meaning of 'coaching' and where the boundaries lie between coaching and mentoring, giving advice and development and the various differences between business coaching, executive coaching, life coaching, counselling and consultancy (Parsloe and Wray 2000).

Whatever meaning emerges, we argue that coaching needs to give sufficient attention to development. If the meaning of coaching is confined to performance and problems, there is the tricky problem of a manager's accountability for the work of staff, which may pose a dilemma for their work as a coach (Phillips 1995). There is significant potential for managers to retreat to task focus, with the possibility of tension if coaching becomes confused with performance assessment for performance management. As Mink *et al* (1993, p.2) suggest, coaching is a 'process by which one individual, the coach, creates enabling relationships with others that make it easier for them to learn', so that it needs to be strongly associated with facilitating learning (Ellinger and Bostrom 1999). Unfortunately, it is not always done well (see Berglas 2002) – but when it is done well, coaching is a powerful and very effective method of developing managers, as shown in the *LMD in Practice* overleaf.

Even if there are potential difficulties in coaching, such is the belief in its value that many organisations are seeking to develop a culture that supports coaching, creating what is referred to as 'the coaching organisation' (Garvey *et al* 2009). Pemberton (2006), for example, suggests that managers need to deliver coaching because staff expect it, partly because they have experienced it elsewhere. Clutterbuck and Megginson (2005) argued that there is a clear business case for creating a coaching culture and, based on a study of major organisations, provided a framework for creating a coaching culture. They suggest that there are six areas to consider (p.28):

COACHING HAS 'PROFOUND' EFFECT ON LEADERSHIP STYLE

Eve Turner

Coaching was 'central' to building self-awareness in Northumbria Water's drive to bring in a new, more engaging and participative leadership style.

The FTSE-250 company, which has an annual turnover of more than £670 million and nearly 3,000 employees, felt a new style of leadership was needed, in order to make an impact on its business culture and to produce a new CEO within the next five years. Leadership and management development, going beyond the acquisition of surface skills, were central to supporting the change, delegates at the CIPD's annual Coaching at Work Conference heard.

Jane Turner from Newcastle Business School said that coaching was key at Northumbria Water in building self-awareness, providing a space for deep personal reflection, helping participants to understand their own identities and how they could be themselves as leaders, honestly and consistently.

At the start of the coaching, leaders at Northumbrian Water were asked to tell their life stories, mapping out their lifelines individually with their high and low points. They paid particular attention to 'trigger events' that could have stimulated positive growth and development. These, along with their proudest moments as leaders, were explored through coaching. Alongside 'connecting the dots' looking backwards, leaders were supported in talking about their values.

Turner said she believes that leaders are resistant to pressure to compromise their values. Therefore, the way their values map onto the organisation will determine how they feel in the organisation and how authentic they are as leaders. The coaching brought out the leaders' emotions and what impact they had in the workplace. Evaluation of the approach is in the early stages but Turner described it as 'profound' and said that deep internal shifts were being achieved, with the leaders' teams judging them more confident and able to take on new responsibilities fully.

Source: *PM Online*, 11 December 2008

- coaching linked to business drivers
- encouraging and supporting coachees
- the provision of training for coaches
- reward and recognition for coaching
- a systemic perspective
- the move to coaching is managed.

Each area has some actions to consider or issues to consider, such as:

- coaching linked to business drivers

    – Integrate coaching into strategy, measures and processes.

    – Integrate coaching and high performance.

    – Coaching has a core business driver to justify it.

    – Coaching becomes the way of doing businesses.

As any reading of the literature on culture change will tell you (Alvesson and Sveningsson 2007), changing an organisation's culture is hardly a step-by-step process and difficult to plan. However, working with such issues can certainly begin a process of change, and coaching can also be fully integrated as a tool in any change programme (Stober 2008). Knights and Poppleton (2008) found in their research of 20 organisations that there were three approaches to structuring coaching, as shown in Figure 9.2.

Figure 9.2 Structured coaching

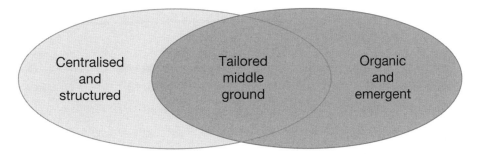

Source: Knights and Poppleton (2008, p.25)

While most organisations were somewhere in the middle, there were clear tendencies towards more or less structure. In organisations with *centralised and structured* approaches, there were formal structures to maintain consistency with senior managers providing high-level and visible support. An example was found in the Metropolitan Police where a strategy for coaching has been developed and a coaching team set up to embed coaching across the service. The concept of leader as coach is promoted so that coaching is viewed as a core skill. The *organic and emergent* approach allows coaching as a varied practice based on differences of context. Informality and personal networks are seen as powerful and slow movement towards a coaching culture seen as necessary. An example is provided from the Cega Group which provides medical risk assessment and travel assistance. Coaching was allowed to evolve, starting with senior management. It was then developed through trainers who could incorporate coaching into their work and then by finding other opportunities to incorporate coaching without formally declaring a strategy for it. The *tailored middle ground* approach is a blend of the two approaches, providing some consistency through direction and structure but also allowing a response to particulars of context. Most organisations have this blend but not in a uniform pattern. For example, the BBC started with a small group of interested and committed coaches which eventually grew and required more structure and direction.

A clear pattern from the research by Knights and Poppleton indicates the importance of context and the fit of coaching with such factors as:

- business priorities
- purpose

- organisation culture
- learning and development climate
- perceptions of coaching
- resource availability
- senior sponsorship.

These are similar to the dimensions provided by Clutterbuck and Megginson (2005), who also provide a questionnaire to allow the diagnosis and consideration of factors.

Another pattern identified by Knights and Poppleton (2008) was the way coaching structures are created. This starts with:

- initiating coaching – one person or a small group who are sufficiently passionate about coaching and want to spread coaching more widely.

If momentum can be established, this allows a second point to be reached:

- first review – taking stock of what has been achieved so far and spreading the story further to involve more people.

If others become involved – and this could involve more structure and an allocation of responsibility – a new phase is started:

- developing momentum and critical mass – this brings in more structure and more processes including training programmes to give life and purpose to coaching. Senior managers especially need to see the value of this since it may also require resources and their support will be vital. A careful approach to evaluation is needed (see Chapter 8).

Success in this phase allows movement towards:

- the tipping-point – coaching becomes 'mainstream' and has evidence of adding value as an activitiy with little remaining resistance or scepticism. In more structured approaches, there may be frameworks for coaching and competences. There may be specialist coaches or 'master-coaches' (Garvey *et al* 2009, p.62) who provide guidance for other coaches but who also continue learning about the coaching process and emerging models (see below).

One possibility in organisations that reach and move beyond the tipping-point is that with a growing number of coaches there needs to be some means of providing support and also learning from their experience. As a result there is growing interest in *coaching supervision* where groups of coaches meet with a 'supervisor' who facilitates the meetings (Hawkins 2006). We find a difficulty with the term 'supervision' here, which we see as a return to more dominating images of hierarchical structures associated with monitoring and control. We accept, however, that the term seems to be widely used even though surveys reveal more of a desire to supervise coaches than practise it (CIPD 2006). Coaching supervision is not without difficulty, and research suggests that there are tensions to be managed such as relationships between coaches, confidentiality and fear about revealing thoughts and opinions (Butwell 2006).

COACHING MODELS

While there are growing variations in the configuration of coaching, the main approach is that of a conversation between one person, the coach, and another, the coachee; it is therefore principally a dyad held together by the interaction which must be valued by both participants. The coach has to take the lead, although this should not imply a dominance by the coach over the coachee. As Stober and Grant (2006, p.3) argue, coaching is 'more about asking the right questions than telling people what to do'.

To help coaches consider how to work with coachees, there are a number of quite well-known models of coaching which have been developed and practised. Most of these are not overly theoretical and so are particularly popular in organisations that want to avoid getting too deep into underlying theories of human interactions. For example, probably the best-known is the GROW model, often attributed to Whitmore (2002). GROW stands for:

- Goal – establishing a clear objective or outcome to be achieved
- Reality – clearly establishing current performance or the current situation
- Options – finding ideas and alternatives before making a choice
- Will or Way forward – the motivation to make things happen and a commitment to action.

This view of coaching is so well known and popular that it is churlish to even attempt to provide criticism. Further, it has been embellished by others such as Passmore (2005) to provide more substance to the actions needed to make it work or incorporated into goal-oriented or solution-focused models of coaching (Greene and Grant 2006). However, we could point out the potential for pushing towards action or solutions when there are difficult or intractable problems to be considered or the lack of consideration for feelings and underlying fears that might be present. Lack of theory is not necessarily a bad thing, although we would point to the ever-present impact of personal or local theories in any interaction, often unrecognised or unchallenged.

 WEB LINK

For a website that has nicely gathered a good variety of coaching models, try **http://www.mentoringforchange.co.uk/classic/index.php** .

Barner and Higgens (2007) suggest that a coach's practice is implicitly based on a theoretical model, and that failure to recognise this can be limiting and constraining to practice. Further, coachees hold implicit ideas of how they expect to be coached, and this will affect how they respond to a coach, with possible adverse consequences if expectations are not met, such as lack of trust and communication breakdowns. Barner and Higgens identify four models which inform coaching practice:

- the clinical model – concerned with helping coachees understand themselves better through self-discloure and exploration of personal history to assess impact on current issues faced

- the behaviour model – concerned with helping coachees understand the impact of their behaviour on others by possibly using feedback data (360-degree, appraisals) before guiding changes in behaviour

- the systems model – concerned with helping coachees understand the context and system in which they work so that any change is set against the possible constraints and the enabling conditions needed, such as support from others

- the social constructionist model – concerned with helping coachees understand the use of language by themselves and others in making meanings where language is used to construct current realities and possibly change them.

Each of these models can provide coaches with a rich understanding of interactions with coachees, if they become more explicit in their understanding. This does require an investment in learning about theories about coaching, but there is a growing number of accredited programmes now available that are based on such models.

It is worth stating here that the social constructionist model gives attention to narrative understanding and stories, which we have referred to in previous chapters. We would argue that the centrality of conversation to interactions between coach and coachee provides a prime resource for considering how meanings are being made and their connection to stories. Drake (2007), for example, provides a model for working with stories in coaching.

 WEB LINK

Try the Center for Narrative Coaching at **http://narrative coaching. com/** .

EXECUTIVE COACHING

One trend in recent years is for managers to seek help from an external consultant, acting as an 'executive coach' (Hall *et al* 1999). Executive coaching (EC)[2] represents an important variation in the coaching movement, and the key idea is that even though he or she has reached the top, a senior manager's performance, like that of a sporting champion, can be sharpened up and improved. In the UK, Carter (2001) suggests that EC has arisen through the failure of more traditional sources of LMD to provide feedback for senior managers who often have to operate in lonely and isolated contexts. There has been a phenomenal growth in EC – although, like many other notions metaphorically transferred from other fields, EC has been subjected to a great deal of confusion and, some would say, mystery (Carter 2001). Perhaps this is part of the reason for a daily charge of £3,300.

Because EC has grown so quickly in the last decade, it is suggested that its practice is more advanced than the research (Feldman and Lankau 2005), with only a few studies completed. One study suggested that EC can lead to more specific goals, more attempts to solicit ideas for improvement and better ratings from staff (Smither *et al* 2003).

At its heart EC remains a dyadic relationship between coach and coachee, drawing either explicitly or implicitly on the model of coaching we considered above. However, there have been attempts to highlight the distinction between EC and other forms of help for managers at senior levels. For example, Feldman and Lankau (2005) suggest that ECs:

- do not provide answers on specific business issues – that is the role of consultants

- do not provide for career counselling; ECs help improve the performance and skills of the manager

- do not act as mentors from within the organisation; ECs are outsiders usually contracted for between six and 18 months

- do not act as therapists; ECs are more focused on performance.

It would appear that ECs are looking to distinguish themselves by their performance and business orientation although, as we noted in the coaching models, it is difficult to maintain a separation between the objective and impersonal aspects of a manager's work and the emotional, subjective, personal aspects. This is recognised by other writers about the practices of EC (Bluckert 2005).

 WEB LINK

Learn more about executive coaching at **http://www. theexecutivecoachingforum.com** and **http://www.execcoach.net/** .

PEER AND TEAM COACHING

These take the coaching idea beyond the exclusive focus of vertical dyads and extend a leader and manager's social capital opportunities laterally. Peer coaching recognises the importance of partners and other managers at the same level of work. According to Parker *et al* (2008), peer coaching is unique because of the mutuality and reciprocity of the relationship between one person and at least one other. This relationship is based on partnership and equality which removes the more objective differences in power, salary and status. They suggest that peer coaching is a good structure for reflection by providing an environment of support as well as challenge. This implies that peer coaching has some connection with Action Learning, although we consider at least five participants necessary for Action Learning. Eaton and Brown (2002) showed how peer groups were used to accelerate culture change at Vodafone, and Peters (1996) shows how National

Semiconductors in the USA incorporated peer coaching to reinforce feedback received from 360-degree assessment.

Perhaps the most powerful aspect of a learning relationship with colleagues revolves around the kind of feedback one offers another. Managers often have quite incorrect ideas about how they achieve what they do. Accurate feedback, particularly if presented in a helpful rather than a negative way, is the first stage of learning and a necessary precursor to learning to do things better. Colleagues may agree to become learning partners, forming a relationship explicitly to support each other. Figure 9.3 shows coaching used with peers in an LMD programme with managers in a professional organisation.

Figure 9.3 A learning partner process

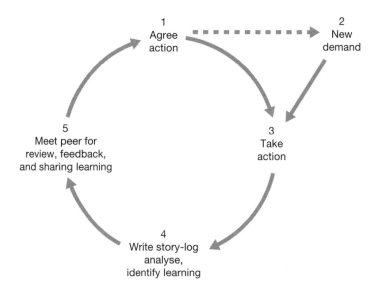

Participants met every two weeks to review and share learning and receive feedback. Actions were agreed but it was accepted that action plans could be changed as new demands were made. The focus of the partnership was to hold a learning conversation with a trusted colleague, having already reflected on key actions by the use of a story-based learning log. Most managers will also be member of a group or team, and we referred to these as constituting a potential learning opportunity in Chapter 7.

 WEB LINK

The website **http://www.peer.ca/coachingnews.html** is a US site but provides interesting links to resources relating to peer coaching, mentoring and networking.

If one-to-one coaching has an analogy with coaching individual athletes, team coaching references football and rugby, perhaps, although often with an obvious difference: the coach is part of the work team too rather than standing on the outside looking in. Team coaching is part of the role of a team leader (Clutterbuck 2007) although it is one that can be easily squeezed out by other activities such as structuring the work, allocating resources and even coaching individual team members (Wageman *et al* 2004). However, according to Hackman and Wageman (2005), an organisation might be missing out on some crucial benefits that come with team coaching. They provide a theory drawing on ideas from group working, team effectiveness and coaching, and suggest that team coaching requires:

- that group performance is not too constrained by task and organisation requirements

- a well-designed team

- that coaching focuses on salient group performance rather than interpersonal relationships

- that coaching is timely – the group is ready for it.

This is a starting point for considering team coaching but there is a need for more research on this practice. Clutterbuck (2007) uses this theory to provide guidance for practice and makes it clear that a team coach is engaged with the task of working with the team and has sufficient expertise to do so. By working with the team, coaching can occur within the process, responding to issues as they arise. He also finds a role for external coaches who can take a wider perspective and can stimulate consideration of alternative options.

COACHING SKILLS AND COMPETENCES

Until recently, frameworks of coaching skills were borrowed from related disciplines such as counselling and therapy. There was an emphasis on listening skills – not least because it may introduce some coaches to the idea of non-directive coaching. The skills involved in active listening and the provision and receipt of feedback are desirable priority items. Mumford (1993) emphasises the non-directive skills of effective coaching and lists them:

- active listening

- reflective listening

- open listening

- drawing out

- recognising and revealing feelings

- giving feedback

- agreeing goals

- deciding which coaching style to use – questioning for reflection, questioning for challenge, instruction

- adapting to preferred learning styles.

As interest in the activity of coaching has increased, so has the quantity of books, journals, e-journals and conferences. Lists of skills and behaviours required for good coaching are frequently presented. For example, the CIPD launched its own *Coaching at Work* magazine, now available on subscription, which, according to its website, provides an 'up-to-date reference archive, practical tips and a place for you to exchange news and views on coaching'.

 WEB LINK

Although a subscription is required, you can gain access to free materials and resources via the website for *Coaching at Work* at **http://www.cipd. co.uk/coachingatwork/** .

There are now a range of programmes and qualifications available for coaches, each with their own versions of coaching models from which knowledge and skills can be derived. We can see that this is very much part of the growing professionalisation of coaching (and mentoring) where defining the distinguishing features of one group against others is very much a part of establishing who is regarded as a professional. As argued by Abbott (1988), control of a profession 'lies in control of the abstractions that generate the practical techniques' (p.9), so the specification of skills and knowledge for coaches is one way of asserting professional control.

In the UK, like other emerging professions, there has been a competition to specify the skills and behaviours for coaching. For example, based on research by Anderson *et al* (2009), the following coaching-type behaviours for line managers were identified:

- sharing decision-making
- making action plans
- listening
- questioning
- giving feedback
- developing staff personally and professionally.

The research also identified barriers which prevented such behaviours and other contextual features which enabled or inhibited a coaching style of management. For example, a key contextual factor is the priority given to coaching by senior managers.

As we saw in Chapter 3, skills and behaviours are usually expressed as competences which are the usual path to providing a specified framework for assessing and developing those who wish to practise. The European Mentoring and Coaching Council (EMCC) has compiled a set of standards (Willis 2005). This followed a two-year consultation process with a range of coaching and mentoring organisations, developers and purchasers of services. They also included coaches and mentors, psychologists and life coaches. We might see the resulting framework as generic competences for all coaches and mentors. It is used as a quality assurance assessment tool for providers who gain a European Quality Award (EQA) if successful. The framework covers six levels, from Foundation – equivalent to National Vocation Qualification Level 3 – to Master Practitioner – equivalent to a Master's Degree. There are four clusters covering:

- Who we are – the incremental hierarchy of personal attributes for coaching and mentoring
- Skills and knowledge – used during the coaching/mentoring process
- How we coach and mentor – how we will demonstrate that we are able to apply what we have learned
- How we manage the process – what we will do as part of our coaching/mentoring practice to maintain and develop an effective and professional approach.

Each cluster is further elaborated at each level. For example, at Master Practitioner level for Who we are:

Beliefs and attitudes:

- formulates own frameworks of techniques, beliefs and values in their approach to coaching and mentoring
- explains their motives to coach/mentor in the context of the wider community.

Self:

- demonstrates through practice and reflection the basics of brain function and human development and how this knowledge can help others to build coaching and mentoring capability.

As we also noted in Chapter 3, there are possible limitations of such approaches to specifying competences. Nevertheless, there is clearly some value in doing this so long as they are reviewed critically over time. In addition, it appears that this framework is meeting a desire for providing some degree of quality assurance among coaching and mentoring providers.

 WEB LINK

Go to **http://www.emccouncil.org/** for more details about the European Mentoring and Coaching Council.

The website of the International Coaching Federation can be found at **http://www. coachfederation.org/** .

The Coaching and Mentoring Network in the UK has a resource centre at **http://www. coachingnetwork.org.uk/ResourceCentre.htm** .

MENTORING

Having considered the possibilities for coaching, we now turn to an activity which covers similar ground (Willis 2005) but with enough difference to warrant separate consideration based on different histories and research (Garvey *et al* 2009). However, there is evidently some confusion with respect to labels and roles, so sometimes 'coaching' might be appropriate and at other times 'mentoring'. In some contexts, such as work with managers in small and medium-sized enterprises, the difference in labels is far less important than the relationship and process (see Chapter 12). 'Mentoring' is often the preferred term in professional contexts such as education and health (Browne-Ferrigno and Muth 2006).

The historical origins of mentoring can be found in the Greek myth of the entrustment of Telemachus, the son of Homer's Odysseus, to the wise Mentor.[3] Since then mentoring has been a developmental process in many walks of life and continues to be so. However, mentoring as an LMD intervention came to prominence in the late 1970s. For example, Roche (1979) found that 66% of respondents in a study of US managers had had a mentor or someone who took an interest in their career and provided guidance and sponsorship. Such studies revealed and named a helping process as mentoring, a process that is most likely to have existed in organisations and elsewhere for many years – an archetypal informal learning process but with elements of deliberation for practice. However, since the late 1970s there has been growing interest in mentoring, again as part of the drive towards making managers responsible for the development of their staff. The result is a growing plethora of ideas, models and prescriptions relating to mentoring in organisations.

There are some issues of definition, and of what is involved, which are very important in establishing mutual expectations. Here are two definitions:

> Off-line help by one person to another in making significant transitions in knowledge, work or thinking.
>
> (Megginson and Clutterbuck 1995; p.13)

> A protected relationship in which experimentation, exchange and learning can occur and skills, knowledge and insight can be developed.
>
> (Mumford 1993; p.103)

There are of course other definitions, but probably the key factors in any mentoring process are:

- a mentor who is a person of experience
- a protégé or mentee who is less experienced
- the relationship between them.

A major issue for some is the need for clarity on the difference between being a mentor and being a direct manager. Much of the American literature has introduced confusion, no doubt repeating what occurs in practice, by including the activities of direct managers operating in a particular style which they then describe as mentoring. There is a crucial difference between the kind of relationship which occurs with an 'off-line' mentor and that which exists with an individual to whom you are directly responsible for managerial performance. That is why Mumford (1993) described it as a 'protected relationship' – the mentor's responsibility is for development, the direct manager's responsibility is for performance, although this may also include coaching. By contrast with coaching, a mentor therefore:

- is able to take a long-term view
- is more informal so that meetings take place as required
- can be more concerned with issues such as career and personal growth
- is more interested in significant and broad issues of performance than in detail
- takes an interest in the general direction of a person's life and all-round development
- is able to offer both distance, independence and perhaps greater clarity of thought about issues.

Kram (1986) distinguishes between career and psycho-social development within a mentor relationship. The career function includes sponsorship, coaching, protection, exposure-and-visibility and challenging work. Psycho-social functions include role modelling, counselling and friendship. The former is more visible and likely to be more formal with a named mentor allocated to a named protégé. It will continue as long as required, at which point the formal relationship ends. This might be a typical approach to graduate development and employees identified to have talent.

The organisation, the mentor, the mentee and the mentee's manager may all have different requirements or understandings about what the purpose of a mentoring relationship should be (Mumford 1997). However, mentoring is most suitable:

- for escaping from sole dependence on the direct manager as developer
- for providing alternative views about leadership and managerial problems, structure, objectives and strategy
- for feedback on the mentee's reported or observed behaviour
- for providing a role model of effective leadership, managerial and learning behaviour
- especially for development purposes grounded in leadership and managerial reality.

While mentoring in organisations was under-researched and the overall benefits little appreciated, it occurred informally and without direction or planning. Mentors have often been door-openers – they try to ensure that their mentees are considered for important jobs, assignments, projects. They ensure that those who make decisions about people know what their mentee has achieved and why that level of achievement is noteworthy. The door-opening role is more that of a sponsor than of someone who provides direct help in learning. Such a process

9.3 REFLECT – CONCLUDE – PLAN

Who has been your 'mentor' over the last three years?

What have been the benefits of this relationship?

Who will be your 'mentor' for the next three years?

could easily lend itself to advancing the power-base of both the mentor and mentee. A critical view of mentoring emphasises the way a mentee is required to adopt the values and norms of a dominant group within an organisation (Townley 1994). Mentoring could also have a discriminatory impact on potential mentees who might not be able to find a compatible mentor – eg females, members of ethnic minorities, etc (Hunt and Michael 1983). Once interest grew and research findings appeared, there was an effort to make mentoring more explicit and turn it from an informal into a formal LMD process. With formality came a degree of specification of roles and skills. Thus in the early 1990s Gibb (1994) was able to show how formal schemes might be defined by either:

- a competency approach – expressed as skills and activities in checklists, usually prescriptive

or

- a typology approach – types of mentoring such as 'instrumental', 'developmental', 'professional', involving roles left for negotiation.

As you might expect, these approaches are very similar to those for coaching indicated above. The EMCC's framework of competences is also presented as mentoring and coaching standards. Further, coaching models such as GROW are also presented as mentoring models.

One of Gibb's interesting findings was that the differences affected the degree of structure and perceptions of value. He presented a continuum between systematic mentoring and process mentoring. The former is highly structured with pre-set requirements. Such schemes were seen as valuable but not important developmentally. By contrast, process mentoring is more concerned with the development of the relationship and the learning within the relationship, which may become the main purpose. This presents organisations with something of a dilemma – how far should mentoring be formally structured, or should the participants themselves be responsible for the process? It is a tension which is unlikely to be fully reconciled. As Gibb (2003, p.48) suggested, 'The theory and practice of mentoring . . . evolves with blooms and with thorns', with different views on how far it is possible to specify and institutionalise its practice.

THE PRACTICE OF MENTORING

As mentoring has gained more recognition, research has started to show some of the benefits. Allen *et al* (2004) completed a meta-analysis of research and found that mentoring had positive implications for compensation, promotions, career satisfaction and commitment, expectations for advance, job satisfaction, and intention to stay. Payne and Huffman (2005) completed a two-year study of over 1,000 US Army officers and found that mentoring supported commitment and continuance commitment. Clutterbuck (2004) points to benefits for the mentee in terms of improvements in knowledge and skills, management of career goals, building a network of influence and growing confidence. Mentors benefit because of the satisfaction of passing on their knowledge and expertise. The rest of the organisation benefits because of the impact on recruitment, retention, commitment and engagement.

A key requirement for the success of mentoring, especially formal programmes, is the support provided by senior managers. Rosser (2005) completed a study of 15 CEOs in large US companies relating to their mentoring experiences and found that mentoring was seen as key to their development, with some relationships more than 40 years old. The findings seemed to suggest that mentoring was viewed as indispensable to achievement, allowing the CEOs to ride above possible constraints. As explained by one respondent (p.532):

> Mentoring is perhaps even one of the most important things that can occur in developing others. Mentoring is giving, giving of yourself. There is no expectation of return.

Interestingly, the CEOs did not see themselves as mentors for others, although they all showed awareness of the roles they played in developing others. This again emphasises the informal aspects of the practice of mentoring. Nevertheless, for formal programmes visible support from senior managers is one of the key requirements for success (Hegstad and Wentling 2005) in addition to teamwork and open communication. Change seems to be the main driving force, often connected to restructuring to provide greater autonomy and teamworking. Garvey (1999)[4] found that there was increased attention to mentors as agents of change.

Mentoring is a highly personal relationship, and problematic as it might be, it forms the focus of considerable research. There are many case study examples, sometimes produced in collaboration with participants (Clutterbuck and Megginson 1999), and large-scale surveys that attempt to measure effectiveness and satisfaction (Ragins *et al* 2000). There are also examples of systematic reviews such as Sambunjak *et al*'s (2006) exploration of mentoring in academic medicine covering 39 studies reported in 42 articles which showed the importance of mentoring for personal development and careers. However, it also showed that fewer than 50% of students had mentors, and there was a perception that women had more difficulty in finding mentors.

Hale's (2000) research was concerned with the match between mentors and mentees. He found that where the aim was to speed the development of the relationship, the emphasis had to be on matching similarities of interests, professional background and function. However, if the aim was to optimise learning, there had to be differences in behaviour and learning styles, strengths and development needs, but there had also to be similarities in terms of values, beliefs and life-goals.

Megginson *et al* (2006) provide a number of cases of mentoring schemes, and one clear finding was the need to ensure that mentors and mentees both have an idea of what they want from the relationship. It was not enough that the mentee wanted to give something or provide others with the benefit of their experience. It is necessary for both parties to be willing to learn.

Data from research allows a degree of model-building seeking to explain the key variables of a mentoring relationship. For example, Borredon (2000) produced a simple model of the mentoring process, shown in Figure 9.4. The model highlights the importance of 'space', where mentors use critical questions to stimulate reflection by the mentee. The result is learning which is shared and becomes mutual for the mentor as well as the mentee. However, this does require mentors who are reflective and have an understanding of the different learning processes and the differing learning preferences of individuals.

Figure 9.4 A model of the mentoring process

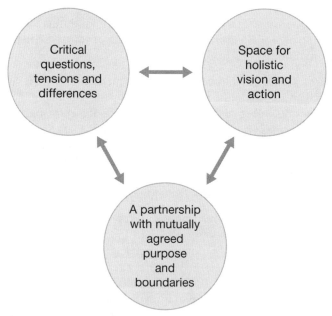

Source: Borredon (2000)

To this point, both coaching and mentoring have tended to be viewed positively for participants and the organisation. However, there are examples of negative experiences. This can be due to a mismatch between participants and such deviant behaviours as deceit by the mentor (Eby *et al* 2000) or sexual harassment. Simon and Eby (2003) explored the mentoring experiences of 73 MBA students and found a range of negative experiences of mentoring, shown listed below (p.1090).

- inappropriate delegation – Mentor delegates too much work to the protégé or does not provide the protégé with enough responsibility for important task
- tyranny – Mentor abuses his/her power and authority over the protégé. For example, the mentor may intimidate the protégé, put the protégé down, and/or constantly remind the protégé of the mentor's control over the protégé
- credit-taking – Mentor takes undue credit for the protégé's accomplishments
- sabotage – Mentor does something intentionally to hinder a protégé's career success or reputation. The act may be malicious or it may be to cover up the mentor's own performance problems
- overt deceit – Mentor lies to the protégé by providing him/her with inaccurate information or telling him/her one thing and doing something different
- intentional exclusion – Mentor intentionally excludes the protégé from important meetings, is not accessible to the protégé, and/or keeps the protégé 'out of the loop' on important issues
- neglect – Mentor does not express interest in the protégé's career, does not provide direction or support, and/or does not do things to help the protégé develop professionally
- self-absorption – Mentor is preoccupied with his/her own career progress, behaves in a self-serving manner, and/or exhibits an exaggerated sense of self-importance
- technical competencies – Mentor lacks the job-related expertise to provide guidance for the protégé
- interpersonal competencies – Mentor lacks skills in dealing effectively with protégé on an interpersonal level
- mismatched values – Poor fit in the mentor–protégé relationship due to different personal and/or professional values (eg ethics, time spent at work versus time with family)
- mismatched personality – Poor fit in the mentor–protégé relationship due to differences in personality
- mismatched work styles – Poor fit in the mentor–protégé relationship due to differences in work styles. For example, one person likes to try new ideas and the other prefers to stick with what has worked in the past
- bad attitude – Mentor has a negative attitude about the organisation and/or the job, and/or is generally bitter or unhappy
- personal problems – Mentor has personal problems that interfere with his/her ability to mentor effectively, such as marital problems or drinking problems
- sexual harassment.

9.4 REFLECT – CONCLUDE – PLAN

Have you had such negative experiences in a mentoring or any other relationship?

How would you deal with a mentor who had a negative attitude?

PEER RELATIONSHIPS

Kram and Isabella (1985) found that relationships between colleagues or peers offered an alternative to traditional mentoring. Such relationships were more likely to be mutual, both parties giving and receiving emotional and information support which helps in career progress. In most cases the help offered by colleagues is not formal LMD but arises from normal leadership or managerial activities – shared problem-solving, discussion of a difficult forthcoming meeting, a chat about a difficult colleague, a review of organisational necessities and political requirements. It is only afterwards that they recognise that they have learned something from a colleague.

Mitchell (1999) provides an example of group mentoring from New Zealand within a women's network. Composed of around 12 participants, each person could choose to take a role of mentee or mentor. The mentee could then present an issue to the rest of the group who could then respond. It was also possible for one-to-one meetings to occur outside the group session. Membership of the group was very flexible and open to any member of the network, initial mentees often becoming mentors after a few visits. Evaluation of the process revealed that mentees valued the support and feelings of not being alone with their issues. Sharing experiences also allowed relationships to be developed. As we noted with peer coaching, this process has some similarity with Action Learning in its concern with problems faced by a manager, who can then receive challenge and support from others who often recognise a connection to their own situations.

E-MENTORING

While most mentoring relationships develop through face-to-face interactions, there is growing interest in the potential of ICT and the Internet to allow such interactions to occur online which allows for a more reflective process to occur (Mueller 2004). It is suggested that e-mentoring provides benefits such as easier access and lower cost, more equality of status, and less emphasis on demographic factors such as age, gender or ethnic background. It can also allow a better record to be kept of interactions (Ensher *et al* 2003). Because participants do not have to be in the same place nor be available at the same time, they can come from any part of the world. This can allow participation in mentoring in organisations with dispersed workforces and those working at home (Headlam-Wells 2004). Clearly, with the spread of Web 2.0 technologies, there would seem to be an even greater opportunity for providing e-mentoring in organisations. Web 2.0 allows ideas to be shared, the promotion of discussion and the development of communities through social networking (Martin *et al* 2008).

Headlam-Wells *et al* (2005) provide a case study of e-mentoring for women which was designed to develop careers and the management potential. It involved 122 participants who were matched into pairs of mentors and mentees within six groups. Most had had mentoring experience and some mentees had been mentors. Each group had an e-moderator who could provide support and guidance. Participants also had the opportunity to meet face to face and learn ICT skills. Evaluation showed the benefits of mentoring for development, and the use of electronic communication facilitated this, although it was also evident that other communication methods were needed and, crucially, the most important factor was the quality of mentoring and the relationships between participants.

BEYOND COACHING AND MENTORING

Help for LMD can be available by establishing relationships with others outside the formal or informal offerings of coaching and mentoring. Within an organisation, a manager can gain useful data for LMD from:

- direct reports
- internal professional advisers
- the wider network
- clients and customers
- external professional advisers and consultants
- participants in training, professional meetings, voluntary activities
- domestic partners.

DIRECT REPORTS

The growing use of 360-degree assessment and multi-source feedback (see Chapter 4) brings about the possibility of using the feedback of direct reports and others for help. Based on the principle that others can see aspects of a leader or manager, especially performance, which they cannot see, staff can provide important information.

INTERNAL PROFESSIONAL ADVISERS

In larger organisations, the HR director ought to direct the development processes and ensure that any separate specialisms are coordinated. This responsibility is not always met, especially where training and development are compartmentalised. The different roles depend on the size of the organisation and more particularly on the amount of resources it is prepared to put into this whole field.

In some cases internal professionals will act as counsellors or advisers to managers on problems concerned with effective performance. So an LMD adviser might help set up a two-day event 'Problems and opportunities to 2010', or 'Clarifying relationships between our divisions'. The adviser might give individual advice on development in terms of a total career plan or in terms of advice on a particular need or a developmental process.

THE WIDER NETWORK

Perhaps a richer source of help and support for LMD can be found outside the organisation. Managers can develop their social capital by networking. This is defined by Orpen (1996, p.245) as the process of:

> building up and maintaining a set of informal, co-operative relationships with persons other than the manager's immediate superior and subordinates in the expectation that such relationships will help or assist the manager to perform his or her job better

– and, we would add, to support the learning process. Every activity undertaken by a manager and every interaction (virtually or otherwise) carries the potential for learning and a widening of the network. Managers who make use of their network are referred to as 'high-dependency managers' (p.246), and it is suggested that by engaging in networking behaviour they are more likely to advance their careers – so long as such behaviour leads to support and co-operation from the network to perform more effectively. There is also increasing interest in networking behaviour in the construction of new knowledge and ideas. Knowledge-based organisations require the continuous production of knowledge to prosper. Managers are often at the hub of different processes and cross-functional/organisational teams, both inside and beyond organisation boundaries. By networking, shared understandings can be co-ordinated into new knowledge (Swan *et al* 1999).

CLIENTS AND CUSTOMERS

The increasing growth of e-business and customer choice highlights the importance of customer relationship management and the use of feedback for learning. It is not always understood that any interaction in providing a product or a service can also be a learning situation. It can be primarily about knowledge – but it might be about the skills observed in those with whom the interaction is taking place. This is of course usually an implicit learning process, not one in which the client or customer is actually asked to structure and provide a learning experience within a work situation – but it could and should be.

EXTERNAL PROFESSIONAL ADVISERS AND CONSULTANTS

One of the reasons for going outside the organisation for help was indicated earlier. The greater the level of intimacy of the development counselling and advice, the greater is the likely worry of managers about the terms under which it is offered. While the internal adviser potentially has the great advantage of knowing much more about the reality of the organisation, the problem of confidentiality inevitably arises. Can a manager really get highly personal advice from an internal adviser and trust that details of her or his thoughts and problems are not going to be passed on or used internally? Or the organisation might wish to test its internal knowledge against the wider view.

PARTICIPANTS IN TRAINING, PROFESSIONAL MEETINGS, VOLUNTARY ACTIVITIES

There is a significant difference between the first of these – participants on a training or education course – and the latter two. In the former case, particularly if the institution providing the course uses learning theory and especially the concept of learning to learn advanced earlier in this book, learning from and with each other becomes a conscious and structured part of the programme. It is a specific element in Action Learning, for example. While individuals often talk about what they have learned from others on courses, it is sadly the case that in few instances the course has been designed explicitly to achieve this. It is something which for both the designers of the course and for the participants is 'expected to happen', rather than being the focus of particular information, discussion or even specific sessions. Courses often get credit for their success in providing opportunities to exchange information and ideas – but they ought to be much more effective than most of them are at ensuring that it happens.

The second and third categories of participation, on professional activities such as attending meetings of the CIPD or the Chartered Management Institute, or voluntary activities such as chairing the trustees of a community organisation, or leading a charitable appeal, do not provide 'helpers' in the same way. They are more people who provide opportunities for others to learn by providing their knowledge or exemplifying skills. Increasingly, however, professional associations are incorporating the idea of the 'reflective practitioner' into their accreditation frameworks.[5]

DOMESTIC PARTNERS

There has been a considerable change in the way partners discuss careers and career moves. The advent of dual-career families is one obvious cause, but in general the trend has been towards a less clear-cut, less autocratic process of decision-making on the career of one partner. Jack Welch (2001) gives an unusual illustration – he improved his own golf by teaching his wife how to play. Most partners carry out a range of roles as listener, prompter, or commentator. Whereas some managers want to leave their work at the office and not discuss it at home, others find it at least therapeutic and sometimes positively helpful to do so. For managers in small businesses, domestic partners and the family as a whole are often a key influence on learning, although usually as part of a problem-solving process (Gibb 1997).[6]

9.5 REFLECT – CONCLUDE – PLAN

Which part of your wider network has provided the most help for you on learning? Which part has provided the least help for you on learning?

Why was the help useful, or not useful? What conclusions do you draw?

In what ways could you change for the better your own use of 'helpers'? In what ways might you help others provide more effective help?

SUMMARY

- There is a significant role for others in providing help for LMD, but there are variations in how managers respond to help.

- The value of relationships with others has been increasingly recognised as a form of 'social capital', and managers are encouraged to engage in social capital development by attending to connections, relationships and interactions as learning opportunities.

- Direct managers have a significant responsibility for LMD, especially through coaching but also through 'developmental interactions' in a variety of activities.

- Coaching is a popular LMD process and has benefits for both managers who coach others and those who are coached. Many organisations are seeking to develop coaching cultures.

- Executive coaching has seen significant growth in recent years.

- Mentoring enables managers to benefit from the experience and guidance of more senior managers.

- There are variations in both coaching and mentoring by which relationships are formed with peers for mutual benefit.

- Use of a wider network enables managers to draw on support for learning and to perform more effectively.

QUESTIONS

For discussion

1 How helpful are organisations in providing support for LMD?

2 *Direct managers' accountability for the performance is bound to conflict with their role as supporter of the managers' learning.* Discuss.

3 Is mentoring simply a way of socialising managers into the 'old boys' network'?

4 What do you see as the advantages and/or disadvantages of formal/informal mentoring?

5 What is the importance of feedback from customers in LMD? How can such learning be optimised?

6 Can managers benefit from joining social networking sites?

GROUP ACTIVITY

Get together in a group of four.

Each person should take a plain sheet of A3 paper and, placing themselves one at a time in the centre, identify who are the key influences on how they perform their work. Consider influences both inside and outside the organisation.

Now identify to what extent such influences have been helpful or a hindrance to learning and development.

Provide an explanation for your classification.

Share your findings and prepare a presentation on help and hindrance in learning at work.

The Campaign for Learning's website may be of interest at **http://www.campaign-for-learning.org.uk/cfl/index.asp** .

NOTES

1 The more recent ideas of 'executive coaching', 'peer coaching' and 'team coaching' are examined later in the chapter.

2 Executive coaching overlaps with other expensive forms of external help for senior managers such as personal coaching and personal mentoring. There is also a connection to career counselling.

3 To add further confusion to the myth, the original Mentor was the female goddess Athene in disguise.

4 Other terms found by Garvey (1999) included 'godfather/mother' scheme and 'sponsorship'.

5 The CIPD refers to the idea of the 'thinking performer'.

6 See also Chapter 12.

 ## FURTHER READING

ALRED, G., GARVEY, B. and SMITH, R. (1998) 'Pas de deux – learning in conversation', *Career Development International*, Vol.3, No.7: 308–13

BALKUNDI, P. and KILDUFF, M. (2006) 'The ties that lead: a social network approach to leadership', *The Leadership Quarterly*, Vol.17, Issue 6: 941–61

GRAY, D. E. (2006) 'Executive coaching: towards a dynamic alliance of psychotherapy and transformative learning processes', *Management Learning*, Vol.37, No.4: 475–97

IVES, Y. (2008) 'What is 'coaching'? An exploration of conflicting paradigms', *International Journal of Evidence-Based Coaching and Mentoring*, Vol.6, No.2: 100–13

SCANDURA, T. A. (1998) 'Dysfunctional mentoring relationships and outcomes', *Journal of Management*, Vol.24, No.3: 449–67

CHAPTER 10

The future supply of leaders and managers

CHAPTER OUTLINE

Introduction
A strategy for talent
Succession planning
Selecting managers
Careers for managers
Self-management of careers
Summary

LEARNING OUTCOMES

After studying this chapter, you should be able to understand, explain, analyse and evaluate:

- the key ideas of talent management
- the importance of succession planning
- approaches to selecting managers
- key ideas on management careers
- the importance of the self-management of careers

INTRODUCTION

Historically, there have been persistent concerns in the UK relating to the supply of managers, who also tend to be under-qualified (Johnson and Winterton 1999) (see Chapter 2). At the micro level, it is up to organisations to ensure that they have the right number of managers with the potential for high performance through LMD. Thus, even though most organisations have been able to recruit staff for leadership and management positions, this provided little indication of their quality (Williams 2002). More recently, a survey of HR professionals and leaders based in larger organisations in the UK found that many managers were below the standard needed for growth and successful international competition (CIPD 2009). However, given uncertain and difficult times for many organisations, more weight is being given to finding more creative ways to attract and select the best talent and the ethical stance of managers (CIPD 2009a). While many organisations have been forced to respond to a downturn by reducing the size of the workforce, including managers, others have looked to recruit talent from other organisations (CIPD 2009b). Within organisations, evidence suggests that a positive psychological contract forms the basis for commitment and motivation (Guest *et al* 1998) and it is during times of selection that managers will form and re-form their expectations of the organisation's offer. At different points in their lives, managers face selection processes. Each time a manager moves to a new area of responsibility, the move needs to be seen as a new beginning to the relationship with his or her employer. Managers on every such occasion are thus able to assess their employer's offer, and part of this assessment will relate to factors such as the potential for further promotion, the opportunities for LMD, and how they will continue to be supported in the management of their careers.

A STRATEGY FOR TALENT

During the 1990s and into the 2000s there were general concerns about skills shortages as well as specific concerns about the quantity and quality of managers. In particular, there was intense competition between organisations to identify, attract and develop those individuals who could add most to organisation performance. Such 'high-potential' individuals were seen as critical to an organisation's success. This was the so-called 'war for talent' (Michaels *et al* 2001). Since that time, talent management (TM) has become a highly popular policy in organisations, with a growing list of books, articles and consultancy offers. There is, however, a view that TM represents a repackaging of traditional HRM concepts such as selection, assessment, development and reward but is part of the struggle by HRM professionals to find credibility and status at work (Chuai *et al* 2008). Certainly, there are concerns about the lack of clarity, critical understanding and cases of effectiveness within organisations that have developed TM strategies (Iles 2007). Nevertheless, recent surveys suggest (CIPD 2009a) that during the downturn, some organisations have responded by:

- developing more talent in-house
- focusing on essential development
- continuing to recruit key talent
- placing an increasing focus on employee retention.

In addition, some evidence is emerging of how organisations develop TM strategies and practices even during recession (Tansley *et al* 2007; CIPD 2009b). For example, one response has been to become more active in strengthening relationships and building the profile of the organisation so that it is in a stronger position to recruit talent when the recession ends. At BT, a 'talent deal' established in 2005 has been maintained and has provided a set of commitments from the company for those in the 'talent pool' – a term we explore below. This includes support for career planning and movement, opportunities for networking, meeting senior managers and mentoring. Members of the talent pool are also expected to support the development of others in the company (see CIPD 2009b for more examples).

There is a debate around the meaning of 'talent' (Ashton and Morton 2005), and this has meant that there are a variety of different perspectives of the term. Michaels *et al* (2001) argue that definitions of talent need to fit an organisation with an approach that is right for its situation. This allows a great deal of choice for any organisation in working out an approach to TM and who is included. Iles and Preece (2010) suggest four possible approaches:

- *Exclusive: people* – a focus on 'key' people with high performance and/or potential
- *Exclusive: position* – the right people in key positions
- *Inclusive: people* – everyone in the organisation is seen as actually or potentially talented
- *Inclusive: social capital* – importance of networks, trust, relationships and teams.

Considering these possibilities, we can see that in terms of LMD an *exclusive: people* perspective is more likely to include managers. TM tends to consider people's potential as well as performance, so although managers are often the focus, consideration of potential could widen the identification of those considered talented. Some organisations pay considerable attention to those they consider 'high-potential' as well as 'high-performing'. The *exclusive: position* perspective shifts attention towards key jobs in key positions. Huselid *et al* (2005) point to the importance of 'A positions', which are strategically critical jobs which have to be filled by 'A players' who are the right staff for such positions, in which case the talent will be displayed. It is possible that such positions are not considered to require managers, even though they probably require people who can work with discretion and judgement which have a significant impact on the organisation's performance. For example, customer service staff may not be considered significant in hierarchical terms but their interactions with customers are important.

The *inclusive* approaches both consider that talent can be found beyond a narrowly identified group. The *people* approach recognises that nearly everyone has talent and this can be identified and developed. The *social capital* approach highlights again the importance of networks and distributed influence which attention to individuals fails to recognise. Groysberg *et al* (2004) showed that in a range of different organisations such as banking, software and the law, it is quite possible that giving attention to hiring a 'star' performer can result in a decline in performance of the person and the organisation. Instead, more important were the relationships, systems, processes, networks and team membership, all aspects of social capital which are needed for effective performance. Collings and Mellahi (2009) suggest that the *position* perspective needs to be given more consideration in developing a strategy for TM. They argue that too much attention is given to non-strategic roles that do not provide above-average impact. The crucial feature of positions of talent is their pivotal role in fulfilling an organisation's strategic intent.

These differing approaches do provide a choice in the development of a strategy for TM, and research has tended to find evidence of each of them in practice. For example, the *LMD in Practice* below illustrates an example of an inclusive approach to talent for managers in a restaurant chain.

LMD IN PRACTICE

TALENT STRATEGY FEEDS GROWTH AT NANDO'S

An inclusive approach to talent management has helped restaurant chain Nando's to achieve sevenfold growth in as many years.

UK Learning and Development Manager Marcelo Borges told delegates that the firm's ability to fill vacancies internally was proof that its approach to talent management has paid off.

Almost half (42%) of Nando's restaurant managers are promoted, as are 63% of area managers and 67% of regional directors. The company enjoys a management retention figure of 22%, almost twice as good as the restaurant sector average.

'Nando's approach to talent management is "Let's assume that everyone who works for us is talented, and let them grow and develop in their own environment,"' Borges said. 'Recruiting *nandocas* [staff] with the right values – pride, passion, courage, integrity and family – is key.'

The skills needed to grill chicken could be acquired in two to three weeks, Borges added, but having the right attitude and behaviour was essential to business performance. The vast majority of staff – 96% – say they have fun working for the company, he said.

The company is recruiting 300 managers throughout the UK this year, and is expecting to recruit half internally, Borges added.

Source: Jill Evans, *People Management* magazine 3 May 2007, p.16

Implementation of strategy usually centres on a number of processes, which Tansley *et al* (2007) present as a 'TM loop', shown in Figure 10.1.

WEB LINK

Talent Management Review is an online magazine devoted to TM at **http://www.talentmanagementreview.com/** . The CIPD's factsheet on TM can be obtained from **http://www.cipd.co.uk/subjects/recruitmen/ general/talent-management.htm** .

Figure 10.1 A talent management loop

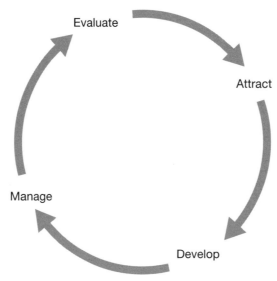

Source: Tansley *et al* (2007, p.19)

SUCCESSION PLANNING

Tansley *et al* (2007) report that succession planning is often presented as the purpose of talent management (TM). This is likely when the TM strategy focuses on the development of future leaders, and during the 2000s succession planning and management were seen as a way of identifying and developing leaders as well as replacing those in senior positions (Fulmer and Conger 2004). With the use of terms such as 'talent pools' and 'talent pipelines', TM could be seen as a replacement for succession planning – a fresh set of ideas for old techniques and tasks by HR managers (Chuai *et al* 2008). However, it is quite possible that the relationship between TM and succession planning is not fully developed with responsibilities for each process allocated to different departments. Tansley *et al* (2007) emphasise the need to 'join up' (p.29) such processes.

For around 50 years there has been an interest in succession in organisations, with debates around the value of a planned approach for the succession, especially of senior managers, for performance, improvement or survival (Giambatista *et al* 2005). Research has tended to suggest that a formal and structured approach to succession, ensuring a smoother fit of managers, provides less disruption to performance. A particular interest in the research is to consider the impact of succession at the level of CEO in organisations quoted on the stock exchange. For example, Ang *et al* (2003) examined CEO succession events in 268 companies listed on the New York Stock Exchange in terms of the pay premium given to a new CEO and future accounting performance, which they hypothesised as positive. Generally, however, the research on succession is described as 'fragmented and variable' (p.981) with uncertainty around whether formal succession can provide more strategic or visionary leaders which might be needed in turbulent future environments or simply to reinforce a stable culture.

A simple view of succession rests on two basic propositions (Hirsh 2000):

- There are fewer management positions as the shape of an organisation's hierarchy narrows.
- There is a pool of staff within an organisation's internal labour market who may have the potential to fill management positions within the hierarchy.

Succession management activities are therefore concerned to reconcile the tensions between identifying the requirements for managers now and in the future in terms of numbers and key skills in relation to business strategy and the desires of managers who aspire to such positions. At the heart of a succession management system lies the succession plan, which is formed by consideration of the direction of the business and future requirements for management and information about the capabilities and potential of the management pool, now likely to be called the talent pool. Common elements of the process to produce the plan are:

- collecting information from appraisals and making an assessment of the individuals concerned[1]
- summarising that information, often by the HR function
- alternatively, presenting the line manager with a chart empty of everything except the name of the job and job-holder, and then asking for the insertion of comments, or asking the manager to talk through his or her comments with an HR adviser
- collating the information to be presented to a decision-making group or to the chief executive alone
- the group or chief executive making a final decision about the comments recorded on the succession plan
- a process by which the succession plan is eventually reviewed and adopted, including a special meeting either of the board or management committee, or of a special LMD committee created for the purpose
- development plans for individual managers.

Of course, there was a time when the shape of an organisation's hierarchy was relatively predictable and sufficiently tall to accommodate enough levels and grades to meet aspirations to 'climb the ladder', with 'fast tracks' available for those identified with the potential to reach the top. In such circumstances, managers could expect frequent promotions into clearly specified jobs until they reached the point where their abilities were matched to the requirement of the role. One approach to measuring the match between people's ability and the task to perform over time is 'career path appreciation' (Stamp 1989). The key idea of this approach is the matching of individual capabilities[2] with challenges the person is to tackle, as measured by the requirements for decision-making. If the challenge is greater than a person's capability, there are negative consequences for individuals and organisations such as stress and rising costs. If the capabilities of the leader or manager are greater than the challenge of the work, resources are wasted and boredom and frustration creep in. Since challenges occur within tasks that are set in an organisation's structure, for balance, flow and effectiveness, managers must be performing work at the right level or stratum for their stage of development with projections to continue the process of development over time. The basic notion of career path appreciation is shown in Figure 10.2.

Figure 10.2 The appreciation of challenge and capability

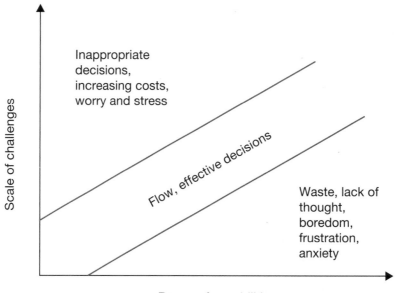

Source: adapted from Stamp (1989)

By the end of the 1980s and into the 1990s succession planning became increasingly problematic. This suggested that continuous learning and development were needed, a theme also highlighted by Hirsh (1990), who pointed to a 'developing potential' (p.18) model of succession as a response to high business uncertainty. Organisations develop all staff as part of a culture of self-development, and succession plans are used only for emergencies; the main onus is on individuals to manage their own careers (see below). Through the 1990s and into the 2000s, varied patterns of succession planning have continued to unfold, often within single organisations. There emerged a segmented pattern of succession. For example, some managers and high-potential staff had their careers managed and supported by their organisation with succession planning to fill senior positions. They faced frequent assessments of their capability, especially where competences provided a link to strategy and a potential means of identifying high-performers. Others faced more limited development opportunities and uncertainty over career paths, with an expectation that they should look after themselves.

In recent years, with the shift in language towards talent management (TM), depending on the TM perspective utilised, those identified as 'talented' become members of a talent pool. Indeed, there can be a number of such pools or there can be movement between pools. Tansley *et al*'s (2007) research of different organisations suggested that talent pools change according to business requirements. Membership of a pool is determined by selection processes including performance reviews, interviews and 360-degree reviews. Google, for example, has a 'universal' talent pool but with different streams for customer services staff and IT specialists. In another organisation researched, a trans-national company, there were specific talent pools at different levels such as:

- business leaders seen as future chief executives
- MBA recruits from business schools
- mid-career hires
- high-potential women.

Succession planning, in terms of developing future managers, therefore requires appropriate categories of talent pools at the different levels connected by a 'talent pipeline', as shown in Figure 10.3.

Figure 10.3 A hierarchy of talent and succession

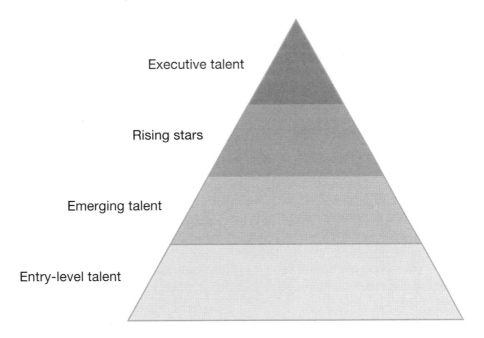

Source: adapted from Tansley *et al* (2007, p.26)

Developing a succession plan based on a talent pipeline between different pools provides an organisation with significant flexibility for appropriate LMD as well as switching attention to motivating internal talent (CIPD 2009b). This is not a hierarchy solely of roles, and there can be considerable lateral movement between roles, departments and projects. Strategically, the organisation becomes what Ready and Conger (2007) refer to as a 'talent factory'. Based on case studies of Proctor & Gamble and HSBC, they suggest that two dimensions should be considered: functionality and vitality. The first is ensuring that the right people are in the right place at the right time, and the second is concerned with attitudes and the mind-sets of those responsible for TM processes.

HIGH-FLYERS

High-flyers are one group that customarily expect few problems with promotion, succession and their careers. Organisations have traditionally spent a great deal of time and money identifying managers of the future who have high potential and are destined to climb the career ladder at a rapid pace; they are on the fast-track to success, starting with graduate entry. Those identified have, until recently, symbolised an ideal of how careers are meant to develop, especially in the Anglo-American context. A good deal of organisational language is action- and achievement-oriented, so high-flyers embody most closely the expectations that such language brings (Altman 1997). However, even in the 1980s the upward path was being superseded by the horizontal path, which implied sideways moves with the opportunity to acquire different skills before advancing upwards (Baruch and Peiperl 1997). By the 1990s many organisations began to close off their fast track because there could not be any certainty about such a track's existing in the future. As Holbeche (1998, p.270) suggested, 'In a "flat" structure, where was a "high-flyer" to "fast track" to?' However, working with the language of TM, during the 2000s many organisations have been seeking to identify 'high-performance and high-potential' employees. A typical approach might be to develop a chart to provide a map of talent within the organisation based on assessments relating to performance and potential, as shown in Figure 10.4.

Figure 10.4 A performance/potential grid[3]

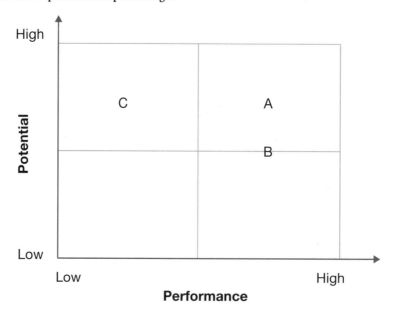

The grid in Figure 10.4 can allow the identification of those who can be considered high-flyers at position A. If the assessment is valid, this is a position of high performance and high potential. At position B, there is high performance and medium potential, and at C, low performance but high potential. The grid is completed by analysing information about each person considered, and for each position on the grid there is a range of possible decisions for learning and development as well as allowing for the formalisation of a succession plan.

10.1 REFLECT — CONCLUDE — PLAN

What development implications might there be for a person considered at positions A, B and C?

Is the performace/potential grid a valid way to assess and develop talent?

How would you deal with people in other positions, such as low potential and medium performance? Or medium potential and medium performance?

For larger numbers of employees that need to be considered, there are software packages now available that allow the processing of massive amounts of data. Pollitt (2007) provides an example from Friesland Foods, a large multinational food company in the Netherlands with over 15,000 staff located around the world. Software was used to track 300 managers in the global talent pool, allowing board-level reporting and discussion for LMD and succession planning. Among its features is graphical talent mapping which can then be used in succession planning to identify blockages.

SELECTING MANAGERS

The availability of a management position provides a range of opportunities for both the organisation and potential recruits. A strategic view would suggest three key questions:

- What is the importance of a role in terms of the value added to the performance of the organisation?
- Should the position be filled internally by developing current staff?
- Should the position be filled by seeking someone externally with the required profile of skills and attributes?

There was a time when the importance of a role could be assessed by its position in a hierarchy as presented on an organisation chart. Each role, if accurately understood by an appropriate evaluation method, could be stated in terms of skills and knowledge required together with its vertical and lateral relationship to other roles. Management roles could be found at higher levels, and so long as markets or context remained relatively unchanging and stable, the importance of a role could be stated clearly and unequivocally. While much of this image remains in place, not least in the way we often talk about organisation roles, it is also becoming clear that new forms of organising and work design within the context of a knowledge-based economy, innovation and technological change on a global scale, are bound to affect how roles are positioned (Valenduc *et al* 2009). Thus project-based organising, virtual organisations and networks all imply a contrast to hierarchical roles and more attention to collaboration and the sharing of influence (Whittington 2002).

Filling a vacancy by internal promotion provides the need for, and justification of, LMD and prevents talented managers from leaving through lack of opportunities (Holbeche 1998). The importance of this 'grow-your-own' approach as a development of the internal labour market is highlighted by the survey of over 500 managers by Thomson *et al* (2001), according to which many managers spent most of their career in the same organisation. Findings from the same survey, however, indicated that nearly half the managers expected to stay less than five years, which suggests that organisations must find ways of retaining managers throughout their careers. There may be certain problems with internal recruitment, though, such as accusations of favouritism or the 'blue-eyed boy' syndrome. For example, Acker (2006) refers to the way an organisation develops a 'gender regime' (p.195) which affects the beliefs and processes that allocate women and men into particular roles. Further, while it may in the short term be more cost-effective to recruit internally, it may also lead to recruitment below the standard required.

The alternative of external recruitment allows an organisation to seek managers with particular skills and attributes that have not been developed internally, such as the formation and implementation of strategy and/or acting as a 'champion of change'. Applicants may be attracted by the 'branding' of an organisation which provides a positive image of an organisation (Edwards 2005). Graduates are a key source of external recruits for the stock of future management. For more senior roles, the initial recruitment might be completed by specialist executive search consultants or 'headhunters'. Over the last 20 years such consultants have exerted a significant but rather unseen influence on the choice of senior managers (McCool 2008).

All applicants, whether internal or external, are assessed against an organisation's model of management (see Chapter 3), frequently expressed as a competency framework which can be used to provide information on the assessment of applicants against the requirements of work (Whiddett and Hollyforde 2003). For internal applicants, information on past and present performance will be available, and this can include 360-degree feedback reports. External applicants can be assessed through various selection instruments such as interviews, psychometric tests, and so on. An assessment centre (AC) provides a way of combining different methods of assessment for selecting managers (see Chapter 4). This also includes selection for participation in LMD programmes and promotion of internal applicants into more senior positions. Indeed, the latter purpose was the original reason for the use of ACs in organisations (Thornton and Gibbons 2009) and there continues to be considerable interest in the use of

ACs in understanding and predicting how managers might learn and perform as they move into more senior positions (Krause *et al* 2006).

WEB LINK

Some useful information on ACs can be obtained at **http://www.jobsite. co.uk/career/advice/ assessment.html** .

CAREERS FOR MANAGERS

It was not so long ago that a manager's career would follow a progressive path through a number of stages. Through selection, assessment and appropriate LMD, a manager could move 'up the ladder', taking on roles of increasing responsibility and rank. Although not everyone could be sure of reaching the top, it was within careers which provided a 'well-made road' (Sennett 1998) that managers could reach their desires for status and fulfilment. Career and managerial identities were thus tightly linked and organisations were expected to support this link by providing a structure for career progression composed of plans for development. In recent years, however, there has been growing scepticism over whether the rules to do with careers and the meanings of 'career management' continue to apply (CIPD 2002). Most organisations advocate a partnership approach to careers, with advice and training provided by the organisation but ownership for career management passed on to the individual. However, surveys suggest little support for careers by senior managers and line managers (CIPD 2003).

THE MEANINGS OF 'CAREER'

Adamson *et al* (1998) have explored the roots of the term 'career' and its implications. They suggest that:

- 'Career' implies a route to be followed which has direction and purpose.
- There is movement over time which has order, logic and meaning between successive positions.
- In organisations, employers and employees can plan the logical progression through work-related events and experiences.
- Over the course of one's life, a career can pass through a number of phases or stages.

Models of career and development have matched such views. For example, Super (1957) suggested that careers were determined by a range of socio-economic factors, mental and physical abilities, personal characteristics and the opportunities from which a person can choose. A key idea in Super's model was that career maturity was achieved by matching tasks with stages of development over a life-span. Career satisfaction could be obtained if, at the appropriate stage of development, people could choose a work role that allowed them to develop their self-concept.[4] Table 10.1 shows Super's stages model.

Table 10.1 Super's stages of career choice

Stage	Characteristics
Growth	Forming the self-concept, developing attitudes, needs, interests and abilities relating to work
Exploration	Trying things out through classes, work experience, hobbies. Beginning to consider work choice
Establishment	Building necessary skills. Stabilising through work experience, adjusting as required
Maintenance	Adjusting to improve position
Decline	Moving towards retirement

Source: adapted from Super (1957)

Super's model has been a significant influence in thinking about careers, and since 1957 the model has been adapted and adjusted several times. One such adjustment related to the flexibility of career stages and the fact that each stage can be repeated or recycled (Super and Kidd 1979). Other writers have also pointed to a more flexible and evolutionary perspective of careers. Kanter (1989) pointed out that the 'bureaucratic career' based on a logic of advancement was only one form of career, and Arthur *et al* (1994, p.8) referred to the 'evolving sequence of a person's work experiences over time', highlighting the importance of the relationship between people and those who provide positions in organisations. That relationships are always subject to change raised the prospect that a career route may have to deviate from an intended path, perhaps coming to a standstill or even closing down altogether.

Adamson *et al* (1998) suggest that during the 1990s, in response to economic and competitive pressure, the notion of a career for life began to disappear. There have been three consequential changes in organisational career philosophy:

- an end to the long-term view of employer–employee relationship
- an end to hierarchical movement as career progression
- an end to logical, ordered and sequential careers.

While the certainty of the single career path disappears, instead the path becomes 'multidirectional' (Baruch 2004), with different ways of achieving a successful career, including how career success is evaluated. This might consider such values as freedom, autonomy, work–life balance, and so on. Those who seek management careers and managers already working cannot rely on organisations for advancement. Instead, they must take more responsibility for their own career management. Arnold (1997, p.16) shifts the emphasis towards individuals by considering a career to be 'the sequence of employment-related positions, roles, activities and experiences encountered by a person'. Arnold includes leisure activities, education and domestic work within the notion of career if they link with employment. It is very much up to individuals to define their careers, and this includes moving around from one post to another and not necessarily seeking promotion. It also shifts the responsibility for managing careers towards the individual – although a variety of stakeholders may influence how a career develops.

During the 1990s the notion of the 'portfolio career' gained prominence (Cawsey *et al* 1995), and it became the responsibility of individuals to develop a range of skills which enhanced their marketability and employability. The more they did this, the less they needed to restrict themselves to employment within one particular organisation: managers could consider their careers 'boundaryless' (Arthur and Rousseau 1996) and therefore less dependent on 'traditional organisational career arrangements' (p.6). The idea of the 'boundaryless career' has attracted considerable interest (Sullivan and Arthur 2006), especially the notions of physical mobility, concerned with the movement between jobs, occupations and locations, and psychological mobility, concerned with how individuals come to understand their abilities to make career movements. The latter gives attention to the subjective perspective of an individual who has to consider current realities in making career choices. Hall (2002) refers to the idea of a 'protean' career where a person self-directs a career based on self-defined goals, values and success. This is similar to a recent idea of the 'subjective career' (Khapova *et al* 2007), where attention is given to the 'individual's own interpretation of his or her career situation at any given time' (p.115). One of the key features of this view is that a career, as interpreted by an individual, can involve a number of different dimensions such as when to undertake LMD, what preferences there are for focus and specialisation and time and commitment for activities such as raising families. Generally, research tends to ignore such features of a career in favour of more objective factors such as pay, status and occupational qualifications (Arthur *et al* 2005).

10.2 REFLECT – CONCLUDE – PLAN

Do you agree with the view that 'a career for life' has disappeared?

What will be the consequences for the management of your career?

What can you do to increase your employability and marketability?

A recent career theory uses the metaphor of a kaleidoscope to consider changes in the patterns of careers in response to individual variations in relationships and the roles of their lives. The Kaleidoscope Career Model (KCM) (Sullivan *et al* 2007) suggests that an individual should consider and evaluate choices, seeking a best fit, based on the parameters of:

1 authenticity – alignment of an individual's internal values with behaviours and the values of the organisation

2 balance – striving to reach an equilibrium between work and non-work demands (eg family, friends, elderly relatives, personal interests)

3 challenge – the need for stimulating work and career advancement.

It is suggested that the prominence and intensity of each parameter shifts over a life-span and that there are variations between different generations in an organisation. For example, research by Sullivan *et al* (2009) found that those considered as 'Generation X' – born between 1965 and 1983 – have a higher preference for authenticity and balance than 'baby boomers' – born between 1946 and 1964.

CAREER MANAGEMENT

Managers perform their work as a part of organised activity, so it should be self-evident that the context and systems of that activity are immensely important to the way a leader or manager's career is managed and developed. Edgar Schein (1978) took a particular interest in career systems, arguing for their strategic importance. He presented a human resource planning and development system which was composed of minimum-level activities to match individual and organisation needs. The activities included:

- at organisational level: organisation planning, human resource planning
- at individual level: individual work history, individual self-assessment
- matching processes: performance appraisal (in respect of present and future performance), human resource inventory.

The outcomes of the system covered individual career plans and a 'specific human resource plan'. Schein argued that because organisations were likely to face increasing turbulence from the environment, it was important to maintain a balance between activities that serve the needs of individuals and those that serve the needs of the organisation. In particular, Schein highlighted the importance of dialogue to achieve such balance in the form of jointly negotiated plans for work and development.

 WEB LINK

For more about the work of Edgar Schein, go to his web page at **http://web.mit.edu/scheine/ www/home.html** which includes links to more work on career dynamics.

Mayo (1997) saw career management activities as a spectrum ranging from those that benefit the organisation, such as succession planning, to those that benefit individuals, such as counselling, and to those that bring the two together, such as appraisal. The key is to ensure that mutual objectives are agreed.

The line manager's role in career management seems particularly important in light of findings relating to perceptions of equity with career management processes. For example, an organisation's concern with the management of careers, especially where it is seen to be fair, has been found to be a significant contributor to satisfaction with career management (Herriot *et al* 1994). There is a clear link between fairness of promotion procedures and honouring agreements and satisfaction with career management, even if managers do not make career progress. Career management can therefore be seen as a feature of the psychological contract between managers and their organisations in respect of attitudes and perceptions towards what each expects from the other. During the 1990s the psychological contract relating to management careers was thrown into flux and, for some, broke down. The need for competiveness, customer service and a response to global change, combined with technological advances, all served to impact on organisational structures and decision-making that had been a source of relatively stable career patterns. Managers' expectations on promotion and job security were changing (Goffee and Scase 1992).

It was during the 1990s that middle managers especially faced serious threats to their careers as many organisations flattened their hierarchies and/or downsized. Some managers found their careers in their preferred organisations curtailed, but even those that remained at work after a period of downsizing might experience lower commitment and insecurity as well as guilt as they felt sympathy for those made redundant – a feeling referred to as 'survivor syndrome' (Thornhill *et al* 1997). Another finding was that middle managers had to take on increased work responsibilities with greater pressure to achieve results (Doherty *et al* 1995). Thomas and Dunkerley (1999) found in their case study research of 50 organisations that middle managers had experienced intensification of work with the loss of a career structure particularly significant in the public sector. For example, in the civil service the loss of a career structure was seen as 'betrayal' by middle managers, little alternative being offered in the form of career development and personal career plans. In some cases, however, restructuring meant an early promotion for middle managers as more senior colleagues took the option of retirement. Appelbaum and Santiago (1997, p.13) suggested that in the context of what they refer to as 'career plateauing', managers had to take control of their career development by becoming 'career strategists'. This included:

- viewing career paths as fragmented and subject to change

- equating career success with personal satisfaction and charting progress by the degree to which career decisions satisfy personal needs

- developing a multi-dimensional plan clustered around several objectives that fulfil career needs at a particular point in life.

For organisations, the experience of middle managers and others in the 1990s had important implications in the 2000s, especially in the context of continuing changes to expectations about careers. One consequence was a movement in what Hirsh and Jackson (1997, p.9) referred to as the 'pendulum of ownership of career development'. Some organisations swung the responsibility for career development towards individuals' taking the initiative for managing their own careers. A new psychological contract for managers was on offer: organisations could provide a job and opportunities, but it was the leader or managers' responsibility to make use of these and develop their own careers – a move which could match a self-development LMD policy. However, Hirsh and Jackson also found that there could be an over-emphasis on individual responsibility, and more shared responsibility where information from career development processes could provide useful data for both the organisation and individuals. For example, 360-degree feedback could be used by individual managers and the organisation. They suggested that career development could be managed in a variety of ways, as shown by Figure 10.5. It is quite possible that variations in responsibility and career development offer exist in the same organisation. Hirsh (2002) argues that the idea of career is still very important to people. Organisations need to combine the achievement of high job performance with active career development, aiming for 'win/win' outcomes (p.49).

Figure 10.5 The career development continuum

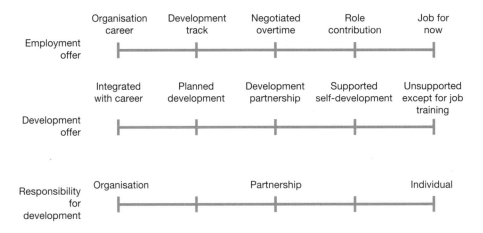

Source: Hirsh and Jackson (1997, p.26)

Hirsh and Rolph (2003) found a confusing and conflicting pattern of career management practices in the UK, most organisations advocating the view that staff should take responsibility for their careers while also emphasising the need to grow future managers and retain key staff. One example of excellent practice was from KPMG, which gave strong input to supporting career development. Everyone had regular discussions with their managers about performance and career aspirations. The organisation also provided internal career coaches, group workshops on career management, one-to-one advice as required, and web-based guidance.

WEB LINK

Check KPMG's approach to careers at **http://www.kpmgcampus.com/** .

The downside to pushing responsibility towards managers for developing their own careers is that there may be a disconnection between success in managing a career and leading groups, teams and organisations. Kaiser *et al* (2008) provide an overview of the research on this possibility and suggest that the

10.3 REFLECT – CONCLUDE – PLAN

Who is responsible for your career development?

What support do you need for career development?

What can you do to help others develop their careers in the future?

relationship between a successful career and being an effective leader varies across organisations, but there is a possibility that a weak relationship between careers and effectiveness can have a negative effect on organisations in terms of morale, strategy, and even corruption. Managers need to be tied in some way to the performance of their teams and staff, and this means that some responsibility must be taken by the organisation for the development of careers.

It is for reasons like these that recent years have seen more interest in organisations for the promotion and movement of managers. As part of the trend towards talent management, it is recognised that as managers move into different roles, usually at higher levels of responsibility, there must be a degree of transformation in how they direct their efforts. Survey research by the CIPD (2007) points to the need to consider career 'transitions' or 'passages' for managers. In a large organisation, such movements can occur:

- from individual contributor to people leader, or 'first-line' leader
- from people leader to operational leader, or 'mid-level' leader
- from operational leader to strategic leader, or 'senior' leader.

Over 80% of 600 managers surveyed agreed that different ways of thinking were needed in transitions for success, although only 30% felt that support was provided. For some there was a negative view of support, with politics and failure to establish networks a particular barrier, both contributing to stress and anxiety as managers seek to develop new skills and ways of understanding. Mentoring and coaching can provide important support processes during transitions in careers.

SELF-MANAGEMENT OF CAREERS

If managers are now faced with a diverse choice in their careers, they require skills of self-management – and since, according to King (2004), career self-management is highly dynamic, a manager will need to perform a number of key behaviours, such as:

- positioning behaviours – concerned with acquiring contacts, skills and experience that are relevant to desired outcomes
- influence behaviours – concerned with influencing the 'gatekeepers' to desired outcomes

● boundary management – concerned with the balance of work demands and life outside work.

There is a clear connection between this view of behaviours and the model of career competences presented by Ball (1997), who used data from case studies that took an individual perspective on career changes to develop four overlapping career competences. These are shown in Figure 10.6.

Figure 10.6 A model of career competences

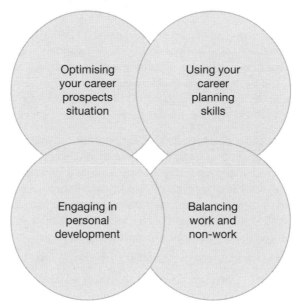

Source: Ball (1997, p.76)

Ball explains the competences as follows:

● *Optimising career prospects*
  – taking a goal-directed approach to career planning, anticipating the future and promoting one's own career interests. In addition, managers can make use of mentors and engage in activities that get them noticed. Further, it is suggested that mentoring is beneficial to career success for those who provide mentoring for others as well as those who receive it (Bozionelos 2004). By mentoring others, managers advance their own careers, and in turn, those they mentor become motivated to mentor others in the future. Networking with others is also considered an important competency for career self-management, especially as a way of increasing visibility at the workplace and being seen to tackle difficult assignments (Forret and Dougherty 2004). However, networking may be more beneficial to males compared with females.

● *Career planning*
  – playing to strengths by frequent reviews of career and personal development. This corresponds to Mumford's (1990) view that the learning process should be prominent in career planning. Managers take advantage of

learning opportunities within work roles and put less reliance on formally constructed plans; we referred to this as practice-based LMD.

- *Engaging in personal development*
  - as well as learning within roles, identifying other learning opportunities both to increase fulfilment and satisfaction and also to enhance marketability. Managers identify needs, learn from the opportunities and find others to support them – such as becoming part of an Action Learning set. Managers who further their human capital by completing a programme such as an MBA are more likely to enjoy career success (Baruch 2009). Of course, membership of an MBA class can also build social capital by providing a network that lasts beyond the completion of the qualification.

- *Balancing work and non-work*
  - using opportunities for learning that might include non-work openings such as voluntary work, although this seems more likely in the USA than in the UK (Whymark and Ellis 1999). It could also be important to counter stress that occurs from working long hours.

10.4 REFLECT – CONCLUDE – PLAN

How far have you developed career competences?

Which career competence do you think requires attention?

What will you do to develop this competence, and what action could others take?

WEB LINK

Achieving work–life balance and flexible working is promoted by the UK Government: the website is located at **http://www.berr.gov.uk/ whatwedo/employment/workandfamilies/flexible-working/index.html** . A number of case studies are provided by the Work Foundation at **http:// www.theworkfoundation.com/difference/e4wlb.aspx** .

Career self-management also implies that careers can be made by managers who have a desire to have control over their careers (King 2004). As Khapova *et al* (2007) suggest, the concern is with careers as a subjective property of managers rather than through objective determination by the organisation. Stewart and Knowles (1999) point to the crucial importance of self-awareness as a process of reflection to match what knowledge and skills a leader or manager has to offer with the work that will provide satisfaction. Self-knowledge is also identified by Butcher and Harvey (1998, p.76) as a meta-ability which is 'a first step toward developing flexibility in dealing with diverse and complex managerial situations'.[5]

One source of self-awareness could be a manager's talents, values and motives which form the self-concept and identity and are acquired through experience and learning. As managers advance through their careers, the self-concept may form into a pattern and provide the basis for decisions about career choices. Schein (1990) refers to the idea of 'career anchors' as features of a person's self-concept which have a significant impact on career choice and behaviour. The crucial impact of a career anchor, according to Schein, is that it is an element of self-concept that 'he or she will not give up' (p.18). This means that where work does not match a career anchor, a person will have a sense that what he or she is doing is 'not really me, not really what I would like to be doing or am capable of doing' (p.19). Eventually, this will cause dissatisfaction and attempts to move to work that matches the career value more closely. Schein (1990) outlines eight career anchors:

- *technical/functional competence* – skills in a technical or functional area that provides a sense of identity
- *general managerial competence* – desire to seek responsibility and accountability for total results
- *autonomy/independence* – the opportunity to define one's own work and remain in work that allows flexibility
- *security/stability* – a concern for security, including financial, and seeking achievement to allow relaxation
- *entrepreneurial creativity* – the desire to create organisation by taking risks and using one's own abilities
- *service/dedication to a cause* – pursuing work that achieves something of value, such as making the world a better place and doing something for others
- *pure challenge* – working on difficult problems and overcoming obstacles
- *lifestyle* – balancing personal, family and career needs into an integrated whole.

Faced with decisions and choices about careers, most managers will have little awareness of their values and self-concept, so completion of an assessment of career anchors is described by Day *et al* (2004) as an 'excellent tool' (p.116) to help increase self-awareness and career motivation.

 WEB LINK

Find out more about career anchors at **http://www.careeranchorsonline. com/SCA/ samplequestionspub.do**, where you can complete sample questions.

COMPLEXITY AND CAREERS

Career anchors offer a degree of persistence and continuity to managers in the face of uncertainty with respect to their careers. In recent years there has been an interest in the application of chaos and complexity theories to provide some explanation of how careers might be developed. Career systems are complex and dynamic, but according to chaos theory such systems follow basic and simple rules even though the effects may seem random and unpredictable. Gibb (1998), for example, argues that the beliefs of people in the system offer an indication of 'attractor states' – that is, of the point at which complex systems settle into an apparent equilibrium. Gibb suggests that the messiness produced by career chaos can be better explored by an examination of beliefs and assumptions of various interests. For individual managers, beliefs and values lie at the heart of a self-organising process that creates the order of their lives. However, this image of the individual must be augmented by the degree of interdependence between managers and others that form a network of relationships. Bloch (2005) works with ideas of complexity and chaos, and views individuals and careers as complex adaptive entities. Career paths may be expected to be predictable but are most likely to be found to follow a trajectory which cannot be explained. Bloch suggests some key elements of chaos, complexity and non-linear dynamics can be applied to careers including participation in networks, self-generation or autopoiesis, transitions between order and chaos and the potential for small changes to bring about large effects. She gives particular emphasis to spirituality which highlights interdependence and connectedness and how this is experienced as a unity. Similarly, Parker and Arthur (2001) present the concept of an 'intelligent career', in which interaction feeds three features of 'ways of knowing' for careers – *knowing-whom* in terms of relationships, *knowing-how* in terms of skills, and *knowing-why* in terms of career motivation. Interactions are non-linear where small actions can have large effects and are subject to feedback which can prevent any degree of settlement or equilibrium.[6]

 WEB LINK

If you want to explore further the way chaos and complexity theories can be used in thinking about careers, you might like to visit *M@n@agement*, an online journal, at **http://www.management-aims.com/vol5_fr.html**, where Vol.5, No.1, 2002 – a special issue on 'Careers and new science' – can be downloaded.

Go to **http://www.humaxnetworks.com/socialcap.html** for more information on social capital and how it is measured.

CAREER SUCCESS

If most managers are unable to gain rapid promotion or achieve hierarchical advance, how do they judge whether they have been successful in developing their careers? This was an issue explored by Sturges (1999) in a UK telecommunications company. Interviewing 36 managers of different ages and both genders, meanings of 'career success' were examined. Managers identified both external and internal criteria for success. External criteria included pay and position but also intangible criteria such as influence and personal recognition. Internal criteria related to accomplishment in terms of feeling good about work carried out, a sense of personal achievement from work, enjoying and finding work interesting, feeling that work was worthwhile and combining work with successful home life. Four orientations for career success were suggested:

- *climbers* – who described success in terms of external criteria, such as moving up the organisation hierarchy to gain status

- *experts* – who saw success as achieving competence in their jobs and being recognised personally for being good

- *influencers* – for whom success was defined as being able to do things that had a clear and positive effect, whatever their hierarchical position

- *self-realisers* – for whom success was based on achievement on their own terms for personal fulfilment, with a balance between work and home life vital.

There is evidence here that managers use criteria other than position in the organisational hierarchy to judge success in their careers thus giving more prominence to a subjective view of career success over an objective view. This may be a response to the reality that managers now face – ie reconciling the limitations on external indicators of success by focusing on what is achievable, such as influence or high competency in work. It also suggests that succession plans and TM systems need to focus less on formal plans and more on the values and beliefs of managers, helping them to understand how they can continue to develop their careers in line with their own criteria for success.

Ng *et al* (2005) completed an analysis of key articles relating to the predictors of career success and found that working hard and receiving sponsorship or support from the organisation played a key role. Working hard suggests the need for learning skills and competencies related to work but sponsorship also highlights the importance of contextual factors such as access to resources and support for career development. For example, some organisations provide career development workshops to deliver a range of processes for the self-management of careers. Career workshops have been identified as one of the most effective interventions to promote career planning (Jackson 1990). As part of a workshop provided for young managers in Leeds, the following processes were used:

- an introduction to career competences, based on Ball (1997)

- a consideration of key influences on the career, surfacing values and beliefs

- a personal SWOT analysis

- the completion and analysis of Schein's Career Anchors Inventory and Honey and Mumford's Learning Styles Questionnaire

- the compilation of a personal action plan, followed two months later by a one-day review.

One interesting finding by Ng *et al* (2005) related to the careers of women. Subjectively, education for women had a stronger impact on career satisfaction than for men. This might reflect the lower availability of career opportunities for women, so that investment in skills and qualifications become more attractive and satisfying. It is also suggested that women, facing disadvantage for promotions at work, have to work harder to prove themselves, and this includes having qualifications. On the basis that women might be expected to work fewer hours than men, those women that work longer hours become more recognised for their commitment. Another finding found less inequality between men and women on pay but a persistent problem of women failing to gain promotion to higher levels within organisations. It is argued that women may decide not to pursue promotions for a variety of reasons such as raising families but also to avoid the politics and power issues that are likely to occur at higher levels of an organisation. Of course, bias and prejudice of male managers can also contribute to this ongoing inequality.

Increasingly, an organisation may support career development by providing access to materials for self-help and continuous learning, often available online, as described in the *LMD in Practice* below.

LMD IN PRACTICE

ONLINE 'CAREER INNOVATION ZONE' HELPS STAFF ASSESS THEIR STRENGTHS, WEAKNESSES

Royal & SunAlliance (R&SA) is encouraging staff to plan their careers with the help of a new intranet site. The 'career innovation zone' contains interactive elements to help users assess their strengths, weaknesses and motivations and set development goals. Katherine Morris, head of HR at R&SA, told *PM* that employee feedback had found that staff wanted more help in understanding the career opportunities available to them.

'Giving people the confidence to develop their careers is one of the most engaging things you can do,' she added. Morris said the site had 'inspired leaders to get involved in career development', and that there were now more conversations between employees and their managers on the topic.

The site also profiles 'career connectors', explaining how various people from across the business arrived at their current role. Staff are invited to contact these 'career connectors' for advice and support. Morris said: 'The most successful people tend to focus on their strengths, but understanding weaknesses also helps people to put themselves in the right space. Also, if weaknesses are knowledge-based, they can be easy to fix.'

One way to address skills gaps is through international secondments, which meets another of R&SA's objectives – encouraging movement within the business. 'In emerging markets we're developing at a faster rate than perhaps the local skills base can accommodate,' Morris explained. 'In order to grow we want to use skills that exist in our UK markets.' She said that although international vacancies were advertised on the intranet, workers who were not actively looking for a new role would not see them. The site now alerts users to these vacancies.

The system, made by provider Career Innovation, went live after a pilot at the end of last year. Employees are encouraged to 'blog' on the intranet and have given positive feedback on their experiences so far, Morris added.

Source: Laura Chubb, *People Management* magazine, 21 February 2008, p.10

Managers can also be more proactive about their careers and futures. Wheelwright (2009) draws on the key ideas of life stages to develop a framework for individuals to use future tools and methods, such as a personal strategic plan and scenarios, so they can make choices at different points in their lives. Again, the subjective position becomes prominent through personal values which influence the vision and direction taken. Awareness of values is a key part of the process provided.

WEB LINK

An online career development e-manual can be found at **http://www.cdm.uwaterloo.ca/steps. asp** .

You can also gain access to Verne Wheelwright's material on personal future and personal strategic planning at **http://www.personalfutures. net/** .

LEARNING FROM REDUNDANCY

Being proactive about careers and personal futures would seem particularly important in recent times when many managers have had to reconsider their options. Research by Kammeyer-Mueller *et al* (2008) highlights the importance of self-esteem and indicators of career success such as income and prestige. Valuing self also affects the motivation to search for work when times are less favourable. Clearly, for some managers in recent years, the illusion of a career for life in an organisation is shattered by the loss of their position, and this is often accompanied by financial, social and psychological losses.

Both the threat and the actuality of redundancy affect a manager's feelings of security, commitment to the company and the working of the psychological contract. Long-serving managers in particular tend to assume that they will be protected from redundancy, even in the face of objective information (Hallier and Lyon 1996). Those that remain may suffer from 'survivor syndrome' (Doherty *et al* 1995)

One way to soften the impact for managers is to take a proactive and creative approach to managing redundancy – one that helps them move to a new stage in their career and that is based on learning and development. For example, an organisation can offer managers help through outplacement.[7] This involves providing a programme of support to develop a CV and review skills, to consider how to access the job market and to receive counselling from qualified occupational psychologists. Managers may receive outplacement support as part of a termination package providing off-site access to specialist consultants.[8] During the 1990s outplacement became a central feature of HRM strategy in managing redundancy (Doherty 1998). While outplacement may lead to a new job, another transitional opportunity is to become an 'interim manager'. This involves managers taking on short-term projects and attempting to transfer their knowledge and experience to a new situation. Sometimes referred to as 'troubleshooters' (Voudson 2002), interim managers may be required to manage projects and carry out mergers using their experience and wisdom.

Most are senior managers in their fifties, and although they may be 'comfortably over-qualified' (p.122), the opportunity offers a leader or manager a chance for LMD. The last few years have seen a growth in such opportunities with the trade body the Interim Management Association (IMA) providing an induction workshop for managers with 15 to 20 years' experience on the meaning and role of interim management, coaching on the value they might bring as well as hearing from other interim managers (Robeson 2008).

 WEB LINK

The website **http://www.ioim.org.uk/** provides a link to the Institute of Interim Management, and **http://www.interimmanagement.uk.com/** is the trade body, the Interim Management Association.

SUMMARY

- Based on concerns about skills shortages as well as specific concerns about the quantity and quality of managers, many organisations have developed talent management strategies and policies.

- Succession planning can range from simple reaction to departures and retirements to a more sophisticated consideration of future supply, succession and development as part of a talent management strategy.

- Managers are recruited and selected from an internal pool or external sources.

- An organisation's competence framework can be used to provide information on the assessment of applicants against the requirements of work. Fuller information about candidates can be obtained from assessment centres and via the use of valid and reliable methods such as psychometrics.

- Models of career and development have tended towards the view that careers have a logical route to follow which can be planned – but more recently, predictable career paths have become difficult to achieve.

- Career management in organisations has to maintain a balance between activities which serve the needs of individuals and those that serve the needs of the organisation.

- Managers can learn skills of career self-management including self-awareness and self-knowledge, especially relating to their talents, values and motives which form the self-concept.

- Managers increasingly set their own subjective criteria for career success.

- Proactive redundancy management though the provision of outplacement and interim management opportunities can help managers move to a new stage in their career, based on learning and development.

QUESTIONS

For discussion

1 How might a talent management strategy ensure a future supply of managers? Are there any difficulties with such an approach?

2 Do succession plans work? What are the requirements for successful succession management?

3 How can assessment centres be made attractive to managers in selection?

4 How can the needs of organisations and the needs of individuals be reconciled in career management?

5 *I am fed up with people asking me about careers in the organisation. There are none.* Discuss, with reference to career development for managers.

6 Why might female managers face barriers to their careers?

GROUP ACTIVITY

Get together in a group of four.

Each person should complete an individual career SWOT analysis.

For *Strengths*, consider all the positive attributes and credentials you can offer an employer.

For *Weaknesses*, examine less positive attributes and credentials which might be considered for improvement.

For *Opportunities*, explore trends, relationships and gaps of which you can take advantage.

And for *Threats*, consider the adverse trends, competition and negative forces you might be able to reduce or make preparations for.

Share your findings within your group.

NOTES

1 Some organisations may require attendance at an assessment or development centre as a qualification for consideration in succession plans. A concomitant factor may be that failure to attend could indicate a lack of desire for promotion.

2 Career path appreciation has its origins in the work of the famous organisational psychologist Elliot Jacques.

3 This grid is often presented as a 3 x 3 matrix providing a nine-box grid and is regarded as a very useful TM tool.

4 In Chapter 4 we highlighted the importance of the self-concept in how managers responded to feedback.

5   In addition to self-knowledge, Butcher and Harvey (1998) identified cognitive skills, emotional resilience and personal drive as four meta-abilities for LMD and taking personal career decisions.

6   This seems to contradict the notion of 'attractor states' and equilibrium mentioned above, although the key point is that the dynamics of a complex system may give the appearance of stability while remaining in flux.

7   Outplacement is often referred to by providers as 'career transition'.

8   Some managers may receive their support within the organisation – sometimes referred to as 'inplacement'.

 FURTHER READING

EDDLESTON, K. A. (2009) 'The effects of social comparisons on managerial career satisfaction and turnover intentions', *Career Development International,* Vol.14 No.1: 87–110

HIGGINS, M. (2005) *Career Imprints: Creating leaders across an industry.* San Francisco, CA: Jossey-Bass

IBARRA, H. (2003) *Working Identity: Unconventional strategies for reinventing your career.* Boston, MA: Harvard Business School Press

KETS DE VRIES, M. (2009) *Reflections on Leadership and Career Development: On the Couch with Manfred Kets De Vries.* London/ New York: John Wiley & Sons

CHAPTER 11

Diversity and ecology

CHAPTER OUTLINE

Introduction
Diversity
Women managers
Black, Asian and minority ethnic managers
National cultures and global management
Green LMD
Professions and LMD
Summary

LEARNING OUTCOMES

After studying this chapter, you should be able to understand, explain, analyse and evaluate:

- the relationship of LMD to diversity management

- the difficulties faced by female and black, Asian and minority ethnic managers

- the importance of national cultures in LMD

- the key ideas of green leadership and management

- approaches to leadership and management within the professions

INTRODUCTION

In Chapter 1 we argued that variations in the configuration of work organisation were likely to affect how leadership and management are understood and how LMD might occur. As Burgoyne *et al* (2004) argued, situation and context can vary significantly, so it becomes difficult to generalise too much about LMD. In this chapter we propose to consider some of the effects of variation of situation and context and what this means for managers. For example, recently in the UK in a rare show of unity, the Confederation of British Industry, the Trades Union Congress and the Equality and Human Rights Commission joined forces to argue that meeting legal and moral requirements on diversity can also have clear business benefits (CBI 2008). However, despite the significant interest in the benefits of diversity, many managers frequently face discrimination or stereotyping on grounds of their gender, race or ethnic background, sexuality or disability, all of which may require particular consideration in LMD. Another key variation is the skills and qualifications of the workforce. Increasingly, work is knowledge-based and often requires the employment of professionally qualified staff (Moynagh and Worsley 2005). Managers in organisations where such work occurs will certainly have different needs. Similarly, managers who work in global settings need to understand how local cultures inform the values and behaviours of the workforce. We will also consider how contextual pressures relating to climate, the environment and responsibility to society are having an important impact on LMD provision.

DIVERSITY

In recent years, there has been a tendency for 'diversity' to replace 'equality' in leadership and management discourse and, in the context of labour market deregulation, for the business case to be popularised (Dickens 1999). Diversity moves beyond the idea of equality of opportunities in organisations, towards the recognition of the value of difference. Such differences, when applied to organisations, may be visible and obvious – such as gender and ethnicity – but they may also be less visible and even suppressed, such as religion and sexuality. What is important is that such differences play a vital part in people's self-concept but also in how others relate to them. Stereotyping and discrimination may be ameliorated by adjustments to structural factors such as job descriptions but may persist in actions and attitudes. Diversity is concerned with making the best use of differences and removing barriers to such use. Singh (2002) suggests that diversity matters for several significant reasons:

- the business case – Including all staff in the development pool is a source of competitive advantage.
- the fairness case – Barriers to those who are different are removed.
- the merit case – Stereotyping of the management role as white and male excludes those of talent who are not.

Singh argues that legislation has not sufficiently changed attitudes and awareness. Diversity must therefore become a strategic issue, and managers must have a vital role in leading progress and changing practices. However, while many organisations now rhetorically express their intent to support diversity or equality, and usually both, there has always been recognition that however expressed, the implementation of policy has been far from unproblematic. Foster and Harris (2005) noted that often employers and employees are confused by the simultaneous focus on equality and the valorisation of difference in the workplace, and question whether diversity is just equality repackaged or genuinely represents something new. Additionally, there is a growing critical engagement with the concept of diversity and its origins (Lorbiecki and Jack 2000) and a warning against the dangers of a 'utilitarian' business argument (Western 2008). Ford *et al* (2009) reported that even the term 'diversity' had the potential to alienate leaders, managers and providers of LMD. They suggest that the argument for diversity needed to be presented in a way that complemented the interests of leaders and managers. They also found that compliance with legal requirements and codes is the normal expectation and is given a begrudging reception. This is supported by findings from a national survey by the CIPD (2007) of 285 respondents who had responsibility for diversity from a variety of private, public and voluntary organisations. The survey found a significant disconnection between the reality of diversity and what was espoused. Most employers were said to 'have a long way to go to make diversity a mainstream business issue' (p.3), many seeing diversity as a way of conforming with the law and therefore a cost. It therefore recommends the need for training in the business case arguments for diversity – a call that we can agree with – however, there needs to be more than formal training. Especially important are managers who can exert influence on others and who are seen to exemplify good practice, behaviours and value-driven attitudes. The *LMD in Practice* opposite provides one example of a programme for leaders which incorporated learning about diversity within a framework of talents and workforce planning.

WOMEN MANAGERS

Over 40% of the UK workforce are women, and over the last 15 years there has been a strong growth in the number of female managers, to around 33% of all managers. Women managers represent around 37% of team leaders and 14.4% of directors (CMI 2005). In the larger organisations that feature in the FTSE-100, in 2008 there were 131 women on the board, representing around 11% of directorships, compared with 66 women in 1998 (Sealey *et al* 2008). While this can be seen as progress, it is also suggested that this is still too slow and betokens a failure to take advantage of the talent of women in positions of influence and power (EHRC 2008). In high-level positions women are frequently under-represented, even in areas of work such as health and social services where most managers are women. It is a pattern repeated throughout public life in the judiciary, civil service and local government. Historically, the view of most managers (of course, predominantly male) was that these differences were in some sense 'natural'. It was perceived to reflect women's actual competence or their own inevitable career choices as actual or potential mothers. This view was gradually challenged as ethically inappropriate and as an ineffective use of a total potential resource for the leadership and managerial population. Recent consideration of the views of male and female management students would suggest that leadership and management roles could be performed by both sexes, and that they expect to be treated fairly in selection, training and promotion (Schein 2007).

'EQUALITY STREET': TALENT AND DIVERSITY FOR LEADERS IN THE NHS

Sue Davison, *Managing Director, ETC Training and Development*

Knowing the value in enjoying the mix of talents at work can be rather like exploring the different centres in a tin of chocolates. This was a reflective comment on what diversity now means to pharmacy managers across NHS Yorkshire and the Humber. They developed their skills through a Leadership Development Programme, with a particular focus on workforce planning. The programme also included the new Managing Equality and Diversity Level 4 Award from the Institute of Leadership and Management, which enables groups to have the opportunity to explore legislation within the context of their own organisations, while also providing a practical range of tools to support implementation in the workplace.

One of the delegates commented that having gone through the programme she valued the process in bringing talent to the fore, which is one of the new tools created by the Business Case for Diversity Group in Leeds.

Benefits in understanding the 'true' meaning of the term 'equality and diversity' have been sustained by the group and taken back to their colleagues. A number of people have enquired about coming on to a similar programme in the future. The communication and messages around recognising differences and not making assumptions seem to be cascading throughout the organisation.

A number of case studies and stories resulting from the way the workshops have had an impact are now embedded into the individual units and being shared as best practice. For instance, one of the delegate's stories is how her unit is buying into flexible working hours in every instance, regardless of circumstances. This has shown a positive result in removing traditional boundaries between part-time and full-time staff and makes it possible to cover early morning and late evening duties from normal hours. It has given them more choices and a better work–life balance.

The impact has been highly positive and Gill Risby, training manager for staff development in the unit, felt that 'This has helped us to reflect on our practice and identify improvements which contribute to supporting the patient needs of a diverse population and staff groups. The programme has helped us understand how we can do this better.'

11.1 REFLECT – CONCLUDE – PLAN

How might you advance the business case for diversity in an organisation?

What steps can you take to make diversity a strategic issue for managers?

OBSTACLES FACING WOMEN MANAGERS

There remain a number of stereotypes about women and their position in organisations which are perceived to work against their development. One view,

WEB LINK

A 'diversity excellence model' can be inspected at **http://www. nationalschool.gov.uk/
downloads/diversity_excellence_model.pdf** . It provides a means of assessing an organisation's
ability to lead and manage diversity.

Also try **http://www.nationalcentrefordiversity.com/iid/about/** for information about an
Investors in Diversity framework.

 WEB LINK

Up-to-date information about gender differences can be found at National Statistics Online at
http://www.statistics.gov.uk/focuson/gender/ . Wider concerns about equality can be found at
the Government Equalities Office at **http://www.equalities.gov.uk/Default.aspx** .

held by some successful women, is that 'the queen rises to the top'. Such people
tend to argue that although there are special problems for women managers,
it is the successful overcoming of those problems that demonstrates that you
are special. One of the authors was told by his own direct manager, when he
proposed some special attention for women managers, 'I got here without that
kind of help – other women should do the same.' Some women – and some
men – deprecate any special measures to redress what others see as problems,
on the grounds that such actions lead to tokenism or even to the view that those
who do progress up the managerial ladder have done so through 'politically
correct processes' rather than their own abilities. Nevertheless, there are common
stereotypical presentations that prevent progress for many women. Probably the
most prevalent is that leadership and management are male roles in contrast to
which women should play supportive followers. This kind of reasoning suggests a
deeply rooted patriarchalism in many organisations, which makes any deviation
from male supremacy appear destabilising and too challenging. Further, it might
be argued that failure to consider and understand this process also allows easy
acceptance of the 'queen bee' label for women who do become senior managers
and can be blamed for being 'more male than men' (Mavin 2006, p.269).

Such perceptions are reinforced by the low numbers of females in senior
positions who can act as role models for others, which restrains their attempts to
make progress (Cooper Jackson 2001). The failure of women to make progress
into such positions is usually referred to by the metaphor of a 'glass ceiling' and
sometimes a 'sticky floor'. It is also worth noting that similar images are applied
to ethnic minority leaders and managers. According to Weyer (2007), there
are three categories of explanation for these phenomena. Firstly, the biological
explanations grounded on the basic idea of differences between men and women
which have evolved through time. Secondly, socialisation explanations, which
consider how men and women acquire different identities through education and

working life. Thirdly, structural/cultural explanations, which consider the way that structures and systems reflect differing meanings, perceptions and values that underpin how we come to expect roles such as leadership and management to be performed and by whom.

The third category in particular provides many of the stereotypes that are biased against women. Women face stereotypes along the whole route of their careers, and it becomes harder – and perhaps more political – the higher women attempt to rise. A key stereotype is based on how roles in society are allocated according to gender or what are referred to as gender-roles (Jolly 2000). Thus it is suggested that women have a more communal role to play and this makes them more suited to more caring and interpersonal behaviours and specialisation in social services roles. By contrast, male roles are proactive and achievement-oriented (Eagly and Karau 2002). It is even suggested that the role of leadership is more in tune with the masculine gender-role, especially if leadership is concerned with action to achieve task outcomes (Weyer 2007). One image that has received attention in recent years is that of women who become CEOs facing an expectation of failure greater than that faced by men – referred to as the 'glass cliff'. Adams *et al* (2009) used stock market information against the appointment of men and women CEOs but found little evidence to support the idea of bias and prejudice against women. Others such as Ryan and Haslam (2009) suggest caution and state that there needs to be a more contextualised investigation of women in such positions. For example, women's tenure in senior positions seemed less secure irrespective of whether the organisation was successful.

 WEB LINK

Exeter University is completing research into the phenomenon of the 'glass cliff'. Go to **http:// psy.ex.ac.uk/seorg/glasscliff/** .

Both gender-roles lead to prejudice and bias, even for men who fail to live up to the role ascribed. These images can feed the identities that managers form for men and women, although most usually they remain in the background and are seldom explored. However, they do affect what people do and how they respond to what happens at work. For example, Davidson and Cooper (1992) pointed out that men may feel threatened by women and may take action to inhibit their progress. A woman's distaste for internal politics may further reinforce perceptions (Ng *et al* 2005). Vinnicombe and Singh (2002) found that although there could be much talk about the value of women and acknowledgement of the importance of equal opportunities, stereotypes and prejudices could still pervade how guidelines are implemented by line managers. A key issue therefore is what factors are consciously and less consciously considered by those who make decisions in organisations about selecting managers for higher positions. One obvious and traditional explanation is based on the idea that managers are selected for higher positions on the basis of an attraction-similarity paradigm

(Byrne 1971). Thus white male managers promote people like themselves, perpetuating a culture of male dominance which devalues women. However, there is emerging evidence from the USA that the 'glass ceiling' is less a result of male prejudice and more related to perceptions held by women that prevent them from applying for top management positions (Powell and Butterfield 2002).

Clearly, the idea of gender-roles and the subsequent bias and prejudices requires a strong degree of critical awareness by managers, and this includes the beliefs held by women themselves which can constrain their efforts to apply for more senior positions. For example, Gold *et al* (2002) explore how critical thinking resulted in one female manager being able to identify how her socialisation in a home environment of dominant males resulted in feelings of low confidence in meetings at work and reticence to put her ideas forward. Even where an organisation espouses equality of opportunity, the contstraints for females and others may be institutionalised and embedded within selection instruments and psychometric tests as well as in the attitudes of those involved in selection. A wider enquiry could make use of the Women as Managers scale (WAMS), a 21-item instrument that measures negative attitudes towards women in management positions, or Moore *et al*'s (2004) adaptation of WAMS to consider stereotypical beliefs such as whether women have ideas challenged more often than men or whether women have to perform better than men to succeed.

11.2 REFLECT – CONCLUDE – PLAN

Are you aware of your own prejudices relating to male and female roles?

How far do stereotypical roles inhibit or constrain your activities?

What can you do to counter such restraints in yourself and others?

There are undoubtedly career choice issues for some women. Some leave employment in order to have children at a crucial time in terms of their development as managers. Organisational attitudes and policies in the past were certainly dominated by an expectation that this would happen. Changes towards policies which make it easier for women (and, indeed, men) to be both managers and responsible for their children are slowly emerging. Liu and Wilson (2001) found that women tend to regard their careers in phases, and that those who choose to have families may find themselves restricted when seeking career advancement. Family women may be prevented from participating in social networks which put them in the 'know' for advancement (p.171). During pregnancy, women may find themselves facing changed views of their abilities and accusations of less commitment to their careers and the organisation. It is therefore argued (Wajcman 1998) that career structures favour males, supporting the male lifecycle, with the family man as norm at senior management levels rather than mothers. Some organisations have gradually become less accepting of traditional views about women's careers, promoting themselves as 'family-friendly'.

Nevertheless, it does appear that for some women to advance their careers as managers, they may need to remain childless, even though there is no certainty that such a sacrifice will be successful (Wajcman 1999). Wood and Newton (2006) considered the issue of marriage and children among Australian managers. They found interesting complexities between what they called an enlightened discourse, which valued equal opportunities and balance, and a maternalist discourse where the responsibility for marriage and family lay with women. However, it was recognised that children could be an 'impediment to a woman's career in management' (p.354), although remaining childless to advance a career was not necessarily a woman's intention.

Critics such as Wajcman (1998) would argue, however, that the various policies that might provide protection against discrimination tend to reinforce the view of women as a problem, preserving the norm of the male manager. Others point to the need to change ideas about careers, understanding the differences between male and female expectations. Women are clearly as well qualified as men, especially at the start of their careers, and there is a business case for helping women reach higher levels of management (Mavin 2001). Increased understanding would utilise research that has shown that women tend to define success in their careers differently (Sturges 1999), giving prominence to the content of work, achievement and personal recognition for their contribution. Women also tended to take a broader view of their careers, defining success as a balance of work and other parts of their lives. Ng *et al* (2005) suggested that education, skills and qualifications had a stronger impact on career satisfaction for women, but this might also indicate the need to work harder to prove themselves.

DIFFERENCES IN LEADERSHIP AND MANAGEMENT BEHAVIOUR

General views about the reason for the lower number of women managers, to some extent depending on folklore, are accompanied by more specific issues about women as managers. How women perform as managers, and how their performance is perceived by their male colleagues, is complicated by further questions. Should women behave like male managers? Do they bring special kinds of behaviour which actually produce more effective results? Perhaps male managers should try to employ some of the behaviours evidenced by some successful women managers.

Both men and women tend to agree that women behave differently from their male colleagues. While women who accept the 'difference' argument will tend to say 'different, but as good as', men will more characteristically say 'different, and less effective than'. However this commonly held view is challenged, for example, by Fraker (1984) who showed no difference in the way women managed as compared with men in a match study of 2,000 managers. Marshall (1991), however, argued that similarities in male and female managerial behaviour have been over-emphasised in order to support women managers. In her view these similarities have been overstated at the expense of legitimate and useful differences:

- Women tend to emphasise people management over task structuring, whereas men have opposite priorities.

- Women are often inhibited in exercising position power because other people reject or undermine their use of authority, or stereotype them in devalued female roles.

Like other authors, she commented on the male emphasis on individualism, competition and control (in contrast to interdependence, collaboration and acceptance) as defining the values to which women managers are supposed to adhere. There has been a tendency to push women into 'caring' functions. To some extent this process is a reflection of social stereotypes of desired female behaviour, of the failure to provide effective choice at school (eg for girls to do science), and of subsequent early career options. Further research by Burke and Collins (2001), based on self-ratings of styles in the use of management skills, found that there were differences between males and females, and that females were more likely to be effective in communicating and coaching and developing staff. They were strong in using contingent reward behaviour to make expectations clear, and in using a transformational leadership style to motivate staff. Females were more likely to:

- be positive role models for staff

- inspire staff to believe in and work for a common purpose

- encourage others to be creative and question assumptions

- spend time developing and coaching.

In the same study, male managers were more likely to engage in monitoring staff and focusing on errors or deviations.

In many respects, these findings reflect and sustain the stereotypical views about leadership and management that we considered above. However, writers such as Mavin et al (2004) suggest that the differences that women can bring leadership and management tend to be suppressed, and that both in theory and practice there is a process of 'gender blindness' (p.294) which tends to cancel out the contribution that a different way of thinking can bring. Despite the progress made by women, they still have to work in a patriarchal context and with processes that reflect male supremacy. In leadership and management theory, some of the key research and ideas – such as McGregor's Theory X and Theory Y or Mintzberg's roles – were based on or assumed managers who were male. This reinforces the masculinity of the qualities of leadership and management which are often found in models and competence frameworks. These feed notions of the 'ideal' manager which is usually a preference for male characteristics of rationality in contrast to female emotionality (Fournier and Keleman 2001). For example, in a study of a local authority during a period of 'modernisation' which included a call for better leadership in public services, Ford (2006) found that following a leadership development programme for 150 managers there was a predominance of a 'macho-management' image based on competitive, controlling and self-reliant' (p.84) individuals with clear targets to achieve and financial motivation. Women participants became aware of this requirement and learned to respond 'like a man' (p.85), and this could also mean ensuring that they did not look 'weak' compared to others. However, in contradiction, and less dominant, Ford also found a more feminine response based on teams, connections, links with staff and 'showing a genuine interest' (p.87).

11.3 REFLECT – CONCLUDE – PLAN

Has your experience of leadership and management education been 'gender-blind'?

Is 'macho-mangement' finished?

How can you embrace a more gender-inclusive view of leadership and management?

WOMEN LEADERS AND MANAGERS: DIFFERENT DEVELOPMENT NEEDS?

The traditional divide between rational male managers and emotional and caring females, with the dominance of the former over the latter, has been challenged by calls for models that value both male and female talents – what Marshall (1995) referred to as the 'androgynous' manager. Singh (2002) suggests that masculinity and femininity can be regarded as two dimensions, and that both male and female managers should consider their styles in relation to both. Senior managers and those responsible for LMD can work to use both dimensions in setting values, assessing needs and designing activities.

A principal route to assessing needs is performance appraisal, usually presented as objective and neutral in its effects but often revealed to be subjective and discriminatory (Brown and Heywood 2005). Sometimes, however, this can work in a woman's favour. For example, if a female manager performs better than expected in a male role, this might lead to a 'gender contrast' effect which over-rates the performance (Heilman *et al* 1988). One possible approach to minimise bias is to use 360-degree feedback. Of course, where this also includes self-appraisal, it is likely that bias will occur, although women might tend to under-rate themselves if they suffer low self-esteem (Baruch 1996) – but the same might apply to men. Millmoore *et al* (2007) provide an exploration of possible gender bias within 360-degree appraisal within a financial services organisation in the UK. Based on the result of 66 managers (33 males, 33 females), it was found that there was a higher performance rating for females over males, suggesting that 360-degree appraisal can ensure a more rounded and balanced source of information for LMD. It was also found that ratings by self tended to be higher for women, suggesting confidence and increasing self-esteem. It also suggests some inconsistency with previous findings.

On LMD courses, male attitudes and behaviour tend to follow the stereotypes about women found in the real world outside. Behaviour that is seen by men in men as normal, such as assertiveness, is seen by men in women as aggressive and strident. Alternatively, women who do not behave like most men are pushed towards the supposedly 'feminine' behaviour corner. Women are expected to be concerned about the comfort of the group, to pour out the tea, and to express emotion rather than to conceal it. They are treated with a form of superficial gallantry that emphasises the fact that they are being treated as women, not as leaders or managers. Or their capacities may be belittled by reference to their sexuality: 'I bet it's difficult having a serious discussion with a beauty like Jane in the group.'

Because of the difficulties women may face in largely male LMD situations, and because of the view that they have special needs anyway, women-only training groups were developed. There are two conflicting arguments over this. One says that since women have to survive in a predominantly male environment, it is unreal to provide them with women-only LMD. Whatever else this may achieve, the absence of men will reinforce the exclusion and isolation of women and create a future problem of transferring any learning achieved (Lewis and Fagenson 1995). The alternative view is that the absence of men removes some unnecessary obstacles to learning, and opens opportunities for more women to be more experimental with behaviour. This may be helpful to them subsequently in the male environment, but it may also reinforce the view that women must change rather than the organisation. Some women feel they have benefited from women-only courses in the ways indicated above. It is also the case that since some women nowadays are less prepared to accept inappropriate male behaviour towards them on courses, mixed courses can sometimes become a battleground for male/female issues rather than a learning experience related to the original objectives (Reynolds and Trehan 2003). Brew and Garavan (1995, p.18) argued that women-only training needs to be 'an integral part of a wider programme for change'.

If women are in a minority in a learning group, they may be dealt with differently from their male colleagues by a tutor, by a facilitator or by participants in the learning group. Hite and McDonald (1995) claim that women are often constrained in the classroom by having to conform to male models, by materials constantly using the pronoun 'he', and by the kind of style favoured by tutors and colleagues. Their research showed further that there was a significant difference in the amount of interaction with the tutor and the kind of response made to their contribution. Moreover, males were more often called on to make a contribution. Tanton (1995) also concludes that male tutors behave differently towards male and female students. She says in addition that women prefer small group discussions where these problems are either less visible or capable of being managed by women themselves. They are said to like role-plays and the keeping of journals. No reasons are given for these preferences (and they are not supported by the Hite and McDonald research). It may be that journal-keeping is particularly favoured because it is a solitary process of learning which is not immediately affected by the intervention of tutors or colleagues.

Case and Thompson (1995) reviewing behaviours on an MBA programme found that women engaged in more frequent self-reflection than men, and that reflecting on their own actions provides a more accurate depiction of their role in events that occur. These two aspects would suggest that women might learn better than men from the same event. One criticism of MBAs and formal management education in general is the lack of women lecturers to present a female view of leadership and management. Miller *et al* (2002) suggest that where MBAs 'replicate patriarchal orthodoxy in the classroom' (p.27), this can engender a sense of alienation among women which is not conducive to learning.

A further proposition is that women are more likely to learn through relationships and empathy, and through collaborative discussion rather than argumentative debate. Tannen (1991) described this as report talk. These points would seem to relate particularly to, for example, a large group case study discussion. Research about women's way of knowing by Belenky (1987) showed that women valued, for example, co-operation rather than competition and discussion over debate. This is interesting in its own right, but there is no comparative analysis of men on the same issues.

In multinationals additional complications arise from the unacceptability of women managers in some countries. Van Velsor and Hughes (1990) and Ohlott *et al* (1994) argue that in relation to large-scale developmental assignments women have to overcome more obstacles. The research was focused on preferred learning experiences rather than on how women actually learned from experiences. Research on whether women learn more or less readily from bosses, colleagues or mentors does not seem to exist. Case and Thompson (1995) do not support the view expressed in Van Velsor and Hughes (1990) that women were more likely than men to learn from others.

Where there is a deficiency of female managers moving into more senior positions, as part of a package of measures to provide support, positive action training programmes for women only can be provided. Such training provides a way for women to explore the organisational systems, structure and culture that they have to work in and that need to change if progress is to be made (Shaw and Perrons 1995). Anderson (2004) describes a positive action programme for women in local government in the UK where, as a result, several achieved promotion and many reported gains in confidence and the benefits of networking (see below).

11.4 REFLECT — CONCLUDE — PLAN

Do you think women-only development activities are appropriate?

To what extent might your experiences and your views about them be affected by your gender?

What conclusions can you draw about gender and LMD?

What action can be taken to enhance LMD for women?

MENTORING, COACHING AND NETWORKING

Mentoring has been a particularly useful method of learning for women. Powerful male mentors may have helped, but some women prefer a female mentor – although it may be difficult to find one within the organisation (see Chapter 10). Within the context of diversity, mentoring by senior and line managers has been identified as a significant contributor to cultural change and the advancement of women (Mattis 2001). Sponsoring women for key positions is described as a key role for senior managers and a vital requirement in driving an initiative through the organisation. Veale and Gold (1998) found that mentoring by senior managers often gave women managers the confidence to aim higher. Recently, Fowler *et al* (2007) considered the effect of different gender combinations in mentoring on such measures as personal and emotional guidance, career development facilitation, strategies and systems advice and friendship. The results found few gender differences except the ability of female mentors to provide more personal and emotional support and career development facilitation whatever the sex of the mentee, and female mentees perceived that they obtained more career development facilitation than males.

In addition to mentoring, coaching is also suggested as a way of supporting women in developing careers and moving into more senior positions. Research by Broughton and Miller (2009) suggested that coaching needs to start early and at key transition points in such areas as building confidence, obtaining access to development opportunities, achieving work–life balance and networking. They also identified the need to coach men as 'gatekeepers' to senior position to help move more women into such positions.

Networking has also been identified in previous chapters as an important LMD activity. The key issue here is that women often find themselves excluded from the so-called 'old boy networks' that seem so important to male managers. Ibarra (1992) found that men were more likely to benefit from networks while women could find themselves caught between a social network of women and a task network of men and women; the consequence was potentially conflicting advice and tension. One problem for women is that they may have less time for networking compared to men. Nevertheless, networking is suggested as a method of improving women's career development (Veale and Gold 1998), breaking down isolation and allowing the sharing of experiences to break down barriers (Linehan 2001). One recent finding identifies age as an important factor for women: younger women managers are more likely to favour a network of other women of a similar age – a 'young woman's network' (Waldstrøm and Madsen 2007). Online networking is also now considered a possible way for women to enhance their careers, although receptivity to such methods and involvement is varied (Donelan *et al* 2009).

BLACK, ASIAN AND MINORITY ETHNIC MANAGERS

It is frequently observed that countries like the UK, the USA and elsewhere are becoming more ethnically and culturally diverse. The recent election of

WEB LINK

Catalyst is a North American organisation working to advance women in business. Its homepage is **http://www.catalyst.org/** .

A formal network for women includes Women in Banking and Finance at **http://www.wibf.org.uk/** .

The European Women's Management Development International Network is located at **http://www.ewmd.org/** .

Barack Obama to the presidency of the USA is deeply symbolic and provides much-needed stimulus and hope to many for the future. Yet in the meantime, many of the difficulties faced by women managers are also faced by black, Asian and minority ethnic (BAME) managers.

According to recent figures, BAME managers in the UK accounted for 6.8% of all managers at the end of 2007, an increase from 4.4% in 2000. The proportion of the total population that is classified as BAME stands at around 10% (RfO 2008). While the proportion of the BAME population is forecast to grow to 15% by 2015, the number of BAME managers is forecast to increase to 11%, thus widening the gap in BAME representation at leadership and management levels. Considering the patterns by sector, BAME managers account for 33% of the total in public administration, education and health, an increase from 25.7% in 2000. In banking, finance and insurance the figures were 25.7% in 2007 and 23.1% in 2000. However, there have been reversals in nearly all other sectors. For example, in 2000 8.4% were employed in transport, but only 6.1% were employed in 2007, and in distribution, retail and restaurants the figures were 20% in 2007 and 23% in 2000.

A benchmarking report on race and diversity covering 99 private and public organisations (RfO 2002) showed that only 44 ethnic managers held posts at senior levels, and there were no black or other ethnic minority chief executives in the private sector organisations, nor black or Asian Permanent Secretaries in any of the central government departments. However, by 2009 there do seem to have been some positive indicators of progress (RfO 2009). Firstly, in March 2009 Tidjane Thiam became the first black CEO of a FTSE-100 company when he was appointed at the insurance company Prudential. Secondly, there was a large increase in the number of BAME employees participating in development and training activities. Thirdly, all organisations in the survey had a clear commitment stated for race equality. Fourthly, 9% of foremen and supervisors were BAME workers – a growing trend.

WEB LINK

Find out more about RfO (Race for Opportunity) at **http://www.bitc.org. uk/workplace/diversity_and_inclusion/race/index.html** .

The disproportionate presence of BAME leaders and managers in certain sectors results in what Singh (2002, p.20) refers to as 'ghettoising'. BAME managers may also face stereotyping and exclusion from certain activities that help in career advancement – eg after-work drinks. In the USA Powell and Butterfield (1997) found that it was probably access to internal networks that gave white managers an advantage over other managers. Of course, many organisations are now able to prevent overt racist practices, but it is more difficult to deal with deep-seated stereotypes and negative images. In the USA, there has been some investigation of the 'glass cliff' phenomenon for black leaders (Cook and Glass 2008) when they are appointed CEOs to large organisations. It was found that the reaction of share prices tended to rise initially but became more strongly negative over time, in contrast to white leaders.

Women managers from BAME groups face something of a double jeopardy. Davidson (1997, 2002) found that ethnicity was a greater hurdle than gender in that such women face not only a glass but also a concrete ceiling. Women managers often felt they were tokens, subject to stereotyping and had to deliver higher performance. There were also fewer role models. However, it was also found that many women could maintain a positive self-image and that their visibility allowed them to make their good performance better known. Mattis (2001), using US findings for 'women of color', highlighted the importance of opportunities for visibility as well as help with career goals and explanation of organisation politics from senior managers.

Positive action for specific BAME managers, consisting of a range of LMD activities, has been shown to provide a route into higher levels of responsibility. In the UK, the Network for Black Professionals developed 'positive action' career development programmes for staff working in the learning and skills sector (NBP 2008). The programmes included mentoring, work shadowing and secondments for staff at all levels of leadership and management. Evaluation of the programmes showed that there had been an impact on career progression associated with increased confidence in abilities and awareness needed for success. Over 90% recommended the programmes to others. Organisations such as LloydsTSB provide support for BAME careers through mentors and a Group Ethnic Minority (GEM) network that provides networking and personal development opportunities.

In the health sector, where large numbers of BAME staff are employed, it is not surprising that LMD activities give attention to diversity issues and have increased BAME representation in leadership positions. Kalra *et al* (2009) draw on evidence from the USA and the UK to show the value of LMD activities such as networking – for instance, the NHS Confederation BAME Forum – and mentoring and identifying future talent. However, a crucial feature of any LMD process is the role of managers in providing development opportunities such as challenging tasks and a supportive culture.

 WEB LINK

Find out more about the Network for Black Professionals at **http://www.nbm.org.uk/** including the Black Leadership Initiative at **http://www.nbm.org.uk/black_leadership_initiative/** .

NATIONAL CULTURES AND GLOBAL MANAGEMENT

Diversity of behaviour and values becomes very apparent when managers work in a multinational company (MNC) or global organisation, and increasingly, leaders and managers will need to learn to work in and with different cultural contexts. According to Colakoglu and Caligiuri (2008) there are 850,000 MNC subsidiaries around the world, with the numbers of managers expected to work abroad or across borders expected to rise (Harvey and Moeller 2009). When managers need to interact with staff, customers and suppliers across international borders, whether face to face or mediated by the Internet or other forms of communication, and consider the behaviour of competitors from around the world, they face a complex and dynamic set of factors which together represent the force of globalisation.

Within the broad term of globalisation there are different meanings or variations in the idea of global managers and what they need to learn. For example, a manager who is assigned to work in an MNC subsidiary which is located in another country will have to understand particular ways of working and interacting with others in that context. By contrast, consider leaders or managers who have responsibility for integration across different subsidiaries in different locations. The former we can call 'international' or 'expatriate' managers, and the latter 'global managers' (Caligiuri and Tarique 2009). Turnbull-James and Collins (2010) suggest that global managers need different capabilities that enable them 'to look and think beyond their local environment' (p.490), although research has tended to show that many organisations promote managers on technical and organisation skills rather than their abilities to work globally (Manning 2003). There is also evidence that lack of understanding of differing cultural assumptions can hamper learning and joint working among managers from different countries (Liu and Vince 1999).

LEADING AND MANAGING WITHIN AND ACROSS CULTURES

Most ideas about LMD for both international and global managers give attention to cultural awareness. Hofstede (1980) provided the major original work on cultural issues still widely used in LMD. Hofstede described culture as 'a collective programming of the mind'. Because his research was conducted in one major organisation with a strong managerial culture, the differences in national style that he drew out were identifiably national rather than influenced by other variables such as organisation structure, techniques or processes. He developed four dimensions from his empirical research across 50 countries:

- *power distance* – being concerned with the extent to which those with less power within a country expect and accept that power is distributed unequally

- *collectivity/individualism* – determining the levels of sharing and achievement, competition and collaboration. Individualist societies lead to expectations that people will look after themselves and their own interests; collective societies give preference to the interest of the group as a source of identity

- *masculinity/femininity* – being concerned with the degree to which gender roles are distinct (masculinity – eg men are tough, women are tender) or overlap (femininity – both men and women are models, tender and concerned with quality of life)

- *uncertainty avoidance* – being concerned with feelings of threat when there is uncertainty or unknown situations.

Organisations can use frameworks such as this to consider how to provide LMD for managers who will work across cultural boundaries. For example, when Volkswagen were seeking to transfer know-how to new operations with Škoda in the Czech Republic, they identified the importance of 'intercultural sensitivity and open-mindedness' as a key competence for managers (Syrett and Lammimam 1999, p.137).

 WEB LINK

Geert Hofstede's homepage can be found at **http://www.geert-hofstede.com/** .

The results of his research for different countries against each of his dimensions can be found at **http://www.geert-hofstede.com/ geert_hofstede_resources.shtml** .

Hofstede's definitions provide a good starting point, although he emphasised that individuals differ within a country 'norm'.[1] Working abroad – or working in your own country with leaders or managers from other countries – creates culture shock because your idea of the right way of doing things differs from that of other nationals.

Allied views to culture awareness are the ideas of emotional and cultural intelligence (Alon and Higgins 2005). We considered emotional intelligence (EI) in Chapter 3, but suffice to say that advocates of EI such as Goleman *et al* (2002) make a strong link between the level of EI and success in leadership. Cultural intelligence (CI), as suggested by Earley and Mosakowski (2004), is concerned with a person's capability to notice and understand different facets of cultural behaviour across different cultures or in multicultural settings. Differences in cultural behaviour can occur within and between organisations as well as between countries and sub-regions within countries. In all cases, such differences will be the result of traditions and history. Alon and Higgins (2005) point to the differences of the Basque, Andalusian, and Catalan sub-cultures in Spain, and any manager working in Spain would need sufficient CI to appreciate and respond to such differences.

Measurement and assessment of such intelligences for LMD can be incorporated into an organisation's global competences framework which, like other competences, can be derived from and linked to an organisation's global strategy (McCall and Hollenbeck 2002). There are also generic competences such as those presented by Kets de Vries and Florent-Treacy (1999), based on their analysis of the lives and work of such leaders as Richard Branson (Virgin) and David Simon (BP). They suggested 12 dimensions of global leadership including envisioning, energising, team-building, outside orientation, emotional intelligence and global mindset. The idea of the global mindset has been further developed by others such as Bowen and Inkpen (2009) and consists of three kinds of characteristics of individuals:

- intellectual (global business savvy, cosmopolitan outlook, and cognitive complexity)
- social (intercultural empathy, interpersonal impact, and diplomacy)
- psychological (passion for diversity, quest for adventure, and self-assurance).

Development of such characteristics can enable leaders to influence others in cross-cultural situations.

WEB LINK

Find out more about a global mindset at **http://www.thunderbird.edu/ about_thunderbird/ inside_tbird/truly_global/global_mindset.htm** .

Also explore **http://www.thunderbird.edu/sites/globe/** . This is the homepage of the Global Leadership and Organizational Behaviour Effectiveness (GLOBE) Research Project, which is a long-term project to examine the inter-relationships between societal culture, organisational culture, and organisational leadership in 61 cultures/countries.

As with all competence frameworks, there are problems in showing their validity, and this extends to global competences where there remain difficulties of finding common agreement of meaning as well as outcomes (Jokinen 2005).

LMD FOR GLOBAL MANAGERS

Over the last 10 years it has been recognised that organisations need to provide more plans and activities for LMD in global leadership and management (Mendenhall 2006). Given the need for acquiring cultural awareness or intelligence, there remains the usual dilemma, common to most LMD, over whether to front-load the learning by specifying clear inputs and providing a package of skill, delivered in a programme of workshops or by adopting a more emergent approach allowing managers to learn through the experience of assignments in other cultures composed of real tasks and projects.

Cross-cultural training (CCT) could also include experiential learning events, but a study by Mendenhall *et al* (2004) of the effectiveness of CCT found that didactic methods such as lectures, presentations, culture assimilators and discussions were the most frequently used. These were seen as less effective in changing behaviour and attitudes and enhancing adjustment and performance. However, it has been found that CCT accelerates the adjustment of managers where they had little prior international experience (Waxin and Panaccio 2005). According to Tarique and Caligiuri (2004, p.285), designing effective CCT involves:

- identifying the type of global assignment for which CCT is needed – Is the position technical, functional, high-potential, or strategic/executive?

- determining specific CCT needs – What is the organisational context, individual needs and level of the assignment?

- establishing goals and measures to determine effectiveness in the short and long term, such as the cognitive, affective and behavioural changes necessary to enhance adjustment and success

- developing and delivering CCT – for example, content, methods and sequencing. Here models of culture may be addressed, as well as mixing didactic and experiential methods seen as appropriate and determining whether these are best delivered pre-departure, post-departure, or both. Basic information may be appropriate pre-departure; deeper learning post-departure

- evaluating the programme's success against stated goals.

However well-designed, it is difficult to escape the systemic constraints of CCT which inevitably include all the difficulties of formal LMD, including transfer to practice, but also the tendency to simplify the complex cultural situations that a manager is likely to encounter (Brockner 2003). This suggests that there ought to be some attempt to provide a more emergent form of LMD through assignments and experiences, although Caligiuri (2006) suggests that managers need to be predisposed toward success for these to be effective – but this is hardly surprising for any form of LMD. However, many multinational companies would consider cross-border assignments the most effective way to develop global managers (Evans *et al* 2002), as do managers themselves (Suutari 2003). To provide support for learning from assignments we would add the availability of a mentor, especially since assignments that require significant travel and residence abroad is likely to involve a reconsideration of career and identity (Kohonen 2005). In addition, Action Learning provides another source of support with challenge when managers face inevitable issues of difficulty. Furthermore, an Action Learning set can operate virtually, making use of Web 2.0 networking sites or VOIP technologies such as Skype. Action Learning can also be used by global team leaders to bring together a culturally diverse and dispersed team (Pauleen 2003).

GREEN LMD

Just as there is a pressing requirement for managers to become sensitive to differences of people, it is also becoming a necessity for managers to prove their understanding of environmental and ecological issues – they need to become 'green managers'. The reasons for this include:

11.5 REFLECT – CONCLUDE – PLAN

What has been your experience of differences in national culture when working on tasks and projects?

How far does your experience confirm or refute the propositions advanced above?

What actions might you take personally, or attempt to introduce, within the next task or project involving participants from different national cultures?

- protecting, saving and sustaining natural resources
- reducing greenhouse gases and carbon emissions to reduce global warming and climate change
- reducing the production and use of harmful substances and toxins
- preserving areas of natural beauty
- recycling waste for re-use.

Of course, these are arguments for the attention of individuals, households and governments as well as managers in organisations. However, it is to the latter that much of the attention is directed, and it is clear that in recent years many organisations have been eager to prove their green credentials. Organisations need to focus on green management to ensure sustainable development for present and future generations (Marcus and Kaiser 2006).

WEB LINK

Go to **http://group.barclays.com/Sustainability** and examine the Barclays Bank Sustainability website. A similar site can be found for Marks & Spencer at **http://corporate.marksandspencer. com/ howwedobusiness/our_policies/sustainable_raw_materials/sustainable_processes** . Note the range of activities covered by their environmental policy. The UK Government has also established, under the Climate Change Act 2008, the Committee on Climate Change to report on setting carbon budgets and on the progress being made in reducing greenhouse gas emissions – go to **http://www.theccc.org.uk/** .

The reasons for green management are hardly recent. It could be argued throughout history, and certainly since the Industrial Revolution, that with every generation 'the environment has been suffering the consequences of selfish and wasteful human behaviour' (Pane Harden *et al* 2009, p.1042). Recent events such as the tsunami and the melting of the polar ice-caps have given added impetus to the argument that organisations in the present should make up for the damage done by organisations in the past (Anderson 2004). Instead of a single focus on profit or a narrow range of production or service outcomes, an organisation needs to widen its perspective against a 'triple bottom line' (Elkington 1994) that requires consideration of the impact of performance against economic, social and environmental measures, and to work towards the achievement of harmony between each of the areas of measurement.

 WEB LINK

Economic, social and environmental measurement and reporting now form the basis of the Global Reporting Initiative (GRI) at **http://www. globalreporting.org/AboutGRI/** .

A key argument here is that, left to the operation of a free market, decisions would be made on purely private economic costs rather than a wider societal cost which considers the external impact of activities on pollution and impacts on the environment such as global warming and deforestation (McWilliams and Siegel 2001). The resulting gap between private and societal cost would warrant some degree of intervention or regulation to reduce market failure, and in recent years there has been more intervention or attempts to find agreement on what is an acceptable level of societal cost in organisation activities. However, there are also choices for organisations on how much green management they can engage in. For example, Siegel (2009) argues that organisations should only adopt green management if there are good business reasons to do so, especially if it is demanded by customers. He states that there are competitive reasons for differentiating products and services on the basis of environmental and social responsibility, such as hybrid cars with reduced pollution. Such policies need to be seen as investment decisions which yield an appropriate return. A contrasting view on green management is presented by Marcus and Fremeth (2009), who argue that there is duty beyond a narrow utilitarian measurement of pay-off. They pose a crucial question: 'Under what circumstances do humans have the right to remove endowments from nature that future generations will need to sustain life?' (p.24).

 11.6 REFLECT – CONCLUDE – PLAN

To what extent do you agree that it is a duty for organisations to adopt green management?

How would you argue for more green management and leadership, even if it reduced profits?

What should be the first steps towards a strategy for green management?

Following Haden *et al* (2009) we would argue that, lacking clear definition, it is best to see green management as a continuum of possible positions by an organisation, summarised in Figure 11.1.

Figure 11.1 A simple/complex green management continuum

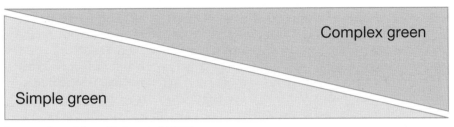

Source: adapted from Haden *et al* (2009)

Thus a simple approach would be a reactive response to regulation (Banerjee 2001) based on mere compliance. This might involve, for example, simple changes to practice on the use of paper for meetings and the sorting of waste. The movement towards complexity would allow progress towards an organisation environmental strategy which itself would be seen as an opportunity for competitive advantage. This might also mean the use of measurement and reports that engender accountability, developing green competences (Marcus and Fremeth 2009) as well as finding opportunities to reconsider practices and structures that incur significant societal costs. We would consider such movements a learning opportunity for managers, but this needs full organisational support including the appointment of senior managers with responsibility for green management, as shown in the *LMD in Practice* below.

LMD IN PRACTICE

TRAVELODGE INVESTS £1M IN GREEN STRATEGY

Budget hotel chain Travelodge has appointed its first director of environment and sustainability in response to a staff survey on green practices. Nicola Stopps was recruited to the position after 79% of staff admitted they would leave the company if it did not show enough commitment to being green. Stopps will be responsible for researching techniques to reduce energy usage in hotels, cutting the organisation's carbon footprint and its £10 million utility bill.

Chief executive Grant Hearn said: 'Our staff tell us that they want Travelodge to tackle this issue in a responsible and determined way.'

The staff survey also found that although 77% were concerned about the impact of

their behaviour on the environment, only 8% of employees were fully aware of how to be environmentally friendly at work. Travelodge has invested £1 million in its environment strategy, with engaging staff a key component of this.

A spokeswoman for the chain, which operates 320 hotels, mainly in the UK, and employs 5,000 staff, said: 'We have a great deal still to do to satisfy consumers' growing demand for green accommodation in the UK, as well as fulfil staff's desire for an eco-friendly employer. ... Transforming the behaviour and attitudes of our customers and staff is central to this, and it will be an enormous task,' she said.

Source: *People Management*, 6 September 2007

In making a move from simple to complex along the continuum, managers are proactively considering a more strategic approach to green management. There are a number of tools to help achieve this. For example, there are a range of environmental management systems that meet recognised standards – such as ISO 14001 – which are supported by a toolkit and training for implementation. There is also Eco-mapping, which allows managers to map their organisation to assess environmental impact. It is a work-based learning process that involves a series of workshops to build an inventory of environmental practices, analyse problems and take action (Koroljova and Voronova 2007). In addition, organisations can work with the idea of a Green Productivity Index which is based on the ratio of productivity to environmental impact, allowing more rigour in analysing the impact on the environment in making decisions and planning for environmental protection (Mohan Das Gandhi *et al* 2006). All these approaches imply a great deal of learning that can be achieved by leaders, managers and others. While there is undoubtedly much that can be accomplished by formal training, the great value of these tools is their relevance to context and application within the organisation.

They also meet the first requirement in taking action suggested by Murray (2010), which is to examine core business activities and determine who are most affected by operations. The second requirement presented by Murray is 'stakeholder engagement', which requires leaders and managers to consider those who are affected by the organisation's practices for good or ill. 'Engagement' means that those who are aggrieved by what the organisation is doing are heard and consideration is given on how to respond. The third step arises from analysing stakeholders' interests and considering who needs to be influenced and how. This provides focus and relevance to any activities and removes the generality of reports and websites. The final step is to set goals, the time-scales for achievement and the overall vision for sustainability.

Green management is clearly an issue that is going to occupy the thoughts and actions of managers for many years to come both because they have to and because they want to. The inclusion of stakeholders in such considerations also raises a fundamental question relating to how organisations as human constructions and entities are considered against the natural environment. By tradition, it has been humans finding ways to control and exploit nature in the interests of a narrow range of stakeholders. However, as Driscoll and Starik (2004) argue, 'the natural environment can be identified as the primary stakeholder' of an organisation (p.56) and so improving an organisation's green performance must be considered by managers more strategically (Banerjee 2002).

PROFESSIONS AND LMD

Professional status is granted to those who have technical and theoretical expertise which is recognised by others to help them tackle what Dietrich and Roberts (1997, p.16) refer to as 'decision-making complexity'. Recognition of expertise grants professionals an authority as a group who, through their professional body, are able to set standards and ethics for practice. They might also attempt to license those who wish to practise, but most provide an education scheme for new entrants to show the acquisition of professional expertise.[2]

LEADERS, MANAGERS AND PROFESSIONALS

A crucial feature of professionals at work is that on the basis of their expertise they are able to act with independence, autonomy and discretion (Middlehurst and Kinnie 1997). These particular features pose certain difficulties and dilemmas for those who wish to lead and manage the work of professionals, as highlighted by Raelin (1986). Many professionals work in managed contexts, where they are employed on the basis of their expertise but are subject to the alternative authority of a line manager, who may not always be professionally qualified. For example, in public services such as health, local government, public administration and education, there are many professional staff who over the last 20 years have experienced what is referred to as 'new managerialism' or 'new public management' (NPM). Managers are made responsible for service delivery and improvement, frequently by setting and monitoring measurable targets (Exworthy and Halford 1999), the achievement of which may be formulated into league tables. Such managers are pressed to take a more proactive stance towards 'modernisation', especially where vested interests are perceived to provide restrictions on reform – eg professionals and trade unions. However, what is apparent is that traditional management styles of command and control are usually not appropriate, especially where staff are themselves highly qualified. More recently, there has been a shift away from NPM, which is described as 'dead' (Dunleavy *et al* 2006) towards what Brookes (2008) calls 'new public leadership' with a great emphasis on collective understanding and collaboration between partners through networks.

The concepts of leadership and management have also spread into other areas of professional life with a shift towards diverse professions such as the law, the Church and the armed services (Dawson 1994). Managerialism is becoming a feature in other sectors such as professional organisations. For example, Cooper *et al* (1996) argued that in the 'managed professional business', professional firms are increasingly organised as a business to be managed with more emphasis on strategy and planning, and managers accountable for the performance of teams and the delivery of results. There is an increased focus on client surveys and feedback and the introduction of organisation and business professionals such as marketing and HRM. Staff, while still working within the framework of their professional standards, may also be accountable to a line manager or 'partner-in-charge' (Hinings *et al* 1999). It is also argued that the change in professional organisations may be somewhat overstated, with evidence of a more partnership and consensus-seeking approach still very much continuing (Pinnington and Morris 2003). Nevertheless, there has been a continuing push to allow professional organisations to become more commercial while at the same time ensuring that a regulatory framework exists to protect consumers. For example, for England and Wales, Clementi (2004) provided a review of the regulatory framework of legal services which recommended a more centralised and independent process for consumer redress against lawyers. It also allowed non-lawyers to become partners in law firms and envisaged that law firms could consist of a range of legal professionals such as solicitors, barristers, licensed conveyancers and others (referred to as legal disciplinary practices or LDPs).

In the health sector, as a response to the 2007 Government White Paper (DoH 2007) which sought to improve regulation, professional associations such as the Royal Pharmaceutical Society have been establishing leadership bodies to support members' interests as distinct from regulation.

WEB LINK

Go to **http://www.pharmacyplb.com/Index.aspx**, the homepage of the Pharmacy Profession Leadership Body.

LEARNING ABOUT LEADERSHIP AND MANAGEMENT IN THE PROFESSIONS

In the UK, the Council for Excellence in Management and Leadership recommended that professional associations introduced 'elements of management and leadership into their pre-qualification and Continuing Professional Development programmes' (CEML 2002, p.23). In addition, the Profession's Working Group set out what they referred to as an 'irreducible core' of management and leadership abilities as a foundation for every professional, shown below (CEML 2001).

Leading strategic direction

- Match external opportunities and threats with internal strengths and weaknesses
- Act as a catalyst for strategic decision-making, innovation and quality

Managing client/customer relations

- Understand who clients/customers are, their environment, what they want and what will make them happy with the service
- Deliver a quality service
- Build relationships
- Measure satisfaction and effectiveness

Managing and leading people

- Inspire shared vision
- Develop shared values
- Support and develop individuals and teams
- Optimise talent and diversity
- Performance management: delegate effectively, set clear stretching objectives, review achievement, give feedback and recognition

Making it happen

- Responsible decision-making

- Operational planning
- Information management
- Resource management
- Project management
- Continuous process improvement

This does rather represent a generic view of the professions, but there are important differences between the professions relating to the knowledge they apply, the work accomplished and the context in which practice is completed. Such differences are bound to affect how professionals are managed and led. Halliday (1987), for example, distinguishes between scientific and normative professions. In the former, the abstractions are derived empirically from observation and experimentation, epitomised by the natural sciences and professions such as engineering. In the latter, abstractions are concerned primarily with matters of value relating to how people should behave, epitomised by professions such as law. In between, there are professions that include both, referred to as syncretic, epitomised perhaps by professions such as auditing. Recently, Malhotra and Morris (2009) considered how these different forms of knowledge influence the organisation of professionals and by implication how they are managed or led. For example, legal work requires an interpretation and application of the law, so much of this is left to the discretion of the individual lawyer in relation to clients. A high degree of autonomy and authority, with minimal hierarchy, is expected. Contrast this with a firm of consulting engineers, or engineers working as employees of an organisation. The knowledge is technical and to some extent prescribed. Projects therefore have a sufficient degree of predictability that allow planning, budgets and roles to be defined. The skill of an engineer is still needed but requires fitting together the key parts to make a whole. The organisation form can be more bureaucratic with roles allocated according to particular criteria. This can provide a clearer remit for managers. Auditing allows a mix of normative and technical knowledge. There are predictable methods within systems to follow, but the process of auditing is important too, and has also been recognised as a way of adding value to the client (Dawson 2000), so there must be some allowance for professional staff to be autonomous and to use their discretion. Auditors need to be led and managed with some degree of bureaucracy but to have authority to make decisions as the work is carried out.

Since many professionals have to work with autonomy and discretion to make judgements that are appropriate for their clients or customers, in many respects they cannot solely be led and managed in traditional styles. As argued by Vermak and Weggeman (1999), these are a recipe for conflict with professionals, although they may be a manager's reflex for dealing with problems. Yet 'it is easy to get into a vicious circle: the manager tries to control things – the professionals sabotage this' (p.33). Instead, managers of professionals and, indeed, of knowledge-based workers need to consider more collective approaches and an understanding of distributed leadership. Much of the research on distributed leadership has occurred within schools where teacher leadership has been identified, and where through collaboration and collegial ways of working all teachers can take the lead and, in so doing, advance a school's capacity for change and development (Harris 2003). There has been growing research and evidence of a positive relationship between distributed leadership and school outcomes (Leithwood *et al* 2006) and normative guidance can be provided (Harris 2008).

 WEB LINK

The National College of School Leadership has a website devoted to distributed leadership at **http://www.nationalcollege.org.uk/index/ leadershiplibrary/leadingschools/leading-an-effective-organisation/ developing-leadership-within-your-school/distrbuted-leadership.htm** .

A US Distributed Leadership Study is located at **http://www.sesp. northwestern.edu/dls/** .

Interestingly, the professions have made a contribution to LMD because of their attention to their professional needs for development. So, for example, the engineering profession and the Chartered Institute of Personnel and Development have contributed the idea of continuing professional development (CPD), in part so that their members can cope with change (Gold *et al* 2001). For some, CPD is a compulsory feature of professional membership, and a growing number of associations provide formal systems to monitor and support CPD activities. Although management is not necessarily a feature of all professional association views of CPD, there are increasing pressures to bring this about. Further, managers can seek a professional standing in the UK through the Chartered Management Institute for which CPD is a core feature.

The ideas and processes involved in CPD have made a significant input to the idea that managers are involved also in continued development – in lifelong learning. There are, however, a number of different approaches to CPD. Firstly, there is what we might call the orthodox approach to CPD which emphasises a planned approach to finding gaps in knowledge and skills to be met through formal learning processes with particular emphasis on off-the-job methods such as lectures, updates and short academic courses (PARN 2000). This is an input-led approach which suffers from the typical difficulties of transfer of learning to work practice. For these reasons, Eraut (2001) considers such models of CPD to be 'one-dimensional' (p.8). A second approach is to use the outcome of learning where a professional must show that learning has taken place and is impacting on practice. This allows informal learning to be used and shared with others. It also allows activities such as mentoring, networking, and learning contracts to be incorporated into CPD schemes. A possible constraint on such learning is where a professional association may specify outcomes in advance which set out the requirements for CPD. This can also turn CPD into a form-filling exercise, often completed and returned via a website. There can even be spot-checks and sanctions for incorrect or non-completion (Taylor 1996). A third approach is concerned with learning in the context of practice, or what in Chapter 7 we called practice-based learning (PBL). This is particularly interesting for professionals as well as all managers because it focuses on a person's 'know-how' and how it is employed in practice. One view is to consider when a professional is required to work under pressure, in a task which is to some extent uncertain but in which the professional is expected to find a right answer. For example, a lawyer in court has to respond when faced with a difficult question or argument, and a surgeon has to deal with a problem in an operation. These are moments of 'hot' action (Beckett 2000, p.42). At such moments learning can emerge, to be surfaced and shared with others. It can also lead to new understandings which advance the skills of a professional or group of professionals. Gold *et* al (2007) explored this idea of PBL with a group of lawyers in Leeds and found that they were often 'put on the spot', or 'under fire', or 'surprised', but through the process were able to find new ideas which were 'an immediate and relevant form of CPD' (p.13).

 WEB LINK

As part of its approach to CPD, the Institution of Electrical Engineers has created a number of online Knowledge Networks, including one on management which you can examine at **http://kn.theiet.org/ management/** . The UK Inter-Professional Group acts as a forum for the major professional and regulatory bodies in the United Kingdom. Its website is located at **http://www.ukipg.org.uk/index** .

The Professional Associations Research Network provides up-to-date information on CPD at **http://www.parnglobal.com/** .

11.7 REFLECT – CONCLUDE – PLAN

Does professional status conflict with management?

What do you conclude about learning to lead and manage professionals?

What would be your first steps as a managing director of a firm of architects?

SUMMARY

- Managers are required to learn about the importance of valuing difference in an organisation as part of the growing interest in the benefits of diversity management.

- Career opportunities are more limited for women managers than for men where women face problems of stereotyping and prejudice.

- There are contrasting views of whether women have different management styles and development needs, and whether there should be separate male/female LMD activities.

- Black, Asian and minority ethnic managers may face stereotyping and exclusion, forcing them into 'career ghettos'.

- Positive action for specific BAME managers, consisting of a range of LMD activities, has been shown to provide a route into higher levels of responsibility.

- Global managers need capabilities that enable them to take responsibility for integrating activities across different subsidiaries in different locations around the world.

- It is becoming a necessity for managers to prove their understanding of environmental and ecological issues.

- There is a recognition that LMD for professionals must take into account the independence, autonomy and discretion of professional work.

QUESTIONS

For discussion

1 How can diversity management contribute to an organisation's ability to achieve strategic advantage? What are the implications for developing managers?

2 Do you think that most management courses are based on a 'masculine' view of management? Should women have separate courses?

3 What LMD activities can be provided to support BAME managers?

4 What are the key skills required for managers in a globalised economy?

5 Is green management worth it?

6 Can managerialism and professionalism ever be reconciled?

GROUP ACTIVITY

Get together in a group of three.

Between the three of you, taking one website each, visit the following websites to explore the strategy of the specified organisation for sustainability and environmentalism.

Sainsbury's: **http://www.j-sainsbury.com/files/reports/cr2005/ index. asp?pageid=5**

BP: **http://www.bp.com/sectionbodycopy.do?categoryId= 6931&contentId=7051661**

York City Council: **http://www.york.gov.uk/environment/ sustainability/**

Share your findings with the others in your group.

NOTES

1 An alternative analysis is offered by Trompenaars (1996). Seven valuing processes are presented as dilemmas that require reconciliation. The seven dilemmas are: universalism *v* particularism, analysing *v* integration,

individualism *v* communitarianism, inner-directed *v* outer-directed orientation, time as sequence *v* time as synchronisation, achieved status *v* ascribed status, and equality *v* hierarchy. See also Trompenaars and Hampden-Turner (2009).

2   In the UK there are around 400 professional bodies all providing a qualification education scheme.

 ## FURTHER READING

GHEMAWAT, P. (2005) 'Regional strategies for global leadership', *Harvard Business Review*, Vol.83, No.12: 98–107

METCALFE, B. D. (2010) 'Leadership and diversity development', in GOLD, J., THORPE, R. and MUMFORD, A. (eds) *A Handbook of Leadership and Management Development*. Aldershot: Gower

SHIEH, C.-J., WANG, I.-M. and WANG, F.-J. (2009) 'The relationships among cross-cultural management, learning organization, and organizational performance in multinationals', *Social Behavior and Personality: An International Journal*, Vol.37, No.1: 15–30

TROMPENAARS, F. and HAMPDEN-TURNER, C. (2009) *Innovating in a Global Crisis: Riding the whirlwind of recession*. Oxford: Infinite Ideas

TURNBULL-JAMES, K. and COLLINS, J. (2010) 'Leading and managing in global contexts', in GOLD, J., THORPE, R. and MUMFORD, A. (eds) *A Handbook of Leadership and Management Development*. Aldershot: Gower

CHAPTER 12

The development of leaders and managers in small and medium-sized enterprises

CHAPTER OUTLINE

Introduction
What are SMEs?
The nature of learning in SMEs
Performance and LMD provision in SMEs
Providing LMD in an SME context
Summary

LEARNING OUTCOMES

After studying this chapter, you should be able to understand, explain, analyse and evaluate:

- the ways in which small and medium-sized enterprises (SMEs) are different from their large firm counterparts

- the implications these differences have on the development of managers in SMEs, and the way in which size affects the leadership process

- the nature of learning in SMEs

- the implications of performance measurement on small firms

- key issues and approaches to LMD in SMEs

INTRODUCTION

For many years the number of small and medium-sized enterprises (SMEs) in Britain has been relatively low in comparison to other European countries and the United States. As a consequence, recognising their value to the economy and the way they can serve to reduce unemployment and create wealth, politicians of

all persuasions have made attempts to support the development of this important
sector of the economy. But this level of support has not always been present. It
was not until the Bolton Report (1971) that the contribution of SMEs, especially
smaller firms, to the economy and employment of the country was recognised.
Prior to this, SMEs were considered extremely marginal to the economy, as, in
a sociological context, were the individual owners and managers who ran them
(Stanworth and Curran 1973). Following the changes to the structure of the
economy that have taken place in recent years, these views have now changed
and SMEs are now regarded as playing an important role in, for example,
contributing to the gross national product through new business starts and small
business growth, providing one of the solutions to unemployment, and through
entrepreneurial development creating new products and services. For many there
is a view that it is from such tiny acorns that large oak trees grow.

According to the most recent statistics (BERR 2008), there were in the UK an
estimated 4.8 million private sector enterprises, with SMEs accounting for 99.9%
of all enterprises, 59.4% of private sector employment and 50.1% of private sector
turnover. Thus employment in SMEs was estimated at 13.7 million. However, we
should note that these figures refer to the start of 2008, well before the onset of
recession later that year. Figure 12.1 shows the share of enterprises, employment
and turnover by size of enterprise at the start of 2008.

Figure 12.1 Share of enterprises, employment and turnover by size of enterprise

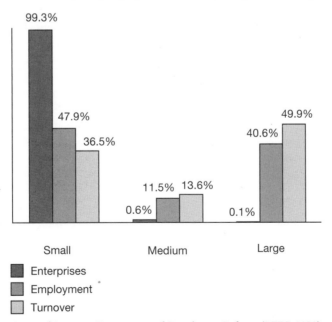

Source: Department of Business Enterprise and Regulatory Reform (BERR 2008)

WHAT ARE SMES?

One of the issues that bedevils any discussion on SMEs is how they might be
defined. There are even whole books related to the difficulties of measurement

WEB LINK

Statistics relating to SMEs are published every year but always lag behind the current time period. Check the latest figures at **http://stats.berr.gov. uk/ed/sme/** .

(Hertz 1986)! More formally in the UK, sections 247 and 249 of the Companies Act 1985 define an SME for the purpose of accounting requirements. These sections have been amended a number of times, most recently by Statutory Instrument 2004/16. According to this, a 'small' company is one that has a turnover of not more than £5.6 million, a balance sheet total of not more than £2.8 million, and not more than 50 employees. A 'medium-sized' company has a turnover of not more than £22.8 million, a balance sheet total of not more than £11.4 million, and not more than 250 employees. A further distinction is often made for organisations with fewer than 10 employees, which are referred to as 'micro-businesses'. There are, of course, many micro-businesses and they account for around 30% of all private sector employment (BERR 2008).[1]

However, it is generally recognised that SMEs are not a homogeneous entity and cannot be compared in any straightforward manner. There will always be differences relating to turnover, sector, size, market structure, and so on that make a single-criterion definition difficult. Although there are a number of commonly used definitions – for example, firms with 249 employees or fewer – this does little to take into account how capital-intensive the business is, such that a high-technology firm employing 200 people could represent a very large company indeed. That might also be true for professional service organisations, such as firms of solicitors. It is for this reason that we prefer to use a more qualitative definition in relation to size which highlights the nature of what it means to be small or medium-sized, and one which genuinely distinguishes small firms from their large firm counterparts. This approach was first suggested by Ganguly and Bannock (1985) and serves to encapsulate three aspects of business life which all SMEs share. These are:

- a relatively small share of the market
- a personalised management style
- independence that gives them a certain level of freedom when making major decisions.

The characteristics relating to an SME's market share means that it normally cannot calculate its market share, nor has it any real need to. Instead, it carves out a proportion of the market sufficient for it to prosper. As a consequence, the impact it makes on the environment is usually relatively small. In respect of the personalised style of the management, this is significant – and the main focus of this chapter. Because the manager or owner is usually active in all the major discussions and activities in the business, there is often very little delegated authority and control, and the strategy and the planning rests firmly with the owner. Independence usually means that the owner controls the business himself or herself, being relatively autonomous in the decision-making. Taken together, then, the way in which we might define an SME – particularly the smaller organisation – is to invoke the notion of a *lonely decision-taker*. This means that a small business is small if the owner-manager or entrepreneur feels isolated and lonely.

Gibb (1983) has operationalised a number of these aspects in a paper that compares and contrasts the impact that size has on a range of variables within the firm. For example, he contrasts the effects of size on such things as whether the firm has any formal management systems, or the extent to which it is able to obtain capital, or the way that managers can influence how tasks are performed.

DIFFERENCES BETWEEN OWNER-MANAGERS AND ENTREPRENEURS

In most media presentations, the terms 'owner-manager', 'small businessman/ woman' and 'entrepreneur' are used interchangeably. However, although there is an overlap between entrepreneurial firms and SMEs (Cartland *et al* 1984), owner-managers may well be entrepreneurs and vice versa. What we feel it is important to recognise is that these two phases have embedded in them decidedly different ways of working, and these ways of working will have implications for the methods of development and support that will be appropriate in terms of development. Failure to distinguish between these two groups could lead to much wasted effort and resource. Entrepreneurship has strong positive connotations of a person who takes risks, recognises opportunities and brings together either factors of production or individuals, or both, into new arrangements (Schumpeter 1934). Cartland *et al* (1984) indicate that an implicit assumption is often made that entrepreneurs make a disproportionate contribution to the wealth of a nation yet in development terms we have perhaps been slow to isolate these development needs. Cartland *et al* (1984) have devised a helpful framework for thinking about entrepreneurial activity related to both individuals and firms, and offer the following four basic classifications:

- *small business venture* – any business that is independently owned and operated, not dominant in the field and engaging in new, innovative practices

- *entrepreneurial ventures* – ventures engaging in one or other of Schumpeter's categories of entrepreneurship, where a principal goal of the business is profitability and growth, and where innovation is a component

- *small business owner* – an individual who creates and manages a business and sees the firm as an extension of himself or herself, and is intrinsically bound up in his/her own identity, motivations and ambitions

- *entrepreneur* – an individual who establishes and manages a business for the purpose of profitability and growth. The entrepreneur is characterised by innovative behaviour, and the policies and strategies employed are all with the aim of growth.

MANAGEMENT, LEADERSHIP AND ENTREPRENEURSHIP

We recognise that organisations need management, leadership and entrepreneurial behaviour if they are to succeed, and in many ways the distinctions we make between them are more academic than real. In reality, the roles typically act simultaneously, suggesting the need for a combination of development interventions. The overlap of skills and competences between entrepreneurship and leadership, for example, was a clear finding of the UK Government's Council for Excellence in Management and Leadership (Perren and Burgoyne 2002), as illustrated in Figure 12.2.

Figure 12.2 The overlap between entrepreneurship and leadership

Entrepreneurship   Leadership

Belief in control of events

Ambiguity tolerance

Need for independence

Identification of market opportunities

Innovation

Personal drive

Risk acceptance

Communication and social skills

Ability to motivate

Honesty and integrity

Knowledge of business

Interest in others

Team orientation

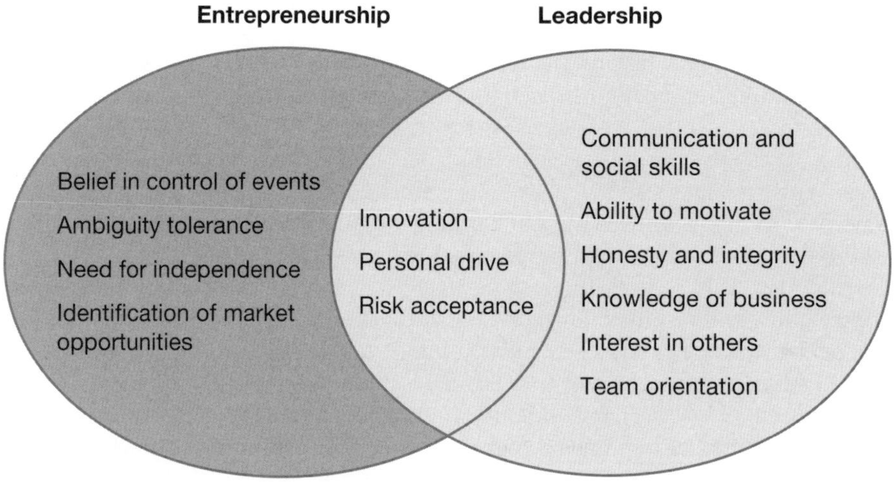

Source: Perren and Burgoyne (2002)

Entrepreneurship draws from management and leadership orientations and extends behaviour towards innovation, networking, visionary commitment and risk management. So, rather than seeing entrepreneurial behaviour or leadership as inherited traits gifted to a few, we argue here for the adoption of a dynamic learning perspective that can be developed and supported over a lifetime as well as in different contexts. By adopting such a perspective, learning and how it takes place become critical to entrepreneurial effectiveness. Such a dynamic view also means that less importance will be afforded to the pursuit of single personality traits, with the focus turning instead to understanding entrepreneurial processes, structures and those contexts where the attitudes we define as leadership and entrepreneurship can be developed and thrive.

THE NATURE OF LEARNING IN SMES

Another aspect of SMEs that is different from their large firm counterparts is the way that the business is closely related to the manager or owner, and very often family-based. This tends to mean that owner-managers run the business day to

12.1 REFLECT – CONCLUDE – PLAN

Do you have any ideas for innovation in any aspect of work?

Will you keep this idea to yourself or share it with someone else?

Do you accept the risk of taking this idea to a next stage?

day in addition to having overall management responsibility (Johnson 1999). Thus, for example, the 'task structure' is likely to be a highly personalised one, as opposed to one that is more objective and rationally prescribed (Gibb and Dyson 1982). This feature of the relationship between the owner and the firm means that if you develop the individual, you have a far greater chance of developing the firm as a consequence.

What becomes important then is to understand the nature of learning within SMEs as well as to understand that the development of SMEs is in many ways synonymous with the development of their owners or managers. That is, it is through the development of the owner that the business as a whole can be developed. However, it is often the case that the managers of SMEs are those least enthusiastic about formal training, which reinforces an absence of a formal HRD culture (Fuller-Love 2006). This is borne out by the proportion of managers who receive training or undertake formal HRD initiatives. Matlay (2004), for example, has shown that formal initiatives such as Investors in People, vocational qualifications and programmes brokered by support agencies such as Business Links only attract marginal interest from SMEs. This is the case even where SME managers are aware of initiaitives and understand them. For some time it has been recognised, therefore, that it is doubtful that HRD activity, in a formal sense, could provide a measurable payback (Gibb 1997).

One of the reasons for this is that SME managers are often short of time and necessarily focused on day-to-day problems. Another is that they don't see the relevance of development, and when they can, they find taking time off work difficult and expensive (Ram 2000). This phenomenon was one identified by the Bolton Report as long ago as in 1971, but it was not until the work of academics such as Gibb (1983, 2009) and the emergence of a more considered understanding of SMEs and how they operated that steps were taken to intervene more effectively. Gibb's work showed how an understanding of the nature of small firms and the attitudes and orientations of their managers, how they acquired knowledge and managed, meant that better, more considered pathways of support could be designed. Before that time interventions all too often emphasised recipes for business improvement available to all, rather than to those businesses with the potential to develop – for example, not distinguishing between entrepreneurial firms that wished to grow and more mature businesses in a steady state that did not.

We have already considered the difference between a small business and an entrepreneurial venture, and an owner-manager and an entrepreneur, and we have suggested that aspects of both are important at different times in the context of SME development. We have also seen that when it comes to understanding SMEs a continuing issue is that they are often referenced against the business practices of larger organisations and that this is not always helpful. What we have come to understand is the way SME managers need to pay attention to both the day-to-day details as well as the longer-term ongoing aspects of governance. So it matters little whether we call what they do 'management' or 'leadership' development. Instead, what is important is how the learning relates to how managers experience and undertake their work (Gold and Thorpe 2008).

There are clearly managers who want to grow their business in markets that are able to sustain growth, but who soon become overwhelmed by the day-to-day issues faced. We also know that there are others with little interest in growth *per se* (although they still might need support). These are businesses that we might characterise as mature – the ones that wish to retain their independence and survive, but for whom major change is either difficult or unattractive. For many SME managers there is a paucity of time for them to stand back and reflect – yet often this is exactly what they need to do if they are to take stock and develop. This often means that most learning in SMEs takes place at work, outside formal educational settings such as universities and colleges, and although in recent years there has been a growth in the number of programmes for 'entrepreneurs', there is still very little support available for the vast numbers of managers in small businesses. Their learning preference appears to be to develop by actively working through problems, and talking to customers, staff and other SME managers they meet during the course of their day. What we know by studying managers is that everyday occurrences offer significant learning opportunities. Moreover, the learning occurs naturally because it is already part of their work, and often goes unrecognised when researching where managers learn their craft from. This everyday phenomenon of learning is learning, nevertheless (Billett 2000). Again there is nothing new in highlighting this: recognising the value of this kind of 'informal learning', Alan Gibb (1997, 2009) and his team at Durham University championed a variety of learner-centred, problem-centred approaches in the 1980s and 1990s. However, in broad terms managers in SMEs learn by doing, exploring, experimenting, copying and problem-solving, through opportunities taken and lessons from mistakes made (Gibb 1997; Beaver *et al* 1998; Dalley and Hamilton 2000).

LEARNING THEORY IN RELATION TO SMALL FIRMS

Gold and Thorpe (2010) have summarised the relationship between learning, training and organisational performance in a small firm. Picking up the themes we have developed in earlier chapters, they outline previous research that shows how significant learning by managers derives in ways other than formal courses (Pavlica *et al* 1998), and the way natural learning (Burgoyne and Hodgson 1983) occurs in relation to 'significant' events that take place at work. The literature on SME learning also recognises that if the learning that takes place through these naturally occurring processes can be captured, then learning can be enhanced and speeded up – a finding that has led management developers to consider what mechanisms might be designed that can effectively intervene and facilitate this learning (Cohen and Sproull 1996).

These considerations would suggest that the most appropriate learning theories for SMEs that we considered in Chapter 5 would be Lave and Wenger's (1991) situated learning theory and Vygotsky's (1978) socio-cultural theory – the first because of the attention given to the idea of learning within a community of practice, where learning and practice are intimately connected to the working of relationships in the situation of practice. Thus learning usually occurs in the face of a problem that occurs within the practice of work. Vygotsky's theory is also concerned with practice and the achievement of goals, mediated by tools that both enable and potentially constrain the achievement of goals. Learning involves a disturbance to the use of existing tools through the introduction of new tools. Writers focusing specifically on learning within SMEs such as Rae (2004) and Down (2006) have pointed to the importance that needs to be placed on developing tools to help managers think and reflect, often critically, about such things as their identity as managers and how to exploit their social networks and working relationships within their organisations (Devins and Gold 2002). Again, Gibb (1997) had earlier pointed out the necessity of drawing on the help of others in SME learning, including family and friends, and professional help such as bankers, solicitors and accountants. These form what has been called the 'network-interdependency' of an SME.

Gold and Thorpe (2010) also point to the historical preoccupation of much of the academic research on individuals within the firm as opposed to understanding the social contexts in which learning takes place and is embedded. This extension of the focus of where and how learning occurs has led writers (Jones *et al* 2010; Jones and Macpherson 2006) to consider how knowledge is gained via an individual's human and social capital, and the role that learning networks play in the development of useful knowledge that will help the owner-manager overcome problems and difficulties at work (Cope 2005; Tell 2000). The focus on issues such as these makes the link between learning and leadership but a short step. Jones *et al* (2010), for example, note that for SMEs to be successful there is a need for them to recognise the value of quite different kinds of capital such as the financial, human and social dimensions which also include the quality of an SME's leadership. It is leadership that is one of the least understood. And so to the importance that must be placed on development practices that deal effectively with the manager in the context of the firm. Such practices must help or facilitate managers to make sense of problems that are often complex and roughly defined (Gold *et al* 2010) and enable them to think outside their current context (Cuniliffe 2002). Anderson (2007) suggests that they also need to be able to reflect, often critically, on the actions and decisions they have taken. A variety of learning environments where this activity can take place have been proposed by Anderson and Gold (2009) and Clark *et al* (2006) and include, for example, Action Learning methods, by which individuals come together to challenge their practice and take action but work on problems that concern them and that if not resolved will affect the development of their organisations. Such approaches also embrace the social dimensions of learning and help owner-managers to learn from the social influence of others.

If most learning in an SME is informal, what does this suggest about more obvious forms of learning such as formal programmes, seminars and courses? Many SME managers are prepared to attend events such as these if they are attracted to them and if it serves their interests and desires. This would suggest a need for flexibility in approaches to learning for SMEs. Figure 12.3 shows the possibilities.

Figure 12.3 Dimensions of learning in SMEs

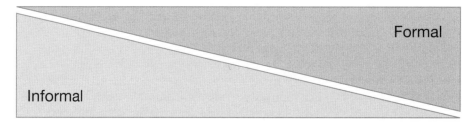

Approaches to learning range from one extreme of highly informal to another extreme of highly formal. Between these poles is a raft of possible approaches The preferred approach to learning will be affected by a number of factors which, according to Gold and Thorpe (2008), include:

- *place* – where the learning takes place
- *problem* – the time period over which the problem needs to be solved
- *sociality* – the social setting and who is involved
- *impact* – how quickly the results must be made manifest.

For example, where the preferred approach for development is mainly informal, it might suggest that coaching and mentoring would be more effective. This would allow situated work with SME managers, usually on a one-to-one basis, on issues of immediate concern which need a solution with immediate impact. Research evidence suggests if SME managers use external advice, it is valued because of the "'soft" (relationship-building and marketing) benefits' which help them cope with problems or improving the ability to manage (Ramsden and Bennett 2005, p.240). Approaches such as coaching and mentoring, working mostly informally, is what the Council for Excellence in Management and Leadership (CEML 2002) saw as joining managers 'in their world' by providing support that reflects their personal aspirations and ambitions and enables managers to take ownership of their own development.

12.2 REFLECT – CONCLUDE – PLAN

Do you think an MBA would be of value to an SME manager?

How could a formal off-the-job programme be of value to an SME manager?

Use the Internet to find out about MBA programmes for SME managers.

PERFORMANCE AND LMD PROVISION IN SMES

Growth in the SME sector is seen by many external agencies to equate to the growth of capital or the generation of employment. Such a view can be both inaccurate and misplaced. Many managers wish simply to consolidate their businesses, and rather than grow into large oak trees, want no more than to remain little bonsais and survive.

Understanding managers and SME owners from the way they construct their reality and adopting a problem-centred and learner-centred approach to their development requires that those undertaking the development also have an understanding of how those managing and leading in small firms view performance. Garengo *et al* (2005) have shown how difficult it is for SME managers to find time to participate in projects even when they are of immediate importance to their development. When they do take an interest, the projects on which they embark are often unfinished. Perhaps most important of all, they also found that the measures SME managers use are often very narrowly focused, with a preference for the use of financial data to the exclusion of some of the more qualitative matters equally important for organisational success – for example, securing a pool of new, young, talented employees who take the business forwards. Often the use of financial data serves to focus on past performance and activities as opposed to more strategic issues. As a consequence, many of the measures used are short term and reflect the pressures the managers face from day to day. What is often not appreciated by business development advisers is that for many SME managers, performance is an idiosyncratic concept (Thorpe 2006) that can only be properly understood through understanding the motivations and aspirations of the manager, and if the manager's horizons are limited, so too will be the ambitions he or she has for the firm. For many the idea of standing back and thinking strategically about the business is anathema, and this in its turn dictates the performance measures used by SMEs – which often reinforces how managers think about their businesses, the opportunities that might be possible and the nature of any LMD undertaken. To collect a wider set of data requires managers to be able to stand back from the hurly-burly of the day-to-day and reflect. As argued by Thorpe *et al* (2008), they *need to be able to create 'space' for themselves*, so that they can think ahead and reflect on the context of the business and the opportunities that might exist for change. This shortage of time to undertake a proper analysis of performance usually means that even when more formal procedures are used, implementation tends to be incomplete. Thorpe *et al*'s (2008) study, conducted in the north-west of England, has been helpful in our understanding about how SME managers lead their firms through crisis and manage to adopt a more strategic orientation. The research highlighted how informal learning, past experiences, systems and engagement with others are central to this strategic learning process, but that actual practices between firms differ. In others words, the research suggested that it is not the adoption of 'best practice' that is key to a firm's success, but rather that a firm's actual learning and leadership activities are largely unique, and that where some firms are more successful than others, it is when they manage to create the resources, time and 'strategic space' (Jones *et al* 2007) to lift their attention towards a more distant horizon. Effective managers in these organisations are able to stand back from day-to-day activities and consider long-term issues which impact on their businesses.

Figure 12.4 illustrates the way performance management thinking might move from something that is short term, partial and operational to something that is longer term, strategic and systems-based.

Figure 12.4 Performance management thinking in SMEs

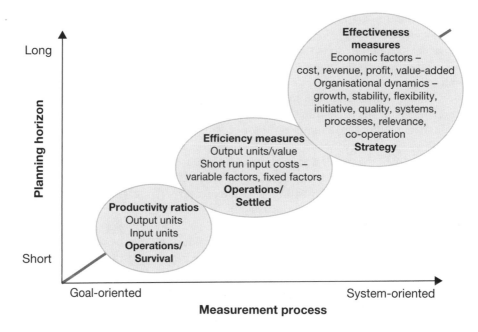

The horizontal axis represents a range of approaches to the evolution of performance, from rather limited short-term goal-based approaches to those at the other end of the axis that increasingly take account of a range of variables and systems in operation within the firm. The vertical axis indicates the planning horizon associated with the use of the measures. Many SMEs depend on achieving a certain weekly turnover for their survival. These measures do give managers information that is key to their survival but they fail to take into account important qualitative considerations that point to a wider context. It is this context that might offer the manager insights into how and where the business might develop. Movement along the diagonal line involves moving from a short-term planning process towards a more long-term process and considering a more complex and system-oriented measurement process.

These insights from Figure 12.4 are important because they form part of the special and rather different context that makes SMEs small and influences the way in which LMD has to be introduced. For example, if survival is the current priority, managers will be concerned to meet short-term operational goals

12.3 REFLECT – CONCLUDE – PLAN

Does this figure explain why so many managers in SMEs fail to grow?

What do you think is needed to help an SME manager adopt a longer-term planning horizon?

What measurement tools could be used for an effectiveness approach?

against clear measures of the 'bottom line'. As a result, LMD needs to respond to the concerns of managers but also to seek to move towards measurements that allow a longer-term and more strategic view to be considered. The challenge is to demonstrate a connection between the immediate pressures faced by a manager while at the same time motivating them to explore new possibilities and discover how the business might develop in the future. These two possibilities can be presented as dimensions along a continuum of provision of LMD, shown in Figure 12.5.

Figure 12.5 A continuum of provision of LMD in SMEs

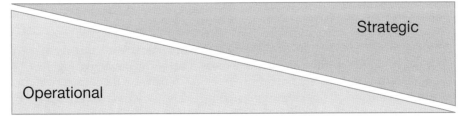

LMD provision can vary from highly operational to highly strategic. Gold and Thorpe (2008) suggest that the kinds of factors a provider will need to consider are:

- *time frame* – how long it will take for the intervention to impact on the manager and the organisation
- *horizon* – how the provision offered might broaden the thinking of the manager
- *measurement* – how performance will be measured
- *ownership* – who owns the problem
- *cost* – how the costs will be justified.

Combining the two dimensions from Figures 12.3 and 12.5 provides a grid showing possible approaches to learning and provision of LMD for SMEs. This is shown as Figure 12.6.

The grid suggests 25 possible combinations of learning and provision, or (following the CEML 2002) 25 SME 'worlds'. This is an over-simplification, since

Figure 12.6 Approaches to learning and provision of LMD for SMEs

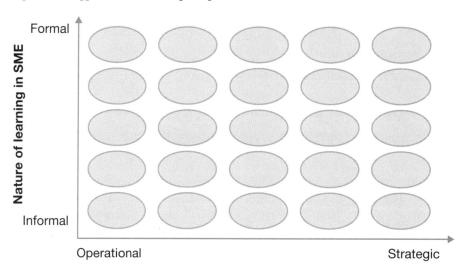

Provision of leadership and management development

all SMEs can be considered unique in some way. However, it does provide some possible ways of considering LMD for SME managers. For example, the lower left corner is perhaps the starting position for many SMEs – this is highly informal learning and highly operational provision. Survival is the main way of operating, and all learning has to be situational and based on practice. Some managers can move from this position and become more strategic by moving along the operational/strategic axis but not perhaps seeking to increase the formality of learning. Such managers might be prepared to 'boldly go' forward, developing their businesses and themselves as 'mature entrepreneurs' without help from external agencies (Thorpe *et al* 2006).

We could contrast such a move with managers who might be prepared to learn from a training course in order to consider small improvements to make their organisations more efficient. However, as we have suggested, most SME managers become trapped in the lower left position on the grid, so the crucial decision is how to engage with them and move them from that position through LMD.

STRETCHING THE HORIZONS OF POSSIBILITIES FOR THE SME MANAGER

If each point in the grid shown in Figure 12.6 can be regarded as a 'world' of the SME, what is important in SME development practice is for those engaged in working with individuals within a firm to begin their development initiatives in the context of each person's current capabilities, and having established what those capabilities are, to enlarge the person's horizons, initially to the outer boundary of their current world (World 1) and then into a new position on the grid (World 2). This 'stretch' is illustrated in Figure 12.7.

Figure 12.7 Stretching SMEs

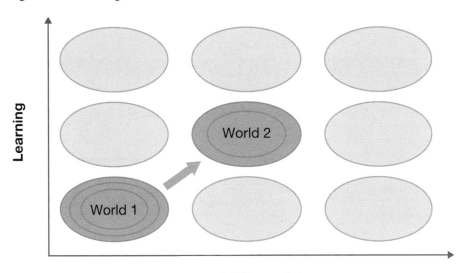

The idea here is that based on some 'early successes' within World 1, and importantly through the establishment of trust, the manager can be engaged in considering World 2. Once some 'safe' interventions have been successful in this domain and the opportunities that emanate from this new World have been established in the mind of the manager, new capabilities appropriate to the new circumstances and opportunities they find themselves in can be exploited through further development (Vygostsky 1978).

For any developer to consider such ideas, initially there has to be a process of engagement – and as we have seen, many SMEs do not undertake formal LMD. While the cost of training is one factor, others relate to the practicalities of the time many managers have available to engage in development activities of any kind. Devins and Gold (2000) have referred to these managers as the 'hard to reach' or the 'tough nuts to crack', where engagement is not easy and awareness of what training and development can offer is limited. Their work and the work of others suggest, however, that even the 'hard to reach' managers can be attracted to development, particularly through intermediaries and brokers (Thursfield *et al* 2004). For example, Gold and Thorpe (2008) report on the work of a group of brokers who they refer to as 'door-knockers'. Such brokers were particularly adept at drawing 'hard-to-reach' SME managers into a conversation. Most striking was the skill at sustaining this conversation, sometimes over several weeks, before the relationship was established which allowed the broker to provide the possibility of support for the manager based on needs identified. Because managers were often suspicious of any approach from an outsider, the brokers had to work to reassure managers and remove the perception of threat to their businesses and the fear of being burdened with excessive paperwork (which often accompanies funding for support provided by the government). If these perceptions can be removed and a good relationship established with a manager, a broker may then be able to help in the formulation of a plan for LMD, based on identified needs, and introduce recommended providers who could help the manager implement the plan.

PROVIDING LMD IN AN SME CONTEXT

The methods that appear relevant in meeting the requirements of SME managers would seem to be coaching and mentoring and other one-to-one methods. These approaches offer significant potential for working with the SME managers because they serve to help them find solutions to the immediate problems they face and can then move them on and offer the 'stretch' which we indicate as desirable for them to consider new possibilities and ways of working. The *LMD in Practice* below provides one example:

LMD IN PRACTICE

MARK MEETS HIS MENTOR

Mark Riley is a well-known hairdresser in Huddersfield, but for many years his views about learning and development were typical of many SME managers – he was highly sceptical of the benefits of such initiatives.

He agreed to meet Brian Wadsworth, a specialist mentor of SME managers, 'over breakfast in a café'. Importantly, through a series of such meetings, Mark's needs and desires became more evident, and he emerged as no longer 'stuck and struggling' but 'a man with a plan for change', which he agreed to implement with Brian.

Working with Brian, Mark soon identified 'major inefficiencies' in current operations that were causing cash-flow problems. Indeed, the business was 'a mess'. One change needed was a supervisory infrastructure which would allow Mark more time to focus on operational and financial performance. He could also take time away from 'cutting hair' to meet with Brian to think strategically and talk business. Part

of this talk was to articulate Mark's special vision of the 'Mark Riley Experience', based on a 'journey of well-being for customers' and growth of the business to over 10 salons across Yorkshire by 2010.

This vision would also need trained staff who could enact the values that went with the vision. So it was not enough that trainees went to college to get their NVQ in Hairdressing – it was also important that trainees understood and worked with Mark's notion of the 'journey' and the experience of 'well-being' for the customers. One way to ensure this was to do more training in-house, rather than at the college. So with Brian's help, a partnership deal was struck with Brighouse College to allow Mark to establish an academy for 20 trainees, with a forecast to expand to 50 as the business grew. As a result, Mark can select trainees against his criteria of quality which reflect his aspirations for growth.

Also important as vehicles for SME development are those that foreground the social aspects of learning – for example, networking. We are aware that many managers find it useful to discuss their problems and learn from other managers (Zhang and Hamilton 2006). We know too that local networks, forums and business clubs also provide opportunities for this to happen, and although managers may not regard the activity as learning while they are there, new knowledge is passed on and retained in a tacit manner. Action Learning programmes are also popular because they provide many of the ingredients discussed earlier (Clark *et al* 2006). In Action Learning there is informality and challenge between peers, but learning has a more central place in the process. The *LMD in Practice* below provides two examples from Action Learning.

LMD IN PRACTICE

MANAGER 1

'I was appointed MD two months before the programme and wanted help to gain the confidence to change the company. This programme has really been invaluable. I have now increased the level of promotional and PR activities – we produce newsletters and ask for referrals. I now give staff briefings to keep them all informed and we are starting to document our procedures. I am now working on a culture change to create a more open style of management and increased staff empowerment. I have found the group feedback sessions really useful in helping me to develop my ideas. Thank you!'

MANAGER 2

'I joined the programme after it had started but soon found it very helpful. I had not been in this role long and was having problems. I am now being appreciated as a leader. I have delegated almost 80% of my old roles and people are now coming to work earlier, probably as a result of changing my style. I seem to be more approachable – people are asking me for help with their problems instead of hiding them. The point of the course seems to be about dealing with *you*, not the shop floor. I have been able to remove my self-made blocks. The business has benefited from reduced wastage and improved production. The programme has really helped me to gain the confidence and achieve these changes.'

Source: *Success Stories*, All-Sector Management and Leadership Skills Development

---

Other possibilities are to combine coaching and mentoring with Action Learning, and to introduce further inputs such as lectures, masterclasses and seminars that seek to open further the managers' horizons and desire for growth, and to make use of genuine 'strategic space'. For example, a programme has been championed at Lancaster University which incorporates coaching, mentoring and peer learning, as well as strategic workshops led by experts. The evaluation of this programme revealed the importance of the 'soft aspects' of formal provision, including acknowledging the need for affirmation and growth in confidence, principally achieved by building relationships and supported by reflective and peer learning. Finally, the concept of 'strategic space' proves to be a key finding from the research literature that suggested that SME managers and leaders crucially need space to think strategically away from the day-to-day, so that new ideas can be considered and absorbed into normal work.

As a conclusion to this chapter, we include seven principles of good practice for those working within the SME community in relation to LMD practice. These principles are based on the evidence collected by the Northern Leadership Academy (Thorpe *et al* 2009) in which we participated. Because they have emerged from evidence of practice, they serve as a guide to both policy-makers and practitioners.

1 ENGAGE WITH THE IDENTITY AND INTERESTS OF THE MANAGER

For managers in SMEs, learning becomes meaningful when it is strongly related to their concerns, problems and desires. It is important to explore their situation and how it has come about.

2 UNDERSTAND THE CONTEXT AND BUILD ON IT

The experience of the SME manager both shapes and is shaped by the context of the organisation, so it is important to understand this before any activity can be provided.

3 RESPOND TO THE TIME-FRAME AS APPROPRIATE

It is important to understand a manager's thinking about time-frames. The reality is that most SMEs have extremely short planning horizons, and order books that barely last more than one or two months at a time.

4 DETERMINE THE MEASUREMENT AND WHAT IS VALUED

How SMEs measure their performance is strongly connected to the managers' response to what they learn. The measures that managers use can constrain and limit learning, especially as research suggests that most SMEs find it difficult to participate in performance-measurement projects due to lack of time for anything other than operational activities.

5 STIMULATE ENTREPRENEURSHIP AND STRETCH

SME managers are generally concerned with present interests, seeking to repair or improve current ways of working. It is important to assess existing capacity and capabilities, and to explore the potential for making an advance.

6 DEVELOP COMMUNITIES OF PRACTICE

Learning by managers in SMEs most often occurs naturally by completing work and solving problems as part of an everyday process. Such learning is the by-product of a work process rather than its focus, and is shared with everyone involved in the process. The accumulation of such learning over time, and the meanings attached to what is done, become accepted by everyone connected to the organisation. SME managers also like to learn with and from others who have similar concerns and face similar issues.

7 ENHANCE BELIEF, CONFIDENCE AND AWARENESS

Any attempt to provide support for SME management and leadership development requires space to attract managers into a conversation. Development intervention must recognise the need for appropriate language and learning contexts (often the manager's own or other businesses') and for pedagogy that is premised on exchanges of experiences and ideas.

SUMMARY

- SMEs are now seen as playing an important role in contributing to the gross national product, in that new business starts and small business growth provide one of the solutions to unemployment, and in that entrepreneurial development creates new products and services.

- There are difficulties in defining an SME but a small business is small if the manager or entrepreneur may be described as isolated and lonely.

- Entrepreneurship draws from management and leadership orientations and extends behaviour towards innovation, networking, visionary commitment and risk management.

- The development of SMEs is in many ways synonymous with the development of their owners or managers.

- Most learning in SMEs is informal and takes place at work, outside formal educational settings such as universities and colleges.

- Performance measurement and management has a key impact on LMD in SMEs.

- LMD provision can vary from highly operational to highly strategic.

- Engagement is an important process to attract hard-to-reach SME managers into development.

- The main approaches to LMD in SMEs are mentoring and coaching, Action Learning and joining networks of other SME managers.

QUESTIONS

For discussion

1 Why isn't LMD for managers in large organisations appropriate for SME managers?

2 How do SME managers learn?

3 Do SME managers consider themselves leaders?

4 What skills are needed to persuade SME managers to undertake LMD?

5 If an SME manager does not wish to grow the business, is LMD needed?

6 How can 'hard-to-reach' SMEs be attracted into LMD activities?

GROUP ACTIVITY

Get together in a group of three.

Between the three of you, taking one website each, visit the following websites to explore the specified organisation's policy and view on how to provide support for managers in SMEs.

The Federation for Small Business, at **http://www.fsb.org.uk** .

Business Link at **http://www.businesslink.gov.uk** .

The Institute for Small Business and Entrepreneurship at **http://www.isbe.org.uk/** .

Share your findings with the others in your group.

NOTES

1   At the start of 2008, the latest reported figures, there were 3.5 million enterprises with no employees and 1.3 million with 1–9 employees.

FURTHER READING

ANDERSON, L. and GOLD, J. (2009) 'Conversations outside the comfort zone: identity formation in SME manager action learning', *Action Learning: Research and Practice*, Vol.6, No.3: 229–42

DEVINS, D. (2008) 'Encouraging skills acquisition in SMEs', in R. BARRETT and S. MAYSON (eds) *International Handbook of Entrepreneurship and HRM*. London: Edward Elgar Publishing

HOQUE, K. and BACON, N. (2008) 'Investors in People and training in the British SME sector', *Human Relations*, Vol.61, No.4: 451–82

STEWART, J. and BEAVER, G. (2004) *HRD in Small Businesses*. London: Routledge

THOMPSON, J. (2006) *Enabling Entrepreneurs*. Huddersfield: University of Huddersfield

CHAPTER 13

Futures learning for leaders and managers

CHAPTER OUTLINE

Introduction
Approaches to learning for the future
Learning in complexity
To boldly go
Summary

LEARNING OUTCOMES

After studying this chapter, you should be able to understand, explain, analyse and evaluate:

- different approaches to learning for the future

- how managers must learn to deal with complexity

- the engagement of managers with others in the face of an unpredictable future

INTRODUCTION

Throughout this book we have considered how managers have faced a number of pressures which carry a high degree of uncertainty but are still expected to provide clarity for others. It is common to cite a range of forces and trends that contribute to this pressure, such as:

- globalisation

- developments in science and technology

- the generative power of ICT

- socio-economic factors such as the diversity and composition of the population and the changing values of the workforce

- climate change and the green agenda
- ethical and social responsibility.

The events of the late 2000s have not removed any of these factors, and to this list we must now add economic uncertainty, unpredictability and concern about survival and sustainability of life on Earth. These have made the need to learn even more prominent. We are reminded of the famous presentation by Reg Revans (1986), who first noted how the rate of learning has to be at least equal to or greater than the rate of change in the environment – or $L \geq C$. Otherwise, Revans predicted, 'failure' would follow. We would also propose that it is not just the rate of change in the environment that requires a response – there is an important difference between change that is incremental or simply an adjustment to restore equilibrium, and change that is more radical, transformational and discontinuous. For the latter, learning involves a challenge to existing assumptions and frames of thinking – what Argyris (1999) referred to as 'double-loop' learning. Managers have a key role in leading and learning from change and setting out the landscape for the future. It is therefore argued that managers need to find a way to identify what lies in the future and take action to prepare themselves and their organisations, as 'strategic leaders' (Boal and Hooijberg 2001; CMI 2008). They will also need cultural awareness and the skills of innovation, managing change and flexibility (Winterton et al 2000).

APPROACHES TO LEARNING FOR THE FUTURE

When Revans was forecasting 'failure', he was engaging in the common practice of forecasting which you will find in abundance on a daily basis, ranging from prediction of football results to the Earth's temperature in 2050. In making such forecasts, it is necessary to draw on patterns of information which form a trend. However, it is also important to use such information carefully and critically (Gordon 2009). Although some of the trends may be clear, there is not always predictability about their impact. How managers respond will depend on how they learn to develop new ways of thinking and acting with others. For example, there is a difference between analytical thinking for predictability and creative thinking where there is unpredictability, complexity and multiple future possibilities (PIU 2001). Figure 13.1 shows this spectrum of approaches to the future.

Analytical approaches work with trends and predictive models which allow managers to attempt to plan and control events. By contrast, creative approaches are required where the presence and interaction of large numbers of factors make prediction, planning and pre-specification more difficult. In such situations managers need to learn to think differently, perhaps drawing on ideas from complexity and chaos theories (Stacey 2002). There is a difference between a future which is uncertain and one which is complex. In the former, there is a search to remove the uncertainty mainly by gathering information and subjecting it to analysis. This can occur even when there are large numbers of

Figure 13.1 A spectrum of approaches to the future

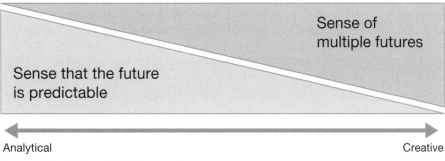

Sense of multiple futures

Sense that the future is predictable

Analytical

Creative

Source: adapted from PIU (2001, p.15)

factors – the crucial point is that uncertainty can be made understandable. With complexity, there are too many factors interacting in a dynamic and non-linear way for analysis to reduce the uncertainty and increase predictability. Patterns of interaction between the factors produce results that cannot be set out in rules of cause and effect. Instead, more creative approaches are required.

Given the difficulty of making predictions about the future with certainty, managers will need to learn new skills, drawing from the field of *futurism*. For example, Dator (2003), a leading futurist, has suggested that various essential attributes and skills are required such as creativity, imagination, the willingness to think new thoughts, to make unmade connections, to be ridiculed and laughed at, and to laugh at yourself

13.1 REFLECT – CONCLUDE – PLAN

How often do you engage in creative and imaginative thinking about the future?

What do you think can be done to enhance your analytical and creative skills?

What will you do to bring this about?

In addition to futurist skills, there are futures tools and techniques. Probably the most well-known of these is the scenario method (van der Heijden *et al* 2002), based on the principle that organisations prepare best for the future by developing different alternative future stories. Scenarios are not forecasts, although there is often a tendency to consider them as such – they are future possibilities, and the process should be considered an opportunity for leaders, managers and others to develop joint conversation about the future.

There are other futures methods, and Mićić (2010) has sought to develop these into a model of Future Management. Based on research with leadership teams over a number of years, the model explores possible futures from a number of different perspectives. The model requires managers to consider assumptions, scan the environment for opportunities, analyse possible surprises and set a vision for the future. Prior to attending a series of workshops, a trend analysis is completed, but once again creativity is engendered through a conversational approach that allows both divergent and convergent thinking.

WEB LINK

The oil company Shell have been working with scenarios for nearly 30 years. Go to **http://www.shell.com/scenarios/** to examine the latest work. Consider more futures methods at **http://www.thinkingfutures.net/ futures-methods** . The UK's Cabinet Office has a Strategic Futures Team at **http://www.cabinetoffice.gov.uk/strategy/work_areas/ strategic_futures/research.aspx** where you can obtain its 2001 publication, *Understanding Best Practice in Strategic Futures Work*.

LEARNING IN COMPLEXITY

Faced with a morass of information, even if organised into discernable patterns as trends, and a high level of unpredictability, it might still be possible for managers to learn to cope – managers can reflect critically on their assumptions, challenge their mental models and find new ways of proceeding. The answer would seem to be to endure a period of discomfort as long-held beliefs are overturned so that eventually leader and managers can return to some form of equilibrium, albeit with new assumptions. The difficulty here is that they might remain with a way of thinking and behaving which continues with the assumption that events can be controlled and engineered by uncovering rules of cause and effect (Antonacopoulou 2004). The influence of this approach to leading and managing persists with the specification of skills and competences that are claimed to link to analysing the work of managers and predicting performance.

In contrast, there is increasing attention being given to discontinuity in the world, the unpredictability of events, and ongoing and continuous flux in which disequilibrium becomes the norm. To help managers cope, a more creative approach to learning is suggested using the idea of complexity and complex systems. According to Cilliers (1998), while not subject to a simple definition, complexity occurs when:

- there are a large number of interacting elements behaving in a non-linear fashion
- interactions can have the effect of feedback that can be positive or negative
- systems are usually open to interaction with the environment
- systems operate far from equilibrium, subject to continuous movement and flux.

One of the main principles of complexity is that interaction between elements produces a sense of order through self-organisation. Such order emerges, but due to the non-linear dynamics cannot be predicted with certainty or planned. Instead, there are a variety of possible effects. Capra (2002) stresses the 'livingness' of organisations, pointing out that as living beings, people have the ability to regenerate, change and evolve, and that these are the characteristics required for survival in a complex, fast-changing and knowledge-intensive environment.

For managers in organisations, this might mean that plans for change do not turn out as expected, the acquisition of particular skills or competences does not produce a desired performance (and may even produce the opposite result), and groups of staff may be beyond control – at least by a top-down command approach to management. As we have argued throughout this book, in many contexts it is not possible to take a traditional view of how work is structured nor retain the idea that expertise is concentrated at higher levels. In knowledge-based and professional organisations, for example, self-organisation has to be seen as the norm with the power and influence to lead and manage distributed throughout the organisation.

 WEB LINK

The Complexity Research Programme at the London School of Economics is focusing on complex social systems to study organisations. The homepage is **http://www.psych.lse.ac.uk/complexity/research.html** .

Go to **http://www.santafe.edu/**, the homepage of the Santa Fe Institute and a key source of ideas on complexity.

We can see the influence of complexity in a number of recent approaches to leadership, management and learning. For example, Watson and Harris (1999) argued that managers need to take a more process-oriented view of organisations and their own positions as managers. Instead of focusing on the idea of fixed things, like teams, the department, the business, or even the self as manager, there is a need to see everything as in a process of continuous movement. Thus a person performing a management role, managing, is never a fixed entity with permanent features such as static and unchangeable skills and competences. He or she is always 'becoming' (p.19). Similarly, Lichtenstein *et al* (2006) present a complexity leadership theory by which leadership emerges as a result of interaction and tension between people and ideas.

How can leaders and managers learn to cope with complexity in the present and the future? Bruner (1986) referred to a narrative mode of thinking, as a contrast to a logico-scientific mode. Narratives give prominence to the way we make sense of what is happening and how events are explained. Some narratives are deeply embedded in the past – for example, in the form of myths and folktales. However, they are often employed to make sense of the present. Recent years have seen significant interest in narrative and stories in organisations, especially in the context of change (Brown *et al* 2009), and we would suggest that in the face of complexity in their work they allow leaders and managers to make sense of ideas, actions and events through reflection. They also provide a resource for sense-making with others (Weick 2005) and provide a way of persuading others on the basis of evidence for a particular source of action (Pfeffer and Sutton 2006). But it is not only managers who use narratives. They have to recognise that far from the common assumption of a unified and single understanding of an organisation, they are more likely to have to respond to and understand a story-telling system that reflects a plurality of viewpoints.

WEB LINK

Find out more about story-telling at **http://cbae.nmsu.edu/~dboje/** . This is the homepage of David Boje, who has been a key writer about story-telling in organisations.

TO BOLDLY GO

It was clear even before the turbulent events of the late 2000s that managers will need to reject or reassess commonly held views about the controllability of the future and give more prominence to creativity and imagination. However, as futurists Rogers and Tough (1996, p.495) stated, 'Facing the future is definitely not for wimps', and as Slaughter (1999, p.845) warns, 'Futures work cannot be based on ego; it is an expression of shared transpersonal aspirations to help create a better world.'

Even if there is greater unpredictability about the future, managers – and especially those appointed as leaders – are expected by others to know what will happen and to be in control of events. As Pfeffer and Sutton (2006a) argue, leaders have to behave so that others believe they will bring about success. They refer to this as their 'leadership control cycle' (p.202) which includes talking and acting as though they were in control, so that any success in change is attributed to the leaders, even if there is evidence that this not the case. They also suggest that leaders can come to believe in the power of their words and actions, although those with more wisdom will remain sceptical about this. Nevertheless, this image is one that many people will recognise.

13.2 REFLECT – CONCLUDE – PLAN

Do you recognise the attribution of success to leaders who talk and act as if they were in control?

Why should you be sceptical about such attributions?

How can managers attain a more complex view of success?

Another image, which we referred to in Chapter 1, is that of the manager as a 'practical author' (Holman and Thorpe 2002), where a manager learns to work in the present and make the future through talk and conversation with others. The beauty of this image for LMD is that every day there are opportunities for managers to engage in conversations with others during which they are able to argue and persuade others of the need to act and respond to what they hear. By reviewing and reflecting on events that occur, through the same processes of talk and conversation, leaders/managers can learn with others how the future can be made. This also applies to thinking about strategy, and there has been growing interest in how strategy emerges and in 'strategy innovation' (Hamel 1998) – the process whereby new value for customers and new wealth for all stakeholders is created. A major implication is the need to shift attention for strategy as a plan or product to strategy as a process. Managers must adopt a learning approach to strategy, like any other activity. However, for new ideas to emerge from activities throughout an organisation requires a climate and processes where learning is designed into activities and given priority (Mumford 2000). Inevitably, this means that managers must delve more deeply into the process of how knowledge is produced within local contexts, especially with those who work closely with customers and key stakeholders on the boundaries of any organisation (Yanow 2004). The leader's conundrum that we referred to in Chapter 1 has therefore to be embraced and recognised if such organisations are going to make best use of their talent and provide a culture for engagement (CIPD 2008). Recent evidence from such organisations as the John Lewis Partnership, Tesco, the London Ambulance Service, Sainsbury's, Standard Chartered Bank, BAE Systems, Toyota, Babcock Marine Clyde and Google point to the importance of managers' engaging with employees on the basis of adult relationships as a requirement for improving production and service delivery in all sectors (MacLeod and Clarke 2009). Leaders and management must learn about the talents of their staff, how they think and feel, and to develop and build on such strengths, referred to as strengths-based development. Further, it is increasingly being recognised that for successful innovation in the future, managers will need to seek talent and expert resources across boundaries, often globally, in a process of co-production and learning for mutual benefit between partners and within networks of shared understanding (Prahalad and Krishnan 2008). In the future, managers will have to learn how to work within and between organisations and networks of partners in an age of mass collaboration (Tapscott and Williams 2006).

 WEB LINK

You can also learn more about employee engagement and the idea of strengths-based development at **http://www.gallup.com/consulting/52/ employee-engagement.aspx** .

There is growing interest in the process of making strategy, sometimes referred to as strategising. More information is available from **http://www.strategy-as-practice.org** .

At the start of the 1990s, Peter Senge advocated the building of learning organisations as the 'leader's new work' (1990, p.7), an idea also presented by Pedler *et al* (1991, p.1) who defined the learning organisation[1] as an organisation which 'facilitates the learning of all its members and continuously transforms itself'. The learning organisation was a key image during the 1990s and proved to be very attractive to many organisations. However, there were always a variety of concerns about the learning organisation – such as that it was perceived as idealistic or elusive (Garavan 1997), and that managers found they simply did not have the access within their organisations to enable them to initiate, promote or sustain approaches that required an organisation that 'continually transformed itself'. One consequence is that it was frequently regarded, in practice, as another training and development initiative concerned with improvement rather than radical change. Keep and Rainbird (2000) point out that although the idea of the learning organisation has value, there are too many factors in UK organisations which prevent its realisation. Such factors include cost-based competition, little space for creativity and a continued reliance on command-and-control approaches to people management. One particular consideration for managers is how far jobs are designed and work is organised to under-utilise skills and talent. The tendency has been for managers to focus on exploiting existing resources and competences, strategically bringing activities into alignment. By contrast, it is now recognised that strategic leaders need to give as much attention to exploring new opportunities for innovation and learning in order to adapt to changing conditions in the environment (Jansen *et al* 2009). Rather than the learning organisation, a new image has emerged for the future – that of the *ambidextrous organisation* (O'Reilly and Tushman 2004). This requires managers (and others) to work with two competing processes. The first is concerned with achieving alignment and efficiency in the present by exploiting existing talents and skills. The second is to become sufficiently adaptive to change in the environment by devoting time and resource to exploring new possibilities for the future. The danger is to trade off one process against the other – for example, by focusing only on the present and taking a short-term view, thus ignoring the need to explore (Gibson and Burkinshaw 2004). Managers have to learn how to consider dynamically the interplay of these two processes by providing support for exploration. Crucially, as primary role models for others, managers have to talk and act by balancing exploitation and exploration so that learning for efficiency can occur in the present and radical learning can occur for the future.

SUMMARY

- There are predictable trends that are affecting the content and delivery of LMD, but managers also face unpredictability.

- In facing the future, managers must learn analytical thinking for predictability and creative thinking for where there is unpredictability, complexity and multiple future possibilities.

- LMD can use ideas from complexity theory to help managers cope with discontinuity in the world, the unpredictability of events and flux where disequilibrium becomes the norm.

- Narrative thinking and story-telling have been presented as approaches to learning for complexity in LMD.

- Managers are expected by others to know what will happen in the future and to be in control of events.
- Recent evidence from organisations points to the importance of managers' engaging with employees on the basis of adult relationships.
- Strategic leaders need to give attention to exploring new opportunities for innovation and learning in order to adapt to changing conditions in the environment.

QUESTIONS

For discussion

1 'We can't predict the future, but we can think more about the sort of future we want, and how to achieve it. In fact, it is vital that we do just that.' What is the value of futurism for managers?

2 How can managers learn the skills of complex thinking?

3 Should leaders appear in control even when the future is unpredictable?

4 *Any useful statement about the future should seem ridiculous.* Discuss the implications of such a statement for LMD.

5 How can managers learn to engage with others for the future of their organisations?

GROUP ACTIVITY

Get together in a group of four to consider various approaches to learning about the future which can be incorporated into a learning programme for managers and others. The four approaches to consider are:

- scenarios
- open space technology
- future search
- search conferences.

Allocate one approach to each member of your group, who should then find out:

- how the approach operates, the main requirements, and the underlying theories
- examples of how the approach has been used, and evidence of outcomes
- advantages, and possible problems.

Share your findings and prepare a presentation with recommendations.

NOTES

1 Pedler *et al* (1991) always preferred the term 'learning company'.

FURTHER READING

GOBILLOT, E. (2009) *Leadershift: Reinventing leadership for the age of mass collaboration*. London: Kogan Page

GRIFFEN, D. and STACEY, R. (2005) *Complexity and the Experience of Leading Organizations*. London: Routledge

HUFF, A. S. and JENKINS, M. (2002) *Mapping Strategic Knowledge*. London: Sage

MIĆIĆ, P. (2010) 'Developing leaders as futures thinkers', in J. GOLD, R. THORPE and A. MUMFORD (eds) *A Handbook of Leadership and Management Development*. Aldershot: Gower

STACEY, R. (2007) *The Challenge of Complexity to Ways of Thinking About Organisations*. Harlow: Prentice Hall

References

ABBOTT, A. (1988) *The System of Professions.* Chicago: University of Chicago Press

ABMA, T. (2000) *Telling Tales: On evaluation and narrative.* Advances in Program Evaluation, Vol.6. Boston, MA: JAI Press

ABRAHAM, S. E., KARNS, L. A., SHAW, K. and MENA, M. A. (2001) 'Managerial competencies and the managerial appraisal process', *Journal of Management Development*, Vol.20, No.10: 842–52

ACKER, J. (2006) 'The gender regime of Swedish banks', *Scandinavian Journal of Management*, Vol.22, No.3: 195–209

ADAIR, J. (2005) *Effective Leadership Development.* London: Chartered Institute of Personnel and Development

ADAMS, K. (1996) 'Competency: discrimination by the back door?', *Competency and Emotional Intelligence Quarterly*, Vol.3, No.4: 34–9

ADAMS, S. M., GUPTA, A. and LEETH, J. (2009) 'Are female executives over-represented in precarious leadership positions?', *British Journal of Management*, Vol.20, No.1: 1–12

ADAMSON, S. J., DOHERTY, N. and VINEY, C. (1998) 'The meanings of career revisited: implications for theory and practice', *British Journal of Management*, Vol.9, No.4: 251–9

ADLER, P. S. and KWON, S. W. (2002) 'Social capital: prospects for a new concept', *Academy of Management Review*, Vol.27: 17–40

AIM (2009) *Closing The UK's Productivity Gap: The latest research evidence.* London: Advanced Institute of Management

ALBERGA, T., TYSON, S. and PARSONS, D. (1997) 'An evaluation of the Investors in People standard', *Human Resource Management Journal*, Vol.7, No.2: 47–60

ALIMO-METCALFE, B. and ALBAN-METCALFE, J. (2005) 'Leadership: time for a new direction', *Leadership*, Vol.1, No.1: 51–71

ALIMO-METCALFE, B. and ALBAN-METCALFE, R. J. (2001) 'The development of a new transformational leadership questionnaire', *The Journal of Occupational and Organizational Psychology*, Vol.74, No.1: 1–27

ALLEN, T., EBY, L., POTEET, M., LENTZ, L. and LIMA, L. (2004) 'Career benefits associated with mentoring for protégés: a meta-analysis', *Journal of Applied Psychology*, Vol.89: 127–36

ALLINSON, C. W. and HAYES, J. (1996) 'The cognitive style index: a measure of intuition-analysis for organizational research', *Journal of Management Studies*, Vol.33, No.1: 119–35

ALLINSON, C. W. and HAYES, J. (1988) 'The learning styles questionnaire: an alternative to Kolb's inventory', *Journal of Management Studies*, Vol.25, No.3: 269–81

ALON, I. and HIGGINS, J. M. (2005) 'Global leadership success through emotional and cultural intelligences', *Business Horizons*, Vol.48: 501–12

ALTMAN, Y. (1997) 'The high-potential fast-flying achiever: themes from the English-language literature, 1976–1995', *Career Development International*, Vol.2, No.7: 324–30

ALVESSON, M. and SVENINGSSON, S. (2007) *Changing Organizational Culture: Cultural change work in progress.* London: Routledge

ANDERSON, L. (2010) 'Evaluation' in Gold, J., Thorpe, R. and Mumford, A. (eds) *Gower Handbook of Leadership and Management Development.* Aldershot: Gower

ANDERSON, L. and Gold, J. (2009) 'Conversations outside the comfort zone: identity formation in SME manager action learning', *Action Learning* Vol. 6, No.3: 229–42

ANDERSON, N. R. and WEST, M. A. (1994) *Team Climate Inventory.* Chiswick, London: nferNelson Publishing

ANDERSON, R. A. (2004) 'Climbing Mount Sustainability', *Quality Progress*, Vol.37, No.2: 32–7

ANDERSON, V. (2007) *The Value of Learning: A new model of value and evaluation.* London: Chartered Institute of Personnel and Development

ANDERSON, V. (2004) 'Women managers: does positive action training make a difference?', *Journal of Management Development*, Vol.23, No.8: 729–40

ANDERSON, V., RAYNER, C. and SCHYNS, B. (2009) *Coaching at the Sharp End: The role of line managers in coaching at work.* London: Chartered Institute of Personnel and Development

ANG, J., LAUTERBACH, B. and VU, J. (2003) 'Efficient labor and capital markets: evidence from CEO appointments', *Financial Management*, Vol.32, No.2: 27–52

ANTONACOPOULOU, E. P. (2004) *Introducing Reflexive Critique in the Business Curriculum Reflections on the Lessons Learned.* London: Advanced Institute of Management

ANTONACOPOULOU, E. P. (2001) 'The paradoxical nature of the relationship between training and learning', *Journal of Management Studies*, Vol.38, No.3: 327–50

ANTONACOPOULOU, E. P. (1999) 'Training does not imply learning: the individual perspective', *International Journal of Training and Development*, Vol.3, No.1: 14–23

ANTONACOPOULOU, E. and BENTO, R. F. (2004) 'Methods of "learning leadership": taught and experiential', in J. STOREY (ed.) *Leadership in Organizations.* London: Routledge

ANTONIONI, D. (1994) 'The effects of feedback accountability on upward appraisal ratings', *Personnel Psychology*, Vol.47: 349–56

APPELBAUM, S. H. and SANTIAGO, V. (1997) 'Career development in the plateaued organization', *Career Development International*, Vol.2, No.1: 11–20

ARGYRIS, C. (2006) *Reasons and Rationalizations: The hints to organizational knowledge*. Oxford: Oxford University Press

ARGYRIS, C. (1999[Chapter 7]) 'Tacit knowledge and management', in R. J. STERNBERG and J. H. A. HORVATH (eds) *Tacit Knowledge in Professional Practice: Researcher and practitioner perspectives*. Mahwah, NJ: Lawrence Erlbaum

ARGYRIS, C. (1999[Chapter 13]) *On Organizational Learning*. Malden, MA: Blackwell

ARGYRIS, C. (1991) 'Teaching smart people how to learn', *Harvard Business Review*, May/June: 99–109

ARGYRIS, C. (1982) *Reasoning, Learning and Action*. San Francisco: Jossey-Bass

ARITZETA, A., SWAILES, S. and SENIOR, B. (2007) 'Belbin's team role model: development, validity and applications for team building', *Journal of Management Studies*, Vol.44, No.1: 96–118

ARNOLD, J. (1997) *Managing Careers into the 21st Century*. London: Paul Chapman

ARTHUR, M. B. and ROUSSEAU, D. M. (1996) *The Boundaryless Career: A new employment principle for a new organizational era*. New York: Oxford University Press

ARTHUR, M. B., HALL, D. T. and LAWRENCE, B. S. (1994) *Handbook of Career Theory*. Cambridge: Cambridge University Press

ARTHUR, M. B., KHAPOVA, S. N. and WILDEROM, C. P. M. (2005) 'Career success in a boundaryless career world', *Journal of Organizational Behavior*, Vol.26, No.2: 177–202

ARTHUR, W. JR, DAY, E. A., MCNELLY, T. L. and EDENS, P. S. (2003) 'A meta-analysis of the criterion-related validity of assessment center dimensions', *Personnel Psychology*, Vol.56, April: 125–54

ASHTON, C. and MORTON, L. (2005) 'Managing talent for competitive advantage', *Strategic HR Review*, Vol.4, No.5: 28–31

ASTLEY, W. (1985) 'Administrative science as socially constructed truth', *Administrative Science Quarterly*, Vol.30: 497–513

ATHERTON, A. and PHILPOT, T. (1997) *MCI and Small Firms Lead Body Standards and SME Development in Practice*. Report to MCI/DfEE. Durham University Business School

ATTWOOD, M. A. (2002) *Declaration on Learning*. Maidenhead: Honey Publications

ATWATER, L. E., WALDMAN, D. A., ATWATER, D. and CARTIER, P. (2000) 'An upward feedback field experiment: supervisors' cynicism, reactions and commitment to subordinates', *Personnel Psychology*, Vol.53, No.2: 275–97

AVOLIO, B. J. and BASS, B. M. (2004). *Multifactor Leadership Questionnaire: Manual and sampler set*, 3rd edition. Redwood City, CA: Mind Garden

AXTELL, C. M., MAITLIS, S. and YEARTA, S. (1997) 'Predicting immediate and longer-term transfer of training', *Personnel Review*, Vol.26, No.3: 201–13

AYAS, K. and ZENIUK, N. (2001) 'Project-based learning: building communities of reflective practitioners', *Management Learning*, Vol.32, No.1: 61–76

BACHKIROVA, K. and COX, E. (2007) 'Coaching with emotion in organisations: investigation of personal theories', *Leadership and Organization Development Journal*, Vol.28, No.7: 600–12

BADGER, B., SADLER-SMITH, E. and MICHIE, E. (1997) 'Outdoor management development: use and evaluation', *Journal of European Industrial Training*, Vol.21, No.9: 318–25

BALDWIN, T. T. and FORD, J. K. (1988) 'Transfer of training: a review, and directions for future research', *Personnel Psychology*, Vol.41: 63–105

BALL, B. (1997) 'Career management competences – the individual perspective', *Career Development International*, Vol.2, No.2: 74–9

BALLANTYNE, I. and POVAH, N. (2004) *Assessment and Development Centres*. Aldershot: Gower

BANDURA, A. (1986) *Social Foundations of Thought and Action*. Englewood Cliffs, NJ: Prentice Hall

BANDURA, A. (1977) *Social Learning Theory*. New York: General Learning Press

BANERJEE, S. B. (2002) 'Corporate environmentalism: the construct and its measurement', *Journal of Business Research*, Vol.55, No.3: 177–91

BANERJEE, S. B. (2001) 'Corporate environmental strategies and actions', *Management Decision*, Vol.39, No.1: 36–44

BANK, J. (1994) *Outdoor Development For Managers*, 2nd edition. London: Gower

BARKER, R. A. (1997) 'How can we train leaders if we do not know what leadership is?', *Human Relations*, Vol.50, No.4: 343–61

BARLOW, G. (1989) 'Deficiencies and the perpetuation of power: latent functions in management appraisal', *Journal of Management Studies*, Vol.26, No.5: 499–518

BARNER, R. and HIGGENS, J. (2007) 'Understanding implicit models that guide the coaching process', *Journal of Management Development*, Vol.26, No.2: 148–58

BARRY, D. (1991) 'Managing the bossless team: lessons in distributed leadership', *Organizational Dynamics*, Vol.20 No.1: 31–48

BARTUNEK, J. M. and LOUIS, M. R. (1989) 'The design of work environments to stretch managers' capacities for complex thinking', *Human Resource Planning*, Vol.11, No.1: 13–22

BARUCH, Y. (2009) 'To MBA or not to MBA', *Career Development International*, Vol.14, No.4: 388–406

BARUCH, Y. (2004) 'Transforming careers: from linear to multidirectional career paths', *Career Development International*, Vol.9, No.1: 58–73

BARUCH, Y. (1996) 'Self-performance appraisal vs direct-manager appraisal: a case of congruence', *Journal of Managerial Psychology*, Vol.11, No.6: 50–65

BARUCH, Y. and PEIPERL, M. (1997) 'High-flyers: glorious past, gloomy present, any future?', *Career Development International*, Vol.2, No.7: 354–8

BASS, B. M. (1985) *Leadership and Performance Beyond Expectations*. New York: Free Press

BASS, B. M. and AVOLIO, B. J. (1997) *Full Range Leadership Development: Manual for Multifactor Leadership Questionnaire*. Redwood City, CA: Mind Garden

BASS, B. M. and AVOLIO, B. J. (1990) *Multifactor Leadership Questionnaire*. Palo Alto, CA: Consulting Psychologists Press

BATESON, G. (1983) *Steps to Ecology of Mind*. London: Paladin

BEAVER, G., LASHLEY, C. and STEWART, J. (1998) 'Management development', in R. THOMAS (ed.) *The Management of Small Tourism and Hospitality Firms*. London: Cassell

BECKETT, D. (2000) 'Making workplace learning explicit: an epistemology of practice for the whole person', *Westminster Studies in Education*, Vol.23: 41–53

BECKETT, D. and HAGER, P. (2002) *Life, Work and Learning*. London: Routledge

BEHRMAN, J. N. and LEVIN, R. I. (1984) 'Are business schools doing their job?', *Harvard Business Review*, January: 140–7

BELBIN. M. (1981) *Management Teams*. London: Heinemann

BELENKY, M. F. (1987) 'Women's ways of knowing', in P. S. LAVER and C. HENDRICK (eds) *Sex and Gender*. London: Sage

BELL, E. (2008) 'Towards a critical spirituality of organization', *Culture and Organization*, Vol.14, No.3: 293–307

BELL, E. and TAYLOR, S. (2004) 'From outward bound to inward bound: the prophetic voices and discursive practices of spiritual management development', *Human Relations*, Vol.57, No.4: 439–66

BELL, L., BOLAM, R. and CUBILLO, L. (2002) 'A systematic review of the impact of school leadership and management on student/pupil outcomes', *Research Evidence in Education Library (online)*. London: Institute of Education, No.1, EPPI-Centre, Social Science Research Unit

BENNETT, N., WISE, C. and HARVEY, J. (2003) *Distributed Leadership*. Nottingham: National College for School Leadership

BENNIS, W. (1989) *On Becoming a Leader*. Reading, MA: Addison-Wesley

BENNIS, W. and NANUS, B. (1985) *Leaders*. New York: Harper & Row

BENNIS, W. and O'TOOLE, J. (2005) 'How business schools lost their way', *Harvard Business Review*, May: 96–104

BERGLAS, S. (2002) 'Dangers of executive coaching', *Harvard Business Review*, June: 87–92

BERR (2008) *SME Statistics 2008*. Available from **http://stats.berr.gov.uk/ed/sme/** [accessed 22 October 2009]

BETTENHAUSEN, K. L. and FEDOR, D. B. (1997) 'Peer and upward appraisals', *Group and Organization Management*, Vol.22, No.2: 236–63

BILLETT, S. (2006) 'Constituting the workplace curriculum', *Journal of Curriculum Studies*, Vol.38, No.1: 31–48

BILLETT, S. (2000) 'Guided learning at work', *Journal of Workplace Learning*, Vol.12, No.7: 272–85

BLAKE, R. R. and MOUTON, J. S. (1964/1985) *The Managerial Grid*. Houston: Gulf Publishing

BLOCH, D. (2005) 'Complexity, chaos, and nonlinear dynamics: a new perspective on career development theory', *Career Development Quarterly*, Vol.53, No.: 194–207

BLUCKERT, P. (2005) 'Critical factors in executive coaching – the coaching relationship', *Industrial and Commercial Training*, Vol.37, No.7: 336–40

BOAL, K. and HOOIJBERG, R. (2001) 'Strategic leadership research: moving on', *Leadership Quarterly*, Vol.11, No.4: 515–49

BOLDEN, R. (2005) *What is Leadership Development?* Exeter: Leadership South West

BOLDEN, R. and GOSLING, J. (2006) 'Leadership competencies: time to change the tune?', *Leadership*, Vol.2, No.2: 147–63

BOLTON, J. (1971) *Report of the Committee of Inquiry on Small Firms*. London: HMSO

BOLTON, R. and GOLD, J. (1994) 'Career management: matching the needs of individuals with the needs of organisations', *Personnel Review*, Vol.23, No.1: 6–24

BORREDON, L. (2000) 'Capturing essential meaning', *Career Development International*, Vol.5, Nos4/5: 194–201

BOSWORTH, D., DAVIES, R. and WILSON, R. (2002) *Managerial Qualifications and Organisational Performance: An analysis of ESS 1999*. Warwick: Warwick Institute for Employment Research, Warwick University

BOUD, D. and SOLOMON, N. (2001) *Work-Based Learning: A new higher education*. Buckingham: Open University Press

BOWEN, D. and INKPEN, A. (2009) 'Exploring the role of "global mindset" in leading change in international contexts', *The Journal of Applied Behavioral Science*, Vol.45, No.2: 239–60

BOWERY, A. M. and THORPE, R. (1986) *Payment Systems and Productivity*. London: Macmillan

BOXALL, P. and PURCELL, J. (2003) *Strategy and Human Resource Management*. Basingstoke: Palgrave

BOYATZIS, R. (2008) 'Competencies in the 21st century', *Journal of Management Development*, Vol.27, No.1: 5–12

BOYATZIS, R. (1982) *The Competent Manager: A model for effective performance*. New York: John Wiley & Sons

BOYATZIS, R. E., SMITH, M. L. and BLAIZE, N. (2006) 'Developing sustainable leaders through coaching and compassion', *Academy of Management Learning and Education*, Vol.5, No.1: 8–24

BOZIONELOS, N. (2004) 'Mentoring provided: relation to mentor's career success, personality, and mentoring received', *Journal of Vocational Behavior*, No.64: 24–46

BRAMLEY, P. (1999) 'Evaluating effective management learning', *Journal of European Industrial Training*, Vol.23, No.3: 145–53

BREW, K. and GARAVAN, T. N. (1995) 'Eliminating inequality: women only training, Part 1', *Journal of European Industrial Training*, Vol.19, No.7: 13–19

BREWIS, J. (1996) 'The "making" of the "competent" manager', *Management Learning*, Vol.27, No.1: 65–86

BROCKNER, J. (2003) 'Unpacking country effects: on the need to operationalize the psychological determinants of crossnational differences', in B. M. STAW and R. M. KRAMER (eds) *Research in Organizational Behavior*. Greenwich, CT: JAI Press

BROOKES, S. (2008) 'Responding to the New Public Leadership challenge'. Paper presented at Herbert Simon 2nd Annual Conference, 16 April

BROOKFIELD, S. (1995) 'Adult learning: an overview', in A. TUIJNMAN (ed.) *International Encyclopedia of Education and Training*. Oxford: Pergamon Press

BROOKFIELD, S. D. (1986) *Understanding and Facilitating Adult Learning*. Milton Keynes: Open University Press

BROUGHTON, A. and MILLER, L. (2009) *Encouraging Women into Senior Management Positions: How coaching can help*. Brighton: Institute for Employment Studies

BROWN, A., GABRIEL, Y. and GHERARDI, S. (2009) 'Storytelling and change: an unfolding story', *Organization*, Vol.16, No.3: 323–33

BROWN, J. S. and DUGUID, P. (1991) 'Organizational learning and communities-of-practice: toward a unified view of working, learning and innovation', *Organization Science*, Vol.2, No.1: 40–7

BROWN, M. and HEYWOOD, J. (2005) 'Performance appraisal systems determinants and change', *British Journal of Industrial Relations*, Vol.43, No.4: 659–79

BROWN, M. and TREVIÑO, L. (2006) 'Ethical leadership: a review and future directions', *Leadership Quarterly*, Vol.17: 595–616

BROWN, M. E., TREVIÑO, L. K. and HARRISON, D. (2005) 'Ethical leadership: a social learning perspective for construct development and testing', *Organizational Behavior and Human Decision Processes*, Vol.97: 117–34

BROWN, P. (2007) 'Strategic management development', in R. HILL and J. STEWART (eds) *Management Development: Perspectives from research and practice*. London: Routledge

BROWN, P. (2005) 'The evolving role of strategic management development', *Journal of Management Development*, Vol.24, No.3: 209–22

BROWNE-FERRIGNO, T. and MUTH, R. (2006) 'Leadership mentoring and situated learning: catalysts for principalship readiness and lifelong mentoring', *Mentoring and Tutoring*, Vol.14, No.3: 275–95

BRUNER, J. (1986) *Actual Minds, Possible Worlds*. Cambridge, MA: Harvard University Press

BRUTUS, S. and DERAYEH, M. (2002) 'Multi-source assessment programs in organizations: an insider's perspective', *Human Resource Development Quarterly*, Vol.13: 187–201

BURGOYNE, J. (1989) 'Creating the managerial portfolio: building on competency approaches to management development', *Management Education and Development*, Vol.20: 56–61

BURGOYNE, J. (1988), 'Management development for the individual and the organisation', *Personnel Management*, June: 40–4

BURGOYNE, J. and HODGSON, V. E (1983) 'Natural learning and managerial action: a phenomenological study in the field setting', *Journal of Management Studies*, Vol.20, No.3: 387–99

BURGOYNE, J. and JACKSON, B. (1997) 'Management development as a pluralistic meeting point', in J. BURGOYNE and M. REYNOLDS (eds) *Management Learning*. London: Sage

BURGOYNE, J. and REYNOLDS, M. (1997[Chapter 2]) 'Introduction', in J. BURGOYNE and M. REYNOLDS (eds) *Management Learning*. London: Sage

BURGOYNE, J. and REYNOLDS, M. (1997[Chapter 5]) *Management Learning: Integrating perspectives in theory and practice*. London: Sage

BURGOYNE, J. and SINGH, R. (1977) 'Evaluation of training and education: macro and micro perspectives', *Journal of European Industrial Training*, Vol.1, No.1: 17–21

BURGOYNE, J., HIRSH, W. and WILLIAMS, S. (2004) *The Development of Leadership and Management Capability and Its Contribution to Performance:*

The evidence, the prospects and the research need. Report 560. London: Department for Education and Skills

BURKE, K. and COLLINS, D. (2004) 'Optimising skills transfer via outdoor management development. Part I : the provider's perspective', *Journal of Management Development*, Vol.23, No.7: 678–96

BURKE, S. and COLLINS, K. M. (2001) 'Gender differences in leadership styles and management skills', *Women in Management Review*, Vol.16, No.5: 244–56

BURT, R. S. (2000) 'The network structure of social capital', in R. L. SUTTON and B. M. STAW (eds) *Research in Organizational Behavior 22*. Greenwich, CT: JAI Press

BUTCHER, D. and HARVEY, P. (1998) 'Meta-ability development: a new concept for career management', *Career Development International*, Vol.3, No.2: 75–8

BUTWELL, J. (2006) 'Group supervision for coaches: is it worthwhile? A study of the process in a major professional organization', *International Journal of Evidence-Based Coaching and Mentoring*, Vol.4, No.2: 43–53

BYRNE, D. (1971) *The Attraction Paradigm.* New York: Academic Press

CABINET OFFICE (2007) *Social Enterprise Action Plan: Scaling New Heights.* London, Cabinet Office

CALDART, A. A. and RICART, J. E. (2004) 'Corporate strategy revisited: A view from complexity theory', *European Management Review*, Vol.1: 96–103

CALIGIURI, P. (2006) 'Global leadership development', *Human Resource Management Review*, Vol.16: 219–28

CALIGIURI, P. and TARIQUE, I. (2009) 'Predicting effectiveness in global leadership activities', *Journal of World Business*, Vol.44: 336–46

CAMPBELL, D. J. and LEE, C. (1988) 'Self-appraisal in performance evaluation: development versus evaluation', *Academy of Management Review*, Vol.13, No.2: 302–14

CANNON, M. and WITHERSPOON, R. (2005) 'Actionable feedback: unlocking the power of learning and performance improvement', *Academy of Management Executive*, Vol.19, No.2: 120–34

CAPRA, F. (2002) *The Hidden Connections.* London: HarperCollins

CARRICK, P. and WILLIAMS, R. (1999) 'Development centres – a review of assumptions', *Human Resource Management Journal*, Vol.9, No.2: 77–92

CARROLL, S. J. and GILLEN, D. J. (1987) 'Are the classical management functions useful in describing managerial work?', *Academy of Management Review*, Vol.12, No.1: 38–51

CARTER, A. (2001) *Executive Coaching: Inspiring performance at work.* Report 379. Sussex: Institute of Employment Studies

CARTLAND, J. W., HOY, F., BOULTON, W. R. and CARLAND, J. C. (1984) 'Differentiating entrepreneurs from small business owners: a conceptualization', *Academy of Management Review*, Vol.9, No.2: 354–9

CASE, S. and THOMPSON, L. (1995) 'Gender differences', in R. BOYATZIS, S. COWEN and D. KOLB (eds) *Innovation in Professional Education*. San Francisco: Jossey-Bass

CAWSEY, T., DESZCA, G. and MAZEROLLE, M. (1995) 'The portfolio career as response to a changing job market', *Journal of Career Planning and Employment*, Fall: 41–7

CBI (2008) *Talent, Not Tokenism: The business benefits of workforce diversity*. London: CBI/TUC/EHRC

CEML (2002[Chapters 1, 2, 3, 6, 11]) *Managers and Leaders: Raising our game*. London: Council for Excellence in Management and Leadership.

CEML (2002a[Chapter 6]) *The Contribution of UK Business Schools to the Development of Managers and Leaders*. London: Council for Excellence in Management and Leadership

CEML (2002[Chapter 12]) *Joining Entrepreneurs in Their World*. London: Council for Excellence in Management and Leadership

CEML (2001) *Meeting the Need*. London: Council for Excellence in Management and Leadership

CHARAN, R. (2009) *Leadership in the Era of Economic Uncertainty*. New York, McGraw Hill.

CHENG, E. W. L. (2000) 'Test of the MBA knowledge and skills transfer', *International Journal of Human Resource Management*, Vol.11, No.4: 837–52

CHIA, R. and MORGAN, S. (1996) 'Educating the philosopher-manager: de-signing the times', *Management Learning*, Vol.27, No.1: 37–64

CHIVERS, W. and DARLING, P. (1999) *360-Degree Feedback and Organisational Culture*. London: Institute of Personnel and Development

CHUAI, X., PREECE, D. and ILES, P. (2008) 'Is talent management just "old wine in new bottles"?', *Management Research News*, Vol.31, No.12: 901–11

CILLIERS, P. (1998) *Complexity and Postmodernism*. London: Routledge

CIPD (2009[Chapters 1, 2, 6; 2009a Chapters 9, 10]) *The War on Talent? Talent management under threat in uncertain times*. London: Chartered Institute of Personnel and Development

CIPD (2009[Chapter 9]) *Learning and Development*. Annual Survey. London: Chartered Institute of Personnel and Development

CIPD (2009b [Chapter 10]) *Fighting Back Through Talent Innovation*. London: Chartered Institute of Personnel and Development

CIPD (2008[Chapters 1, 10]) *UK Highlights: Global Leadership Forecast 2008–09: The typical, the elite and the forgotten.* London: Chartered Institute of Personnel and Development

CIPD (2008[Chapter 3]) *Competency and Competency Frameworks* Fact Sheet. Available online from **www.cipd.co.uk/subjects/perfmangmt/competnces/comptfrmwk.htm** [accessed 16 October 2009]

CIPD (2008[Chapter 6]) *Web 2.0 and HR.* London: Chartered Institute of Personnel and Development

CIPD (2008[Chapter 13]) *Engaging Leadership.* London: Chartered Institute of Personnel and Development

CIPD (2007[Chapter 9]) *Coaching in Organisations.* London: Chartered Institute of Personnel and Development

CIPD (2007[Chapter 10]) *Leadership Transitions: Maximising HR's contribution.* London: Chartered Institute of Personnel and Development

CIPD (2007[Chapter 11]) *Diversity in Business.* London: Chartered Institute of Personnel and Development

CIPD (2006) *Coaching Supervision: Maximising the potential of coaching.* London: Chartered Institute of Personnel and Development

CIPD (2005) *Performance Management.* London: Chartered Institute of Personnel and Development

CIPD (2004) *Inclusive Learning for All.* London: Chartered Institute of Personnel and Development

CIPD (2003) *Managing Employee Careers.* London: Chartered Institute of Personnel and Development

CIPD (2002[Chapters 2, 3]) *Developing Managers for Business Performance.* London: Chartered Institute of Personnel and Development

CIPD (2002[Chapter 10]) *The Future of Careers.* London: Chartered Institute of Personnel and Development

CLARK, J., THORPE, R., ANDERSON, L. and GOLD, J. (2006) 'It's all action, it's all learning: Action Learning in SMEs', *Journal of European Industrial Training*, Vol.30, No.6: 441–55

CLARK, T. (2008) 'Performing the organization: organizational theatre and imaginative life as physical presence', in D. BARRY and H. HANSEN (eds) *The Sage Handbook of New Approaches in Management and Organization.* London: Sage

CLARKE, A. (1999) *Evaluation Research.* London: Sage

CLARKE, M., BUTCHER, D. and BAILEY, C. (2004) 'Strategically aligned leadership development', in J. STOREY (ed.) *Leadership in Organizations.* London: Routledge

CLEMENTI, D. (2004) *Review of the Regulatory Framework of Legal Services*. London: Legal Services Commission

CLUTTERBUCK, D. (2007) *Coaching the Team at Work*. London: Nicholas Brealey

CLUTTERBUCK, D. (2004) *Everyone Needs a Mentor: Fostering talent in your organisation*, 4th edition. London: Chartered Institute of Personnel and Development

CLUTTERBUCK, D. and MEGGINSON, D. (2005) *Making Coaching Work*. London: Chartered Institute of Personnel and Development

CLUTTERBUCK, D. and MEGGINSON, D. (1999) *Mentoring Executives and Directors*. Oxford: Butterworth-Heinemann

CMI (2008) *Management Futures*. London: Chartered Management Institute

CMI (2005) *National Management Salary Survey*. London: Chartered Management Institute/Remuneration Economics

COFFIELD, F. (2002) *The Necessity of Informal Learning*. Bristol: Policy Press

COFFIELD, F., MOSELEY, D., HALL, E. and ECCLESTONE, K. (2004) *Learning Styles and Pedagogy in Post-16 Learning: A systematic and critical review*. London: Learning and Skills Research Centre

COGHLAN, A. T., PRESKILL, H. and CATSAMBAS, T. T. (2003) 'An overview of appreciative inquiry in evaluation', *New Directions For Evaluation*, No.100: 5–22

COHEN, D. and PRUSAK, L. (2001) 'How to invest in social capital', *Harvard Business Review*, Vol.79, No.6: 86–93

COHEN, M. and SPROULL, L. (1996) *Organisational Learning*. London: McGraw-Hill

COLAKOGLU, S. and CALIGIURI, P. (2008) 'Cultural distance, expatriate staffing and subsidiary performance: the case of US performance in multinational corporations', *International Journal of Human Resource Management*, Vol.19: 223–39

COLEMAN, S. and KEEP, E. (2001) Background literature review for PIU project on workforce development. London: Cabinet Office, Performance and Innovation Unit

COLLINGS, D. G. and MELLAHI, K. (2009) 'Strategic talent management: a review and research agenda', *Human Resource Management Review*, Vol.19, No.4, May: 304–13

COLLINS, H. M. (2001) 'Tacit knowledge, trust, and the Q of sapphire', *Social Studies of Science*, Vol.31, No.1: 71–85

COLTHART, I., CAMERON, N., MCKINSTRY, B. and BLANEY, D. (2008) 'What do doctors really think about the relevance and impact of GP appraisal three years on? A survey of Scottish GPs', *The British Journal of General Practice*, Vol.58: 82–7

CONGER, J. A. and FULMER, R. M. (2003) 'Developing your leadership pipeline', *Harvard Business Review*, Vol.81, No.12: 76–85

CONSTABLE, J. and MCCORMICK, R. (1987) *The Making of British Managers*. London: BIM/CBI

CONTE, J. (2005) 'A review and critique of emotional intelligence measures', *Journal of Organizational Behavior*, Vol.26: 433–40

CONWAY, J. M. (1999) 'Distinguishing contextual performance from task performance for managerial jobs', *Journal of Applied Psychology*, Vol.84: 3–13

COOK, A. and GLASS, C. (2008) 'But can s/he lead? Market assessments of black leadership in corporate America', *Journal of Workplace Rights*, Vol.13, No.3: 337–51

COOPER, D., GREENWOOD, R., HININGS, C. R. and BROWN, J. (1996) 'Sedimentation and transformation in organizational change: the case of Canadian law firms', *Organization Studies*, Vol.17, No.4: 623–47

COOPER JACKSON, J. (2001) 'Women middle managers' perception of the glass ceiling', *Women in Management Review*, Vol.16, No.1: 30–41

COOPERRIDER, D. L., SORENSEN, P. F., WHITNEY, D. and YAEGER, T. F. (2000) *Appreciative Inquiry: Rethinking human organization toward a positive theory of change*. Champaign, IL: Stipes

COPE, J. (2005) 'Towards a dynamic learning perspective of entrepreneurship', *Theory and Practice*, Vol.29, No.4: 373–98

CROSBIE, R. (2005) 'Learning the soft skills of leadership', *Industrial and Commercial Training*, Vol.37, No.1: 45–51

CROSSAN, M., LANE, H. and WHITE, R. (1999) 'An organizational learning framework: from intuition to institution', *Academy of Management Review*, Vol.24: 522–37

CUNLIFFE, A. L. (2002) 'Reflexive dialogical practice', *Management Learning*, Vol.33, No.1: 35–61

CUNLIFFE, A. L. and JUN, J. (2005) 'The need for reflexivity in public administration', *Administration and Society*, Vol.37: 225–42

CUNNINGHAM, I. (1999) *Wisdom and Strategic Learning*, 2nd edition. Aldershot: Gower

CURRY, L. (1987) *Integrating Concepts of Cognitive Learning Styles: A review with attention to psychometric standards*. Ottawa: Canadian College of Health Services Executives

D'ABATE, C. P., EDDY, E. R. and TANNENBAUM, S. I. (2003) 'What's in a name? A literature-based approach to understanding mentoring, coaching, and other constructs that describe developmental interactions', *Human Resource Development Review*, Vol.2, No.4: 360–84

DALLEY, J. and HAMILTON, B. (2000) 'Knowledge, context and learning in the small business', *International Small Business Journal*, No.71: 51–9

DANIELS, H. (2004) 'Cultural historical activity theory and professional learning', *International Journal of Disability, Development and Education*, Vol.51, No.2: 185–200

DATOR, J. (2003) 'Futures studies and sustainable community development'. Available at **http://www.soc.hawaii.edu/future/dator.html**

DAUDELIN, M. (1996) 'Learning from experience through reflections', *Organizational Dynamics*, Winter: 36–48

DAVIDSON, M. J. (2002) 'The black and ethnic minority women manager', in R. J. BURKE and D. L. NELSON (eds) *Advancing Women's Careers: Research and practice*. Oxford: Blackwell

DAVIDSON, M. (1997) *The Black and Ethnic Minority Woman Manager: Cracking the concrete ceiling*. London: Sage

DAVIDSON, M. J. and COOPER, C. L. (1992) *Shattering the Glass Ceiling*. London: Paul Chapman

DAVIES, J. and EASTERBY-SMITH, M. P. V. (1983) 'Learning and developing from managerial work experiences', *Journal of Management Studies*, Vol.21, No.2: 169–82

DAVIES, L. (2008) *Informal Learning*. Aldershot: Gower

DAWSON, R. (2000) *Developing Knowledge-Based Client Relationships*. Woburn: Butterworth-Heinemann

DAWSON, S. (1994) 'Changes in distance: professionals reappraise the meaning of management', *Journal of General Management*, Vol.20, No.1: 1–21

DAY, C., HARRIS, A., HADFIELD, M., TOLLEY, H. and BERESFORD, J. (2000) *Leading Schools in Times of Change*. Milton Keynes: Open University Press

DAY, D. V. (2001) 'Leadership development: a review in context', *Leadership Quarterly*, Vol.11, No.4: 581–613

DAY, D. V. and O'CONNOR, P. M. (2003) 'Leadership development: understanding the process', in S. E. MURPHY and R. E. RIGGIO (eds) *The Future of Leadership Development*. Mahwah, NJ: Lawrence Erlbaum

DAY, D., ZACCARO, S. J. and HALPIN, S. M. (2004) *Leader Development for Transforming Organizations: Growing leaders for tomorrow*. Mahwah, NJ: Lawrence Erlbaum

DEFILLIPPI, R. J. (2001) 'Introduction: Project-based learning, reflective practices and learning outcomes', *Management Learning*, Vol.32, No.1: 5–10

DENISI, A. S. and KLUGER, A. N. (2000) 'Feedback effectiveness: can 360-degree feedback be improved?', *Academy of Management Executive*, Vol.14, No.1: 129–39

DERRY, S. (1996) 'Cognitive schema theory in the constructivist debate', *Educational Psychologist*, Vol.31, Nos.3/4: 163–74

DEVINS, D. and GOLD, J. (2002) 'Social constructionism: a theoretical framework to underpin support the development of managers in SMEs', *Journal of Small Business and Enterprise Development*, Vol.9, No.2: 111–19

DEVINS, D. and GOLD, J. (2000) '"Cracking the tough nuts": mentoring and coaching the managers of small firms', *Career Development International*, Vol.5, Nos.4/5: 250–5

DICKENS, L. (1999) 'Beyond the business case: a three-pronged approach to equality action', *Human Resource Management Journal*, Vol.9, No.1: 9–19

DIERENDONCK, D., HAYNES, C., BORRILL, C. and STRIDE, C. (2007) 'Effects of upward feedback on leadership behaviour toward subordinates', *Journal of Management Development*, Vol.26, No.3: 228–38

DIETRICH, M. and ROBERTS, J. (1997) 'Beyond the economics of professionalism', in J. BROADBENT, M. DIETRICH and J. ROBERTS (eds) *The End of the Professions?* London: Routledge

DIXON, N. (1998) *Dialogue at Work*. London: Lemos & Crane

DoH (2007) *Trust, Assurance and Safety: The regulation of health professionals*. London: Department of Health

DOHERTY, N. (1998) 'The role of outplacement in managing redundancy', *Personnel Review*, Vol.27, No.4: 343–53

DOHERTY, N., BANK, J. and VINNICOMBE, S. (1995) *Managing Survivors: The experience of survivors in BT and the British financial sector*. Bedford: Cranfield University

DONELAN, H., HERMAN, C., KEAR, K. and KIRKUP, G. (2009) 'Patterns of online networking for women's career development', *Gender in Management Review: An International Journal*, Vol.24 No.2: 92–111

DONNELLON, A. (1996) *Team Talk: The power of language in team dynamics*. Boston, MA: Harvard Business School Press

DOWN, S. (2006) *Narratives of Enterprise: Crafting entrepreneurial identity in a small firm*. Cheltenham: Edward Elgar

DOYLE, M. (1995) 'Organisation transformation and renewal', *Personnel Review*, Vol.24, No.6: 6–18

DRAKE, D. B. (2007) 'The art of thinking narratively: implications for coaching psychology and practice', *Australian Psychologist*, Vol.42, No.4: 283–94

DREYFUS, H. L. and DREYFUS, S. E. (1986) *Mind Over Machine: The power of human intuition and expertise in the era of the computer*. Oxford: Blackwell

DRISCOLL, C. and STARIK, M. (2004) 'The primordial stakeholder: advancing the conceptual consideration of stakeholder status for the natural environment', *Journal of Business Ethics*, Vol.49, No.1: 55–73

DULEWICZ, V. and HIGGS, M. (2005) 'Assessing leadership styles and organisational context', *Journal of Managerial Psychology*, Vol.20, No.2: 105–23

DUNLEAVY, P., MARGATTS, H., BASTOW, S. and TINKLER, J. (2006) 'New public management is dead; long live digital-era governance', *Journal of Public Administration Research and Theory*, Vol.16, No.3: 467–94

EAGLY, A. H. and KARAU, S. J. (2002) 'Congruity theory of prejudice toward female leaders', *Psychological Review*, Vol.109, No.3: 573–98

EARLEY, P. C. and MOSAKOWSKI, E. (2004) 'Cultural intelligence', *Harvard Business Review*, Vol.82, No.10: 139–40

EASTERBY-SMITH, M. (1994) *Evaluating Management Development, Training and Education*, 2nd edition. Aldershot: Gower

EASTERBY-SMITH, M., BRAIDEN, E. and ASHTON, D. (1980) *Auditing Management Development*. Farnborough: Gower

EATON, J. and BROWN, D. (2002) 'Coaching for a change with Vodafone', *Career Development International*, Vol.7, No.5: 283–6

EBY, L. T., MCMANUS, S., SIMON, S. A. and RUSSELL, J. E. A. T. (2000) 'The protégé's perspective regarding negative mentoring experiences: the development of a taxonomy', *Journal of Vocational Behavior*, Vol.57: 1–21

EDEN, C. and HUXHAM, C. (1996) 'Action Research for the study of organizations', in S. CLEGG, C. HARDY and W. NORD (eds) *Handbook of Organization Studies*. Beverly Hills, CA: Sage

EDGAR, F. and GEARE, A. (2005) 'HRM practice and employee attitudes: different measures – different results', *Personnel Review*, Vol.34, No.5: 534–49

EDMONDSON, A., BOHMER, R. and PISANO, G. (2001) 'Speeding up team learning', *Harvard Business Review*, Vol.79, No.9: 125–32

EDWARDS, M. (2005) 'Employer and employee branding: HR or PR?', in S. BACH (ed.) *Managing Human Resources*, 4th edition. Oxford: Blackwell

EHRC (2008) *Sex and Power Report*. London: Equality and Human Rights Commission

ELKINGTON, J. (1994) 'Toward the sustainable corporation', *California Management Review*, Vol.36, No.2: 90–100

ELLINGER, A. and BOSTROM, R. P. (1999) 'Managerial coaching behaviors in learning organizations', *Journal of Management Development*, Vol.18, No.9: 752–71

ENGESTRÖM, Y. (2001) 'Expansive learning at work: toward an activity-theoretical reconceptualization', *Journal of Education and Work*, Vol.14, No.1: 133–56

ENGESTRÖM, Y. (1987) *Learning by Expanding: An activity-theoretical approach to developmental research*. Helsinki: Orienta-Konsultit

ENSHER, E. A., HEUN, C. and BLANCHARD, A. (2003) 'Online mentoring and computer-mediated communication: new directions in research', *Journal of Vocational Behavior*, Vol.63, No.2: 264–88

EOC (2003[Chapter 11]) *Women and Men in Britain: Management*. Manchester: Equal Opportunities Commission

EOC (2003a[Chapter 11]) *Facts About Women and Men in Great Britain*. London: Equal Opportunities Commission

ERAUT, M. (2001) 'Do Continuing Professional Development models promote one-dimensional learning?' *Medical Education*, Vol.35: 8–11

ERAUT, M. (2000) 'Non-formal learning, implicit learning and tacit knowledge in professional work', in F. COFFIELD (ed.) *The Necessity of Informal Learning*. Bristol: Policy Press

EVANS, P., PUCIK, V. and BARSOUX, J.-L. (2002) *The Global Challenge. Frameworks for International Human Resource Management*. New York: McGraw-Hill

EVERED, R. D. and SELMAN, J. C. (1989) 'Coaching and the art of management', *Organizational Dynamics*, Autumn: 16–32

EXWORTHY, M. and HALFORD, S. (1999) *Professionals and the New Managerialism in the Public Sector*. Buckingham: Open University Press

FAYOL, H. (1949) *Administration Industrielle Générale*, English translation. London: Pitman Harper

FELDMAN, D. and LANKAU, M. J. (2005) 'Executive coaching: a review and agenda for future research', *Journal of Management*, Vol.31, No.6: 829–48

FERLIE, E. and MCGIVERN, G. (2007) 'Playing tick-box games: interrelating defences in professional appraisal', *Human Relations*, Vol.60, No.9: 1361–85

FERRARIE, K. E. (2005) 'Processes to assess leadership potential keep Shell's talent pipeline full', *Journal of Organizational Excellence*, Vol.24, No.3: 17–22

FERRARO, F., PFEFFER, J. and SUTTON, R. I. (2005) 'Economics language and assumptions: how theories can become self-fulfilling', *Academy of Management Review*, Vol.30, No.1: 8–24

FIEDLER, F. E. (1967) *A Theory of Leadership Effectiveness*. New York: McGraw-Hill

FINCH-LEES, T., MABEY, C. and LIEFOOGHE, A. (2005) 'In the name of capability: a critical discursive evaluation of competency-based management development', *Human Relations*, Vol.58, No.9: 1185–222

FINEMAN, S. (1997) 'Emotion and management learning', *Management Learning*, Vol.28, No.1: 13–25

FISHER, S. G., MACROSSON, W. D. K. and SHARP, G. (1996) 'Further evidence concerning the Belbin Team Role Self-perception Inventory', *Personnel Review*, Vol.25, No.2: 61–7

FLETCHER, C. (1998) 'Circular argument', *People Management*, 1 October: 46–9

FLETCHER, C. and WILLIAMS, R. (1996) 'Performance management, job satisfaction and organizational commitment', *British Journal of Management*, Vol.7, No.2: 169–79

FORD, J. (2006) 'Discourses of leadership: gender, identity and contradiction in a UK public sector organization', *Leadership*, Vol.2, No.1: 77–99

FORD, J. K. and WEISSBEIN, D. A. (1997) 'Transfer of training: an update review and analysis', *Performance Improvement Quarterly*, Vol.10, No.2: 22–41

FORD, J. K., QUIÑONES, M., SEGO, D. and SPEER SORRA, J. (1992) 'Factors affecting the opportunity to perform trained tasks on the job', *Personnel Psychology*, Vol.45: 511–27

FORD, J., TOMLINSON, J., SOMMERLAD, H. and GOLD, J. (2009) '"Just don't call it diversity": developing a programme for the business case for diversity in West Yorkshire'. Paper presented to the HRD in Europe Conference, Newcastle

FORRET, M. L. and DOUGHERTY, T. W. (2004) 'Networking behaviors and career outcomes: differences for men and women?', *Journal of Organizational Behavior*, Vol.25: 419–37

FOSTER, C. and HARRIS, L. (2005) 'Easy to say, difficult to do: diversity management in retail', *Human Resource Management Journal*, Vol.15, No.3: 4–17

FOUCAULT, M. (1980) *Power/Knowledge: Selected interviews and other writings, 1972–1977*. Edited by Colin Gordon. New York: Pantheon

FOURNIER, V. and GREY, C. (2000) 'At the critical moment: conditions and prospects for critical management studies', *Human Relations*, Vol.53, No.1: 7–32

FOURNIER, V. and KELEMAN, M. (2001) 'The crafting of community: recoupling discourses of management and womanhood', *Gender, Work and Organization*, Vol.8, No.3: 267–90

FOWLER, L. J., GUDMUNDSSON, J. A. and O'GORMAN, G. J. (2007) 'The relationship between mentee-mentor gender combination and the provision of distinct mentoring functions', *Women in Management Review*, Vol.22, No.8: 666–81

FOX, S. (1997) 'From management education and development to the study of management learning', in J. BURGOYNE and M. REYNOLDS (eds) *Management Learning*. London: Sage

FRAKER, S. (1984) 'Why women aren't getting to the top', *Fortune*, April

FULLER, A. and UNWIN, L. (2003) 'Learning as apprentices in the contemporary UK workplace: creating and managing expansive and restrictive participation', *Journal of Education and Work*, Vol.16, No.4: 407–26

FULLER-LOVE, N. (2006) 'Management development in small firms', *International Journal of Management Reviews*, Vol.8, No.3: 175–90

FULMER, R. and CONGER, J. A. (2004) *Growing Your Company's Leaders: How great organizations use succession management to sustain competitive advantage.* AMACOM

FURNHAM, A. (2004) 'Performance management systems', *European Business Journal*, Vol.16, No.2: 83–94

GABRIEL, Y. (2000) *Storytelling in Organizations.* Oxford: Oxford University Press

GANGULY, P. and BANNOCK, G. (1985) *UK Small Business Statistics and International Comparisons.* London: Harper & Row

GARAVAN, T. (1997) 'The learning organization: a review and evaluation', *The Learning Organization*, Vol.4, No.1: 18–29

GARAVAN, T. and MCCARTHY, A. (2007) 'Multi-source feedback and management development: managers discourse on context and development intentions', in R. HILL and J. STEWART (eds) *Management Development: Perspectives from research and practice.* London: Routledge

GARAVAN, T. N. and MCGUIRE, D. (2001) 'Competencies and workplace learning: some reflections on the rhetoric and the reality', *Journal of Workplace Learning*, Vol.14, No.4: 144–63

GARAVAN, T. N., BARNICLE, B. and O'SUILLEABHAIN, F. (1999) 'Management development contemporary trends issues and strategies', *Journal of European Industrial Training*, Vol.23, No.4: 191–207

GARDNER, W. and SCHERMERHORN, J. (2004) 'Performance gains through positive organizational behavior and authentic leadership', *Organizational Dynamics*, Vol.33, No.3: 270–81

GARENGO, P., BIAZZO, S. and BITITCI, U. S. (2005) 'Performance measurement systems in SMEs: a review for a research agenda', *International Journal of Management Reviews*, Vol. 7, No.1: 25–47

GARRICK, J. (1998) *Informal Learning in the Workplace.* London: Routledge

GARVEY, B. (1999) 'Mentoring and the changing paradigm', *Mentoring and Tutoring*, Vol.7, No.1: 41–53.

GARVEY, B. and WILLIAMSON, B. (2002) *Beyond Knowledge Management.* Harlow: Financial Times/Prentice Hall

GARVEY, R., STOKES, P. and MEGGINSON, D. (2009) *Coaching and Mentoring.* London: Sage

GEORGE, B. (2003) *Authentic Leadership: Rediscovering the secrets to creating lasting value.* San Francisco: Jossey-Bass

GEORGE, B., SIMS, P., MCLEAN, A. N. and MAYER, D. (2007) 'Discovering your authentic leadership', *Harvard Business Review*, February: 129–38

GHOSHAL, S. (2005) 'Bad management theories are destroying good management practices', *Academy of Management Learning and Education*, Vol.4, No.1: 75–81

GIAMBATISTA, R. C., ROWE, W. G. and RIAZ, S. (2005) 'Nothing succeeds like succession: a critical review of leader succession literature since 1994', *The Leadership Quarterly*, Vol.16: 963–91

GIBB, A. (2009) 'Meeting the development needs of owner managed small enterprise: a discussion of the centrality of action learning', *Action Learning: Research and Practice*, Vol. 6, No. 3: 209–28

GIBB, A. A. (1997) 'Small firms training and competitiveness: building upon the small business as a learning organisation', *International Small Business Journal*, Vol.15, No.3: 13–29

GIBB, A. A. (1983) 'The small business challenge to management education', *Journal of European and Industrial Training*, Vol.7, No.5

GIBB, A. A. and DYSON, J. (1982) 'Stimulating the growth of owner-manager firms'. Research paper. Durham University Business School

GIBB, S. (2008) *Human Resource Development: Process, practices and perspectives*. Basingstoke: Palgrave

GIBB, S. (2003) 'What do we talk about when we talk about mentoring? Blooms and thorns', *British Journal of Counselling and Guidance*, Vol.31, No.1: 39–49

GIBB, S. (1998) 'Exploring career chaos: patterns of belief', *Career Development International*, Vol.3, No.4: 149–53

GIBB, S. (1994) 'Inside corporate mentoring schemes: the development of a conceptual framework', *Personnel Review*, Vol.23, No.3: 47–60

GIBSON, C. and BURKINSHAW, J. (2004) 'The antecedents, consequences, and mediating role of organizational ambidexterity', *Academy of Management Journal*, Vol.47, No.2: 209–26

GILPIN-JACKSON, Y. and BUSHE, G. R.(2007) 'Leadership development training transfer: a case study of post-training determinants', *Journal of Management Development*, Vol.26, No.10: 980–1004

GOFFEE, R. and SCASE, R. (1992) 'Organisational change and the corporate career: the restructuring of managers' job aspirations', *Human Relations*, Vol.45, No.4: 363–85

GOLD, J. (2001) 'Storying Systems: Managing Everyday Flux Using Mode 2 Soft Systems Methodology', *Systemic Practice and Action Research*, Vol. 14, No. 5: 557–73

GOLD, J. and HOLMAN, D. (2001) 'Let me tell you a story: an evaluation of the use of story-telling and argument analysis in management education', *Career Development International*, Vol.6, No.7: 384–95

GOLD, J. and THORPE, R. (2009) 'Collective CPD, professional learning in a law firm', in D. JEMIELNIAK and J. KOCIATKIEWICZ (eds) *Handbook of Research on Knowledge-Intensive Organizations*. Hershey, PA: IGI Global/Information Science Reference

GOLD, J. and THORPE, R. (2008) '"Training, it's a load of crap!": the story of the hairdresser and his "suit"', *Human Resource Development International*, Vol.11, No.4: 385–99

GOLD, J. and THORPE, R. (2010) 'Leadership and management development in small and medium-sized enterprises: SME worlds' in Gold, J., Thorpe, R. and Mumford, A. (eds), *Gower Handbook of Leadership and Management Development*, Aldershot: Gower

GOLD, J., HOLMAN, D. and THORPE, R. (2002) 'The role of argument analysis and story-telling in critical thinking', *Management Learning*, Vol.33, No.3: 371–88

GOLD, J., HOLT, R. and THORPE, R. (2007) 'A good place for CHAT', in M. REYNOLDS and R.VINCE (eds) *Handbook of Experiential Learning and Management Education*. Oxford: Oxford University Press

GOLD, J., RODGERS, H. and SMITH, V. (2001) *The Future of the Professions*. London: Council for Excellence in Management and Leadership

GOLD, J., SMITH, V. and RODGERS, H. (2001) 'Strategy and struggle: exploring strategic learning with participatory action research'. Paper presented to the 2nd Researching Work and Learning Conference, Calgary, July

GOLD, J., THORPE, R. and HOLT, R. (2007) 'Writing, reading and reason: the "three Rs" of manager learning', in R. HILL and J. STEWART (eds) *Management Development: Perspectives from research and practice*. London: Routledge

GOLD, J., THORPE, R. and MUMFORD, A. (2010) *A Handbook of Leadership and Management Development*. London: Gower

GOLD, J., THORPE, R., WOODALL, J. and SADLER-SMITH, E. (2007) 'Continuing professional development in the legal profession: a practice-based learning perspective', *Management Learning*, Vol.38, No.2: 235–50

GOLDSTEIN, I. L. (1993) *Training in Organizations, Needs Assessment, Development and Evaluation*. Pacific Grove, CA: Brooks/Cole Publishing

GOLEMAN, D. (1998) *Working With Emotional Intelligence*. London: Bloomsbury

GOLEMAN, D. (1996) *Emotional Intelligence*. London: Bloomsbury

GOLEMAN, D., BOYATZIS, D. and MCKEE, A. (2002) *Primal Leadership: Realizing the power of emotional intelligence*. Cambridge, MA: HBR Press

GORDON, A. (2009) *Future Savvy*. New York: AMACOM

GRAEN, G. B. and UHL-BIEN, M. (1995) 'Relationship-based approach to leadership: development of leader-member exchange (LMX) theory of leadership over 25 years: applying a multi-level multi domain perspective', *Leadership Quarterly*, Vol.6: 219–47

GRAY, C. (2000) 'Formality, intentionality and planning: features of successful entrepreneurial SMEs in the future?'. ICSB World Conference, Brisbane, Australia

GREEN, A. (2002) 'The many faces of lifelong learning: recent education policy trends in Europe', *Journal of Education Policy*, Vol.17, No.6: 611–26

GREENE, J. and GRANT, A. M. (2006) *Solution-Focused Coaching: Managing people in a complex world*. London: Chartered Institute of Personnel and Development

GREENLEAF, R. (1982) *The Servant as Leader*. Westfield, IN: Robert K. Greenleaf Center

GREY, C. (1996) 'Introduction', *Management Learning*, Vol.27, No.1: 7–20

GRINT, K. (2005) 'Problems, problems, problems: the social construction of "leadership"', *Human Relations*, Vol.58, No.11: 1467–94

GRONN, P. (2009) 'Leadership configurations', *Leadership*, Vol.5, No.3: 1–13

GRONN, P. (2008) 'The future of distributed leadership', *Journal of Educational Administration*, Vol.46, No.2: 141–58

GRONN, P. (2000) 'Distributed properties: a new architecture for leadership', *Educational Management and Administration*, Vol.28, No.3: 317–38

GRONN, P. and HAMILTON, A. (2004) 'A bit more life in the leadership: co-principalship as distributed leadership practice', *Leadership and Policy in Schools*, Vol.13, No.1: 3–35

GROYSBERG, B., NANDA, A. and NOHRIA, N. (2004) 'The risky business of hiring stars', *Harvard Business Review*, Vol.82, No.5: 93–100

GRUGULIS, I. (2000) 'The management NVQ: a critique of the myth of relevance', *Journal of Vocational Education and Training*, Vol.52, No.1: 79–99

GUEST, D., DAVEY, K. and PATCH, A. (1998) *The Impact of New Forms of Employment Contract on Motivation and Innovation*. London: ESRC

GUEST, D., MICHIE, J., SHEEHAN, M. and CONWAY, N. (2000) *Getting Inside the HRM-Performance Relationship*. Working Paper 8, ESRC Future of Work Programme. Swindon: ESRC

HACKMAN, J. R. and WAGEMAN, R. (2007) 'Asking the right questions about leadership', *American Psychologist*, Vol.62, No.7: 43–7

HACKMAN, J. and WAGEMAN, R. (2005) 'A theory of team coaching', *Academy of Management Review*, Vol.30, No.2: 269–87

HADEN, S. S. P., OYLER, J. D. and HUMPHREYS, J. H. (2009) 'Historical, practical, and theoretical perspectives on green management', *Management Decision*, Vol.47, No.7: 1041–55

HALE, R. (2000) 'To match or mis-match? The dynamics of mentoring as a route to personal and organisational learning', *Career Development International*, Vol.5, Nos.4/5: 223–34

HALES, C. (1993) *Managing Through Organisation*. London: Routledge

HALL, D. T. (2002) *Careers In and Out of Organizations*. Thousand Oaks, CA: Sage Publications

HALL, D. T., OTAZO, K. L. and HOLLENBECK, G. P. (1999) 'What really happens in executive coaching', *Organizational Dynamics*, Winter: 39–53

HALLIDAY, T. C. (1987) *Beyond Monopoly: Lawyers, state crises and professional empowerment*. Chicago: University of Chicago Press

HALLIER, J. and LYON, P. (1996) 'Job insecurity and employee commitment: managers' reactions to the threat and outcomes of redundancy selection', *British Journal of Management*, Vol.7, No.2: 107–23

HALMAN, F. and FLETCHER, C. (2000) 'The impact of development centre participation and the role of individual differences in changing self-assessments', *Journal of Occupational and Organizational Psychology*, Vol.73: 423–42

HAMBLIN, A. C. (1974) *Evaluation and the Control of Training*. London: McGraw-Hill

HAMEL, G. (1998) 'Strategy innovation and the quest for value', *Sloan Management Review*, Vol.39, No.2: 7–14

HAMLIN, B. (2009) 'Evidence-based leadership and management development', in J. GOLD, R. THORPE and A. MUMFORD (eds) *A Handbook of Leadership and Management Development*. Aldershot: Gower

HAMLIN, R., ELLINGER, A. D. and BEATTIE, R. S. (2009) 'Towards a profession of coaching? A definitional examination of "Coaching," "Organization Development," and "Human Resource Development"', *International Journal of Evidence-Based Coaching and Mentoring*, Vol.7, No.1: 13–38

HAMMOND, V. and HOLTON, V. (1992) *Information Technology Environments*. Berkhamstead: Ashridge Management Research

HANDY, C. (1987) *The Making of Managers*. London: NEDO

HANDY, L., DEVINE, M. and HEATH, L. (1996) *360-Degree Feedback: Unguided missile or powerful weapon?* Berkhamsted: Ashridge Management Research Group

HANNUM, K., MARTINEAU, J. and REINELT, C. (2006) *The Handbook of Leadership Development Evaluation*. Hoboken, NJ: John Wiley

HARRIS, A. (2008) 'Distributed leadership: according to the evidence', *Journal of Educational Administration*, Vol.46, No.2: 172–88

HARRIS, A. (2003) 'Teacher leadership and school improvement', in A. HARRIS, C. DAY, M. HOPKINS, M. HADFIELD, A. HARGREAVES and C. CHAPMAN (eds) *Effective Leadership for School Improvement*. London: Routledge

HARRISON, R. (2005) *Learning and Development*, 4th edition. London: Chartered Institute of Personnel and Development

HARTER, S. (2002) 'Authenticity', in C. R. SNYDER and S. J. LOPEZ (eds) *Handbook of Positive Psychology*. London: Oxford University Press

HARTLEY, J. (2009) 'Public sector leadership and management development', in J. GOLD, R. THORPE and A. MUMFORD (eds) *A Handbook of Leadership and Management Development*. Aldershot: Gower

HARVEY, M. and MOELLER, M. (2009) 'Expatriate managers: a historical review', *International Journal of Management Reviews*, Vol.11, No.3: 275–96

HAWKINS, P. (2006) 'Coaching supervision', in J. PASSMORE (ed.) *Excellence in Coaching: The industry guide*. London: Kogan Page

HAYES, C., ANDERSON, A. and FONDA, N. (1984) *Competence and Competition: Training and Education in the Federal Republic of Germany, USA and Japan*. London: NEDO

HEADLAM-WELLS, J. (2004) 'E-mentoring for aspiring women managers', *Women in Management Review*, Vol.19, No.4: 212–18

HEADLAM-WELLS, J., GOSLAND, J. and CRAIG, J. (2005) '"There's magic in the web": e-mentoring for women's career development', *Career Development International*, Vol.10, No.6/7: 444–59

HEALTHCARE COMMISSION (2009) *Investigation into Mid Staffordshire NHS Foundation Trust*. London: Healthcare Commission

HEGSTAD, C. D. and WENTLING, R. M. (2005) 'Organizational antecedents and moderators that impact on the effectiveness of exemplary formal mentoring programs in Fortune 500 companies in the United States', *Human Resource Development International*, Vol.8, No.4: 467–87

HEILMAN, M., MARTELL, R. and SIMON, M. (1988) 'The vagaries of sex bias: conditions regulating the undervaluation, equivaluation and overvaluation of female job applicants', *Organizational Behaviour and Human Decision Processes*, Vol.41, No.1: 98–110

HERRIOT, P., GIBBONS, P., PEMBERTON, C. and JACKSON, P. R. (1994) 'An empirical model of managerial careers in organizations', *British Journal of Management*, Vol.5: 113–21

HERRMANN, N. (1996) *The Whole Brain Business Book*. New York: McGraw-Hill

HERSEY, P. and BLANCHARD, K. (1982) *Management of Organization Behaviour*. Englewood Cliffs, NJ: Prentice Hall

HERSEY, P and BLANCHARD, K. H. (1981) 'So you want to know your leadership style?', *Training and Development Journal*, Vol.35, No.6: 34–54

HERTZ, L. (1986) *The Business Amazons*. London: André Deutsch

HININGS, C. R., GREENWOOD, R. and COOPER, D. (1999) 'The dynamics of change in large accounting firms', in D. M. BROCK, M. J. POWELL and C. R. HININGS (eds) *Restructuring the Professional Organization*. London: Routledge

HIRSH, W. (2002) 'Careers in organisations – time to get positive', in CIPD, *The Future of Careers*. London: Chartered Institute of Personnel and Development

HIRSH, W. (2000) *Succession Planning Demystified*. Brighton: Institute for Employment Studies

HIRSH, W. (1990) *Succession Planning: Current practice and future issues*. Report 184. Brighton: Institute of Manpower Studies

HIRSH, W. and JACKSON, C. (1997) *Strategies for Career Development: Promise, practice and pretence*. Report 305. Brighton: Institute of Manpower Studies

HIRSH, W. and ROLPH, J. (2003) 'Snakes and ladders', *People Management*, Vol.9, No.9: 36–7

HITE, M. and MCDONALD, K. S. (1995) 'Gender issues in management development', *Journal of Management Development*, Vol.14, No.4: 5–15

HODGKINSON, G. P. and CLARKE, I. (2007) 'Exploring the cognitive significance of organizational strategizing: a dual-process framework and research agenda', *Human Relations*, Vol.60: 243–55

HOFSTEDE, G. (1980) *Culture's Consequences*. London: Sage

HOLBECHE, L. (2008[Chapter 1]) 'Developing leaders for uncertain times', *Impact*, No.23: 6–9

HOLBECHE, L. (2008[Chapter 2]) 'The leadership paradox', *Futures*, Issue 1: 2–4

HOLBECHE, L. (1999) *Aligning Human Resources and Business Strategy*. London: Butterworth-Heineman

HOLBECHE, L. (1998[Chapter 4]) *Motivating People in Lean Organizations*. Oxford: Butterworth-Heinemann

HOLBECHE, L. (1998[Chapters 3, 10; 1998a Chapter 4]) *Aligning Human Resources and Business Strategy*. Oxford: Butterworth-Heinemann

HOLMAN, D. (2000) 'Contemporary models of management education in the UK', *Management Learning*, Vol.31, No.2: 197–217

HOLMAN, D. and HALL, L. (1996) 'Competence in management development: rites and wrongs', *British Journal of Management*, Vol.7, No.2: 191–202

HOLMAN, D. and THORPE, R. (2002) *Management and Language*. London: Sage

HOLMAN, D., GOLD, J. and THORPE, R. (2002) 'Full of characters: identity and talk in practical authoring', in D. HOLMAN and R. THORPE (eds) *Management and Language*. London: Sage

HOLMAN, D., PAVLICA, K. and THORPE, R. (1997) 'Rethinking Kolb's theory of experiential learning in management education', *Management Learning*, Vol.28, No.2: 135–48

HOLMES, L. (1995[Chapter 2]) 'The making of real managers: ideology, identity and management development'. Available online at **http://www.re-skill.org.uk/ relskill/ realmgr.htm** [accessed 28 August 2002]

HOLMES, L. (1995[Chapter 3]) 'HRM and the irresistible rise of the discourse of competence', *Personnel Review*, Vol.24, No.4: 34–49

HOLTON, E. F., BATES, R. A., BOOKTER, A. I. and YAMKOVENKO, V. B. (2007) 'Convergent and divergent validity of the learning transfer system inventory', *Human Resource Development Quarterly*, Vol.18, No.3: 385–419

HOLTON, E. F. III, BATES, R. A., SEYLER, D. L. and CARVALHO, M. B. (1997) 'Towards construct validation of a transfer climate instrument', *Human Resource Development Quarterly*, Vol.8: 95–113

HONEY, P. and LOBLEY, R. (1986) 'Learning from outdoor activities: getting the balance right', *Industrial and Commercial Training*, Vol.18: 7–12

HONEY, P. and MUMFORD, A. (1996[Chapter 5]) *Manual of Learning Styles*, 3rd edtion. Maidenhead: Honey Publications

HONEY, P. and MUMFORD, A. (1996[Chapter 7]) *How to Create a Learning Environment*. Maidenhead: Honey Learning

HONEY, P. and MUMFORD, A. (1995[Chapter 6]) *The Opportunist Learner*, 2nd edition. Maidenhead: Honey Publications

HONEY, P. and MUMFORD, A. (1995[Chapter 9]) *Managing Your Learning Environment*. Maidenhead: Honey Publications

HÖPFL, H. and DAWES, D. (1995) '"A whole can of worms!": the contested frontiers of management development and learning', *Personnel Review*, Vol.24, No.6: 19–28

HOULDSWORTH, L. and BURKENSHAW, S. (2008) 'Taking a human resource management perspective on performance management', in R. THORPE and J. HOLLOWAY (eds) *Performance Management Multidisciplinary Perspectives*. London: Palgrave Macmillan

HOUSE, R. J. and MITCHELL, T. R. (1974) 'Path-goal theory of leadership', *Journal of Contemporary Business*, Vol.3, Fall: 81–97

HUCZYNSKI, A. (2001) *Encyclopaedia of Development Methods*. Aldershot: Gower

HUCZYNSKI, A. (1977) 'Organisational climates and the transfer of learning', *BACIE Journal*, Vol.31, No.6: 98–9

HUNT, D. M. and MICHAEL, C. (1983) 'Mentorship: a career training and development tool', *Academy of Management Review*, Vol.8, No.3: 475–85

HUSELID, M. A., BEATTY, R. W. and BECKER, B. E. (2005) 'A players or A positions? The strategic logic of workforce management', *Harvard Business Review*, Vol.83, No.12: 110–17

IBARRA, H. (1992) 'Homophily and differential returns: sex differences in network structure and access in an advertising firm', *Administrative Sciences Quarterly*, Vol.37: 422–47

IBBETSON, A. and NEWELL, S. (1999) 'A comparison of a competitive and non-competitive outdoor management development programme', *Personnel Review*, Vol.28, Nos.1/2: 58–76

IDS (2003) *Leadership Development*, Incomes Data Services No.753, July

ILES, P. A. (2007) 'Employee resourcing and talent management', in J. STOREY (ed.) *Human Resource Management: A critical text*, 3rd edition. London: Thomson Learning

ILES, P. (1992) 'Centres of excellence? Assessment and development centres, managerial competence and human resource strategies', *British Journal of Management*, Vol.3, No.2: 79–90

ILES, P. A. and AULUCK, R. K. (1988) 'Managing equal opportunity through strategic organization development', *Leadership and Organization Development Journal*, Vol.4, No.3: 3–10

ILES, P. A. and PREECE, D. (2010) 'Talent management and career development', in J. GOLD, R. THORPE and A. MUMFORD (eds) *A Handbook of Leadership and Management Development*. Aldershot: Gower

ILES, P. A. and PREECE, D. (2006) 'Developing leaders or developing leadership? The Academy of Chief Executives' programmes in the north-east of England', *Leadership*, Vol.2, No.3: 317–40

JACKSON, C. (1990) *Career Counselling in Organisations*. Report 198. Brighton: Institute of Manpower Studies

JACKSON, C. and YEATES, J. (1993) *Development centres: assessing or developing people*. Brighton: Institute of Manpower Studies

JACOBS, R. (1989) 'Getting the measure of management competence', *Personnel Management*, June

JACOBS, T. O. and JAQUES, E. (1990) 'Military executive leadership', in K. E. CLARK and M. B. CLARK (eds) *Measures of Leadership*. West Orange, NJ: Leadership Library of America

JANSEN, J., VERA, D. and CROSSAN, M. (2009) 'Strategic leadership for exploration and exploitation: the moderating role of environmental dynamism', *The Leadership Quarterly*, Vol.20: 5–18

JARZABKOWSKI, P. and SPEE, P. A. (2009) 'Strategy-as-practice: a review and future directions for the field', *International Journal of Management Reviews*, Vol.11, Issue 1: 69–95

JOHNSON, S. (1999) *Skills Issues for Small and Medium-sized Enterprises*. London: Skills Task Force

JOHNSON, S. and WINTERTON, J. (1999) *Management Skills*. Research Paper 3. London: Skills Task Force

JOKINEN, K. (2005) 'Global leadership competencies: a review and discussion', *Journal of European Industrial Training*, Vol.29, No.3: 199–216

JOLLY, S. (2000) '"Queering" development: exploring the links between same-sex sexualities, gender, and development', *Gender and Development*, Vol.8, No.1: 78–88

JONES, O. (1996) 'I was upward appraised and survived!', *Career Development International*, Vol.1, No.2: 47–8

JONES, O. and MACPHERSON, A. (2006) 'Inter-Organisational Learning and Strategic Renewal in SMEs: Extending the 4I Framework', *Long Range Planning*,Vol. 39, No. 2: 155-75

JONES, O., MACPHERSON, A. and THORPE, R. (2010) 'Learning in the owner-managed small firms: mediating artefacts and strategic space', *Entrepreneurship and Regional Development* (forthcoming)

JONES, O., MACHPHERSON, A., THORPE, R. and GHECHAM, A. (2007) 'The evolution of business knowledge in SMEs: conceptualising strategic space', *Journal of Strategic Change*, Vol.16, No.6: 281–94

JUDGE, T. A., LOCKE, E. A. and DURHAM, C. C. (1997) 'The dispositional causes of job satisfaction: a core evaluation approach', *Research in Organizational Behaviour*, Vol.19: 151–88

KAISER, R. B., HOGAN, R. and CRAIG, S. B. (2008) 'Leadership and the fate of organizations', *American Psychologist*, Vol.63, No.2: 96–110

KALRA, V. S., ABEL, P. and ESMAIL, A. (2009) 'Developing leadership interventions for black and minority ethnic staff', *Journal of Health Organization and Management*, Vol.23, No.1: 103–18

KAMMEYER-MUELLER, J. D., JUDGE, T. A. and PICCOLO, R. F. (2008) 'Self-esteem and extrinsic career success: test of a dynamic model', *Applied Psychology: An International Review*, Vol.5, No.2: 204–24

KANTER, R. M. (1989) *When Giants Learn to Dance*. New York: Simon & Schuster

KEEP, E. and RAINBIRD, H. (2000) 'Towards the learning organization?', in S. BACH and K. SISSON (eds) *Personnel Management*. Oxford: Blackwell

KEERS, K. (2007) 'Using Appreciative Inquiry to measure employee engagement', *Strategic HR Review*, Vol.2, No.6: 10–11

KEMPSTER, S. (2009[Chapter 7]) *How Managers Have Learnt To Lead*. Basingstoke: Palgrave

KEMPSTER, S. (2009a[Chapter 7]) 'Observing the invisible', *Journal of Management Development*, Vol.28, No.5: 439–56

KETS DE VRIES, M. F. R. and FLORENT-TREACY, E. (1999) *The New Global Leaders: Percy Barnevik, Richard Branson, and David Simon, and the Making of the International Corporation*. San Francisco, CA: Jossey-Bass

KETTLEY, P. (1997) *Personal feedback: Cases in Point*. Brighton: Institute of Manpower Studies

KHAPOVA, S. N., ARTHUR, M. B. and WILDEROM, C. P. M (2007) 'The subjective career in the knowledge economy', in H. GUNZ and M. PEIPERL (eds) *Handbook of Career Studies*. Thousand Oaks, CA: Sage Publications

KIM, H. and CERVERO, R. M. (2007) 'How power relations structure the evaluation process for HRD programmes', *Human Resource Development International*, Vol.10, No.1: 5–20

KIM, H. and CERVERO, R. M. (2007a[Chapter 8]) 'Understanding the impact of organizational power on evaluation outcomes', *International Journal of Lifelong Education*, Vol.26, No.1: 45–58

KING, Z. (2004) 'Career self-management: its nature, causes and consequences', *Journal of Vocational Behavior*, No.65: 112–33

KIRKPATRICK, D. L. (1983) 'Four steps to measuring training effectiveness', *Personnel Administrator*, November: 19–25

KIRTON, M. J. (1999) *Kirton Adaption-Innovation Inventory Manual*. Berkhamsted: Occupational Research Centre

KIRWAN, C. and BIRCHALL, D. (2006) 'Transfer of learning from management development programmes: testing the Holton model', *International Journal of Training and Development*, Vol.10, No.4: 252–68

KNIGHTS, A. and POPPLETON, A. (2008) *Developing Coaching Capability in Organisations*. London: Chartered Institute of Personnel and Development

KNOWLES, M. (1998) *The Adult Learner*, 5th edition. Houston: Gulf Publishing

KNOWLES, M. S. (1986) *Using Learning Contracts*. San Francisco: Jossey-Bass

KNOWLES, M. (1984) *Andragogy in Action*. San Francisco: Jossey-Bass

KOHONEN, E. (2005) 'Developing global leaders through international assignments', *Personnel Review*, Vol.34, No.1: 22–36

KOLB, D. (1984) *Experiential Learning*. Englewood Cliffs, NJ: Prentice Hall

KOLB, D. (1982) 'Problem management: learning from experience', in S. SRIVASTVA (ed.) *The Executive Mind*. San Francisco: Jossey-Bass

KOROLJOVA, A. and VORONOVA, V. (2007) 'Eco-mapping as a basis for environmental management systems integration at small and medium enterprises', *Management of Environmental Quality: An International Journal*, Vol.18, No.5: 542–55

KOTTER, J. P. (1990) *A Force for Change*. New York: Free Press

KOTTER, J. P. (1982) *The General Managers*. New York: Free Press

KOUZES, J. M. and POSNER, B. Z. (1995) *The Leadership Challenge*. San Francisco: Jossey-Bass

KRAM, K. E. (1986) 'Phases of the mentor relationship', *Academy of Management Journal*, Vol.26, No.4: 608–25

KRAM, K. E. and ISABELLA, L. A. (1985) 'Mentoring alternative: the role of peer relationships in career development', *Academy of Management Journal*, Vol.28, No.1: 110–32

KRAUSE, D. E., KERSTING, M., HEGGESTAD, E. D. and THORNTON, G. C. (2006) 'Incremental validity of assessment center ratings over cognitive ability tests: a study at the executive management level', *International Journal of Selection and Assessment*, Vol.14, No.4: 360–71

KUR, E. and BUNNING, R. (2002) 'Assuring corporate leadership for the future', *Journal of Management Development*, Vol.21, Nos.9/10: 761–79

LAURENT, A. (1986) 'The cross-cultural puzzle of international human resource management', *Human Resource Management*, Vol.25, No.1: 91–102

LAVE, J. and WENGER, E. (1991) *Situated Learning: Legitimate peripheral participation*. Cambridge: Cambridge University Press

LAWLER, J. (2005) 'The essence of leadership? Existentialism and leadership', *Leadership*, Vol.1, No.2: 215–31

LAWRENCE, T., MAUWS, M.K., DYCK, B. and KLEYSEN, R.F. (2005) The Politics of Organizational Learning: Integrating Power into the 4I Framework, *Academy of Management Review*, Vol. 30, No. 1: 180–91

LEARY, M., BOYDELL, T., VAN BOESCHOTEN, M. and CARLISLE, J. (1986) *The Qualities of Managing*. Sheffield: Manpower Services Commission

LEES, S. (1992) 'Ten faces of management development', *Management Education and Development*, Vol.23, No.2: 89–105

LEITCH, S. (2006) *Prosperity for All in the Global Economy – World Class Skills*. London: HM Treasury

LEITHWOOD, K., MASCALL, B. and STRAUSS, T. (2008) *Distributed Leadership According to the Evidence*. London: Routledge

LEITHWOOD, K., DAY, C., SAMMONS, P., HARRIS, A. and HOPKINS, D. (2007) *Leadership and Student Learning Outcomes*. Interim Report. London: DCSF

LEITHWOOD, K., DAY, C., SAMMONS, P., HARRIS, A. and HOPKINS, D. (2006) *Successful School Leadership: What it is and how it influences pupil learning*. London: DFES

LESKEW, S. and SINGH, P. (2007) 'Leadership development: learning from best practices', *Leadership and Organization Development Journal*, Vol.28, No.5: 444–64

LEVINSON, H. (1970) 'Management by whose objectives?', *Harvard Business Review*, July/August: 125–34

LEWIS, A. E. and FAGENSON, E. A. (1995) 'Strategies for developing women managers: how well do they fulfil their objectives?', *Journal of Management Development*, Vol.14, No.2: 39–53

LICHTENSTEIN, B. B., UHL-BIEN, M., MARION, R., SEERS, A., ORTON, J. D. and SCHREIBER, C. (2006) 'Complexity leadership theory: an interactive perspective on leading in complex adaptive systems', *Emergence: Complexity and Organization*, Vol.8, No.4: 2–12

LINDKVIST, L. (2004) 'Governing project-based firms: promoting market-like processes within hierarchies', *Journal of Management and Governance*, Vol.8, No.1: 3–25

LINEHAN, M. (2001) 'Networking for female managers' career development: empirical evidence', *Journal of Management Development*, Vol.20, No.10: 823–9

LIU, J. and WILSON, D. (2001) 'The unchanging perceptions of women as managers', *Women in Management Review*, Vol.16, No.4: 163–73

LIU, S. and VINCE, R. (1999) 'The cultural context of learning in international joint ventures', *Journal of Management Development*, Vol.18, No.8: 666–75

LONDON, M. (1986) 'The boss's role in management development', *Journal of Management Development*, Vol.5, No.3: 25–34

LONDON, M. and SMITHER, J. W. (1995) 'Can multi-source feedback change perceptions of goal accomplishment, self-evaluation and performance-related outcomes? Theory-based applications and directions for research', *Personnel Psychology*, Vol.48: 803–36

LORBIECKI, A. and JACK, G. (2000) 'Critical turns in the evolution of diversity management', *British Academy of Management Journal*, Vol.11: 17–31

LSC (2006) *Impact Evaluation of the National Phase of the Leadership and Management Development Programme.* Coventry: Learning and Skills Council National Office

LUMBY, J. (2003) 'Distributed leadership in colleges', *Educational Management and Administration*, Vol.31, No.3: 283–92

LUTHANS, F. (1988) 'Successful vs effective real managers', *Academy of Management Executive*, Vol.2, No.2: 127–32

LUTHANS, F. and PETERSON, S. J. (2004) '360-degree feedback with systematic coaching: empirical analysis suggests a winning combination', *Human Resource Management*, Vol.42, No.3: 243–56

LYONS, M. (2007) *Place-Shaping: A shared ambition for the future of local government.* London: The Stationery Office

MABEY, C. (2005) *Management Development That Works: The evidence.* London: Chartered Management Institute

MABEY, C. (2002) 'Mapping management development practice', *Journal of Management Studies*, Vol.39, No.8: 1139–60

MABEY, C. and FINCH-LEES, T. (2008) *Leadership and Management Development*. London: Sage

MABEY, C. and RAMIREZ, M. (2005) 'Does management development improve organizational productivity? A six-country analysis of European firms', *International Journal of Human Resource Management*, Vol.16, No.7: 1067–82

MABEY, C. and THOMSON, A. (2000) 'Management development in the UK: a provider and participant perspective', *International Journal of Training and Development*, Vol.4, No.4: 272–86

MACBEATH, J. (1998) *Effective School Leadership: Responding to change*. London: Paul Chapman

MACHIN, S. and VIGNOLES, A. (2001) *The Economic Benefits of Training to the Individual, the Firm and the Economy: The key issues*. London: Centre for the Economics of Education

MACLEOD, D. and CLARKE, N. (2009) *Engaging for Success*. London: Department of Business

MACPHERSON, A. and JONES, O. (2008) 'Object-mediated learning and strategic renewal in a mature organization', *Management Learning*, Vol.39, No.2: 177–202

MAIER, N. R. F. (1985) 'Three types of appraisal interview', *Personnel*, Vol.35, No.4, March/April: 27–40

MALHOTRA, N. and MORRIS, T. (2009) 'Heterogeneity in professional service firms', *Journal of Management Studies*, Vol.46, No.6: 895–922

MANNING, T. T. (2003) 'Leadership across cultures: Attachment style influences', *Journal of Leadership and Organizational Studies*, Vol.9, No.1: 20–32

MANZ, C. and SIMS, H. P. (1981) 'Vicarious learning: the influence of modeling on organizational behavior', *Academy of Management Review*, Vol.6, No.1: 105–13

MARCUS, A. A. and FREMETH, A. R. (2009) 'Green management matters regardless', *Academy of Management Perspectives*, Vol.23, No.4, August: 17–26

MARCUS, A. and KAISER, S. (2006) *Managing Beyond Compliance: The ethical and legal dimensions of corporate responsibility*. Garfield Heights, OH: North Coast

MARSHALL, J. (1995) 'Researching women and leadership: some comments on challenges and opportunities', *International Review of Women and Leadership*, Vol.1, No.1: 1–10

MARSHALL, J. (1991) 'Women managers', in A. MUMFORD (ed.), *The Handbook Of Management Development*. Aldershot: Gower

MARSHALL, K. (1991) 'NVQs: an assessment of the outcomes approach to education and training', *Journal of Further and Higher Education*, Vol.15, No.3: 56–64

MARSICK, V. J. (2009) 'Toward a unifying framework to support informal learning theory, research and practice', *Journal of Workplace Learning*, Vol.21, No.4: 265–75

MARSICK, V. and WATKINS, K. (1990) *Informal and Incidental Learning in the Workplace*. London: Routledge

MARSICK, V. and WATKINS, K. (2001) Informal and incidental learning, *New Directions for Adult and Continuing Learning*, Vol. 89: 25–34

MARSICK, V., VOLPE, M. and WATKINS, K. (1999) 'Reconceptualizing informal learning', in V. MARSICK and M. VOLPE (eds) *Informal Learning in the Workplace*. Advances in Human Resource Development Series. San Francisco: Berrett-Koehler

MARTIN, G., REDDINGTON, M. and KNEAFSEY, M. B. (2008) 'Web 2.0 and HR: a discussion paper'. London: Chartered Institute of Personnel and Development

MARX, R. D. (1982) 'Relapse prevention for managerial training: a model for maintenance of behavior change', *Academy of Management Review*, Vol.7, No.3: 433–41

MATLAY, H. (2004) 'Contemporary training initiatives in Britain: a small business perspective', *Journal of Small Business and Enterprise Development*, Vol.11, No.4: 504–13

MATTIS, M. C. (2001) 'Advancing women in business', *Journal of Management Development*, Vol.20, No.4: 371–88

MAVIN, S. (2006) 'Venus envy: problematizing solidarity behaviour and queen bees', *Women in Management Review*, Vol.21, No.4: 264–76

MAVIN, S. (2001) 'Women's career in theory and practice: time for change?', *Women in Management Review*, Vol.16, No.4: 183–92

MAVIN, S., BRYANS, P. and WARING, T. (2004) 'Gender on the agenda 2: unlearning gender blindness in management education', *Women in Management Review*, Vol.19, No.6: 293–303

MAYER, J. D. and SALOVEY, P. (1997) 'What is emotional intelligence?', in P. SALOVEY and D. SLUYTER (eds) *Emotional Development and Emotional Intelligence: Implications for educators*. New York: Basic Books

MAYO, A. (1997) *Managing Careers*. London: Institute of Personnel and Development

MCCALL, M. W. and HOLLENBECK, G. P. (2002) *Developing Global Executives: The lessons of international experience*. Boston, MA: Harvard Business School Press

MCCALL, M., LOMBARDO, M. M. and MORRISON, A. M. (1988) *The Lessons of Experience*. Lexington, KY: Lexington Books

MCCLURG, L. M. (2001) 'Team rewards: how far have we come?', *Human Resource Management*, Vol.40, No.1: 73–86

MCCOOL, J. (2008) *Deciding Who Leads: How executive recruiters drive, direct, and disrupt the global search for leadership talent.* Mountain View, CA: Davies-Black

MCCULLUM, S. and O'DONNELL, D. (2009) 'Social capital and leadership development', *Leadership and Organization Development Journal*, Vol.30, No.2: 152–66

MCGREGOR, D. (1957) 'An uneasy look at performance appraisal', *Harvard Business Review*, Vol.35, May/June: 89–94

MCLAUGHLIN, H. and THORPE, R. (1993) 'Action Learning – a paradigm in emergence: the problems facing a challenge to traditional management education and development', *British Journal of Management*, Vol.4, No.1: 19–27

MCPHERSON, M. and NUNES, J. (2008) 'Critical issues for e-learning delivery: what may seem obvious is not always put into practice', *Journal of Computer Assisted Learning*, Vol.24: 433–45

MCWILLIAMS, A. and SIEGEL, D. S. (2001) 'Corporate social responsibility: a theory of the firm perspective', *Academy of Management Review*, Vol.26, No.1: 117–26

MEGGINSON, D. and BOYDELL, T. A. (1979) *Manager's Guide to Coaching.* London: BACIE

MEGGINSON, D. and CLUTTERBUCK, D. (1995) *Mentoring in Action.* London: Kogan Page

MEGGINSON, D. and PEDLER, M. (1992) *Self-Development.* Maidenhead: McGraw-Hill

MEGGINSON, D., CLUTTERBUCK, D., GARVEY, B., STOKES, P. and GARRETT-HARRIS, R. (2006) *Mentoring in Action*, 2nd edition. London: Kogan Page

MENDENHALL, M. E. (2006) 'The elusive, yet critical challenge of developing global leaders', *European Management Journal*, Vol.24, No.6: 422–9

MENDENHALL, M. E., STAHL, G. K., EHNERT, I., ODDOU, G., OSLAND, J. S. and KÜHLMANN, T. M. (2004) 'Evaluation studies of cross-cultural training programs: a review of the literature from 1988 to 2000', in D. LANDIS, J. M. BENNETT and M. J. BENNETT (eds) *Handbook of Intercultural Training*, 3rd edition. Thousand Oaks, CA: Sage Publications

MEYER, H. H. (1980) 'Self-appraisal of job performance', *Personnel Psychology*, Vol.33: 291–5

MEYER, H. H., KAY, E. and FRENCH, J. R. P. (1965) 'Split roles in performance appraisal', *Harvard Business Review*, Vol.43, No.1, January/February: 123–9

MEZIROW, J. (1990) *Fostering Critical Reflection.* San Francisco: Jossey-Bass

MICHAELS, E., HANDFIELD-JONES, H. and BETH, A. (2001) *The War For Talent.* New York/London: McKinsey & Co/Boston, MA: Harvard Business School

MIĆIĆ, P. (2010) 'Developing leaders as futures thinkers', in J. GOLD, R. THORPE and A. MUMFORD (eds) *A Handbook of Leadership and Management Development*. Aldershot: Gower

MIDDLEHURST, R. and KINNIE, T. (1997) 'Leading professionals: towards new concepts of professionalism', in J. BROADBENT, M. DIETRICH and J. ROBERTS (eds) *The End of the Professions?* London: Routledge

MILLER, L., RANKIN, N. and NEATHEY, F. (2001) *Competency Frameworks in UK Organisations*. London: Chartered Institute of Personnel and Development

MILLER, P. and ROSE, N. (1990) 'Governing economic life', *Economy and Society*, Vol.19, No.1: 1–31

MILLER, S., ROUELLA, H. and JOHNSON, M. (2002) 'Divergent identities? Professions, management and gender', *Public Money and Management*, January–March: 25–30

MILLMORE, M., BIGGS, D. and MORSE, L. (2007) 'Gender differences within 360-degree managerial performance appraisals', *Women in Management Review*, Vol.22, No.7: 536–51

MINGERS, J. (2000) 'What is it to be critical? Teaching a critical approach to management undergraduates', *Management Learning*, Vol.31, No.2: 219–37

MINK, O. G., OWEN, K. Q. and MINK, B. P. (1993) *Developing High-Performance People: The art of coaching*. Reading, MA: Addison-Wesley.

MINTZBERG, H. (2004[Chapter 1]) 'Enough leadership', *Harvard Business Review*, November: 1–2

MINTZBERG, H. (2004[Chapter 6]) *Managers, Not MBAs: A hard look at the soft practices of managing and management development*. San Francisco, CA: Berrett-Koehler

MINTZBERG, H. (1987) 'Crafting strategy', *Harvard Business Review*, July/August: 66–75

MINTZBERG, H. (1983) *Structure in Fives: Designing effective organisations*. Englewood Cliffs, NJ: Prentice Hall

MINTZBERG, H. (1975) 'The manager's job: folklore and fact', *Harvard Business Review*, July/August

MINTZBERG, H. (1973) *The Nature of Managerial Work*. New York: Harper & Row

MINTZBERG, H. and WATERS, J. A. (1985) 'Of strategies, deliberate and emergent', *Strategic Management Journal*, Vol.6: 257–372

MINTZBERG, H., AHLSTRAND, B. and LAMPEL, J. (1998) *Strategy Safari*. London: Prentice Hall

MITCHELL, H. (1999) 'Group mentoring – does it work?', *Mentoring and Tutoring*, Vol.7, No.2: 113–20

MOHAN DAS GANDHI, N., SELLADURAI, V. and SANTHI, P. (2006) 'Green productivity indexing', *International Journal of Productivity and Performance Management*, Vol.55, No.7: 594–606

MOORE, S., GRUNBERG, L. and GREENBERG, E. (2004) 'Development and validation of a scale to measure beliefs about women managers', *Current Psychology*, Vol.23, No.3: 245–57

MORAN, A. (1991) 'What can learning styles research learn from cognitive psychology?', *Educational Psychology*, Vol.11, Nos.3/4: 239–45

MOYNAGH, M. and WORSLEY, R. (2005) *Working in the Twenty-first Century*. Leeds: ESRC Future of Work Programme

MUELLER, S. (2004) 'Electronic mentoring as an example for the use of information and communication technology in engineering education', *European Journal of Engineering Education*, Vol.29, No.1: 53–63

MUMFORD, A. (2001) *How to Produce Personal Development Plans*. Maidenhead: Honey Publications

MUMFORD, A. (2000) 'A learning approach to strategy', *Journal of Workplace Learning*, Vol.12, No.2: 265–71

MUMFORD, A. (1997) *How to Choose the Right Development Method*. Maidenhead: Honey Publications

MUMFORD, A. (1993) *How Managers Can Develop Managers*. Aldershot: Gower

MUMFORD, A. (1990) 'Making a career through learning', *International Journal of Career Management*, Vol.2, No.1: 8–16

MUMFORD, A. (1988) *Developing Top Managers*. Aldershot: Gower

MUMFORD, A. (1987) 'Using reality in management development', *Management Education and Development*, Vol.18, Part 3: 223–43

MURRAY, A. (2010) 'Leadership and management development for the environment', in J. GOLD, R. THORPE and A. MUMFORD (eds) *A Handbook of Leadership and Management Development*. Aldershot: Gower

NAHAPIET J. and GHOSHAL, S. (1998) 'Social capital, intellectual capital and the organisational advantage', *Academy of Management Review*, Vol.23: 242–66

NAILON, D., DELAHAYE, B. and BROWNLEE, J. (2007) 'Learning and leading: how beliefs about learning can be used to promote effective leadership', *Development and Learning in Organizations*, Vol.21, No.4: 6–9

NBP (2008) *Positive Action Report*. London: Network for Black Professionals

NEVIS, E. C., DIBELLA, A. J. and GOULD, J. M. (1995) 'Understanding organizations as learning systems', *Sloan Management Review*, Vol.36, No.2: 73–85

NEWELL, S., SCARBROUGH, H. and SWAN, J. (2009) *Managing Knowledge Work*, 2nd edition. Basingstoke: Palgrave

NEWTON, T. and FINDLAY, P. (1996) 'Playing God? The performance of appraisal', *Human Resource Management Journal*, Vol.6, No.3: 42–58

NG, T. W. H., EBY, L. T., SORENSEN, K. L. and FELDMAN, D. C. (2005) 'Predictors of objective and subjective career success: a meta-analysis', *Personnel Psychology*, Vol.58: 367–408

NICOLINI, D., GHERARDI, S. and YANOW, D. (2003) *Knowing in Organizations: A practice-based approach*. New York/London: Armonk/M. E. Sharpe

NONAKA, I., TOYAMA, R. and KONNO, N. (2000) 'SECI, Ba and leadership: a unified model of dynamic knowledge creation', *Long Range Planning*, Vol.33: 5–34

NORTHOUSE, P. G. (2004) *Leadership Theory and Practice*, 3rd edition. Thousand Oaks, CA: Sage Publications

NSTF (1998) *Towards a National Skills Agenda*. London: Department for Education and Employment

OHLOTT, P. J., RUDERMAN, M. N. and MCCAULEY, C. D. (1994) 'Gender differences in managers' developmental job experiences', *Academy of Management Journal*, Vol.37, No.1: 46–67

OLIVIER, R. and VERITY, J. (2008) 'Rehearsing tomorrow's leaders: the potential of mythodrama', *Business Strategy Series*, Vol.9, No.3: 138–43

ONS (2003) *New Earnings Survey 2002*. London: Office for National Statistics

O'REILLY, C. and TUSHMAN, M. (2004) 'The ambidextrous organization', *Harvard Business Review*, April: 74–83

ORPEN, C. (1996) 'Dependency as a moderator of the effects of networking behavior on managerial success', *Journal of Psychology*, Vol.130, No.3: 245–8

OSBORN, R. N., HUNT, J. G. and JAUCH, L. R. (2002) 'Toward a contextual theory of leadership', *Leadership Quarterly*, Vol.13, No.6: 797–837

OWEN, H. (2008) *Open Space Technology: A User's Guide*, 3rd edition. San Francisco: Berrett-Koehler

PANE HARDEN, S., OYLER, I. and HUMPHREYS, J. (2009) 'Historical, practical and theoretical perspectives on green management', *Management Decision*, Vol.47, No.7: 1041–55

PARKER, P. and ARTHUR, M. B. (2001) 'Bringing "New Science" into careers research', *M@n@gement*, Vol.5, No.1: 105–25. Available online from **http://www.dmsp.dauphine. fr/management/PapersMgmt/51Parker.html**

PARKER, P., HALL, D. T. and KRAM, K. E. (2008) 'Peer coaching: a relational process for accelerating career learning', *Academy of Management Learning and Education*, Vol.7, No.4: 487–503

PARN (2000) *Continuing Professional Development*. Bristol: Professional Associations Research Network

PARSLOE, E. (1999) *The Manager as Coach and Mentor*. London: Chartered Institute of Personnel and Development

PARSLOE, E. and WRAY, M. (2000) *Coaching and Mentoring*. London: Kogan Page

PASSMORE, J. (2005) 'The heart of coaching: developing a coaching model for the manager', *The Coaching Psychologist*, Vol.2, No.2: 6–9

PATON, R., PETERS, G., STOREY, J. and TAYLOR, S. (2005) *Handbook of Corporate University Development: Managing strategic learning initiatives in the public and private domains*. Aldershot: Gower

PATTON, M. (1997) *Utilization-Focused Evaluation*, 3rd edition. Newbury Park, CA: Sage Publications

PAULEEN, D. (2003) 'Leadership in a global virtual team: an Action Learning approach', *Leadership and Organization Development Journal*, Vol.24, No.3: 153–62

PAVLICA, K., HOLMAN, D. and THORPE, R. (1998) 'The manager as a practical author of learning', *Career Development International*, Vol.3, No.7: 300–7

PAVLOV, I. P. (1927) *Conditioned Reflexes: An investigation of the physiological activity of the cerebral cortex*, translated and edited by G. Anrep. London/Oxford: Oxford University Press

PAYNE, S. and HUFFMAN, A. (2005) 'A longitudinal examination of the influence of mentoring on organizational commitment and turnover', *Academy of Management Journal*, Vol.48: 158–68

PEDLER, M. (1996/2008) *Action Learning for Managers*. Aldershot: Gower

PEDLER, M. and TREHAN, K. (2008) 'Action learning, organisational research and the "wicked" problems', *Action Learning Research and Practice*, Vol.5, No.3: 203–5

PEDLER, M., BURGOYNE, J. and BOYDELL, T. A. (2006) *A Manager's Guide to Self-Development*, 5th edition. Maidenhead: McGraw-Hill

PEDLER, M., BURGOYNE, J. and BOYDELL, T. A. (2004) *A Manager's Guide to Leadership*. London: McGraw-Hill

PEDLER, M., BURGOYNE, J. and BOYDELL, T. (1991) *The Learning Company: A strategy for sustainable development*. Maidenhead: McGraw-Hill

PEDLER, M., BURGOYNE, J., BOYDELL, T. and WELSHMAN, G. (1990) *Self-Development in Organisations*. London: McGraw-Hill

PEIPERL, M. A. (2001) 'Getting 360-degree feedback right', *Harvard Business Review*, Vol.79, No.1, January: 142–7

PEMBERTON, C. (2006) Coaching *to Solutions: A manager's toolkit for performance delivery*. Oxford: Butterworth-Heinemann

PERREN, L. (2001) *Management and Leadership in the UK Professions*. London: Council for Excellence in Management and Leadership

PERREN, L. and BURGOYNE, J. (2002[Chapter 3]) *Management and Leadership Abilities: An analysis of texts, testimony and practice.* London: Council for Excellence in Management and Leadership

PERREN, L. and BURGOYNE, J. (2002[Chapter 12]) *The Management and Leadership Nexus: Dynamic sharing of practice and principle.* London: Council for Excellence in Management and Leadership

PERREN, L. and GRANT, P. (2001) *Management and Leadership in UK SMEs.* London: Council for Excellence in Management and Leadership

PETERS, H. (1996) 'Peer coaching for executives', *Training and Development*, March: 39–42

PETTIJOHN, L. S., PARKER, S., PETTIJOHN, C. E. and KENT, J. L. (2001) 'Performance appraisals: usage, criteria and observations', *Journal of Management Development*, Vol.20, No.9: 754–71

PFEFFER, J. and FONG, C. T. (2002) 'The end of business schools? Less success than meets the eye', *Academy of Management Learning and Education*, Vol.1, No.1: 78–96

PFEFFER, J. and SUTTON, R. (2006[Chapter 13]) 'Evidence-based management', *Harvard Business Review*, Vol.84, No.1: 62–74

PFEFFER, J. and SUTTON, R. (2006a[Chapter 13]) *Hard Facts, Dangerous Half-Truths, and Total Nonsense.* Boston, MA: Harvard Business School Press

PHILLIPS, J. (1996) 'Measuring ROI: the fifth level of evaluation', *Technical and Skills Training*, April: 10–13

PHILLIPS, R. (1995) 'Coaching for higher performance', *Executive Development*, Vol.8, No.7: 5–7

PINNINGTON, A. and MORRIS, T. (2003) 'Archetype change in professional organizations', *British Journal of Management*, Vol.14, No.1: 85–99

PIU (2001) *Benchmarking UK Strategic Futures Work.* London: Cabinet Office, Performance and Innovation Unit

PIU (2000) *Leadership in Delivering Better Public Services.* London: Cabinet Office

POLANYI, M. (1967) *The Tacit Dimension.* Garden City, NY: Doubleday

POLKINGHORNE, D. E. (1997) *Narrative Knowing and the Human Sciences.* New York: University of New York Press

POLLARD, E. and HILLAGE, J. (2001) *Exploring e-Learning.* Brighton: Institute for Employment Studies

POLLITT, C. (2000) 'Is the emperor in his new underwear? An analysis of the impacts of public management reform', *Public Management*, Vol.2, No.2: 181–99

POLLITT, D. (2007) 'Software solves problem of global succession planning at Friesland Foods', *Human Resource Management International Digest*, Vol.15, No.6: 21–3

POON, J. M. (2004) 'Effects of performance appraisal politics on job satisfaction and turnover intention', *Personnel Review*, Vol.33, No.3: 322–34

PORTER, M. E. (2003) 'UK competitiveness: moving to the next stage', LSE Lecture, 22 January

POWELL, A., PICCOLI, G. and IVES, B. (2004) 'Virtual teams: a review of current literature and directions for future research', *The DATABASE for Advances in Information Systems*, Vol.35, No.1: 6–36

POWELL, G. N. and BUTTERFIELD, D. A. (2002) 'Exploring the influence of decision-makers' race and gender on actual promotions to top management', *Personnel Psychology*, Vol.55: 397–428

POWELL, G. N. and BUTTERFIELD, D. A. (1997) 'The effect of race on promotions to top management in a federal department', *Academy of Management Journal*, Vol.40, No.1: 112–29

PRAHALAD, C. K. and HAMEL, G. (1990) 'The core competence of the corporation', *Harvard Business Review*, May/June: 79–91

PRAHALAD, C. K. and KRISHNAN, M. S. (2008) *The New Age of Innovation: Driving co-created value through global networks*. New York: McGraw-Hill

PRESKILL, H. (2008) 'Evaluation's second act: a spotlight on learning', *American Journal of Evaluation*, Vol.29, No.2: 127–38

PRESKILL, H. and CATSAMBAS, T. T. (2006) *Reframing Evaluation Through Appreciative Inquiry*, Thousand Oaks, CA: Sage Publications

PUN, A. (1990) 'Managing the cultural differences in learning', *Journal of Management Development*, Vol.9, No.5

PUN, K. F. and WHITE, A. S. (2005) 'A performance measurement paradigm for integrating strategy formulation: A review of systems and frameworks', *International Journal of Management Reviews*, Vol.7, No.1: 49–71

PURCELL, J. and HUTCHINSON, S. (2007) 'Front-line managers as agents in the HRM-performance causal chain: theory, analysis and evidence', *Human Resource Management Journal*, Vol.17, No.1: 3–20

RACKHAM, N. (1973) 'Recent thoughts on evaluation', *Industrial and Commercial Training*, Vol.5, No.10: 454–61

RAE, D. (2004) 'Entrepreneurial learning: a practical model from the creative industries', *Education and Training*, Vol. 46, No.8/9: 492–500

RAELIN, J. (2007) 'Toward an epistemology of practice', *Academy of Management Learning and Education*, Vol.6, No.4: 495–519

RAELIN, J. (2004) 'Don't bother putting leadership into people', *Academy of Management Executive*, Vol.18, No.3: 131–5

RAELIN, J. (1997) 'A model of work-based learning', *Organization Science*, Vol.8, No.6: 563–78

RAELIN, J. (1986) *The Clash of Cultures: Managers and professionals*. Boston, MA: Harvard Business School Press

RAGINS, B. R., COTTON, J. L. and MILLER, J. S. (2000) 'Marginal mentoring: the effects of type of mentor, quality of relationship and program design on work and career attitudes', *Academy of Management Journal*, Vol.43, No.6: 1177–94

RAM, M. (2000) 'Investors in People in small firms', *Personnel Review*, Vol.29, No.1: 69–91

RAMSDEN, M. and BENNETT, J. R. (2005) 'The benefits of external support to SMEs: "hard" versus "soft" outcomes and satisfaction levels', *Journal of Small Business and Enterprise Development*, Vol.12, No.2: 227–43

RANKIN, N. (2001) 'Raising performance through people: the eighth competency survey', *Competency and Emotional Intelligence Annual Benchmarking Survey 2000/01*, pages 2–23

READY, D. and CONGER, J. (2007) 'Make your company a talent factory', *Harvard Business Review*, June

REBER, A. S. (2003) 'Implicit learning and tacit knowledge', in B. J. BAARS (ed.) *Essential Sources in the Scientific Study of Consciousness*. Boston, MA: MIT Press

REDMAN, T., SNAPE, E., THOMPSON, D. and KA-CHING YAN, F. (2000) 'Performance appraisal in an NHS hospital', *Human Resource Management Journal*, Vol.10, No.1: 48–62

REED, J. (2007) *Appreciative Inquiry*. London: Sage

REILLY, R. R., SMITHER, J. W. and VASILOPOULOS, N. L. (1996) 'A longitudinal study of upward appraisal', *Personnel Psychology*, Vol.46: 599–611

REVANS, R. (1998) 'Sketches in Action Learning', *Performance Improvement Quarterly*, Vol.11, No.1: 23–7

REVANS, R. (1986) 'Action Learning in a developing country', *Management Decision*, Vol.24, No.6: 3–7

REVANS, R. (1982) *The Origins and Growth of Action Learning*. Bromley: Chartwell-Bratt

REYNOLDS, M. (1997) 'Learning styles: a critique', *Management Learning*, Vol.28, No.2: 115–33

REYNOLDS, M. and TREHAN, K. (2003) 'Learning from difference', *Management Learning*, Vol.34, No.2: 162–80

REYNOLDS, M. and VINCE, R. (2007[Chapter 1]) *The Handbook of Experiential Learning and Management Education*. Oxford: Oxford University Press

REYNOLDS, M. and VINCE, R. (2007[Chapter 6]) 'Introduction', in M. REYNOLDS and R.VINCE (eds) *The Handbook of Experiential Learning and Management Education*. Oxford: Oxford University Press

RfO (2009) *Benchmarking Report 2009*. London: Race for Opportunity

RfO (2008) *Race to the Top*. London: Race for Opportunity

RfO (2002) *Race: Creating business value*. London: Race for Opportunity

RIGG, C. (2007) 'Corporate technocrats or world stewards?', in R. HILL and J. STEWART (eds) *Management Development: Perspectives from research and practice*. London: Routledge

RITTELL, H. and WEBBER, M. (1973) 'Dilemmas in a general theory of planning', *Policy Sciences*, Vol.4: 155–69

ROBERTSON, I. T. and SADRI, G. (1993) 'Managerial self-efficacy and managerial performance', *British Journal of Management*, Vol.4: 37–45

ROBESON, N. (2008) 'Interim management: is it the right career move?', *Industrial and Commercial Training*, Vol.40, No.6: 300–2

ROBINSON, S. (2010) 'Leadership ethics', in J. GOLD, R. THORPE and A. MUMFORD (eds) *A Handbook of Leadership and Management Development*. Aldershot: Gower

ROCHE, G. R. (1979) 'Much ado about mentors', *Harvard Business Review*, January/February: 14–28

RODGERS, H., FREARSON, M., GOLD, J. and HOLDEN, R. (2003) *International Comparator Contexts: The Leading Learning Project*. London: Learning and Skill Research Centre

ROGERS, M. and TOUGH, A. (1996) 'Facing the future is not for wimps', *Futures*, Vol.28, No.5: 491–6

ROHRBACH, D. (2007) 'The development of knowledge societies in 19 OECD countries between 1970 and 2002', *Social Science Information*, Vol.46, No.4: 655–89

ROSS, L., RIX, M. and GOLD, J. (2005) 'Learning distributed leadership, Part 1', *Industrial and Commercial Training*, Vol.37, No.3: 130–7

ROSSER, M. H. (2005) 'Mentoring from the top: CEO perspectives', *Advances in Developing Human Resources*, Vol.7, No.4: 527–39

ROSSETT, A. (2002) *The ASTD E-learning Handbook*. New York: McGraw-Hill

ROTHMAN, J. (1997) *Resolving Identity-Based Conflict in Nations, Organizations and Communities*. San Francisco: Jossey-Bass

ROUNCE, K., SCARFE, A. and GARNETT, J. (2007) 'A work-based learning approach to developing leadership for senior health and social care professionals', *Education & Training*, Vol.49, No.3: 218–26

ROUSSEAU, D. (2006) 'Is there such a thing as "evidence-based management"?', *Academy of Management Review*, Vol.31, No.2: 256–69

ROY, D. (1952) 'Quota restriction and gold-bricking in a machine shop', *American Journal of Sociology*, Vol.57: 427–42

RUBIN, R. S., MUNZ, D. C. and BOMMER, W. H. (2005) 'Leading from within: the effects of emotion recognition and personality on transformational leadership behavior', *Academy of Management Journal*, Vol.48: 845–58

RUSS-EFT, D. and PRESKILL, H. (2005) 'In search of the Holy Grail: return on investment evaluation in human resource development', *Advances in Developing Human Resources*, Vol.7, No.1: 71–85

RYAN, M. K. and HASLAM, S. A. (2009) 'Glass cliffs are not so easily scaled: on the precariousness of female CEOs' positions', *British Journal of Management*, Vol.20, No.1: 13–16

RYLE, G. (1949/1984) *The Concept of Mind*. Chicago: University of Chicago Press

SADLER-SMITH, E. (2006) *Learning and Development for Managers*. Oxford: Blackwell

SADRI, G. and LEES, B. (2001) 'Developing corporate culture as a competitive advantage', *Journal of Management Development*, Vol.20, No.10: 853–9

SALA, F. (2002) *Emotional Competence Inventory: Technical manual*. Philadelphia, PA: McClelland Center For Research

SALAMAN, G. and BUTLER, J. (1990) 'Why managers won't learn', *Management Education and Development*, Vol.21, Part 3: 183–91

SALAMAN, G. and TAYLOR, S. (2002) 'Competency's consequences: changing the character of managerial work'. Paper presented at ESRC Workshop on Managerial Work, Critical Management Studies Seminar, Cambridge, June

SALOVEY, P. and MAYER, J. D. (1990) 'Emotional intelligence', *Imagination, Cognition and Personality*, Vol.9: 185–211

SAMBROOK, S. (2006) 'Management development in the NHS: nurses and managers, discourses and identities', *Journal of European Industrial Training*, Vol.30, No.1: 48–64

SAMBROOK, S. (2003) 'E-learning in small organisations', *Education and Training*, Vol.45, Nos.8/9: 506–16

SAMBUNJAK, D., STRAUS, S. and MARUŠIĆ, A. (2006) 'Mentoring in academic medicine', *Journal of American Medical Association*, Vol.296, No.9: 1103–15

SBS (2004) *Government Action Plan for Small Businesses*. London: Small Business Service/DTI

SCARBROUGH, H., SWAN, J., LAURENT, S., BRESNEN, M., EDELMAN, L. F. and NEWELL, S. (2004) 'Project-based learning and the role of learning boundaries', *Organization Studies*, Vol.25, No.9: 1579–1600

SCHEIN, E. (1990) *Career Anchors*. San Diego, CA: Pfeiffer

SCHEIN, E. (1978) *Career Dynamics: Matching individual and organisation needs*. Reading, MA: Addison-Wesley

SCHEIN, V. (2007) 'Women in management: reflections and projections', *Women in Management Review*, Vol.22, No.1: 6–18

SCHÖN, D. A. (1987) 'Educating the reflective practitioner'. Paper presented to the American Educational Research Association, Washington

SCHÖN, D. A. (1983) *The Reflective Practitioner: How professionals think in action*. London: Temple Smith

SCHÖN, D. A. and REIN, M. (1994) *Frame Reflection*. New York: Basic Books

SCHRIESHEIM, C. A., WU, J. B. and SCANDURA, T. A. (2009) 'A meso measure? Examination of the levels of analysis of the Multifactor Leadership Questionnaire (MLQ)', *The Leadership Quarterly*, Vol.20, No.4: 604–16

SCHUMPETER, J. A. (1934) *The Theory of Economic Development*. Cambridge, MA: Harvard University Press

SEALY, R., VINNICOMBE, S. and SINGH, V. (2008) *Female FTSE Index and Report 2008*. Bedford: Cranfield University

SENGE, P. (1999) 'The gurus speak (panel discussion): complexity and organizations', *Emergence*, Vol. 1, No.1: 73–91

SENGE, P. (1992) 'Mental models', *Strategy and Leadership*, Vol.20, No.2: 4–44

SENGE, P. (1990) 'The leader's new work: building learning organizations', *Sloan Management Review*, Fall: 7–23

SENNETT, R. (1998) *The Corrosion of Character*. New York: Norton

SHAW, J. and PERRONS, D. (1995) *Making Gender Work*. Buckingham: Open University Press

SHOTTER, J. and CUNLIFFE, A. (2003) 'Managers as practical authors: everyday conversations for action', in D. HOLMAN and R. THORPE (eds) *Management and Language*. London: Sage

SIEBERS, P.-O., AICKELIN, U., BATTISTI, G., CELIA, H., CLEGG, C. W., FU, X., DE HOYOS, R., IONA, A., PETRESCU, A. and PEIXOTO, A. (2008) *Enhancing Productivity: The role of management practices*. AIM Working Paper No.65. London: Advanced Institute of Management

SIEGEL, D. S. (2009) 'Green management matters only if it yields more green: an economic strategic perspective', *Perspectives*, Vol.23, No.3: 5–16

SIMON, S. and EBY, L. (2003) 'A typology of negative mentoring experiences: a multidimensional scaling study', *Human Relations*, Vol.56, No.9: 1083–1106

SIMPSON, P. and BOURNER, T. (2007) 'What Action Learning is not in the twenty-first century', *Action Learning: Research and Practice*, Vol.4, No.2: 173–87

SIMPSON, P. and LYDDON, T. (1995) 'Different roles, different views: exploring the range of stakeholder perceptions on an in-company management development programme', *Industrial and Commercial Training*, Vol.27, No.4: 26–32

SINGH, V. (2002) *Managing Diversity for Strategic Advantage*. London: Council for Excellence in Management and Leadership

SKINNER, B. F. (1974) *About Behaviourism*. London: Jonathan Cape

SLAUGHTER, R. (1999) 'Professional standards in futures work', *Futures*, Vol.31: 835–51

SMITH, A. (1993) 'Management development evaluation and effectiveness', *Journal of Management Development*, Vol.12, No.1: 20–33

SMITH, A. (1990) 'Evaluation of management training – subjectivity and the individual', *Journal of European Industrial Training*, Vol.14, No.1: 12–15

SMITH, B. and DODDS, B. (1993) 'The power of projects in management development', *Industrial and Commercial Training*, Vol.25, No.10

SMITHER, J. W., BRETT, J. F. and ATWATER, L. E. (2008) 'What do leaders recall about their multisource feedback?', *Journal of Leadership and Organizational Studies*, Vol.14, No.3: 202–18

SMITHER, J. W., LONDON, M. and REILLY, R. R. (2005) 'Does performance improve following multisource feedback? A theoretical model, meta-analysis, and review of empirical findings', *Personnel Psychology*, Vol.58: 33–66

SMITHER, J., LONDON, M., FLAUTT, R., VARGAS, Y. and KUCINE, I. (2003) 'Can working with an executive coach improve multi-source feedback ratings over time? A quasi-experimental field study', *Personnel Psychology*, Vol.56, No.1: 23– 44

SNELL, R. (1988) 'The emotional cost of learning at work', *Management Education and Development*, Vol.19, No.4

SPACKMAN, T. (2010) 'Crafting a leadership and management development strategy, II', in J. GOLD, R. THORPE and A. MUMFORD (eds) *A Handbook of Leadership and Management Development*. Aldershot: Gower

SPARROW, P. and PETTIGREW, A. (1987) 'Britain's training problem: the search for a strategic human resources management approach', *Human Resource Management*, Vol.26, No.1: 109–27

SPENDER, J.-C. (2008) 'Organizational learning and knowledge management: whence and whither?', *Management Learning*, Vol.39, No.2: 159–76

SPILLANE, J. P. (2006) *Distributed Leadership*. San Francisco: Jossey-Bass

SPILLANE, J. P., CAMBURN, E. M., PUSTEJOVSKY, J., PAREJA, A. S. and LEWIS, G. (2008) 'Taking a distributed perspective', *Journal of Educational Administration*, Vol.46, No.2: 189–213

STACEY, R. (2002) 'The impossibility of managing knowledge'. Paper presented to the Royal Society of Arts, London, 27 February

STAKE, R. (1975) *Evaluating the Arts in Education: A responsive approach*. Columbus, OH: Merrill

STAMP, G. (1989) 'The individual, the organisation and the path to mutual appreciation', *Personnel Management*, July: 28–31

STANWORTH, J. and CURRAN, J. (1973) *Management: Motivation in the smaller business*. Aldershot: Gower

STEIN, S. J., PAPADOGIANNIS, P., SITARENIOS, G. and YIP, J. A. (2009) 'Emotional intelligence of leaders: a profile of top executives', *Leadership and Organization Development Journal*, Vol.30, No.1: 87–101

STEWART, J. (2010) 'E-learning for leaders and managers', in J. GOLD, R. THORPE and A. MUMFORD (eds) *A Handbook of Leadership and Management Development*. Aldershot: Gower

STEWART, J. and KNOWLES, V. (1999) 'The changing nature of graduate careers', *Career Development International*, Vol.4, No.7: 370–83

STEWART, R. (1999) *The Gower Handbook of Teamworking*. Aldershot: Gower

STEWART, R. (1975) *Contrasts in Management*. Maidenhead: McGraw-Hill

STOBER, D. R. (2008) 'Making it stick: coaching as a tool for organizational change', *Coaching: An International Journal of Theory, Research and Practice*, Vol.1, No.1: 71–80

STOBER, D. and GRANT A. M. (2006) *Evidence-Based Coaching Handbook*. New York: John Wiley

STOGDILL, R.M. (1974) *Handbook of Leadership*. New York: The Free Press

STOREY, J. (2004[Chapter 1]) 'Signs of change', in J. STOREY (ed.) *Leadership in Organizations*. Oxford: Routledge

STOREY, J. (2004[Chapter 2]) 'Changing theories of leadership and leadership development', in J. STOREY (ed.) *Leadership in Organisatations*. London: Routledge

STOREY, J. and TATE, W. (2000) 'Management development', in S. BACH and K. SISSON (eds) *Personnel Management*. Oxford: Blackwell

STOREY, J., EDWARDS, P. and SISSON, K. (1994) *Managers in the Making*. London: Sage

STREBLER, M. and BEVAN, S. (2001) *Performance Review: Balancing objectives and content*. Report 37. Brighton: Institute of Employment Studies

STREBLER, M. and BEVAN, S. (1996) *Competence-Based Management Training*. Report 302. Brighton: Institute of Manpower Studies

STREBLER, M., ROBINSON, D. and HERON, P. (1997) *Getting the Best Out of Your Competences*. Report 334. Brighton: Institute of Manpower Studies

STREUFERT, S. and SWEZEY, R. (1986) *Complexity, Managers and Organizations*. Orlando: Academic Press

STUART, R. (1984) 'Towards re-establishing naturalism in management training and development', *Industrial and Commercial Training*, July/August: 19–21

STURGES, J. (1999) 'What it means to succeed: personal conceptions of career success held by male and female managers at different ages', *British Journal of Management*, Vol.10, No.3: 239–52

SULLIVAN, S. and ARTHUR, M. (2006) 'The evolution of the boundaryless career concept: examining physical and psychological mobility', *Journal of Vocational Behavior*, Vol.69: 19–29

SULLIVAN, S. E., FORRET, M. L., CARRAHER, S. M. and MAINIERO, L. A. (2009) 'Using the kaleidoscope career model to examine generational differences in work attitudes', *Career Development International*, Vol.14, No.3: 284–302

SULLIVAN, S. E., FORRET, M. L., MAINIERO, L. A. and TERJESEN, S. (2007) 'What motivates entrepreneurs? An exploratory study of the kaleidoscope career model and entrepreneurship', *Journal of Applied Management and Entrepreneurship*, Vol.12, No.4: 4–19

SUPER, D. E. (1957) *The Psychology of Careers*. New York: Harper & Row

SUPER, D. E. and KIDD, J. M. (1979) 'Vocational maturity in adulthood: toward turning model into a measure', *Journal of Vocational Behavior*, Vol.14: 255–70

SUUTARI, V. (2003) 'Global managers: career orientation, career tracks, life-style implications, and career commitment', *Journal of Managerial Psychology*, Vol.18, No.3: 185–207

SUUTARI, V. and VIITALA, R. (2008) 'Management development of senior executives: methods and their effectiveness', *Personnel Review*, Vol.37, No.4: 375–92

SWAILES, S. and BROWN, P. (1999) 'NVQs in management', *Journal of Management Development*, Vol.18, No.9: 794–804

SWAN, E. (2007) 'Blue-eyed girl? The experiential methods of Jane Elliott and anti-racist training', in M. REYNOLDS and R.VINCE (eds) *Handbook of Experiential Learning and Management Education*. Oxford: Oxford University Press

SWAN, J., NEWELL, S., SCARBROUGH, H. and HISLOP, D. (1999) 'Knowledge management and innovation: networks and networking', *Journal of Knowledge Management*, Vol.3, No.4: 262–75

SYRETT, M. and LAMMIMAM, J. (1999) *Management Development*. London: Profile/The Economist Books

TAMKIN, P. and DENVIR, A. (2006) *Strengthening the UK Evidence Base on Leadership and Management Capability*. IES Report. Brighton: Institute of Employment Studies

TAMKIN, P., YARNELL, J. and KERRIN, M. (2002) *Kirpatrick and Beyond: A review of models of training evaluation*. Brighton: Institute for Employment Studies.

TAMS, S. (2008) 'Constructing self-efficacy at work: a person-centered perspective', *Personnel Review*, Vol.37, No.2: 165–83

TANNEN, D. (1991) *You Just Don't Understand: Women and men in conversation.* London: Virago

TANSLEY, C., TURNER, P., FOSTER, C., HARRIS, L., STEWART, J., SEMPIK, A. and WILLIAMS, H. (2007) *Talent Strategy, Management and Measurement.* London: Chartered Institute of Personnel and Development

TANTON, M. (1995) *Women in Management.* London: Routledge

TAPSCOTT, D. and WILLIAMS, A. (2006) *Wikinomics.* London: Atlantic Books

TARIQUE, I. and CALIGIURI, P. (2004) 'Training and development of international staff', in A. HARZING and J. VAN RUYSSEVELDT (eds) *International Human Resource Management.* London: Sage

TAYLOR, F. J. W. (1994) *Management Development to the Millennium: The Taylor Working Party Report.* London: Institute of Management

TAYLOR, N. (1996) 'Professionalism and monitoring CPD: Kafka revisited', *Planning Practice and Research*, Vol.11, No.4: 379–89

TAYLOR, S. (1998) *Employee Resourcing.* London: Institute of Personnel and Development

TEJEDA, M. J., SCANDURA, T. A and PILLAI, R. (2001) 'The MLQ revisited: psychometric properties and recommendations', *The Leadership Quarterly*, Vol.12, No.1: 31–52

TELL, J. (2000) 'Learning networks: a metaphor for inter-organisational development in SMEs', *Enterprise and Innovation Management Studies*, Vol.1, No.3: 303–17

TEMPORAL, P. (1978) 'The nature of non-contrived learning and its implications for management development', *Management Education and Development*, Vol.9: 93–9

TENGBLAD, S. (2006) 'Is there a new managerial work? A comparison with Henry Mintzberg's classic study 30 years later', *Journal of Management Studies*, Vol.43: 1437–61

TESSMER, M. (1993) *Planning and Conducting Formative Evaluations.* London: Kogan Page

THOMAS, R. and DUNKERLEY, D. (1999) 'Middle managers' experiences in the downsized organization', *British Journal of Management*, Vol.10, No.2: 157–69

THOMSON, A., MABEY, C., STOREY, J., GRAY, C. and ILES, P. (2001) *Changing Patterns of Management Development.* Oxford: Blackwell

THOMSON, A., STOREY, J., MABEY, C., GRAY, C., FARMER, E. and THOMSON, R. (1997) *A Portrait of Management Development.* London: Institute of Management

THORNHILL, A., SAUNDERS, M. N. K. and STEAD, J. (1997) 'Downsizing, delayering – but where's the commitment?', *Personnel Review*, Vol.26, No.1: 81–98

THORNTON, G. and GIBBONS, A. (2009) 'Validity of assessment centers for personnel selection', *Human Resource Management Review*, Vol.19, No.3: 169–87

THORPE, R. and HOLLOWAY, J. (2008) *Performance Management: Multidisciplinary perspectives*. London: Palgrave

THORPE, R., COPE, J., RAM, M. and PEDLER, M. (2009) 'Leadership development in small and medium-sized enterprises: the case for Action Learning', *Action Learning, Research and Practice*, Vol.6, No.3: 201–8

THORPE, R., GOLD, J., HOLT, R. and CLARKE, J. (2006) 'Immaturity, the constraining of entrepreneurship', *International Small Business Journal*, Vol.24, No.3: 232–52

THORPE, R., JONES, O., MACPHERSON, A. and HOLT, R. (2008) 'The evolution of business knowledge in SMEs', in H. SCARBROUGH (ed.) *The Evolution of Business Knowledge*. Oxford: Oxford University Press

THORPE, R., GOLD, J., ANDERSON, L., BURGOYNE, J., WILKINSON, D. and MALBY, R. (2009) *Towards Leaderful Communities in the North of England*, 2nd edition. Cork: Oaktree Press

THURSFIELD, D., HOLDEN, R. J. and HAMBLETT, J. (2004) *Learning Brokerage in the Workplace: Some preliminary reflections*. London: Learning and Skills Research Centre

TOMLINSON, K. (2003) *Effective Interagency Working: A review of the literature and examples from practice*. LGA Research Report 40. Slough: NFER

TORRES, R. T. (2006) 'Continous learning', in K. HANNUM, J. MARTINEAU, C. REINELT and L. C. LEVITON (eds) *The Handbook of Leadership Development Evaluation*. Hoboken, NJ: John Wiley & Sons

TORRES, R. T., PRESKILL, H. and PIONTEK, M. E. (2005) *Evaluation Strategies for Communicating and Reporting: Enhancing learning in organizations*. Thousand Oaks, CA: Sage

TOULMIN, S. (1958) *The Uses of Argument*. Cambridge: Cambridge University Press

TOVEY, L. (1993) 'Competency assessment: a strategic approach – Part 1', *Executive Development*, Vol.6, No.5

TOWNLEY, B. (1994) *Reframing Human Resource Management: Power, ethics and the subject at work*. London: Sage

TOWNLEY, B. (1993) 'Performance appraisal and the emergence of management', *Journal of Management Studies*, Vol.30, No.2: 221–38

TREHAN, K. and PEDLER, M. (2009) 'Animating critical Action Learning: process-based leadership and management development', *Action Learning: Research and Practice*, Vol.6, No.1: 35–49

TREHAN, K. and RIGG, C. (2007) 'Working with experiential learning', in P. M. REYNOLDS and R. VINCE (eds) *Handbook of Experiential Learning and Management Education*. Oxford: Oxford University Press

TROMPENAARS, F. (1996) *Riding the Waves*. London: Nicholas Brealey

TROMPENAARS, F. and HAMPDEN-TURNER, C. (2009) *Innovating in a Global Crisis: Riding the whirlwind of recession*. Oxford: Infinite Ideas

TUC (2002) *The Low Road, TUC Employment Research*. Available online from **http://www.tuc.org.uk/em_research/tuc-5459-f0.cfm** [accessed 10 September 2002]

TUCKMAN, B. (1965) 'Developmental sequence in small groups', *Psychological Bulletin*, Vol.63, No.6: 384–99

TURNBULL-JAMES, K. and COLLINS, J. (2010) 'Leading and managing in global contexts', in J. GOLD, R. THORPE and A. MUMFORD (eds) *A Handbook of Leadership and Management Development*. Aldershot: Gower

TYMON, W. G. and STUMPF, S. A. (2003) 'Social capital in the success of knowledge workers', *Career Development International*, Vol.8, No.1: 12–20

VALENDUC, G., VENDRAMIN, P., PEDACI, M. and PIERSANTI, M. (2009) *Changing Careers and Trajectories*. Leuven/Louvain, Belgium: Leuven Catholic University, Higher Institute of Labour Studies

VAN DER HEIJDEN, K., BRADFIELD, R., BURT, G., CAIRNS, G. and WRIGHT, G. (2002) *The Sixth Sense: Accelerating organizational learning with scenarios*. London: John Wiley

VANDEWALLE, D. and CUMMINGS, L. L. (1997) 'An empirical test of goal orientation as a predictor of feedback-seeking behavior', *Journal of Applied Psychology*, Vol.82, No.3: 390–400

VANDEWALLE, D., GANESAN, S., CHALLAGALLA, G. N. and BROWN, S. P. (2000) 'An integrated model of feedback-seeking behavior: disposition, context and cognition', *Journal of Applied Psychology*, Vol.85, No.6: 996–1003

VAN VELSOR, E. and HUGHES, M. W. (1990) *Gender Differences in the Development of Managers: How women managers learn from experience*. Greensboro, NC: Center for Creative Leadership

VEALE, C. and GOLD, J. (1998) 'Smashing into the glass ceiling for women managers', *Journal of Management Development*, Vol.17, No.1: 17–26

VERMAK, H. and WEGGEMAN, M. (1999) 'Conspiring fruitfully with professionals: new management roles for professional organisations', *Management Decision*, Vol.37, No.1: 29–44

VICTOR, B. and BOYNTON, A. (1998) *Invented Here: Maximizing your organization's internal growth and profitability*. Boston, MA: Harvard Business School Press

VINCE, R. (2004) 'Action Learning and organisational learning: power, politics and emotion in organisations', *Action Learning, Research and Practice*, Vol.1: 63–8

VINCE, R. (2002) 'The impact of emotion on organisational learning', *Human Resource Development International*, Vol.5, No.1: 73–85

VINCE, R. and REYNOLDS, M. (2010) 'Leading reflection: developing the relationship between leadership and reflection', in J. GOLD, R. THORPE and A. MUMFORD (eds) *A Handbook of Leadership and Management Development*. Aldershot: Gower

VOCI, E. and YOUNG, K. (2001) 'Blended learning working in a leadership development programme', *Industrial and Commercial Training*, Vol.33, No.5: 157–60

VOUDSON, P. (2002) 'Interim management: now a permanent feature of the workplace', *Industrial and Commercial Training*, Vol.34, No.3: 120–2

VROOM, V. H. and YETTON, P. W. (1973) *Leadership and Decision-Making*. Pittsburgh, PA: University of Pittsburgh Press

VYGOTSKY, L. S. (1982) *Collected Works*. Moscow: Pedagogica

VYGOTSKY, L. S. (1978) *Mind in Society: The development of higher psychological processes*, edited by M. Cole, V. John-Steiner, S. Scribner and E. Souberman. Cambridge, MA: Harvard University Press

WAGEMAN, R., HACKMAN, J. R. and LEHMAN, E. V. (2004) *Development of the Team Diagnostic Survey*. Hanover, NH: Tuck School of Business Administration, Dartmouth College

WAJCMAN, J. (1999) *Managing Like a Man: Women and men in corporate management*. Cambridge: Polity

WAJCMAN, J. (1998) *Managing Like a Man*. Oxford: Blackwell

WALDSTRØM, C. and MADSEN, H. (2007) 'Social relations among managers: old boys and young women's networks', *Women in Management Review*, Vol.22, No.2: 136–47

WALTON, J. (2005) 'Would the real corporate university please stand up', *Journal of European Industrial Training*, Vol.29, No.1: 7–23

WALUMBWA, F. O., AVOLIO, B. J., GARDNER, W. L., WERNSING, T. S. and PETERSON, S. J. (2008) 'Authentic leadership: development and validation of a theory-based measure', *Journal of Management*, Vol.34, No.1: 89–126

WARR, P., BIRD, M. and RACKHAM, N. (1970) *Evaluation of Management Training*. Epping: Gower Press

WARZYNSKI, C. C. (2004) 'Future-search conferences at Cornell University', *New Directions For Institutional Research*, No.123: 107–12

WATKINS, J. (2003) 'Get with the programme', *People Management*, Vol.9, No.12: 14–15

WATSON, A. and VASILIEVA, E. (2007) 'Wilderness thinking: inside-out approach to leadership development', *Industrial and Commercial Training*, Vol.39, No.5: 242–5

WATSON, T. J. (2001) 'The emergent manager and processes of management pre-learning', *Management Learning*, Vol.33, No.2: 221–35

WATSON, T. J. (1994) *In Search of Management.* London: Routledge

WATSON, T. J. (1980) *On Weber: Sociology, work and industry.* London: Routledge

WATSON, T. and HARRIS, P. (1999) *The Emergent Manager.* London: Sage

WAXIN, M. F. and PANACCIO, A. (2005) 'Cross-cultural training to facilitate expatriate adjustment: it works!', *Personnel Review*, Vol.3, No.1: 51–67

WEICK, K. (2005) *Making Sense of the Organization.* San Francisco, CA: Wiley-Blackwell

WEICK, K. (1995) *Sensemaking in Organizations.* San Diego: Sage Publications

WEISBORD, M. and JANOFF, S. (2000) *Future Search: An action guide to finding common ground in organizations and communities.* San Francisco: Berrett-Koehler

WEISS, C. H. (1972) *Evaluation Research.* Englewood Cliffs, NJ: Prentice Hall

WELCH, J. (2001) *Jack: What I've Learned Leading a Great Company and Great People.* London: Headline

WENGER, E. C. and SNYDER, W. M. (2000) 'Communities of practice: the organizational frontier', *Harvard Business Review*, Vol.78, No.1: 139–45

WESTERN, S. (2008) *Leadership: A critical text.* London: Sage

WEYER, B. (2007) 'Twenty years later: explaining the persistence of the glass ceiling for women leaders', *Women in Management Review*, Vol.22, No.6: 482–96

WHEELWRIGHT, V. (2009) 'Futures for everyone', *Journal of Futures Studies*, Vol.13, No.4: 91–104

WHETTEN, D. and CAMERON, K. S. (2005) *Developing Management Skills.* Upper Saddle River, NJ: Pearson Education

WHIDDETT, S. and HOLLYFORDE, S. (2003) *A Practical Guide to Competencies: How to enhance individual and organisational performance.* London: Chartered Institute of Personnel and Development

WHIDDETT, S. and HOLLYFORDE, S. (1999) *The Competencies Handbook.* London: Chartered Institute of Personnel and Development

WHITMORE, J. (2002) *Coaching for Performance: Growing people, performance and purpose*, 3rd edition. London: Nicholas Brealey

WHITTINGTON, R. (2002) *Organising for Success in the Twenty-First Century: A starting point for change.* London: Chartered Institute of Personnel and Development

WHYMARK, K. and ELLIS, S. (1999) 'Whose career is it anyway? Options for career management in flatter organisation structures', *Career Development International*, Vol.4, No.2: 117–20

WHYTE, W. F. (1991) *Participatory Action Research.* San Diego: Sage Publications

WILLIAMS, S. (2002) *Characteristics of the Management Population in the UK: Overview Report*. London: Council for Excellence in Management and Leadership

WILLIS, P. (2005) *European Mentoring and Coaching Council, Competency Research Project*. Watford: European Mentoring and Coaching Council

WINTERTON, J. and WINTERTON, R. (1997) 'Does management development add value?', *British Journal of Management*, Vol.8, Special Issue: 65–76

WINTERTON, J., PARKER, M., DODD, M., MCCRACKEN, M. and HENDERSON, I. (2000) *Future Skills Needs of Managers*. Research report RR182. Sheffield/Nottingham: Department for Education and Employment

WOOD, G. and NEWTON, J. (2006) 'Childlessness and women managers: "choice", context and discourses', *Gender, Work and Organization*, Vol.13, No.4: 338–58

WOOD, M. (2005) 'The fallacy of misplaced leadership', *Journal of Management Studies*, Vol.42, No.6: 1101–21

WOODRUFFE, C. (2000) *Development and Assessment Centres*, 3rd edition. London: Chartered Institute of Personnel and Development

WOODRUFFE, C. (1992) 'What is meant by a competency?', in R. BOAM and P. SPARROW (eds) *Designing and Achieving Competency*. Maidenhead: McGraw-Hill

WORK FOUNDATION (2005) *Cracking the Performance Code*. London: Work Foundation

YANOW, D. (2004) 'Translating local knowledge at organizational peripheries', *British Journal of Management*, Vol.15, S9–S25

ZALEZNIK, A. (1977) 'Leaders and managers: are they different?', *Harvard Business Review*, September/October: 67–78

ZHANG, J. and HAMILTON, E. (2006) 'Entrepreneurial learning through peer networks: a process model'. Paper presented at the British Academy of Management Conference in Belfast, September

Index

The CIPD would like to thank the following members of the CIPD Publishing editorial board for their help and advice:

Caroline Hook, Huddersfield University Business School; Edwina Hollings, Staffordshire University Business School; Pauline Dibben, Sheffield University Business School; Simon Gurevitz, University of Westminster Business School; Barbara Maiden, University of Wolverhampton Business School; Wendy Yellowley and Marilyn Farmer, Buckinghamshire New University School of Business and Management.